W9-ANM-898

Contemporary Theory in INTERNATIONAL RELATIONS

EDITED BY
Stanley Hoffmann
Associate Professor of Government
Harvard University

Contemporary Theory in INTERNATIONAL RELATIONS

Prentice-Hall, Inc.
Englewood Cliffs, N. J.

Library of Congress Catalog Card No. 59-15939

PRINTED IN THE UNITED STATES OF AMERICA

17083—C

Second printing, October, 1960

Preface

The study of international relations has developed considerably in the United States during the last twenty years. The increasing number of textbooks, theoretical essays, and monographs dealing with the most varied problems, the many analyses of the present international situation and of nineteenth century diplomacy, the studies advocating discordant policies—all these efforts tend to make of the discipline an overcrowded shopping center, much like political science in the days when departments of government were characterized by an accumulation of unrelated courses.

This book has grown out of the two feelings which such luxuriant growth has instilled in me: dissatisfaction with the present state of the discipline, and hope for a more fruitful approach. It is my conviction—a conviction shared by most writers—that many of our problems in the discipline of international relations can be solved only by more systematic work than has been done in the past. This book is a plea for theory understood as a set of interrelated questions capable of guiding research both of the empirical and of the normative variety.

There are two sides to this book, and three parts. There is on the one hand a selection of readings: articles and excerpts from books which present the general problems of the discipline, discuss the need for theory, describe contemporary theoretical efforts. On the other hand, I have conveyed my own point of view on these various problems and assessed those theoretical attempts as well as suggested directions of research. Hence the somewhat unorthodox result: a book of selected readings whose editor in some cases criticizes rather harshly the selections he has made.

The first part argues the need for theory in connection with the general problems of scope and purpose of the discipline. The second part presents and discusses the main contemporary approaches to a general theory of international relations. The third part offers some suggestions for less ambitious but perhaps more satisfactory efforts toward theory and includes a tentative program of systematic research in areas I consider crucial for the development of the discipline. In each part the reader will find first my own commentary, then a set of selected readings, and finally a short bibliography.

Much of the discussion involves problems of the method and purpose common to most of the social sciences. Precisely because the discipline of international relations is in poorer shape than most of the other social sciences, these problems are particularly important here.

The emphasis throughout is on the field as a whole: there is no study of specific areas (such as the foreign policies of certain nations, the phenomenon of nationalism, international organization), nor am I concerned with theories applicable to a limited section of the field, such as theories of international law or of imperialism. Some of the readings relate to what looks like a mere section of the field: the problem of war and peace, but this is not really an exception since the ever present possibility of war is one of the most essential characteristics of international relations. No attempt is made to discuss in detail the respective contributions which various disciplines (ranging, according to a recent survey, from literary criticism to technology) can make to the field.

Neither in the selected readings nor in my commentaries is this book trying to discuss or propose answers to the questions of substance which are at the heart of the discipline, such as the nature of the national interest, the influence of domestic affairs on foreign policy, the role of ideologies in world politics, or how can the cold war be won (or ended). This book is concerned with a very different question: *how should one go about studying world politics?* The consideration of substantive issues here is either incidental or—in some of the readings in the third part—included only because the issues are those on which attention should be concentrated for the sake of the discipline, whatever one's opinion may be on the points which these issues raise.

Since only contemporary theories are examined, there is no detailed examination of the theories held by various political thinkers in the past, although the usefulness of their theories (both in their empirical and in their normative aspects) for an understanding of international politics is heavily stressed in the commentary and readings of Part III. Similarly, the liberal theory of international relations which dominated nineteenth century thought and, under the influence of men like Wilson, part of twentieth century world politics, is mentioned but not analyzed in any detail.

Finally, only those theories which are presented in a reasonably systematic and explicit fashion are studied here. Many works in international relations or political philosophy contain valuable implicit theories, but another and different kind of book should be devoted to such a task. The reader will not find any statement of the present Communist theory of international relations, for ever since Lenin's *Imperialism* Soviet pronouncements have been both unsystematic and subject to the countless tactical shifts and somersaults imposed by political imperatives.

I have chosen to select a small number of readings and to reprint either articles *in toto* or with minor cuts, or fairly long excerpts from books, rather than including numerous short selections. I have tried to present readings which are sufficiently representative samples, yet avoiding that shopping center aspect which I have criticized earlier.

The idea of this publication originated with Mr. Donald Hammonds. I want to thank both him, and Mr. Al Goodyear of Prentice-Hall, for their useful comments and their cooperation. I would also like to acknowledge my huge intellectual debt to, and admiration for, Professor Raymond Aron of the Sorbonne, and to thank Miss Inge Schneier, Research Associate at MIT, for most helpful suggestions on the points discussed in Part III. Finally, I am grateful to the editors of *World Politics* who have kindly allowed me to include in my contribution to this book the substance of an article published in the April 1959 issue of this quarterly.[1]

[1] "International Relations: The Long Road to Theory," Vol. XI, No. 3 (pp. 346-77).

Contents

Part III. Suggestions for the Study of International Relations

Part I

International Relations

as a Discipline

A. COMMENTARY

In his book, *The Study of International Relations,* Quincy Wright remarks that "at the least a discipline implies consciousness by the writers that there is a subject with some sort of unity," [1] even though disagreement and uncertainty might exist about the criterion, the limits, and the methods of the discipline. I think that it is possible to consider international relations as a largely autonomous field within the sprawling and loose science of politics. This is precisely the reason why there is a great need for theory.

1. The case for an autonomous discipline

Arguments about the degree of autonomy of international relations, both as an area of human activity and as an intellectual discipline, can go on forever. No one will argue that the field can be isolated, or that the problems asked by political science and political philosophy in general are not relevant here too. However, for those who are interested in trying to develop the discipline in the same way in which political science has been growing for two thousand years, and sociology during the last century, the two following points should be decisive.

First, the field *can* be sufficiently distinguished for analytical purposes. International relations owe their character to the fact that the milieu in which they take place is a decentralized one. It may be easy to exaggerate the degree to which, within a nation, the supreme political authority effectively controls the lesser centers of power; nevertheless such an authority exists. This is not the case in the international sphere: international relations owe their distinctive character to the fact that power has been fragmented into competing or independent groups throughout

[1] Quincy Wright, *The Study of International Relations,* New York, 1957, p. 23.

the world's history. The nature of the basic units has changed; what has not disappeared is the coexistence of multiple units; no empire has ever stretched across the whole world. Also, past and present empires, which do indeed possess at their center a supreme authority, are nevertheless no exception to the rule, since their establishment normally proceeds from one community's drive to subjugate others, and their structure generally reflects this origin. An empire is "a creation of force artificially superimposed upon a multiplicity of unwilling national societies," [2] not the realization of a community which transcends such societies.

It is the very lack of a supreme and generally accepted authority which explains why the rules of the game in world politics differ so sharply from the rules of domestic politics: the overriding loyalty of each of the groups into which the world has been divided, belongs to the group rather than to the world as a whole. Even in the period when those groups had a common ideal transcending their boundaries, such as "the majestic conception of the unity of the Christian community," [3] political authority remained fragmented; the common ideal, at best, was no more than a restraint on the actions of the groups—not the expression of a supreme temporal power. Hence, in particular, the striking differences between domestic law and international law, whose elaboration, interpretation and enforcement continue to depend on the will and consent of its very subjects. Hence also the difference in perspective between the disciplines of world politics and "domestic" political science. As one writer has put it, the former begins with the context and is then led to consider the content: its interest is in the environment and in the interrelatedness of everything within; the latter begins within the basic unit and is then led to consider the setting: its interest is in the individual organism and in its relationships with everything without.[4] Certainly the contrast should not be exaggerated; there are twilight periods, and even in times of sharply distinguished multiple sovereignties, there are twilight zones, such as the areas in which a federalizing process goes on. Nevertheless the basic distinction remains normatively valid.

Second, since the prerequisite can be met, *i.e.,* since it is intellectually possible to distinguish the field, I would argue that the field *should* be treated as an autonomous discipline. This does not mean that it should necessarily be taught in separate departments. Indeed, the fragmentation of the social sciences into sovereign units has begun to resemble the present state of world affairs. Paradoxically enough, this trend comes at a time when the specialists in each field realize that their own subjects—political science, sociology, or even economics, the most autonomous of

---

[2] Hans J. Morgenthau, *Politics Among Nations,* 2nd ed., New York, 1955, p. 482.

[3] Charles de Visscher, *Theory and Reality in Public International Law,* Princeton, 1957, p. 3.

[4] C. A. W. Manning, *The University Teaching of Social Sciences: International Relations,* Paris, 1954, p. 74.

all—really require both a separate set of theories and techniques *and* a considerable dose of interdisciplinary cooperation. Certainly the autonomy of any field within the social sciences, in so far as it arbitrarily isolates and elevates one sector of social activity, performs a kind of vivisection.

However, the difference in perspective which I have mentioned justifies a separate treatment. The great historian Marc Bloch quoted an economist's remark to the effect that an epidemic would be interpreted differently by a doctor and by a sociologist; the former would see the spreading of microbes as the cause, and the country's poverty as a condition, the latter would find exactly the reverse.[5] A similar contrast can be obtained when the same event, for instance a country's decision to attack its neighbor, is studied both from the viewpoint of domestic affairs and from the perspective of international politics: internal tensions (such as the pressure of social conflicts and the need to find a diversion from them) could be seen as the cause and external insecurity as the condition in the first case, and the reverse might be found in the second.

There is a much more important reason for advocating autonomy. No social scientist can work without having in mind at least an implicit model of his field. If we look at the two social sciences whose contributions have been most vital for the development of international relations—political science and sociology—we see that these disciplines use as a model the image of the integrated community. The norm for scientific analysis, and also, usually, for implicit or explicit evaluation, is the society which agrees on a certain notion (more or less extensive) of the common good. The norm is the society in which political power is institutionalized and law made for the realization of this common good, and in which the conflicts of ideas and interests are both dampened by the underlying agreement on fundamentals and ultimately resolved in a way which confirms this consensus and the equilibrium of the system. In this society, social functions are differentiated and carried out in such a way that the unity, harmony, or internal consistency of the society is achieved and maintained. Now, whatever else the nature of international relations may be, it is not an integrated system. It would be very dangerous in the long run to continue to work in our field with a model that does not fit. Many of the mistakes of contemporary theoretical attempts in international relations and international law come from the systematic misapplication of the model of the integrated *Rechtsstaat*—the modern state characterized by a sense of common purpose, a rational organization of power, a bureaucracy and the rule of law—to the decentralized international milieu, either as a norm for analysis or as a goal. The most extreme and revealing example is provided by Hans Kelsen's theory of international law, which assumes that the international legal order is already supreme. In order to explain the obvious differences between such a legal order (which is backed neither

[5] Marc Bloch, *The Historian's Craft,* New York, 1953, p. 193.

by a sense of community nor by any central system of power) and domestic legal orders, he is obliged to resort to an impressive gamut of fictions and to reason "as if" there existed a superpower over and above the units of the world. The gap between theory and practice becomes so great that the former ceases to have any value as an interpretation of the latter. For he did not ask the indispensable previous question, "whether an international community exists capable of supporting a legal order." [6]

There is a last and, I think, decisive reason for advocating an autonomous treatment of international relations. Without wanting to sound like an imperialist for a relatively green science, I would add that the architectonic role Aristotle attributed to the science of the Polis might well belong today to international relations, for these have become in the twentieth century the very condition of our daily life. To philosophize about the ideal State in isolation, or to theorize about political systems in the abstract, has become almost meaningless. If, in the study of politics, we were to put the primary emphasis on world affairs, and to treat domestic politics in the light of world affairs, we might produce a Copernican revolution even bigger than the change that transformed economics when macroanalysis replaced microanalysis. This should not be taken as a plea to treat domestic affairs as a by-product of world politics, for to do so would be just as mistaken as to study domestic political systems in isolation. The relations between internal and world affairs are highly complicated. One of the crucial features and paradoxes of politics today is that whereas internal politics are conditioned and affected by world problems more than ever before, the foreign policies of nations remain largely dictated by the domestic experience and by the nation's image of itself. World problems become domestic issues, but the nation's reaction to these issues and the nation's conduct on the world stage can often be explained only by internal history and by the values developed in those happier days when the outside world did not press so heavily on each country. The impossibility of unscrambling domestic and world affairs is not an argument against an autonomous discipline of international relations; it merely shows that we do indeed need an architectonic conception of our discipline.

2. Problems of scope, method, and purpose

As a discipline, international relations are not in very fine shape. There is, first of all, broad disagreement on a definition of the field. I confess that this does not worry me very much, for debates which try to determine the scope of a social science are rather pointless. Writers argue for their respective definitions as if there were an immutable essence of world politics, or sociology, and so on. Recent arguments concerning the criterion of political science, in particular, cannot be said to have led anywhere; for such arguments normally end with formulas even more ambiguous than the absence of any definition. If one calls political science the study of

[6] Julius Stone, *Legal Controls of International Conflicts,* New York, 1954, p. 34.

the state, one runs into the objection that there are one hundred and forty-five discernible definitions of the state, and that furthermore political science deals with phenomena which no such definition of the state can embrace.[7] If one sees in political science the science of power, or of the phenomena of control, one is left with the burden of distinguishing this discipline from the other social sciences, in which power and control are also important concepts. To speak of the "authoritative allocation of values in a society" as the proper criterion raises the further question of a definition of the society which one selects as the focus of analysis.[8]

Similar problems arise in connection with current definitions of the domain of international relations. Some say that the discipline is concerned with the relations among states. But this glosses over the fact that states are not monolithic blocs and that within them and often side by side with them, individuals and ideological or interest groups are the real decision-makers. Some see in power the criterion of international politics and thus define international relations as the discipline concerned with those relations among nations (i.e. between their governments or between individuals or groups belonging to different nations) which involve the power of states. Such a definition does not quite conceal the fact that it is not always obvious whether a certain activity involves the power of states or not. It is pretty clear that international postal communications do not, and it is clear today that international trade does, but in the nineteenth century, international politics and law operated largely under the assumption that the commercial activities of the nations' citizens did not concern, at least directly, the power of the states, except in the case of incidents of which these citizens were the victims in a foreign country. If we try to avoid all these difficulties by defining international relations as "relations between powerful groups," [9] we are then faced with a discipline so broad that the need would soon arise to distinguish the relations that are political from the others, and to give more precision to the concept of powerful groups. Should we, finally, try to answer those two questions by saying that the discipline of international politics is concerned with the relations between *all* groups in so far as they affect international society, but *only* with those relations among groups which are indeed important for world society[10]—we would then be back exactly where we started, and the quest of a definition of world society would decamp us into a new and formidable jungle.

A nominalist approach to the problem makes more sense: the best definition is the statement which, without violating common sense notions about the substance and purpose of the discipline, leads to the most perceptive investigations. The function of a definition is to indicate proper

[7] David Easton, *The Political System,* New York, 1953, p. 107.
[8] *Ibid.,* pp. 129 ff.
[9] Wright, *The Study of International Relations,* p. 7.
[10] George Schwarzenberger, *Power Politics,* New York, 1951, p. 4.

areas of inquiry, not to reveal the essence of the subject. How could one agree once and for all upon the definition of a field whose scope is in constant flux, indeed a field whose fluctuation is one of its principal characteristics? The basic units—city-state, empire, nation-state, et cetera—have changed frequently; the range of problems with which these units have been concerned in their external affairs, and the intensity and the geographical scope of the relations among them have also known great variations. Today, Sweden and Indonesia are likely to join in a multilateral convention for the regulation of labor conditions within their respective territories; a century ago, world affairs did not cover such a subject matter, and Indonesia was part of the Dutch empire.

Thus for practical purposes here is what I would suggest as a purely operational definition: The discipline of international relations is concerned with the factors and the activities which affect the external policies and the power of the basic units into which the world is divided. Such a formula (which solves nothing and *can not* solve anything) indicates only what I think we should investigate. It shows that we should deal, for instance, with the United Nations, but not *necessarily* with the World Meteorological Organization; or that we should deal with private groups such as the United Fruit Company or the Socialist Internationale, but not *necessarily* with a group such as the International Political Science Association—at least until political scientists begin to play the role of grey eminences and social engineers to which some of them aspire.

Next to the problem of definition, there is a second and much larger area of confusion: the confusion that concerns the proper method and purposes of the discipline. We find in our field a bewildering multitude of contributions from all kinds of disciplines. A chart drafted by Quincy Wright makes room for twenty-three "disciplines concerned with international relations"; at the four corners of the chart, we have technical aid, international propaganda, the art of war, and the control of foreign relations.[11] Another recent survey gives "specific examples of possible approaches" and after a cautionary note which denies any claim to providing a definitive list, enumerates no less than twenty-seven approaches—alphabetically ranged from "action analysis" and "analytical field" to "structural-functional requisite analysis" and "war and peace." [12] Such a conglomeration of partial approaches makes little sense. No one will deny that most fields have something to offer, but a flea market is not a discipline. Interdisciplinary cooperation is not good under all conditions.

On the one hand, unless there is a discipline which supervises all those "approaches," each one of them will consider international relations from a perspective that is parochial. There is no point at all in wondering why, for

---

[11] Q. Wright, *op. cit.*, p. 506.

[12] Charles O. Lerche and Burton M. Sapin (eds.), "Some Problems in the Study and Teaching of International Politics" (mimeographed), Emory University, 1958, pp. 10-12.

instance, studies in international communication or in international trade answer so few of the questions which political scientists have in mind with respect to international relations: such studies normally do not *try* to answer these questions, and the juxtaposition of the answers which such studies give to their own questions does not necessarily amount even to a partial answer to our questions. If no effort at harmony is ever made, the mixture of notes can hardly fail to produce cacophony. On the other hand, the purposes which the various approaches try to achieve are very different and sometimes conflicting. Some of these approaches are purely descriptive. Others represent attempts at explaining scientifically the role of certain factors, or certain types of behavior, in international affairs. Others try to define what such behavior ought to be, from the viewpoint of morality or of law. Others still are oriented toward practical action and manipulation. It is not surprising that many of these attempts should never really intersect, like planes flying in different directions, and that the contributions of other such attempts should be somewhat contradictory, like planes colliding in the air.

Work in many of these contributing fields may be very exciting indeed, especially if there are new disciplines exploring unknown areas, but from the viewpoint of international relations, this might not get us anywhere. Much can be said for toiling "at the frontiers of knowledge," but all too often what the researcher finds at those frontiers is a land of mirages, and he is faced with such arid prospects as the rediscovery of platitudes or the capitulation to "the technical fad, in which a new device is taken up so widely that a researcher feels deficient if his study does not contain an application of the latest gadget, whether or not it is relevant to his substantive problem." [13] Before we can send researchers on such frontiers and into such dangers, we should find a way of making their contributions relevant, a way of making each one of the partial disciplines aware of the findings of the others—in other words a way of asking the right questions, so that the other fields can be used for the benefit of the discipline of international relations, and not just of their own. There must be a core, which is missing at present.

Such a core, such a "principle of order" is precisely what we mean by theory. In each of the social sciences, "the word theory threatens to become emptied of meaning." [14] It has to be defined with reference first to its scope, and secondly to its purpose. As for *scope,* the word "theory" often refers to "logically interconnected propositions" designed to synthesize a more or less vast amount of data. This is not the only legitimate definition. A theory is *primarily* (in both meanings of the word primarily: first in time

---

[13] David Truman, "The Impact on Political Science of the Revolution in the Behavioral Sciences," in S. Bailey (ed.), *Research Frontiers in Politics and Government,* Washington, 1955, p. 227.

[14] Robert K. Merton, *Social Theory and Social Structure,* revised ed., Glencoe, 1957, p. 5.

and first in importance) a systematic effort at asking questions which will allow us to organize our knowledge, to orient our research, and to interpret our findings. Theory should help us order the data we have accumulated. It should identify the main factors or variables in the field and concentrate our attentions and research on the most important problems. Although it might not give us all at once a master key to the meaning of world politics, theory should at least lead us to a coherent understanding of the data. Thus the reader will find the word "theory" used here indifferently with reference to: (1) conceptual frameworks understood as such a set of *questions* capable of guiding research; (2) conceptual frameworks defined more ambitiously as "a system of working *hypotheses*" [15] whose main function is also to orient research (such as the "systems theory," and the theories of decision-making and equilibrium to be discussed in Part II); (3) even more ambitious sets of interrelated *propositions* which purport to explain a range of behavior, to account for part or even for the whole of the field; such propositions can be either deduced from the kind of conceptual framework described in (2) or derived from the kind of research to which any adequate framework leads—in other words "theory" in this third sense is a set of answers to the questions which theory in the first or second senses asks.

As for the *purpose,* we can again distinguish three kinds of efforts to which the word "theory" applies: (1) *"normative"* or "value" theory, defined by Kenneth Thompson in his essay reproduced below as the study of politics "in terms of ethical desiderata"—the kind of theory produced by political philosophy. A good example would be Kant's theory of perpetual peace in a world federation of representative republics; (2) *"empirical"* or "causal" theory, which tries to analyze actual political behavior and to identify the main variables, such as the theory of the balance of power offered as the key to eighteenth and nineteenth century international relations; (3) "*policy* science" or theory as a set of recipes for action, as systematic advice on statecraft. This kind of theory tries to contribute "to the intelligence needs of the time" [16]; research on psychological warfare or military strategy provides us with contemporary examples.[17]

The reader will find here no plea for theory for its own sake. Theory is no more than "a set of tools whose usefulness is tested in their ability to solve concrete problems." [18] But these tools are indispensable. Scholars

[15] Easton, *The Political System,* p. 57.

[16] Harold Lasswell, "The Policy Orientation" in D. Lerner and H. D. Lasswell (eds.), *The Policy Sciences* (Stanford, 1951), p. 4.

[17] On these distinctions see Easton, *op. cit., passim;* Hans J. Morgenthau, "Reflections on the State of Political Science," *Review of Politics,* Vol. 17, No. 4 (October 1955), pp. 431-60; S. Hoffmann, "Tendances de la Science Politique aux Etats-Unis," *Revue Française de Science Politique,* Vol. VII, No. 4 (October-December 1957), pp. 913-32.

[18] Barrington Moore, Jr., "Social Theory and Contemporary Politics," *American Journal of Sociology* (September 1955), pp. 107-115. See also Hans J. Morgenthau, *Dilemmas of Politics,* Chicago, 1958, pp. 88 ff.

in every social science have recognized that collecting facts is not enough and that it is not helpful to gather answers when no questions have been asked. Without theory, we will have to take whatever the other disciplines may see fit to dump into our plate. Indigestion is the only possible result. With adequate theory, we will help ourselves.

However, when we look at theory in our discipline and examine the questions theory asks, we find ourselves once more in an area of confusion. First, most past attempts at theory have been implicit rather than explicit. Second, existing theories of international relations can, like the partial approaches we have mentioned, be compared to planes flying at different altitudes and in different directions. There are, at the highest elevation, numerous speculative works concerned either with the proper place of ideals and moral standards in world affairs, or with master key explanations of what moves statesmen and people, coupled with normative exhortations or advice on statecraft. At a lower altitude, we find more rigorous analyses of limited and unconnected areas within the field: theories of nationalism and imperialism, of international law and organization, systematic inquiries into the decision-making processes of some nations, or into the nature and varieties of war.

This survey reveals the following facts:

First, if we take a global view of the field, its state is exactly as if, in the study of comparative government, we had only the arsenal of conflicting philosophical reflections from Plato to de Jouvenel, plus empirical studies of such scattered areas as electoral laws, the amending process, and two-party systems. We must try to link and expand the scattered studies of the latter type and we must try to connect these earth-bound theories with the sky-bound works of the former type.

Second, it is impossible to keep completely apart the three kinds of theory which we distinguished analytically from the viewpoint of purpose.

Third, even though empirical theory cannot be entirely separated from value theory and from policy theory, the inevitable cocktail made of all three includes at present very little of the first. It is the state of empirical theory which is particularly distressing; if we go back to our distinction of types of theory according to their scope, we find here very few frameworks or sets of interrelated propositions that try to cover the field as a whole, and a larger number of frameworks or sets of propositions applicable to small segments of the field only. It is my contention that progress in our discipline requires more emphasis on *general* empirical theory—theory which tries to account for major parts of the field. *Partial* theory—theory applicable to smaller areas—will develop best in the framework provided by such general theory. However, as I will try to show in Parts II and III, I do not believe that we can at this stage hope to produce an adequate general theory in the sense of an over-all explanation or even a global set of working hypotheses. A general explanation or model of the main phenomena will have to wait until we have many more partial explanations than we have now. But my point is that such partial explanations will be achieved most satisfactorily if we develop first a general theory in the more modest sense of a conceptual framework which asks relevant questions. The only alternative to the premature panacea of a global explanatory theory is *not* a reduction of the level of generality of the problems to study. There is obviously room and need for such more limited "middle range" or "narrow gauge" explanations, but work on the most general problems should also be undertaken, for two reasons: the interdependence of the phenomena and the messy condition in which the discipline would continue if only limited problems were dealt with; for the total is always *different* from the sum of its parts—even though it might be less rather than more. Therefore research of "middle" or "narrow" problems should be guided by a "total" set of interrelated questions.

Part III of this book will try to outline what kind of general empirical theory can be undertaken at present. I would suggest that there is a previous condition to such work and to any improvement of the discipline's state, in its normative as well as in its empirical aspects: a clear recognition of the scholar's purpose.

His primary duty, in our discipline as in all others, is to seek knowledge and understanding for their own sake. This implies that the main purpose of research should not be "policy scientism." The fighting of crusades, the desire to advise policy-makers, or the scholar's dedication to national or international causes can and perhaps even should be the occasion, but they should not be the purpose, of theoretical research. Policy scientism has been fed by two strong traditions. On the one hand, the creation of departments of government in this country has frequently come from a desire for reform and therapy; political science grew largely out of a curative urge and an engineering itch—but it outgrew them, too. On the other hand, what has survived is the old "scientist" dream of a discipline endowed with the power to predict, and with the function of guiding an equally scientific society, in which the social scientist would be a kind of spiritual leader, as Auguste Comte had wished. Once political studies have become scientific, what could be more natural than to want politics to be scientific too?

The arguments for the policy sciences are powerful. Our knowledge of totalitarian or underdeveloped countries owes very much to studies produced for policy-making agencies. A type of research which brings together the academicians and the practitioners (diplomats or experts working in the field) has much that can be said in its favor. Nevertheless, the distinction between "what is worth knowing intellectually and what is useful for practice," [19] between understanding and doctoring, remains essential, both for practical and for ethical reasons. One of the major perils

[19] Morgenthau, "Reflections on the State of Political Science," p. 440.

of policy scientism, frequently found in specialized studies, is the advocacy of policies based on a view of the situation which is too limited, either because only certain of the factors have been taken into account, or because the assumptions behind the measures suggested have not been made sufficiently explicit, or because the value implications of such advice have not been spelled out.[20] This shows that too heavy an emphasis on the applied sciences is dangerous as long as the "pure" science remains rather nebulous. Concentration on the "policy" periphery of our discipline is premature as long as we know little about the theoretical center that commands the periphery. Impatience, the vice of reformers, is the worst enemy of systematic theory in any field, and the worst temptation of American social scientists. Policy scientism is one form of impatience.

The other major danger, which affects the more ambitious attempts at turning social science into policy sciences, raises a fundamental ethical problem. It is the danger of slipping from the legitimate, indeed indispensable study of the ways in which certain values, posited by the scholar, can be realized in the world as it is, to a study of manipulation, through excessive emphasis on the skills of policy-making available to the political elites to whom advice is offered. From there, it is all too easy to slip further into the unsavory task of justifying the decisions made by such elites. The policy scientist often starts with the Faustian dream of becoming the intellectual leader of his society through "a configurative approach to the decision process" [21] which aims at "providing intelligence and making recommendations to all who have the will and capacity of decision," [22] and he then develops such wide-eyed fascination for the strategies of power that he shifts his glance from the values he posited to the tools which decision-makers use. Thus in the end he will, at best, "turn into an administrator, distinguished from some of his colleagues only by having been recruited from the intellectual community," [23] or turn into a gadfly, or become the politician's Peeping Tom. At worst, he will become the docile or deceived "expert" who obligingly shows to the decision-makers how they can best use for their purposes the techniques of his own field, and who shows to his colleagues how the decision-makers' purposes and his original goals really amount to the same thing. The result, I submit, is a violation of the scholar's duty to serve truth and of his necessary commitment to freedom without which the search for truth is a farce.

---

[20] On this point see Easton, *The Political System,* pp. 78 ff.

[21] Harold D. Lasswell, "The Political Science of Science," *American Political Science Review,* Vol. L, No. 4 (December 1956), p. 979.

[22] Myres S. McDougal and Harold D. Lasswell, "The Identification and Appraisal of Diverse Systems of Public Order," *American Journal of International Law,* Vol. 53, No. 1 (January 1959), p. 28.

[23] Henry A. Kissinger, "The Policy Maker and the Intellectual," *The Reporter,* Vol. 20, No. 5 (March 5, 1959), p. 35.

However, the relations between the scholarly center and the "policy" periphery are far from simple. My critique of policy scientism is not a plea for "paralyzing aloofness." [23] It would be a mistake, as we will suggest again later, to try to find theory in an ivory tower. The very usefulness of theory depends on its ability to illuminate the concrete empirical problems of the field. My point is that our first purpose should be to throw light on these problems, because we cannot dream of solving them as long as we have not elucidated them. To put it in other terms, there is a difference between an intellectual solution of an empirical problem, and the kind of solution which policy-makers are supposed to define with the help of the intellectual tools social scientists can devise. But my point is definitely *not* that emphasis on theory entails the neglect of empirical problems, for the only alternative to a theory oriented toward the intellectual elucidation of such problems is an irrelevant theory.

Furthermore, it would be foolish and unrealistic to ask for a total suspension of policy-oriented works until we have a reasonably coherent, general and accepted body of theory; theory-building is long and difficult, and no one can expect a moratorium on even dangerously incomplete discussions of practical issues in the meantime. Finally, precisely because of the difference between an intellectual solution and a "policy-solution," it would also be foolish and unrealistic to believe that once we had an adequate and relevant theory we could at last deduce from it "the specific requirements of policy (and the requirements of policy are always specific)." [24] Such a simple deduction is impossible for two reasons. First, the definition of a policy presupposes a decision about the ends which our policy should serve. Now, theory can help us understand what we can do and show us the implications of alternative ends, but it cannot dictate our choice among possible ends nor predict what will follow from our choice. Secondly, one of the functions of theory is to distinguish between the essential and the accidental factors in world affairs. But in a concrete instance the weight of the latter might well be decisive for the shaping of policy at the moment. This is not a reason for abandoning the effort toward theory. On the contrary, the limited services theory can render would be enough to justify the effort, even from the viewpoint of the practitioner. But the mistake of expecting a "direct and perceptible connection" between a general analysis and a concrete policy requirement would be as great as the mistake of repudiating theory altogether and sticking to *ad hoc* prescriptions just because more systematic and ambitious efforts do not automatically furnish concrete solutions. The same policies can be advocated on behalf of opposing theories; one of the roles of theory should be, not to indicate "good policies," but to help the policy-makers understand the situations and the alternatives among which they will have to choose.

---

[24] Robert W. Tucker, "The Study of International Politics," *World Politics,* Vol. X, No. 4 (July 1958), pp. 644-5.

B. READINGS

The article by Professor Frederick S. Dunn discusses some of the problems touched upon in the preceding commentary: the nature of the field, its scope, the kinds of problems with which the study of international relations should deal. The article by Mr. Kenneth W. Thompson is a thorough discussion of the need for theory and of the meaning and types of theory.

1. FREDERICK S. DUNN

The Scope of International Relations

. . . What I shall do here is merely to state certain propositions about the nature and scope of *IR* which seem to represent the present views of some mature scholars in the field. In setting these forth I do not mean to imply they incorporate the correct or final form of the subject. In my own view, the present basic divisions of the field are far from satisfactory from the standpoint of creative scholarship and the next few years are apt to witness the development of more imaginative classifications. But in the early stages of any subject it is the wisest course to make use of existing terms and categories. To try to invent a set of new ones at the start usually results in an inability to communicate with anyone else.

The following statements are dogmatically phrased for the reason that sufficient space is not available to express all the possible qualifications. For the same reason, no attempt has been made to squeeze out the last drop of ambiguity from them.

1. *IR* may be looked upon as the actual relations that take place across national boundaries, or as the body of knowledge which we have of those relations at any given time.

The latter is always more restricted in extent than the former, and its contents will depend, among other things, upon the intellectual trends of the times and the point of view and purpose of the observer.

2. As a branch of learning, *IR* consists of both a subject-matter and a set of techniques and methods of analysis for dealing with new questions.

Published in *World Politics,* Vol. I, No. 1 (October 1948), pp. 142-6.

The subject-matter consists of whatever knowledge, from any sources, may be of assistance in meeting new international problems of understanding old ones. It includes both general knowledge about the behavior of political groups or individuals and particular information about events or policy questions.

In the case of questions of general knowledge, the techniques and methods of analysis include the logical devices for arriving at hypotheses and for testing and verifying or rejecting them. In the case of practical questions they include the devices for revealing the issues involved, classifying the value objectives, indicating the alternative courses of action available and their probable consequences, and selecting the one most likely to lead to the desired end.

3. The distinguishing characteristic of *IR* as a separate branch of learning is found in the nature of the question with which it deals.

IR is concerned with the questions that arise in the relations between autonomous political groups in a world system in which power is not centered at one point.

4. An *IR* analyst is one who purports to have some skill in dealing with the questions that arise out of the relations of nations.

The core of his interest lies in the conflict, adjustment and agreement of national policies. When he concerns himself with related subjects, such as demography, anthropology and sociology, it is to the extent that these throw light on international questions. This distinguishes his interest in these fields from that of the professional demographer, anthropologist or sociologist.

5. The technical knowledge of *IR* is not merely the extension to a wider geographical scale of knowledge of social relations inside the national community, but has unique elements of its own.

Thus international politics is concerned with the special kind of power relationships that exist in a community lacking an overriding authority; international economics deals with trade relations across national boundaries that are complicated by the uncontrolled actions of sovereign states; and international law is law that is based on voluntary acceptance by independent nations.

6. Since the questions with which *IR* deals arise primarily out of social conflicts and adjustments, its approach is in large part instrumental and normative in character.

IR is concerned primarily with knowledge that is relevant to the control and improvement of a particular set of social conditions. Its goal is not merely knowledge for its own sake but knowledge for the purpose of molding practical events in desired directions. In this sense it is a policy science. As such it does not differ from traditional politics, economics, jurisprudence, and similar social disciplines, all of which had their origin in a desire to improve a particular segment of social relations.

7. The normative character of *IR* refers to the kinds of questions dealt

with and does not imply that the subject-matter is associated with any particular ideal conception of the international community.

The study of *IR* has been inspired from the beginning by a deep interest in how wars may be avoided. The early students of *IR* tended to conceive of ideal social systems in which wars did not exist and then to evaluate existing practices in the light of these ideal conceptions. The present tendency among scholars is to give primary attention to the ascertainable facts of international life and the forces and conditions that influence behavior among nations, as well as the ways in which these can be used for desired ends.

8. Foreign policies can only be understood in the light of knowledge of internal conditions of the states involved.

For many purposes it is possible to talk about the relations of states as if they were relations between solid bodies with wills of their own apart from human wills. Thus it is possible to discuss the operation of the balancing process among sovereign states, the relative value of different power positions, and, to some extent, the legal rights and duties of nations, without looking beneath the surface of the state.

In general, however, it is not possible to understand the course of international events without a careful study of the local factors and influences that enter into the formation of national policies.

9. All international relations can be described in terms of decision-making by identifiable individuals or groups of individuals.

This reveals the fact that the study of *IR* is basically the study of human behavior in a particular social setting.

10. By focusing on decision-making it is possible to devise ways of improving the chances of getting more intelligent decisions.

The study of decision-making reveals the specific kinds of skills and talents needed in staffing the government service. It indicates the kinds of training that should be undertaken by those who intend to follow professional careers in the field. In addition, it helps us to understand the extent to which the personality and predispositions of the decision-maker enter into his choices of action.

11. It is equally important to study the processes of decision-making in other countries.

Decision-making in *IR* generally involves the interaction of the officials of two or more states. Agreement is facilitated by a knowledge of the factors and considerations that influence the policy-makers of other countries.

12. The average decision-maker tends to operate on the basis of a speculative model of the general type of decision-makers from other communities he expects to meet in international negotiations. The accuracy of this model determines in large degree his success in achieving his objectives.

In the past such models have tended to follow two extreme types: the "Machiavellian" character whose sole aim was the enhancement of his own power or that of his nation and who used any means, however immoral, for these ends; and the "statesman" who paid little attention to power considerations but sought the settlement of issues solely on the basis of law and justice and the good of the greatest number.

Neither of these speculative models has been of much use in calculating action, since only a few policy-makers met in actual life resemble them to any extent. The study of decision-making should greatly improve the mental pictures which negotiators have of those whom they are likely to encounter in their negotiations.

13. The question "What is the scope of *IR* as a body of knowledge?" is different from the question "What is the proper scope of an educational program in the subject?"

The kind of a program to be offered by any particular institution should depend primarily on whether its aim is to offer *IR* as a cultural subject, or to train professionals, or both.

14. As a cultural subject, the aim should not be to turn out skilled decision-makers but to introduce the students to the general field and the methods available for analyzing its problems.

The subject-matter of *IR* has high cultural value both in teaching the ways of effective thinking and in enabling the student to come to terms with an important part of his environment. As a citizen in a democracy he is constantly faced with the necessity of arriving at sensible opinions on questions of foreign affairs.

15. As professional training for those who intend to follow careers in the field, *IR* contains an essential core of five subjects: international politics, international economics, international law and organization, diplomatic history, and political geography. In addition, it calls for some knowledge of the socio-psychological subjects—sociology, anthropology, psychology and social psychology, and ethics.

The *IR* analyst must acquire enough knowledge of the core subjects to enable him to move freely across the boundaries that separate them and to be able to think effectively about the whole questions. In addition, he should have mastered at least one of the accepted disciplines so that he may become familiar with the basic intellectual virtues. Only after such training will he become sensitive to the need for maintaining the highest standards of rigorous scholarship if *IR* is to earn its place as a useful branch of higher learning.

2. KENNETH W. THOMPSON

Toward a Theory of International Politics

Recently a group of scholars, analysts, and diplomatists met for a week-end conference on theoretical approaches to international politics.[1] Their discussion was inspired by the widespread and growing interest in conceptual and theoretical problems illustrated by parallel efforts in the study of politics, economics, law, and human relations. In the field of foreign relations the impulse toward theory comes from practitioners as well as philosophers. Indeed a former Secretary of State maintains that our most urgent need is for "an applicable body of theory in foreign policy." Practical men with first-hand diplomatic experience point to the need for rational generalizations and intellectual structures to extract meaning from the jet stream of contemporary events. The intellectual processes by which practical judgments are made along a moving front of events clearly demand inquiry and analysis. Theory in the study of international politics perhaps deserves a special priority because of the urgency of the problem and the stridency of the debate generated by competing approaches each claiming to have preempted the field. Perhaps what is called for is a sorting out and assessment of the intellectual factors that go into diverse theories of international politics at varying levels of abstraction and generality. This sorting out was one of the objectives of the conferees. Similarly this paper seeks to review the nature and purpose of theory, its limitations, and the characteristics of the chief types of theory in international politics.

Until comparatively recently most publicists and scholars had given little thought to formulating a theory of international relations. "Men have generally dealt with international relations on one of three levels, all alien to theory: history, reform, or pragmatic manipulation." [2] History is seldom considered theoretical, for its paramount goal is to illuminate the uniqueness of events. It is true that historians like Ranke have stressed the in-

Published in the *American Political Science Review*, Vol. XLIX, No. 3 (September 1955), pp. 733-746; copyright, 1955, by the *American Political Science Association;* reprinted by permission of the author and of the *American Political Science Review*.

[1] Robert Bowie, Dorothy Fosdick, William T. R. Fox, Walter Lippmann, Hans J. Morgenthau, Reinhold Niebuhr, Paul H. Nitze, Don K. Price, James B. Reston, Dean Rusk, Kenneth W. Thompson, and Arnold Wolfers. George F. Kennan was not in attendance but submitted a paper.

[2] Hans J. Morgenthau, unpublished paper, "The Theoretical and Practical Importance of the Theory of International Relations," p. 1.

terdependence of theory and history, ascribing to history the role of checking and illustrating theory and imputing to theory the function of integrating and directing history. However, theory in these terms is seldom explicit; it is almost always fragmentary and implicit in character. "In such historians of international relations, theory is like the skeleton which, invisible to the naked eye, gives form and function to the body." [3] History differs from theory in its resort to a chronological recital of events to demonstrate its oftentimes unavowed theoretical propositions. By comparison, the theorist turns from chronology to modes of analysis that can use the events of widely separated periods despite the fact that their only bond is their relationship to a principle and not proximity in time. History is past politics and as such provides the raw stuff of theory. But fundamentally history and theory are unlike in purpose and in form.

Reformers, in contrast to historians, make their theories explicit. They focus, however, on international relations not as they are but as they ought to be. Hence reformers, like historians, are not primarily theoreticians. Practitioners look to the present more than do reformers; statesmen, at least some of the greatest, conceive of international relations in terms of a generalized picture of the international scene. They see concrete cases as examples of more general or theoretical principles. They are inhibited, however, in their concern with the theoretical by the imperatives of practice and policy and only rarely when these immediate demands recede into the background can they afford to make their theories explicit. Statesmanship, as history, can serve as the handmaiden of theory for "those engaged in practice may have insights derived from concentrated experience and thought on the particular nodes where action was significant and possible, which can both assist the theoretician and serve as test checks on his theories." [4] Their practical concerns, however, prevent them from developing theories general enough to account for behavior on the international scene. Only scholars who analyze, compare, and evaluate the words and deeds of leaders like Bismarck, Churchill, or Wilson can uncover the essence of their approach, i.e., their theory.

The purpose and functions of theory. Observers can point to intellectual activities which are not primarily theoretical more readily than they can define or identify theory. Those who assert the possibility of theory for the field of international relations confront the same obstacles, ambiguities, and contradictions on which all past theories of history and politics have suffered shipwreck. The material with which the theorist must deal confounds and frustrates his task at almost every point. The substance of theory is history, composed of unique events and occurrences. An episode in history and politics is in one sense never repeated. It happens as it does only once; it is nonrecurrent in that it has never happened before nor will

---

[3] *Ibid.*, p. 2.

[4] Paul H. Nitze, unpublished paper, "The Implications of Theory for Practice in the Conduct of Foreign Affairs," p. 4.

it be repeated again. In this sense, history is beyond the reach of theory. Underlying all theory, however, is the assumption that these same unique events are also concrete instances of more general propositions. The wholly unique, having nothing in common with anything else, is indescribable, for we know that all analysis (and even description) is made in terms of predicates, class concepts, and repeatable relations. Both recurrence and uniqueness are present in history as in everything else, and the logical difficulty in reconciling them is neither greater nor smaller in international relations than in other fields.

The purpose and function of theory is not to provide a "substitute for the art of decision-making in foreign affairs, which, in view of the infinite number of combinations of multitudes of variables that form any concrete solution, must always remain in part a matter of risky choices based on more or less rational hunches." [5] Theory may serve to enhance the rationality of choice of decision-makers by helping them in the articulation of a more fully consistent view of the factors of the external environment. Yet the statesman is bound to a world of contingencies and pressures. He must express his philosophy from time to time as rough guides and rules-of-thumb that can only be limited and restricted in character. Whether this is a permanent condition, the conference was not agreed. It was suggested that the field of medicine offers an interesting parallel to decision-making. The medicine man of an earlier age was turned into physician as philosophical and scientific inquiry gave him new insights and resources. In the same way the policy-maker today is handicapped by the fact that his rough generalizations are sometimes drawn from a single experience. With better data and more accurate theories he can become more nearly "a physician of policy." It should be noted that this analogy was not accepted by those members of the conference who resisted the notion that the realms of nature and human behavior can readily be equated.

The function of theory as conceived and discussed by the participants is threefold. First, and perhaps most basic, it makes possible the ordering of data. It is a useful tool for understanding. It provides a framework for systematic and imaginative hypothesizing. It gives order and meaning to a mass of phenomena which without it would remain disconnected and unintelligible. This function is one emphasized particularly by Professors Fox and Morgenthau. The ordering of data can help the observer to distinguish uniformities and uniquenesses. In one scheme of analysis, for instance, it helps us to understand and distinguish the relatively fixed, the changing but uncontrollable, and the manipulatable aspects of world politics. In another, it guides us in considering the manifold social configurations of politics by offering an organizing principle founded on the most distinctive characteristic of politics, the struggle for power. Theory holds out the tools whereby the observer can discover in the welter of events that

[5] Arnold Wolfers, unpublished paper, "Theory of International Politics: Its Merits and Advancement," p. 1.

which is recurrent and typical. It satisfies man's need for intellectual orientation in a vital sector of existence.

Second, theory requires that the criteria of selection of problems for intensive analysis be made explicit. It is not always recognized that whenever a particular problem is selected for study and analysis in some context or other, there is practically always a theory underlying the choice. The idea of a presuppositionless social science has often been warmly embraced by prominent and aggressive research groups, but has tended more to mislead than to clarify the true nature of most research. It must be obvious that while social scientists should steel themselves to be as objective as possible, the notion that one band of observers goes about its task with a heavy baggage of biases and preferences whereas another starts free from all theories and presumptions is of course a grotesque caricature of social studies. Theory can serve to make more fully explicit the implicit assumptions underlying a research design and thus bring out dimensions and implications that might otherwise be overlooked.

Third, theory can be an instrument for understanding not only uniformities and regularities but contingencies and irrationalities as well. It can make possible "the creative elaboration of fruitful hypotheses which bear on the relationship between specified variables." [6] In modern politics there is a need for specific knowledge of contingent factors. It is argued, for example, that an anatomy of tyranny that deals only with general laws and similarities cannot adequately illuminate the differences between a nihilistic philosophy like nazism and a utopian one like communism. Present-day ideologies and revolutionary forces are variables that complicate the traditional roles of the major powers and must therefore be seen as they relate to other constants and variables. The function that theory serves will be determined by the problem and the intellectual interest of the observer.

. . . *Types of theory.* Walter Lippmann, speaking from a rich familiarity with both theory and practice, reminded the conference of the existence of at least three forms of theory. Normative theory is one form. Another form could be a general theory of politics. He noted: "There might or might not be a general theory that will tell you how the world will behave whether you like it or not. And another use of the word theory concerns theory, conscious or unconscious, on which a man, nation, or government is acting." [7] Mr. Lippmann observed that behind almost every act is an implicit theory. It is useful and important to know more about this field. The conferees adopted Mr. Lippmann's formulation and went on to discuss in some detail the three types of theory.

1. *Normative theory.* Normative theory is the study of politics in terms of ethical desiderata. It is perhaps alarming that political scientists, by

---

[6] *Ibid.,* p. 5.

[7] Transcript of Conference, p. 5.

allegedly confining themselves to the study of facts as contrasted with values, so often fail to take stock of this realm. The scientific approach blunts the fact that ethics and purpose relate to practical matters. The conferees agreed that it is blatant hypocrisy to say that the study of ends, purposes, and values is not a field of theory. They affirmed that we need a theory for the evaluation of norms as they are evolving in society. We need to consider the nature and content of national purposes and objectives at crucial points in our history. We need to understand the processes and standards of moral discrimination and the criteria by which we measure good and evil. We must perceive the levels at which normative thinking is necessary and possible and the hierarchy of values in a society. We need to face the moral issue in the peculiar context of international relations.

"The moral issue is so persistently raised, both in the theory and in the practical conduct of international affairs, not only because men honestly seek to do the right in their collective, as well as in their individual, life; but because they cannot follow their interest without claiming to do so in obedience to some general scheme of values." [8] This invites the two baffling and inescapable problems of moral pretension and moral cynicism. Nations are more inclined than individuals to follow their own interests; the imperatives of national security and survival require the statesman to distinguish his personal and public responsibilities. There is no clearer and more poignant example than Lincoln's subordination of his private views on slavery to the goal of the preservation of the Union. Nations always pretend to have a purer devotion to morality than they actually have. They are not as pure in their actions as they claim to be in their intentions. Moral pretension arises from the claims of a nation that it has acted not from self-interest or national security but in obedience to some higher purpose like "civilization" or "justice." When the conduct of foreign policy is democratic, this tendency increases rather than diminishes. Some authorities say that those responsible for postwar American foreign policy have claimed more benevolence for our policies than they deserve. This pretension inevitably arouses the resentments of people who envy our wealth and fear our power. In France and Asia, in the conduct of the Marshall Plan, and with technical assistance, we are sometimes accused of "compounding the sin of imperialism with the sin of hypocrisy." The antidote to pretension may be to remind ourselves that "though the exercise of our hegemony is a splendid example of the application of a wise self-interest when informed by loyalty to principles transcending national interests, it is important not to claim too much for the moral quality of our policies." [9] The moral issue in international relations consists as much in moderating moral pretensions as in erecting norms for man's collective life.

[8] Reinhold Niebuhr, unpublished paper, "The Moral Issue in International Relations," p. 1.

[9] *Ibid.*, p. 4.

Yet hypocrisy is "the inevitable by-product in the life of any nation which has some loyalty to moral principles, but whose actions do not fully conform to those principles. The price of eliminating those hypocrisies entirely is to sink into a consistent cynicism in which moral principles are not operative at all.[10] We might ask ourselves if it is significant that over the last decade no United Nations delegation has spoken out against the Charter, and in particular against the aims and purposes set forth in Articles 1 and 2. Is it true that national interest involves a range of concerns inclusive not only of specific geographical and power objectives but also of the world system and standards of behavior under which we can act most effectively? Is moral cynicism assuaged by the loyalties of peoples operative in their moral life to prevent the national interest from being conceived too narrowly and selfishly? Ought we to strive to make more rigorous distinctions between what is possible for governments inescapably accountable for security and survival, and the people at large whose ends may transcend national boundaries? Does this awareness present both the problem of reducing popular enthusiasm to the limits of practical statesmanship and the possibility of encouraging the state to find the point of concurrence between its interests and the more universal interest? Has this sensitivity marked the difference between German policies, when they have ostentatiously rejected moral principles if they did not serve concrete selfish interests, as compared with appeals to moral principles by the English inviting at the same time hypocrisy and those qualities institutionalized and preserved in a Commonwealth of nations? [11]

Nations display a continued ambivalence, claiming in one moment to hold moral obligations without regard to selfish interests and in the next moment insisting that only security and survival govern their conduct. Nations are not often subject to the idea that "He that loseth his life shall find it." Yet there is some general impulse behind self-interest illustrated and exaggerated by the Utilitarian presumption that "a wise man determines his interest so broadly that it includes everybody's." In the fact of the moral anguish revealed by this ambivalence, what is the role of normative theory? In plain words, what would a normative theory look like amidst the bewildering issues of modern international life? One American theologian has ventured to give some form and content to such a theory and the conference turned its attention briefly to the main elements of his conception of a normative theory.

For Reinhold Niebuhr, the theorist must come to grips with his subject on at least two levels. In the more ultimate dimension of pure morality, he must face the questions of the source and content of moral standards

---

[10] *Ibid.*, p. 5.

[11] "One could make similar comparisons between the inevitable pretensions involved in our failure to realize the 'American Dream' in our race relations, so poignantly described in Myrdal's *American Dilemma,* and the consistent realism and unhypocritical cruelty of the South African approach to this problem." *Ibid.*, p. 5.

and the nature of a definition of the good. At the level of a proximate political and social morality, he must deal with the factors of interest and power. Niebuhr rejects what he considers the Aristotelian attempt to define the good as "conformity to a preestablished ontological pattern of being." Instead he insists on looking for a more flexible definition of the good and finds it in Santayana's phrase "the harmony of the whole which does not destroy the vitality of the parts." The unique vitality and freedom of the parts and the harmony that results when the coercive force of tyranny does not decisively constrain them provide the criterion of moral value. Justice or the good is possible when liberty and equality are preserved.

Social or political justice, however, is attainable in a context where community or order must prevail, and the organization of any community, whether national or international, demands the inevitable subordination of one man to another or the parts to the whole. Liberty and equality in the political context become regulative principles, not simple possibilities. Justice in concrete international situations involves "giving each man his due." We arrive through the process of endless discrimination, debate, and what philosophers call political prudence, at a tolerably acceptable concept of man's due wherein general principles provide us with at most guides to action.

Liberty is a proposition that arises in western culture because of the Christian and Hebraic traditions. Nevertheless a proposition that is true transcends its presuppositions and Nehru, for example, who prefers to reject western presuppositions, demands liberty for India. Liberty, it appears, is an inevitable norm or regulative principle without being sufficient in itself. National self-determination became an absolute, co-extensive with justice, for some post-World War I western statesmen. It led to the breakdown of the European economy when it obscured the harmonizing role that had been played by the Austro-Hungarian Empire. It brought on a resentful and impractical order. In a situation characterized by the choice between self-determination and order, the statesman can only play by ear. Similarly, too much equality may sometimes be an evil. Those nations who oppose the United States today because it has too much power conceal the fact that without American power western civilization might be destroyed.

Put in more general terms: "Political morality contains an inevitable ambiguity because the factors of interest and power, which are regarded as an irrelevance in pure morality, must be at least tentatively admitted to the realm of social morality. Self-interest may be a source of discord ultimately; but it is tentatively necessary to prevent the harmony of the whole from destroying the vitality of the parts." [12] Power can serve as a counter-weight against power in the interests of justice. It may facilitate coercion when the order of a community is in danger. Tyranny is some-

[12] *Ibid.*, p. 2.

times more desirable than chaos. For instance, some observers maintain that the sole alternative to chaos in some Far Eastern countries has been tyranny. Moreover, the legitimacy of a traditional society that is in a state of neither tyranny nor chaos but is governed by custom, myth, or tradition confronts the west with yet another alternative. It is clear that the good is some kind of harmony, but the emphasis in normative theory must ultimately be on the *kind* of harmony. Specifically, in normative terms it must be a particular kind of harmony that includes equality and liberty.

In view of the infinite contingencies in the historical situation, a normative theory cannot take on more content or body than is possessed by these regulative principles. An historical situation cannot produce a theory which can tell you how much you should trust the future against the present or the past against the present or future. A good theory would have to recognize the existential fact of the difference between interests and ideals. It could clarify the assumption in a democracy that the resort to violence is immoral. It might help nations avoid ideological taint, as when they formalize their own national principles into the contractual rules of international relations. It might provide an estimate of the cost of one set of values as against another. It could test the efficiency of a given set of means for the achievement of a particular end. It would help statesmen find the point where the general good and the national interest come together—if they do.

In his paper, George F. Kennan reminded the group that the conduct of foreign relations ought not be conceived of as an end in itself, but rather as one of the means through which a higher purpose was preserved. Foreign policy, in brief, is a means to an end. He argued that among the overall purposes of sovereign states had been the glorification of dynasties, the fostering and employment of military virtues, and the spread of a particular social theory. The object of this government for the founding fathers was to serve as a means for protecting the individual in his exercise of certain rights, including life, liberty, and the pursuit of happiness. The problem of foreign policy amounted simply to determining what could be done in the handling of foreign relations to promote these objects. The first answer was to safeguard the national soil from military or political intrusion, for only if the nation's security was upheld could the political processes of freedom be preserved. Second, it called for the protection and assistance of our citizens when their activities spilled over beyond the national boundaries. These two functions—promoting national security and private American activities abroad—were all that flowed directly from the original objects of American society. Foreign policy in these terms was moderate, restrained, and ever attuned to the realities and limits of power.

All this was to change with the twentieth century. A posture deriving strictly from the objectives of society ceased to be satisfying when a spirit of romanticism seized the nation. We began to flaunt the American dream. We were content with our expanded borders. We chose to picture the rest of the world as of necessity as content as we were. All that was needed for world peace was a set of contractual relations whereby this happy status quo might be formalized and preserved. A world parliament, constitution, and framework of treaties of arbitration and conciliation would do for others what their national models had done for us. The cultivation of these utopian schemes, flattering to the nation's image of itself, took place at the cost of our feeling for reality. We closed our eyes to the menacing realities of ambition and power.

A normative theory calling for clarity on the objects and purposes of society might help states to remember what was basic to their national lives and to distinguish among a society's means and ends. It is barely possible that the element of moral pretension may be a more consistent cause of conflict between nations than the competition between frankly avowed national interests. Normative theory causes men to cross the threshold to wider questions of philosophy and ontology, for "moral pretension is but one aspect of the general inclination of modern men, who are undoubtedly agents in history, to forget that they are also creatures in the very historical process in which they must take responsible action."

2. *A general theory of international politics.* The prospects of a general theory of international politics are foreshadowed in our earlier discussion. The ambiguity of historical experience presents students of both normative or general theory with a welter of data from which to choose. The events he essays to compare and evaluate are at one and the same time unique and similar. It is only because historical experience contains an element of normality, regularity, and rationality that we can understand it as a continuum susceptible to abstraction and generalization. The pitfall of theory is obviously one of distinguishing by means of appropriate criteria of selection and relevance the repetitive from the unique. The conference was somewhat at odds on the point of the level at which a general theory was most likely to transcend these obstacles and difficulties.

It was maintained by some participants that theory is possible only at the level of general abstractions on the rational character of international politics. If the theorist attempts to become too specific, he is confronted with experiences for which general laws or principles cannot be successfully erected. The unique occurrences in history are accidental and display no element of rationality. There are, however, events in history that show a rational sequence and causal relationship; for these events, observation and generalization is possible. The practical application of some general principles that are tenable at one level may be difficult. Take the principle of Machiavelli that one should "never make an alliance with a stronger nation." The calamitous experiences of the Italian and Greek city states when they departed from this principle provide evidence of its relevance. At the level of practice, however, there are circumstances where weaker nations probably are obliged to make such alliances even though there is basic uniformity between their situation and that of the city states.

The most rational approach is highly discriminatory in relation to the real situation we can know. Principles or "laws" in a general theory partake of many of the same qualities as regulative principles in normative theory. The benefits which flow from over-abstraction were discussed. Several discussants noted that sometimes the "maximizing procedure" in theory was essential, as when one assumes that the USSR wishes to maximize its power and then traces the variables—for example, recent changes in Soviet tactics.

This approach to theory was vigorously challenged by proponents of another view. Spokesmen of this other approach argued that what is lacking in theory today is "the predictability and variability of concepts and thinking." They argued for the behavorial social sciences and pointed to recent successes in the classification of behavior. Theory is no less rational when it employs a great number of variables than when it deals with single variables. Special criticism was leveled at pernicious abstractions that characterize "Britain" or "France" as real entities (reification). Far more complex models, based on the irrationality of a multitude of actors, must be constructed. Instead of looking at the essence of statehood, the observer should consider the "human element." Individuals have loyalties that ramify through the varieties of human communities including the family, church, or labor union; the state is merely one datum point on this spectrum. This approach insists upon dealing with specific, middle-range theoretical problems subject to testing and research. For example, theorists might study the proposition that "totalitarian governments overestimate their own power and underestimate the power of others." Or "democratic governments are influenced by the assumption that peace is more desirable than violence." In the present state of thinking, these problems present theorists with the challenge to come down from the highest level of abstraction and confront problems more concrete in character. The emphasis is upon empirical verification, use of insights from other social sciences, and model building at a more sophisticated level. Here "behavioral or psychological aspects centering on the unmistakable existence of individual persons and methodological problems . . . [are] pushed to the fore." [13]

The swing of the pendulum toward a full-fledged behavioral science of international behavior may have led to the neglect of the situational components of international relations. The hiatus currently existent between the two major approaches to a general theory has left fallow ground unplowed by either group. Studying the relatively changeless features of a nation's foreign policy or the more or less objective factors of the international landscape provides a fixed point of reference. When individuals with quite different political philosophies conduct foreign policies which are similar or even identical in basic objectives, the situation of international politics has clearly imposed direction and limitations upon the actors.

---

[13] Wolfers, p. 4.

Theorists who may be prone to conceive of foreign policy as a mere reflection of the political philosophies or irrationality of particular actors would do well to inquire into substantive problems cast up by the social forces and conditions of the external environment. In turn, those who begin with general principles about major foreign powers should not be oblivious of changing or unique factors. For instance, the theorist must recognize communism as a unique factor influencing historic Russian policies. A closer union between the philosophical and behavioral approaches might go a long way toward solving the unfinished business of current theoretical work.

3. *Theory as the basis for action.* A third type of theory concerns the relationship between the assumptions or theories of statesmen and their conduct of foreign policy. Such an approach attempts to clarify the connection and interrelation between words and deeds through the theoretical treatment of historical personalities and their policies. Inquiries of this kind throw light on the vacillation between idealism and realism in American theory and practice. What is the relationship between the two and what are the decisive elements which make them different? What were the tragic choices in Lincoln's political life arising from this conflict, or in the policies of Adams or Hamilton? A significant analysis might cut both ways to lay bare the illusions in the American tendency to think that history is more malleable than it is [idealism] or that it is characterized by certain immutable laws [realism]. The fascination and appeal of the intellectual trend inherent in this approach to theory is its close relevance and application to history as over against the remoteness of pure conceptualization.

C. SELECTED BIBLIOGRAPHY

Dunn, Frederick S., "The Present Course of International Relations Research," *World Politics,* Vol. II, No. 1 (October 1949), pp. 80-95.

Easton, David, The Political System (New York: Alfred A. Knopf, Inc., 1953).

Fox, William T. R., "Interwar Research: The American Experience," *World Politics,* Vol. II, No. 1 (October 1949), pp. 67-99.

Fuller, Dale C., *Training of Specialists in International Relations* (Washington: American Council on Education, 1957).

———, *The Study of International Relations in American Colleges and Universities* (New York: Council on Foreign Relations, 1947).

Kirk, Grayson, "Materials for the Study of International Relations," *World Politics,* Vol. I, No. 3 (April 1949), pp. 826-30.

Manning, C. A. W., *The University Teaching of Social Sciences: International Relations* (Paris: UNESCO, 1954).

Mathisen, Trygve, *Methodology in the Study of International Relations* (Oslo: Oslo University Press, 1959).

Morgenthau, Hans J., *Dilemmas of Politics* (Chicago: University of Chicago Press, 1958).

Schwarzenberger, George, *Power Politics* (especially the introduction) (New York: Frederick A. Praeger, 1951).

Thompson, Kenneth W., "The Study of International Politics: A Survey of Trends and Developments," *Review of Politics,* Vol. 14, No. 4 (October 1952), pp. 433-67.

Truyol, Antonio, "La Teoría de las Relaciones Internationales Como Sociologia," *Revista de Estudios Politicos,* Vol. 96 (November-December 1957), pp. 293-336.

Wandycz, Piotr S., "The Theory of International Relations," *Review of Politics,* Vol. 14, No. 2 (April 1955), pp. 189-205.

Wright, Quincy, *The Study of International Relations* (New York: Appleton Century Crofts, 1955).

Zimmern, Alfred, *The Study of International Relations* (Oxford: Oxford University Press, 1934).

Part II

Contemporary Theories of International Relations

A. COMMENTARY

One of our arguments for theory and against excessive emphasis on policy-scientism was that the latter tendency reflected unwise impatience. But if we turn to those general theoretical efforts which have been made in recent years and which, on the surface, seem untouched by "policy" drives, we see that they too are marred by impatience. Perhaps because there is too little of it, general empirical theory too often seems like a hasty effort at accounting for everything at once. Consequently, instead of a key opening the doors of science, it is like a sledgehammer that only crushes one or two nuts, and breaks apart in the process.

Our discussion here will be limited to the main general efforts of predominantly "empirical" or "causal" orientation. These efforts can be divided into two main groups. There are on the one hand those which try to produce a "conceptual framework within which a whole discipline is cast," [1] in the form of a set of explanatory hypotheses which purport to reveal the rules of the game of international politics. Here theory is not just an attempt at asking crucial questions, it is also an effort to give us an answer. On the other hand, there are efforts which are apparently less ambitious (although we shall see that the appearances are rather deceptive). They try only to devise a right way of studying the phenomena of world affairs. They try to define the right angle, the method, the model, the concepts which should be the most fruitful for an analysis of the data; they concentrate on the most important variables, even though no attempt is made at the outset to present any laws governing the behavior of those variables: such laws, we are told, can be found only after much more empirical research, and theories of this type pretend only to put into the hands of the researchers an adequate tool for their studies.

[1] David Easton, *The Political System*, New York, 1953, p. 57.

1. Theory as a set of answers

In recent years, there have not been many *general* theoretical efforts at explaining world politics. Partial explanatory theories, such as theories of imperialism, have been more frequent. If we concentrate on the former, we can distinguish two rather different types, which have in common the desire to provide us with master keys: the "realist" theory of power politics, and modern philosophies of history.

(1) The "realist" theory of international politics. The theory which has occupied the center of the scene in this country during the last ten years is Professor Morgenthau's "realist" theory of power politics. It is an attempt at providing us with a reliable "map" of the landscape of world affairs; an effort at catching the essence of world politics. The master key is the concept of interest defined in terms of power. To what extent does the theory accomplish its mission? It succeeds in focusing attention on the units which remain the principal actors in world affairs: the States. The theory also stresses the factors that account for the large degree of autonomy of International Relations: the differences between domestic and world politics which thwart the operation in the latter of ideas and institutions that flourish in the former, the drastic imperatives of survival, self-preservation and self-help which are both the causes and the products of such differences.

However, as a general theory, the "realist" analysis fails because it sees the world as a static field in which power relations reproduce themselves in timeless monotony. The map is inadequate for two main reasons. First, the "realist" analysis of power is a very debatable one. The cornerstone of the realist theory is the statement that the political sphere is just as autonomous as the respective spheres of the economist, or the lawyer, or the moralist. This we can certainly accept. But what kind of an autonomy are we talking about? There are two possible versions: a sphere can be autonomous either because it is concerned with a specialized and limited set of variables, or because it is concerned with *all* the variables with which the various specialized spheres deal—it then differs from these spheres by its own generality and by the way in which all these different variables are combined here. When Mr. Morgenthau discusses the need for theory and for a hierarchical integration of the various disciplines which contribute to the study of international relations, he rightly says that politics must play the role of the common, integrating core and thus adopts the second version.[2] But in the bulk of his writings, and particularly in his statement of the realist theory which the reader will find below, he interprets autonomy in the first sense: the political realist "thinks in terms of interest defined as power, as the economist thinks in terms of utility; the lawyer, of conformity of action with legal rules; the moralist, of conformity of action with moral principles."

[2] Hans J. Morgenthau, *Dilemmas of Politics,* Chicago, 1958, pp. 98-100.

Now, the decision to equate politics and power would be acceptable only if power were analyzed, not as a limited and specific set of variables, but as a complex and diffuse balance between all the variables with which the social sciences are concerned.[3] Political man should properly be seen as the "integrator" of moral man, economic man, religious man, and so on —not as a creature reduced to one special facet of human nature. Unfortunately such an Aristotelian position is not adopted here: the decision to equate politics and the effects of man's "lust for power" is combined with a tendency to equate power and evil or violence—a combination which mutilates reality. A "power monism" does not account for all politics, when power is so somberly defined; even in world affairs, the drive for participation and community plays a part, and the image of political man interested exclusively in the control of the actions of others for the sake of control, is simply not acceptable as a basis for theory.

Furthermore, the extent to which power as a carrier of evil and violence expresses a basic human instinct is questionable. Much of the international (or domestic) evil of power is rooted not in the sinfulness of man but in a context, a constellation, a situation, in which even good men are forced to act selfishly or immorally. Discrimination between the inherent or instinctive aspects of the "power drive," and the situational or accidental ones, is an important task. However, reactions to shifting situations are scarcely considered by the theory.

Also, it is dangerous to put in a key position a concept which is merely instrumental. Power is a means toward any of a large number of ends (including power itself). The quality and quantity of power used by men are determined by men's purposes. It would have been more logical to begin with a theory of ends rather than with the notion of power, which is here both ambiguous and abstracted from its ends. The "realist" theory neglects all the factors that influence or define purposes. Why statesmen choose at times to use national power in a certain way (say a policy of "imperialism") rather than in another is not made clear. The domestic considerations that affect national power: the nature of the regime, the structure of power, beliefs and values which account in great measure for the nation's goals and for the statesmen's motivations, are either left out or brushed aside. For instance it is not enough to say that "the political cohesion of a federal system is the result of superior power located in some part of it," [4] for what remains to be explained is how such superior power got to be located there, what convergence of interests or what community of values led to its establishment and underlies its authority. Similarly, internationally shared beliefs and purposes are left out. Reality comes out oversimplified, for we get a somewhat mechanistic view of international

[3] See Talcott Parsons, *The Social System,* Glencoe, 1951, pp. 551 ff.

[4] Hans J. Morgenthau, "Another 'Great Debate': The National Interest of the United States," *American Political Science Review,* Vol. XLVI, No. 4 (December 1952), p. 968.

affairs in which the statesmen's role consists of adjusting national power to an almost immutable set of external "givens." Professor Morgenthau's metaphor about theory which, like a portrait, and unlike a photograph, should try to show "one thing that the naked eye cannot see: the human essence of the person portrayed" is most revealing. It is quite possible that there is a human essence of the person; but even if we had been able to discover it, we would still have to account for all the twists and vagaries of the person's existence and we cannot assume that they would be easily deducible from the "human essence" discovered. The same is true in world politics. Unfortunately, the "realist" world is a frozen universe of separate essences.

Even if the role of power were as determining as the theory postulates, the question arises whether any scheme can put so much methodological weight upon one concept, even a crucial one; for it seems to me that the concept of power collapses under the burden. It is impossible to subsume under one word variables as different as: power as a condition of policy and power as a criterion of policy; power as a potential and power in use; power as a sum of resources and power as a set of processes. Power is a most complex product of other variables, which should be allowed to see the light of the theory instead of remaining hidden in the shadow of power. Otherwise the theory is bound either to mean different things at different steps of the analysis (or when dealing with different periods), or else to end by selecting for emphasis only one aspect of power: either military force or economic strength.[5] Thus, instead of a map which simplifies the landscape so that we can understand it, we are left with a distortion.

There is a second reason for the inadequacy of the map. The rigidity that comes from the timeless concept of power is compounded by the confusing use of other concepts that are dated in more ways than one, and which the theory applies to situations in which they do not fit. The model of the "realists" is a highly embellished ideal-type of eighteenth and nineteenth century international relations. This vision of the golden age is taken as a norm, both for empirical analysis and for evaluation. A number of oddities of the theory are explained thereby. First, the lack of an adequate discussion of ends; for when all the actors have almost the same credo, as they did during most of that period, it becomes easy to forget the effects of the common credo on the actors' behavior, and to omit from among the main variables of the theory a factor whose role seems constant. It is nevertheless an optical illusion to mistake a particular historical pattern for the norm of a scientific system. When we deal with a period such as twentieth century world politics, whose main characteristic may well be the division of an international society which had previously been rather coherent into rival groups devoted to mutually exclusive purposes and values, the neglect of ends is a fatal mistake.

[5] On this point, see for instance Mr. A. F. K. Organski's economic power monism in his *World Politics* (New York, 1958).

Second, the analysis of power apart from the processes and pressures of domestic politics follows from the same optical illusion. It is easy to understand why public philosophers should bemoan the days when no visible and organized groups challenged the primacy of foreign affairs, the continuity of diplomatic action, unsentimental equilibrium calculations, and privacy. But these principles are not eternal; the Greek city-states did not observe them—at their own peril, of course, but then the world restored in 1815 balanced its power and played its cards into the abyss of 1914; and no one has yet found a way of reversing the trend and of insulating the experts on Olympus from the germs carried by the common men in the swamps below.

Third, the conception of an objective and easily recognizable national interest, the reliable guide and criterion of rational policy, is one which makes sense only in a stable period in which the participants play for limited ends, with limited means, and without domestic kibitzers to disrupt the players' moves. In such a period, the survival of the main units is rarely at stake in the game, and a hierarchy can rather easily be established among the other more stable and far less vital interests that are at stake. In such a period, the influence on foreign policies of factors such as geography, natural resources, industrial capacity, and inherited traditions of national principles is particularly strong and relatively constant. Today, however, survival is almost always at stake, and technological leaps have upset the hierarchy of "stable" factors. The most divergent courses of action can be recommended as valid choices for survival. Ordinarily less compelling objectives, such as prestige, or an increment of power in a limited area, or the protection of private citizens abroad, all become tied up with the issue of survival, and the most frequent argument against even attempting to redefine a hierarchy of national objectives so as to separate at least some of them from survival, is the familiar fear of a "chain of events" or a "row of dominoes falling." In such circumstances of mutual fear and technological turmoil, interpretations of the national interest become almost totally subjective and the relative weight of "objective" factors which affect the states' capabilities and thereby influence state policies is almost impossible to evaluate. Consequently, a scholar attempting to use the theory as a key to the understanding of, or successful influence upon, contemporary realities risks being in the unhappy position of a Tiresias who recognizes interests which the parties concerned refuse to see, who diagnoses permanence where the parties find confusing change and whose ex post facto omniscience is both irritating and irrelevant.

Fourth, the idea that the national interest carries its own morality is also one which makes sense almost only in a stable period. For it is a period in which an international consensus assures at least the possibility of accomodation of national objectives; the conflicts of interests which are involved are not struggles between competing international moralities. The philosophical pluralism implicit in the "realist" theory (which purports to be both normative and empirical) is not sufficiently thought through. For in periods of stability and moderation, which bloom only because of a basic agreement on values, the national interest can be said to be moral and legitimate only because it expresses aspirations of a community which do not rule out those of another group. What is moral is not the national interest as such but its reasonableness, which insures its compatibility with the interests of other states and with the common values of international society; and what is legitimate is the possibility for each group to have such temperate aspirations recognized. This is, at best, the kind of pluralism which is implied by *one* particular set of values—those of liberalism. As for periods of "nationalistic universalism," of secular religions and incompatible ideologies—here the tolerance characteristic of liberal pluralism makes no sense whatsoever. It is one thing to say that ideological differences do not justify crusades which would push the world into the chaos of total war; it is quite another to suggest that *all* national interests (as they are defined by statesmen) are to be given free play and recognition, in a period when one state's interest all too often resides in eliminating another state. A difference must be made between the pluralism of harmony, and the pluralism of the jungle.

Fifth, the emphasis on the "rationality" of foreign policy and the desire to brush aside the irrational elements as irrelevant intrusions or pathological deviations are understandable only in terms of cabinet diplomacy, where such deviations appear (especially with the benefit of hindsight) to have been rare. There, rationality seemed like the simple adjustment of means to stable and generally recognized ends. These concepts are far less applicable to a period in which the political struggles involve primarily the determination of ends.[6] In such a period, a conception of rationality adequate only for the selection of means cannot help us evaluate and classify the ends of states (the narrowness of the theory's conception of rationality makes it even more easy to understand why ends are insufficiently examined). Also, revolutionary periods are often characterized by the selection of means which are perfectly irrational from any point of view, *including* that of the adequacy of those means to the previously selected ends. Forgetting these two facts can entail serious mistakes. Thus, on the one hand, to apply a rationality of means to the selection of ends can have disastrous consequences in areas such as contemporary strategic doctrines. For instance, it can lead us to advocate limited nuclear war as the most rational way of employing the military resources of the West in the case of a conflict, without however having faced the previous question: whether such a strategy fits entirely the purposes the West has set for its relations both with the Communist camp and with the uncommitted nations, or, to put it somewhat differently, whether the purpose of this strategy—

[6] These arguments are developed by Henry A. Kissinger, *A World Restored,* Boston, 1957.

economy of force—is the highest end the West pursues. On the other hand, to forget that a nation might at some point select totally irrational means and be pushed by the dark logic of mutual fears into the very abyss of war that it wanted to avoid, is to assume too lightly that cool calculations of interest necessarily guide a nation's policy, or that mistaken calculations do not occur. Now, as the reader will see, debates among sociologists about the nature of war are not conclusive enough to allow us to assume that nations make war only because, and when, their leaders see in war a rational instrument of policy. In other words, a theory of world politics should certainly be rational but there is no need to suppose that reality is generally rational too.

Finally, the exclusion from the pale of world politics of those activities which were not undertaken by the states as such (i.e., by their governments), or which do not represent an obvious attempt to gain control over other nations (such as the signing of extradition treaties, or exchanges of goods and services, to use Mr. Morgenthau's own examples), is also understandable in certain periods only. It makes sense when a considerable range of activities which do, if only indirectly, affect the political power of the state, is left to private citizens (as was the case in the century of the liberal states). It makes sense when these activities are carried out unobtrusively within the common framework in which "power politics" operate, instead of serving as counters in the struggle for the establishment of a new framework. Nevertheless, even in the study of stable periods, the total exclusion of these acts is a mistake, because their temporary removal from the range of issues that involve directly the states' power is precisely the underpinning and one of the defining features of international relations in these periods—the submerged part of the iceberg. Behind the claim to realism, we thus find a reactionary utopia.

The consequence of this inadequacy of the map is that the theory's usefulness as a general theory for the discipline is limited. In the first place, from the point of view of systematic empirical analysis, it is too static. The price one has to pay for identifying the "timeless features" of the political landscape is the sacrifice of understanding the processes of change in world affairs. The theory stresses the autonomy of international relations to the point of leaving outside its pale the forces which work for change and which, cutting across the states, affect the states' behavior. Consequently the study of international relations tends to be reduced to a formalized ballet, where the steps fall into the same pattern over and over again, and which has no story to tell. To be sure, we are informed that the dancers do not have to remain the same: there might someday be other units than the nation states; but we cannot deal with the problem of knowing how the dancers will change. On the contrary, we are instructed that in the meantime "the national interest as such must be defended against usurpation by non-national interests"; in other words, new dancers might well appear but there is no intermission in which the turnover could happen and while they are on stage their duty is to stay on the job. To change the metaphor, we are presented both with a single key to the closed room of politics among nations, and with a warning that the room is in a house whose key we cannot have, or whose opening must be left to the "workmanlike manipulation of perennial forces." We are not told what they are, or how they operate. Consequently, when they disturb the model, the model's builders are reduced to imprecations against these forces, or to devil explanations.

We reach at this point one of the most fundamental ambiguities of the theory. Realism quite correctly denounces the utopian's mistake of swinging from the goal of a universal harmony to the assumption that in the world as it is the conditions for such harmony already exist. Realism commits exactly the opposite mistake. The postulate of the permanence of power politics among nations as the core of international relations, tends to become a goal. The static qualities of the theory lead to confusion between the phenomenon of power conflicts and the transitory forms and institutions in which such conflicts have been taking place in recent centuries. Why should the sound reminder that power is here to stay mean that the present system of nation states will continue, or change only through forces that are of no concern to us? Such an attitude evades both the empirical duty of accounting for change, and the normative task of assessing whether the present system should indeed continue. It is one thing to say that change will have to be sifted through the slow procedures of present world politics, and meet with the states' consent. It is quite another thing to suggest diplomacy as the only effective procedure and the only meaningful restraint. I cannot help but feel that in spite of Mr. Morgenthau's qualifying statements, there is behind his theory the old position that whatever has been, must continue.

This brings us to a second limitation. A theory which stresses necessity in policy-making rather than choice, and adjustment to the environment or to the existing element of national power, rather than value objectives and the adjustment of the "givens" to such purposes, a theory concerned with the preservation of the present units rather than with change, has disturbing normative implications. It is something of a success philosophy. The criterion of a good foreign policy is its rationality, but the touchstone of rationality is success. Unfortunately the standards of success and failure are not made clear. First, how will we distinguish between the follies of straight utopianism and the fallacies of wrong realism—realism that did not work? Secondly, from what viewpoint shall we decide whether a statesman has succeeded or failed? Shall we turn to history alone? But at what stage? Metternich had succeeded by 1825, and failed by 1848, and writers disagree whether he had succeeded or failed by 1914. If we want an answer from history alone, we will be driven either to pure irrationalism ("it is a tale full of sound and fury . . ."), or to passive contemplation, or to elementary Machiavellianism: "within itself, history has no standard of value but success, and no measure of success but the attainment of power, or survival for a little longer than rival individuals or institutions have survived." [7] If, as we must, we set our standards outside and above history, then we must avoid trying to prove that history will inevitably recompense policies that meet our standards. Otherwise, we become salesmen for a philosophical stand, who travel the roads of history in search of a clientele of confirmations; we are no longer either scholars testing a hypothesis, or philosophers interested in an ideal which history cannot promise to bless at all times.

The former position we wish to avoid. It is particularly uncomfortable when one's basic postulate about human nature is such that history cannot be anything but a tale full of sound and fury, signifying nothing. For it is a postulate which stresses the inevitability and universality of evil, and which assumes that reason, "far from following its own inherent impulses, is driven toward its goal by the irrational forces the ends of which it serves." [8] Now, this view makes it almost impossible to understand how there could be a rational theory of rational human behavior. This is not the last contradiction: the "realist" theory combines a Hobbesian image of naked power politics with an attempt to show that states are nevertheless not condemned to a life that is "nasty, brutish, and short"; "realism" thus puts its faith in voluntary restraints, moderation, and the underlying assumption of possible harmony among national interests—points scarcely admitted by the original postulate, and justified only by a view of power and politics that makes some place for, let us say, a reasonable view of reason. The key to this riddle is to be found in another contradiction which our previous discussion should have suggested: the sharp contrast between the original postulate, whose logic is a permanent clash of forces of evil, and the norm of eighteenth and nineteenth century international relations—the period in which the world's state of nature was most Lockian or Humean, and Mr. Morgenthau's view of human nature most unjustified.

With such flaws and contradictions, the policy guidance the realist theory is able to afford is limited. "Realism" allows us to eliminate those policies that would foolishly forget the prerequisite of power; but it does not go much further. Too often, it is possible to build alternative and conflicting cases of "realist" policies, or to justify in "realist" terms a policy that can also be defended on "utopian" grounds. Too many factors are left out for "realist" policy advice to avoid the dilemma of homilies and admonishments, or suggestions inappropriate for revolutionary periods, such as the advocacy of "peace through accomodation," diplomacy and compromise—a policy which runs against some of the facts of present international life, in particular against the unwillingness of the Soviet side

[7] Alfred Cobban, "The Decline of Political Theory," *Political Science Quarterly*, Vol. LXVIII, No. 3 (September 1953), p. 333.

[8] Hans J. Morgenthau, *Scientific Man vs. Power Politics*, Chicago, 1946, p. 154.

to accept such rules and to seek such deals. The light that illuminated the landscape in the quiet obscurity of nineteenth century politics, is blown out by today's tempest.

(2) Philosophies of history. There are other attempts at providing us with a master key, and at explaining as large an amount of data as possible. I refer to philosophies of history, to which specialists in international relations have sometimes turned and are likely to turn. Like Hegel and Marx, Spengler and (especially) Toynbee are in the process of being adopted by political scientists after having been repudiated by historians. They avoid many of the shortcomings of "realism." Whereas the latter is too much concerned with timeless propositions and permanent necessities, the former are rightly dealing with problems of time and change, and with the effects of changes within the units of the world on the relations between these units. Whereas "realism" puts the State at the center of its analysis, philosophies of history remind us that world politics is more than the intersection of various foreign policies, and that these policies often depend on whether the states address themselves to other members of the same civilization or culture, or to complete outsiders. If it is true that "only a universalist perspective permits a scientific understanding of international reality," [9] these philosophies are indispensable. They are useful also because of their method: the comparison of cultures or civilizations as if they were contemporary carries a lesson for international relations. Finally, philosophers of history have a disarming way of making explicit, and even central, assumptions about man, society, and history which are often repressed but nevertheless operating in all social scientists' schemes. Such candor is to be commended.

However, we are once more in the presence of a short cut. Here, a teleological interpretation which discourages further research and twists the facts into a predetermined pattern is substituted for careful and systematic explanation. It is "a set of advance-judgments," [10] a flaw we found already in "realism." Hence many similarities. First, the net is too wide to catch all the main factors in world affairs and to account for the main forces at work in a given period. Thus, it has been remarked that Toynbee's formula of challenge and response as the explanation of the genesis of civilizations amounts in practice to the arbitrary selection of one cause only: "in every given historical situation it refers to only one element, one out of many, one which, when we are concerned with historical presentation, cannot be abstracted from the others." [11]

Second, history is again ransacked for confirmation of a postulate, and

[9] Antonio Truyol, "La teoria de las relaciones internacionales como sociologia," (here trans. by S. H.), *Revista de Estudios Politicos,* Vol. 96, (November-December 1957), p. 335.

[10] Ernest Barker in M. F. Ashley Montagu (ed.), *Toynbee and History,* Boston, 1956, pp. 94-95.

[11] Peter Geyl in Geyl, Toynbee, and Sorokin, *The Pattern of the Past,* Boston, 1949, p. 23.

facts that do not fit are left out or thrown together under headings that are sometimes more tautological than explanatory, such as the notion of withdrawal-and-return, used to describe the action of creative individuals and minorities—an umbrella under which such different actors as Buddha, Dante, Kant, and England in modern history are supposed to find shelter. As for the postulate which history is begged to demonstrate, the difference with "realism" lies mainly in its nature: organic metaphors or spiritual revelations replace the power drive. The value of such sweeping hypotheses as explanations of reality is dubious; references to a permanent lust for power in human nature, or to a necessary cycle of birth, growth, maturity and decline, or to successive civilizations as steps in religious progress represent an escape from the task of causal explanation rather than the victorious accomplishment of this task. Indeed Spengler denied altogether the possibility of causal analysis and systematic understanding in history, when he stated that causes operate only in the natural sciences and destiny in history.

Third, it is not surprising that the criteria of fitness of civilizations or nations should once again be success or survival, for philosophies of history of the kind we are discussing try at the same time to assert the purposiveness of the universe, and the possibility of deducing historical laws from empirical reality; now any attempt to find purposiveness in history itself rather than in man's moral nature crashes into the impasse and inconsistency of setting up "a normative pattern for the evaluation of laws derived empirically" [12]—and the usual result consists of seeing in the success or the decline of cultures and peoples the sanction of their conformity to the great design which reveals itself in history.

Since philosophers of history see in history the unfolding of a design rather than the mere repetition of a basic pattern, the world is treated no longer as a field, but as a plan in which certain forces work toward an end wanted by God, nature, or history itself. Consequently, the main units of analysis are entities less likely to resist such a scheme than the ordinary units of historians or social scientists. The units of analysis used by the philosophers are huge aggregates such as classes, peoples, civilizations, cultures. Sometimes these units are useful to us; nevertheless they cannot be our only analytical tools, since we must deal primarily with those more modest but less hypothetical basic communities into which the world has been divided: the states, the empires. Sometimes the philosophers' units are altogether artificial congeries whose construction, number, existence, homogeneity and use are open to challenge, such as Spengler's Magian culture, whose reality remains in doubt. Thus we can pick out of these schemes useful insights, and think about suggestive hypotheses. But this road ends in the sky, not in a theory for international relations.

---

[12] Henry A. Kissinger, *The Meaning of History,* unpublished dissertation, Harvard University, 1950, p. 143.

2. Theory as a set of questions

There is another road which is supposed to end in theory. It is beginning to be much traveled. In a way, it seems less pretentious. Those who take it do not claim to have a thesis, a general explanation. The over-all theory is to be but the final salary of long and hard labor. But, it is said, we shall earn our salary only if we begin with a broad and detailed conceptual framework, a scheme "within which it may be possible to organize a theory" and "which specifies the variables which a theory will employ." We start with a central concept, or a set of central related concepts which will allow us to ask the right questions and to analyze the data systematically. We should end with a refined set of laws and propositions "capable of refutation or confirmation by means of controlled experiment or systematic observation." [13]

There is much in these ideas that is sound. But their ultimate usefulness depends on how they are being applied. Attempts made so far seem to me both discouraging and dangerous. There have been two main varieties: on the one hand, an attempt inspired by "general systems theory" (applied to international relations, interpreted in terms of "systems of action") as a first step toward a "system of theory"; on the other hand, attempts at using as a conceptual scheme one particular concept, supposedly strategic enough to allow the organization of the whole field around it. These two varieties will be discussed separately; but they have common characteristics, and many remarks on the first group apply at least in part to the second group as well.

(1) "Systems theory" in international relations. "Systems theory" has progressed mainly in social sciences other than those concerned with politics. It is a spectacular development of the behavioral sciences. Its advocate in international relations is primarily Mr. Morton Kaplan. The reader will find in the selection of Mr. Kaplan's book a description of the main characteristics of systems theory, which a psychologist has described as a series of related definitions, assumptions and postulates about all levels of systems (such as cells, organs, individuals, groups, and so on) and in particular living systems. In the case of international relations, I believe that "systems theory" is a huge misstep in the right direction—the direction of systematic empirical analysis.

It is an effort that raises fundamental questions about the proper purpose and methods of the social sciences in general, and international relations in particular. A writer has recently wondered whether the purpose of "scientism" such as systems theory was to produce systems rather than to achieve understanding of the social world; [14] or, as Alfred Cobban has

[13] See below, p. 104, the selection from Mr. Morton Kaplan's *System and Process in International Politics.*

[14] Norman Jacobson in Roland Young (ed.), *Approaches to the Study of Politics,* Chicago, 1958, pp. 115 ff.

remarked, the political scientist's effort to be a pure scientist is "mostly a device for avoiding politics without achieving science." [15] It is a fact that such efforts tend to invest almost all the scholars' energy in the building of models and boxes and the discussion of method. It is not sure that the systems thus constructed do contribute to our understanding, for in the process "the new scholastic tends . . . to conceptualize about concepts, regressing even further from empirical reality until he finds the logical consummation of his endeavour in mathematical symbols and other formal relations." [16] As a consequence only those problems that are relevant to the systems are being considered, whatever their relevance to the field. "The actual process is primarily one of splitting verbal hairs with an axe." [17] The complexity and barrenness of such efforts reminds me of the fabulously complicated machine built a few years ago by an American engineer. Its only point was that it had no point.

For more than a century, debate has been going on among philosophers as to the relations between the natural and the cultural sciences. Recently, two writers whose conception of the latter is very similar, nevertheless disagreed completely on the issue of the unity of method in natural and social science; Friedrich Hayek asserted that their respective methods were radically different; Karl Popper on the contrary stressed the similarities.[18] It seems to me that what is common to all scientific efforts, whatever their field, is an attitude of the mind—the desire to achieve knowledge, which implies the resort to methods of verification of the hypotheses derived from observation, experimentation or reasoning. However, the methods by which hypotheses are obtained and checked vary from science to science, because the kind of knowledge which one can hope to achieve varies from field to field. Now, the error made by "scientism" in the social sciences lies in a confusion between the *methods* of the physical sciences and the *purposes* of the social sciences: "systems theorists" have mistakenly identified the two, with the paradoxical result that whereas physical scientists shape their tools in order to promote discoveries and produce results, many social scientists tend to lose sight of their subject and to do a job of methodological byzantinism. Such a trend misunderstands the nature of the results that can be obtained in our field. Aristotle's warning has been forgotten: "look for precision in each class of things just so far as the nature of the subject admits." [19]

The scientific purposes of the representatives of this trend (admirably

[15] Cobban, "The Decline of Political Theory," p. 335.

[16] Hans J. Morgenthau, "Reflections on the State of Political Science," *Review of Politics,* Vol. 17, No. 4 (October 1955), p. 443.

[17] Barrington Moore, Jr., "The New Scholasticism and the Study of Politics," *World Politics,* Vol. VI, No. 1 (October 1953), p. 129.

[18] See Friedrich Hayek, *"The Counter-revolution of Science,"* (Glencoe 1952) and Karl Popper, *"The Poverty of Historicism"* (Boston, 1957).

[19] Quoted by Carl J. Friedrich, "Political Philosophy and the Science of Politics," in Young (ed.), *Approaches to the Study of Politics,* p. 176.

summed up by Mr. Kaplan's work) are: to discover laws, recurrent patterns, regularities, high-level generalizations; to make of predictability a test of science; to achieve as soon as possible the ideal of a deductive science, including a "set of primitive terms, definitions and axioms" from which "systematic theories are derived." [20] These objectives, it seems to me, are the wrong ones.

The search for laws is based on a misunderstanding, by social scientists, of the nature of laws in the physical sciences; these laws are seen as far more strict and absolute than they are. The best we can achieve in our discipline is the statement of trends. Because the experimental methods available in the social sciences are "not capable of *demonstrating* any causal laws," we can only eliminate certain hypotheses (i.e. find "negative laws"), and thus define limits, within which certain trends can be suggested with "some degree of approximation" only.[21] Max Weber's resort to "ideal types," for example, was an attempt to suggest the *influence* of certain factors by comparing "the real situation or action" with the construct he called "ideal type" and which consisted of the "accentuation" of those factors whose role he wanted to isolate. But his purpose was not to prove that those factors had "caused" the phenomena found in the real situation or action—for instance that Protestantism was the cause of capitalism. From his method, which many of his disciples have misunderstood, no system of laws "explaining" social reality can be derived. Indeed the reduction of our field to a system of laws, even if it could be done, would be an impoverishment. Max Weber himself warned that the knowledge of social laws was not the knowledge of social reality, but merely an aid for attaining this end.[22] The most general "laws" of international relations are bound to be fairly trivial generalizations, for in the social sciences "regularities are found only at the level of wholes," which must be broken up if we want to understand reality.[23] Exclusive emphasis on regularities leads to the rediscovery of platitudes—often an excellent point of departure, always an execrable destination.

The same remarks can be made about the great yearning for prediction. Again it springs from a misunderstanding of the natural sciences. First of all, not all of them are capable of yielding effective predictions (in this connection, we may remark that Mr. Kaplan's vocabulary shows greater inclination toward biology or astronomy than toward the much more elusive science of meteorology). Second, not even the most precise of the natural sciences predicts "what will actually happen": it only forecasts "what would happen if conditions were such and such." [24] Thus predictability is possible

[20] See below, p. 104, the selection from Mr. Morton Kaplan's book.

[21] M. Cohen and E. Nagel, *An Introduction to Logic and Scientific Method,* New York, 1934, pp. 266-7.

[22] See Shils and Finch (eds.), *Max Weber on the Methodology of the Social Sciences,* Glencoe, 1949, pp. 73 ff.

[23] Raymond Aron, *Introduction à la philosophie de l'histoire,* Paris, 1948, p. 227.

[24] See C. J. Friedrich, *Constitutional Government and Democracy,* Boston, 1946, pp. 571-2.

only in areas (such as military action) where the number of variables is limited and known in advance—two conditions which are rarely met in the social sciences, and never at the level of a general theory. "Even if our science of human nature were theoretically perfect, that is, if we could calculate any character as we can calculate the orbit of any planet, *from given data;* still, as the data are never all given, nor even precisely alike in different cases, we could neither make positive predictions, nor lay down universal propositions."[25] We can say that *z* will happen if *x* and *y* do; that *x* will occur if *a* and *b* do, and *y* if *c* and *d* do; but we always reach a stage when we must confess that we cannot predict whether *a*, or *b*, or *c*, or *d* will happen. Here again, the best we can do is to project into the future a limited number of possible trends, and rank them conditionally ("other things being equal . . ."). "Social scientists sometimes feel themselves to be second class citizens in the scientific community because they cannot make as firm predictions as their colleagues. There is no need for this if they define their task as making accurate assessments of the limits and possibilities of effective human behavior."[26] Prediction is a frustrating exercise, and it should not become the touchstone of adequate theory.

The ideal of a deductive science raises two sets of serious problems. On the one hand, even if one recognizes that every science rightly wants to become a closed system of hypotheses, the real question remains whether many social scientists do not show undue haste in trying to begin with a closed system, deprived of sufficient empirical referents. The construction of purely abstract hypotheses based on a small number of axioms, from which a number of propositions are deduced, is fraught with dangers which John Stuart Mill had listed in his critique of the "abstract and concrete deductive methods" in the social sciences. The abstract deductive method, which assumes that social phenomena result from only one force, tends to present in the form of logical propositions statements which are highly debatable because they neglect all the other forces which operate in reality. The concrete deductive method (which is rather badly named since it is not really concrete, but consists of deducing propositions "from many, not from one or a very few, original premises") can produce only hypotheses; now, "considering . . . in how accelerating a ratio the uncertainty of our conclusions increases as we attempt to take the effect of a greater number of concurrent causes into our calculations, the hypothetical combinations of circumstances on which we construct the general theorems of the science cannot be made very complex without so rapidly accumulating a liability to error as must soon deprive our conclusions of all value."[27]

Far from presenting to us testable hypotheses based on empirical observation, these abstract models are either a strange form of parlor game, too remote from reality to be testable, or else they are based on postulates

---

[25] J. S. Mill, *A System of Logic,* London, 1930, p. 554.

[26] Barrington Moore, Jr., *Political Power and Social Theory,* Cambridge, 1958, p. 151.

[27] Mill, *op. cit.*, p. 587.

about the behavior of the included variables, which are either too arbitrary or too general: the choice here is between perversion and platitude. It is the price of haste.

Indeed, when one combines the ideal of a deductive science and the desire to predict, one risks achieving perversion and platitude simultaneously, by committing what I would call the sin of the tautological prediction. If one builds a model of the behavior of certain groups (for instance, nations) based on a set of hypotheses about the variables which are supposed to determine the behavior of the groups, if, further, some of these hypotheses are highly questionable, and if, finally, the model rests on the assumption that these groups are interchangeable, then the "predictions" about the groups' behavior will be a mere restatement in the future tense of the original hypotheses, and thus comprise a totally arbitrary set of propositions about the groups concerned.[28] Such is the danger of "formal models of imaginary worlds, not generalizations about the real world." [29] It is the triumph of form over substance.

On the other hand, if we should agree that the science of international relations cannot be deductive at the outset, we are still faced with a second problem; what methods should we use now in trying to reduce the mass of facts to scientific analysis and order? It seems to me that "systems scientism," even in its more concrete or inductive aspects, uses totally inappropriate techniques. There are two sorts of aberrations. The first is a mixture of methods borrowed from other sciences. Thus Mr. Kaplan grafts concepts torn from sociology, economics, cybernetics, biology, and astronomy onto a very different subject—a strange method for believers in systems. The previous question: whether these concepts fit our field, has not been asked; consequently this interdisciplinary arsenal serves a pointless invasion of our field by uprooted foreign methods rather than a guided raid into neighboring fields by a rigorous method of our own. In a methodological version of the Catharic heresy, social scientists turn to other fields in order to find concepts more refined, more pure, more precise, more value-free than the traditional tools of analysis in international relations—and demonstrate that efforts at strict definition and conceptual purity in the social sciences lead to infinite regression, or startling mutilations, or fictions.

All too often the reasoning behind such efforts goes like this: "our science is not yet as advanced as economics (or sociology, or physics); therefore in order to progress in our discipline, let us treat our basic concepts—for instance, political power—as if they were assimilable to the clear and calculable concepts of the more advanced disciplines." And one

---

[28] For an example see Harold Guetzkow, "Isolation and Collaboration: a Political Theory of Inter-nation Relations," *Conflict Resolution,* Vol. I, No. 1 (1957), pp. 48-68.

[29] Ralf Dahrendorf, "Out of Utopia: Toward a Reorientation of Sociological Analysis," *American Journal of Sociology,* Vol. LXIV, No. 2 (September 1958), p. 120.

ends by treating political matters in anything but political terms, just as in Kelsen's theory of international law rules which do not exist are treated *as if* they existed and gaps which are big enough to swallow even the least utopian idealist are treated *as if* they did not exist. A pure science of politics, divorced from actual politics, is as objectionable as the pure theory of law, divorced from existing law.

Another aberration is the mushrooming of mathematical models, supposed to account for large parts of the field. Often, the scientist includes in his model only the variables that can be measured; in this case, he is likely to leave out some of the more decisive ones, and to put in satellite factors, which merely reflect, or result from, more important variables which are left out because they are not measurable.[30] Hence, far from explaining reality, many such models seem only to give mathematical substance to shadows, and to drive research into the chase and measurement of shadows. This, it seems to me, is one of the dangers of Mr. Karl Deutsch's recent efforts at arriving at a quantitative theory of national integration, and at taking measurable factors as indices of community formation.[31] For instance, a sudden increase in the flow of communications between neighboring areas (mail, trade, travel, intermarriage, and so on) may well reflect a collective desire for integration or a determination on the part of the leaders in those areas to promote integration; but it may not: we can find out only if we look at such non-measurable factors as the role of political elites, the attitudes and mores of various groups, the nature and effects of political and economic organization, and so on. This example shows also another danger of the emphasis on measurable variables: the reduction of the level of the problems examined; for example, excessive emphasis on the (measurable) communication channels can easily ensure the neglect of the substance and purposes of what is communicated.

Sometimes the model builders try to measure all the important variables; but this involves some fantastic assumptions, such as the postulate that in our discipline quantification always entails a gain in precision rather than a possible loss, or that quantities measured independently can be added or combined meaningfully. The result is quite literally a dismemberment of reality, due to the mistake of treating history, in Barrington Moore's words, as "a storehouse" in which facts are piled up as separate and discrete units,[32] and to the mistake of believing that political phenomena can be reduced to a measurable common denominator comparable to the currency unit in economics.

---

[30] See Jean Rivero, "Introduction to a Study of the Development of Federal Societies," *International Social Sciences Bulletin,* Vol. IV, No. 1 (Spring 1952), pp. 14-15.

[31] Karl Deutsch, *Nationalism and Social Communication,* Cambridge, Mass., 1953.

[32] Moore, *Political Power and Social Theory,* p. 132. The study by Karl Deutsch et al., *Political Community and the North Atlantic Area,* Princeton, 1957, which is nonmathematical, suffers slightly from the same tendency: considering the effect on integration of various factors treated one by one.

Finally, in most cases such models are based on postulates which are correct only in limited periods or in limited parts of the field. Thus, in game theory, which is discussed briefly in the excerpt of Jessie Bernard's study, the assumptions are that the rules of the game are not at stake, that the values are given at the outset and do not change, that all relevant information is available to the players, that the costs in the conflict can be calculated accurately, and that the conduct of the players is rational. These assumptions might fit a limited conflict in a nonrevolutionary era; but they hardly apply to a war in a revolutionary era in which all the previous rules of the game of world politics are challenged, or in which it is precisely the establishment of new rules by trial and error which is at stake. Nor do such assumptions fit those aspects of world politics which cannot be simply analyzed as games of strategy. Before the theory can be useful, qualitative elements will have to be reintroduced, for they play a crucial role in political games. "Human mathematics"—the mathematics which establish "rigorous relations between classes of individuals separated by discontinuous values, discontinuity being one of the essential properties of qualitative ensembles which distinguish them from one another" [33]—will have to be far more advanced than it is at present. Meanwhile, the results of such efforts is always a timeless and closed mathematical universe.

Not only are the purposes and methods of systems scientism open to criticism, but the results achieved so far are also questionable, on three counts. First, the map these efforts produce does not allow us to recognize the landscape. Precisely because they aim at a high level of generality and use tools coming from other disciplines, these systems do not capture the stuff of politics. The political patterns they study are always reduced to something else, because their enterprises are built on the shaky foundations of metaphors taken too seriously. "We cannot think creatively without metaphors, but any metaphor is in danger of becoming a categorical imperative." [34] It is significant that mechanics provide the dominant metaphor or the model which commands the vocabulary of the social scientists discussed here—a tendency which can be traced back to Pareto and Durkheim, and even further to the sixteenth and seventeenth centuries. Mechanism today has a new aspect which reflects the sophistication of modern technology: both in Mr. Kaplan's and in some of Mr. Deutsch's earlier works, men and societies are reduced to communication systems, without much concern for the substance of the "messages" these networks carry. Maybe communications theory will prove to be the common framework for efforts that seek to interpret the behavior of all systems "from atomic

---

[33] See Claude Levi-Strauss, "Les mathématiques de l'homme," *Esprit* (October 1956), p. 532.

[34] David Riesman, "Some Observations on the 'Older' and the 'Newer' Social Science," in Leonard D. White (ed.), *The State of the Social Sciences,* Chicago, 1956, p. 338.

particles to galaxies," from viruses to planets.[35] But this is not what we are interested in here. The definition of values as the operating preferences according to which certain messages are transmitted first[36] is a fine example of a statement which may be useful for cybernetics, but is merely tautological in international relations.

In addition to communications theory Mr. Kaplan has transplanted into alien soil some aspects of structural-functional theory. Even though he starts with one good idea, and one sound warning: the idea that there are various types of international systems, and the warning that these types are not integrated social systems, he soon forgets the warning and overextends the idea. He borrows his vocabulary from a discipline whose model is the integrated society. Concepts which fit such a model (and which are even within their own realm open to the challenge that most living societies cannot be analyzed in so simplified and static a way) do not fit at all the small international milieu characterized by "the extraordinary diversity of national situations." [37] Such heterogeneity vitiates an abstract discussion in terms of general "role functions." For the specialist in international relations, from the viewpoint of the "total system," the differences between the basic units are as important as the similarities; the opposite is true when the sociologist looks at the actors playing a role in the social system. Mr. Kaplan's roles, systems, and processes are assumed but not examined.

Consequently "sociologism" operates here too—in the most unlikely field. Systems are discussed as if they had a compulsive will of their own; the implicit God, Society, who gave its stuffy oppressiveness to the universe of Comte and Durkheim, is again at work, under the incognito of System. Each system assigns roles to actors; the structure of the system sets its needs, its needs determine its objectives, and "the objectives of a system are values for the system." [38] The old and mistaken habit of treating social facts like things is back again. It is not too surprising that the only processes discussed are processes of maintenance, integration, and disintegration; for the implied supreme value is stability: mechanical stability, since purposes and values other than preservation of the system are left out. It is the usual penalty for the double attempt to drive the consideration of values out of the subject matter, and to present a value-free theory: the status quo becomes an empirical and normative pivot. For only the closed society can be compared to an organism, or dealt with in terms which assume a closed system. International systems are always open and moving —at least sufficiently to force us to abandon the model and the vocabulary

---

[35] James G. Miller, *"Toward a General Theory for the Behavioral Sciences,"* in White, *op. cit.*, pp. 31-2.

[36] Karl Deutsch, "Mechanism, Organism and Society: Some Models in Natural and Social Science," *Philosophy of Science*, Vol. 18, No. 3 (July 1951), pp. 230-52.

[37] Edwin Dickinson, *Law and Peace*, Philadelphia, 1951, p. 6.

[38] Kaplan, *ibid.*, p. 149.

of the closed system. Such a model, which starts with the hypotheses of integration and equilibrium, proves totally unable to account for patterns of change and conflict, and tends to treat as disturbances the processes of change which are, in world affairs, certainly more a rule than an exception.

Second, the inadequacy of the results can be shown by pointing to their inability to *explain* world politics. On the one hand, excessive use of Occam's razor (i.e., a desire to reduce the theory to as few hypotheses as possible, and to prefer a single hypothesis to a complex one, because such simplicity makes a theory easier to use even though it might imply sheer formalism) and the tendency to reduce politics to what it is not, entail a loss of such vital elements as institutions, culture, and the action of individuals as autonomous variables rather than social atoms. As in the "realist" theory, Mr. Kaplan's emphasis on international systems also involves a neglect of the domestic determinants of the "national actors," and his model of "action" leaves out the forces of change operating within or across the "actors." [39] On the other hand, the striving for total objectivity (which almost means the reduction of subjects to objects), the desire to retain mainly measurable elements and the effort to build "systems" combine in the production of models in which many variables are interrelated, but where no hierarchy is established among the variables. The principle of "indetermination" [40] is followed with rigorous "scientism," as if it were compatible with the goal of predictability. It does not allow us to determine first what variables will be submitted to the standard scientific methods of verification and validation which determine whether these variables will be included in or excluded from our scheme; nor does it allow us to decide later whether the correlations we have discovered are meaningful or relevant or not.

Furthermore all the variables tend to be treated alike; it is only in their weight that they differ; factors which limit the range of political choices and affect the decision which is ultimately made among such alternatives are treated as if they were of the same kind as those decisions themselves: hence the mechanistic aspect of the models, concatenations of functions and correlations which distort reality far more than they account for it. Here, whatever its ambiguities, obscurities, and perils, the need for the method of "understanding" stressed by Max Weber cannot be denied.[41] We must interpret the correlations we have established; we must present hypotheses as to what variables are the most significant, and how the various correlations discovered between isolated phenomena are interrelated in the area which we try to explain. Otherwise we will end with overstuffed boxes, or with static schemes or, at best, with comparative statics. What is hidden

[39] See the similarities between Mr. Morgenthau's and Mr. Kaplan's conception of the national interest. Mr. Kaplan concludes that it is "objective": *ibid.*, p. 165.

[40] H. Lasswell and A. Kaplan, *Power and Society*, New Haven, 1950, p. xvii.

[41] See Shils and Finch, *Max Weber*, p. 57 ff. Talcott Parsons, *The Structure of Social Action*, New York, 1937, pp. 581 ff. H. Stuart Hughes, *Consciousness and Society*, Cambridge, 1958, pp. 310 ff.

behind the building of "indetermined" schemes is the belief or wish that a correct scientific analysis of a field would reveal all by itself the truth about the field. The subject, if it is submitted to the proper type of scrutiny, will divulge its essence without making it necessary for the specialist to do any interpreting of his own—and to run the frightful risks of subjectivity implied. All he needs is the most advanced form of scientific equipment. Without it, he would be lost; with it, the subject will obligingly disclose its true structure and its laws.

Thirdly, the inadequacy of the results of "systems theory" is also revealed, more indirectly but no less effectively, by the strange underground connection which exists between this theory and a particularly objectionable form of policy scientism. A view of the social universe as the interplay of impersonal forces, the lack of concern for the substance of politics, the procedural and mechanical analogies, the implied norm of stability lead the social scientist almost inevitably to a therapeutic and manipulative approach—to the belief that the control of the variables he has identified would push society in the direction he, or social "elites," deem desirable.[42] The connection between the cool and detached objectivity of the theorist and the *"engagement"* of the policy scientist is often made through another set of metaphors: metaphors about the health and sickness of societies and systems.[43] This is another part of Durkheim's heritage, another consequence of the assumption of equilibrium and integration as the norm: for what disturbs or denies the norm tends to be treated as abnormal. This is a way of arguing which can hardly have any claim to scientific positivism, for it is neither consistent with the pretense of value-freedom, nor does it make sense analytically as long as we do not know the laws of change from one system to another.

Indeed, it is a course which leads to highly unscientific results. On the one hand, precisely because the schemes established by systems theorists are static and not explanatory, when these writers want to suggest policies, they tend to jump from the extreme of indetermination to the extreme of "single-trend" analysis. They suddenly give crucial importance to one factor, without realizing that such a decision postulates both the existence of a general law which states "what kind of change in human culture will regularly follow upon specific changes" [44] in the selected factor, and the possibility of isolating this factor. On the other hand, reliance on system and method is so great that there is a tendency to assume that the "laws of equilibrium" of the system or the methods of scientific analysis will set by themselves the objectives to be attained. What happens instead is that the scientist mistakes for the objectives of his scientific system, the objectives

[42] See discussion of this tendency in Gunnar Myrdal, *An American Dilemma,* New York, 1949, pp. 1041 ff.

[43] See Morton Kaplan, *System and Process,* pp. 4 and 256 ff. See also Harold Lasswell, *World Politics and Personal Insecurity,* New York, 1935.

[44] Carl G. Hempel, "The Function of General Laws in History," *Journal of Philosophy,* Vol. XXXIX, No. 2 (January 1942), pp. 35-47.

of the social system in which he lives and which, not infrequently, he has more or less unconsciously taken as a point of departure for his system-building; the "nationalist celebration" [45] is one of the most curious practical consequences of systems theory. The result is bound to be either very dubious advice, or a considerable number of platitudes, all predicated on the fancy conception of the social scientist as an all-knowing, though democratic, brain-washer.[46]

(2) The approach of "unifying concepts." Attempts at organizing the discipline around a central "unifying concept" are less ambitious but not much more promising. First, as we have seen before, the field is too huge for even only its principal features to be subsumed under one key concept. Second, the choice of one central idea is inevitably based upon a postulate which is too debatable to serve as the single philosophical underpinning of a theoretical system.

There have been two such attempts recently. The first is M. Liska's equilibrium theory.[47] Although by contrast with the "realist" theory the central concept is supposedly used only as an analytical tool, and not as an explanation, the difference becomes almost invisible in practice. For the basic postulate is formulated in terms comparable to the basic assumption of "realism": states seek to secure the best attainable position of equilibrium (instead of: states seek to secure the best power position), and they should seek such a position as "a desirable policy for safe-guarding humane values" [48] (a statement which echoes the "realist" philosophy of the moral national interest). It seems to me that this double analytic and evaluative norm is also based on the model of the world of cabinet diplomacy, as the closest approximation of the norm. The "old teleological beliefs" in harmony which are behind this norm are far too open to criticism to be accepted without qualifications. In particular, the norm imposes a static bias on the data, since it assumes that international relations tend toward equilibrium and stability, and neglects the fact that here as elsewhere efforts toward equilibrium are often likely to produce change instead.

Since the concept presents itself also as the norm of a desirable policy, it runs into the objection that because of the countless varieties of "desirable" equilibrium such a norm must be infinitely more refined before it can be accepted.[49] In particular, it remains to be explained *why* equilibrium has

[45] This phrase is from C. W. Mills, *The Power Elite,* New York, 1956.

[46] See: George Lipsky, "The Theory of International Relations of Harold D. Lasswell," *Journal of Politics,* Vol. 17, No. 1 (February 1955), pp. 43-59; and Bernard Crick, "The Science of Politics in the United States," *Canadian Journal of Economics and Political Science,* Vol. XX, No. 3 (August 1954), pp. 308-20.

[47] M. Liska, *International Equilibrium,* Cambridge, 1957.

[48] See the excerpts, pp. 137-49, from *International Equilibrium.*

[49] See Thomas I. Cook's criticism of the concept, "The Political System: the Stubborn Search for a Science of Politics," *Journal of Philosophy,* Vol. 21, No. 4 (February 1954), pp. 128-37.

been selected as the supreme value (a philosophical "previous question" which the study dodges, just as almost all the efforts affected by "sociologism" and by its impossible striving for total objectivity, avoid any discussion of the values implied in the model or theory presented); it also remains for the writer to explain what particular form of equilibrium he considers ideal. Finally, there is more than a possibility of contradiction between the analytic and the evaluative aspects of the norm. The best attainable position of equilibrium which states do seek to secure is quite likely to conflict with that equilibrium "surviving and evolving by no other than peaceful means into higher forms of community," which states *should* seek.

Here we meet the more technical defects of the scheme. Again like that of power, the concept of equilibrium is both too broad and too narrow to serve as a useful central tool. Too broad: in order to make it meaningful, one has to distinguish various types of equilibrium, and soon the theory becomes as over-complicated as "realism" was over-simplified.[50] Infinite regression sets in, and the reader wonders how the equilibrium between all the partial equilibria is ever going to be assured. Too narrow: the risk of putting at the core of a system a mechanical concept is as great as the danger of emphasizing an instrumental concept like power; for it entails neglect of the purposes of the actors, whose objectives largely determine the nature of the final "equilibrium." Again, most of the processes of change are left out of the analysis, although they usually prevent international systems from attaining equilibrium.

There is a final flaw peculiar to equilibrium analysis. This framework is largely a product of metaphoric thinking—this time an import from economics. The concept of equilibrium makes sense in a universe of measurable variables, in which human behavior can be treated as a parameter, and whose rules are determined by the political and social universe which includes it. Such analysis makes little sense in the political universe, for here the establishment of these rules is one of the main stakes, human behavior must be treated as uncertain, most variables are not measurable, and the empirical verification of equilibrium is limited to very small sectors of behavior. For instance, the "balance between the power of the principal Great Powers and their sense of responsibility and self-restraint," which Professor Liska mentions, is hardly a measurable quantity. Attempts at treating political affairs as an equivalent of economics, at measuring power as if it were wealth, at analyzing political processes as if they were an exchange of goods, at studying the "ingredients of power" (such as political commitments and "contingent support") in the same way as the factors of production, or the types of power (security, the control of facilities, and so on) in the same way as shares of income, can only, like other borrowings from various neighboring disciplines, end in platitudes or

[50] See the distinction of various equilibria in Liska, *International Equilibrium,* pp. 13-14. 52, 57, and 132 ff.

in questionable hypotheses based on too small a selection of variables or too distorting a set of assumptions.[51]

With the second attempt, Mr. Snyder's decision-making approach, we move back to a scheme which is largely inspired by modern theories of organization and communication. We can no longer accuse the author of leaving out too many crucial variables, or of putting at the heart of his scheme a concept whose value implications and empirical significance interfere with each other. Indeed, the framework suffers from exactly the opposite defects. The box built by Mr. Snyder is so filled with smaller boxes within boxes that before it can be used, much has to be thrown out.[52] First, this approach obeys the principle of indetermination and fails to suggest which one of the numerous elements that go into the many sides of the box are likely to be most relevant. One of the paradoxes of the search for pure "interrelatedness" is that the scheme ends with a mere enumeration of factors: we are being shown the pearls, and we are told that they are somehow connected. Secondly, the combined disadvantage of this "value-free" central concept and of the loan from organization and communication theories is proceduralism—the consideration, once more, of world politics as a set of procedures (easily represented by circles and arrows) irrespective of the substance of the "messages" carried or decisions made.

As for the assumption behind the concept, it is that "action" in international relations can be defined as a set of decisions made by recognizable units. This postulate can be attacked both for what it includes and for what it excludes. First, it implies that politics is normally made of highly conscious moves and choices that can be analyzed in terms of neat categories. I am not sure that this is the way things happen, that actions can easily be isolated in time, pinned down like butterflies, broken up into clear elements, and compared as if the measurement of alternatives and preferences in politics had been invented. Mr. Snyder explains that his scheme is intended to recreate the world of the decision-makers as they view it, rather than to recreate the situation "objectively, i.e., by the observer's judgment." [53] It seems to me however that the very nature of the "box" and of its categories implies at least a recreation of the mental universe of the decision makers (if not of the world at large as seen through their mental universe) by the user of the scheme. Second, the postulate leaves out of international relations everything that is not the mere addition

[51] See a critique of these attempts by Bruno Leoni, "The Meaning of 'Political' in Political Decisions," *Political Studies,* Vol. V, No. 3 (October 1957), pp. 225-39. Mr. Talcott Parsons' recent attempt to analyze the "polity" as a "subsystem of society" parallel with the economy (a reversal of his previous position as presented in *The Social System*) is to be found in his essay in Young (ed.), *Approaches to the Study of Politics,* pp. 298 ff.

[52] Compare Mr. Snyder's scheme with the simpler and more convincing framework in Bernard Cohen, *The Political Process and Foreign Policy,* Princeton, 1957.

[53] See page 150, the excerpt from *Decision-Making as an Approach to the Study of International Politics.*

of separate decisions made by various units. Many patterns and rules of world politics, such as the balance of power, or international law, are only in part a deliberate product of the statesman's will. In part, the balance of power is a broad automatic device, and international law the accretion of customs that cannot be explained by Mr. Snyder's "phenomenological" approach. The theory's focus might be right for foreign-policy analysis, but it is too weak for the rest of international relations. Generalizations based on comparative studies of decision-making will be misleading if the international context which conditions the behavior of the units is not studied more adequately. All this does not mean that decision-making is not a highly useful tool of analysis. In fact, Mr. Snyder's scheme is most impressive. But it is impressive as a detailed approach to the study of decision-making, not to the whole of international relations.

B. READINGS

The selections reprinted here illustrate the main contemporary theories of international relations.

A first group of three selections deals with the "great debate" which raged a few years ago around Professor Morgenthau's theory of power politics. I have included an excerpt from his book, *Politics Among Nations* (2nd ed.), which contains the author's definition of realism and his definition of political power. An excerpt from Professor Morgenthau's rebuttal of his critics, published in 1952, will be found next; the passage deals with his conception of the national interest. The third piece is an article by Raymond Aron which gives a sharply critical view of both realism and idealism, and concentrates particularly on the ambiguities of the concept of the national interest. The translation of Professor Aron's article from the original French is mine; I have eliminated certain passages in which Professor Aron commented on aspects of the world situation as it was at the time of his writing, and I have slightly condensed certain other passages.

Mr. Thompson's article on Toynbee is included here as an example of the lessons which students of international relations can draw from the works of philosophers of history. Mr. Thompson is a most skillful partisan of political "realism," and it is therefore not surprising that he should have tried to stress in Mr. Toynbee's enormous works those aspects which bolster the arguments of "realism." Other "laws" and points could be derived from Toynbee; nevertheless Mr. Thompson's article represents, I think, the sharpest attempt at using philosophies of history for the purposes of our discipline—and selecting reasonably short, coherent, and suggestive passages from Toynbee (or Spengler) directly would be almost impossible.

The third group of readings deals with contemporary efforts at building conceptual frameworks largely from the materials provided by sociological theory and social communications. The reader will find here a rather long excerpt from Mr. Morton Kaplan's book, *System and Process in International Politics;* it contains a general presentation of the book, a general discussion of the meaning of theory, and an analysis of political systems in the perspective chosen by Mr. Kaplan ("systems" theory). Next comes an excerpt from a survey, by Professor Jessie Bernard, of recent sociological research on international conflict; in this excerpt she describes and briefly discusses two kinds of research to which I have alluded in my commentary: mathematical studies and game theory. Finally, the reader will find a selection from George Liska's book, *International Equilibrium,* in which he outlines an equilibrium theory for international relations and describes its advantages; and a selection from the monograph of Professors Snyder, Bruck, and Sapin, *Decision-Making as an Approach to the Study of International Politics,* in which some of the principal elements in this complicated scheme, such as the state, the situation, the setting, decision-making, the organization unit, and the limitations on decision-making, are discussed and defined.

1. HANS J. MORGENTHAU

Politics Among Nations

A Realist Theory of International Politics

This book purports to present a theory of international politics. The test by which such a theory must be judged is not *a priori* and abstract but empirical and pragmatic. The theory, in other words, must be judged not by some preconceived abstract principle or concept unrelated to reality, but by its purpose: to bring order and meaning to a mass of phenomena which without it would remain disconnected and unintelligible. It must meet a dual test, an empirical and a logical one. Do the facts as they actually are lend themselves to the interpretation the theory has put upon them, and do the conclusions at which the theory arrives follow with logical necessity from its premises? In short, is the theory consistent with the facts and with itself?

The issue this theory raises concerns the nature of all politics. The his-

Reprinted from Hans J. Morgenthau, *Politics Among Nations* (2nd ed.), pp. 3-13 and 25-34, by permission of Alfred A. Knopf, Inc., New York.

tory of modern political thought is the story of a contest between two schools that differ fundamentally in their conceptions of the nature of man, society, and politics. One believes that a rational and moral political order, derived from universally valid abstract principles, can be achieved here and now. It assumes the essential goodness and infinite malleability of human nature, and blames the failure of the social order to measure up to the rational standards on lack of knowledge and understanding, obsolescent social institutions, or the depravity of certain isolated individuals or groups. It trusts in education, reform, and the sporadic use of force to remedy these defects.

The other school believes that the world, imperfect as it is from the rational point of view, is the result of forces inherent in human nature. To improve the world one must work with those forces, not against them. This being inherently a world of opposing interest and of conflict among them, moral principles can never be fully realized, but must at best be approximated through the ever temporary balancing of interests and the ever precarious settlement of conflicts. This school, then, sees in a system of checks and balances a universal principle for all pluralist societies. It appeals to historic precedent rather than to abstract principles, and aims at the realization of the lesser evil rather than of the absolute good.

This theoretical concern with human nature as it actually is, and with the historic processes as they actually take place, has earned for the theory presented here the name of "realism." What are the tenets of political realism? No systematic exposition of the philosophy of political realism can be attempted here; it will suffice to single out six fundamental principles, which have frequently been misunderstood.

1. Six principles of political realism

1. *Political realism* believes that politics, like society in general, is governed by objective laws that have their roots in human nature. In order to improve society it is first necessary to understand the laws by which society lives. The operation of these laws being impervious to our preferences, men will challenge them only at the risk of failure.

Realism, believing as it does in the objectivity of the laws of politics, must also believe in the possibility of developing a rational theory that reflects, however imperfectly and one-sidedly, these objective laws. It believes also, then, in the possibility of distinguishing in politics between truth and opinion—between what is true objectively and rationally, supported by evidence and illuminated by reason, and what is only a subjective judgment, divorced from the facts as they are and informed by prejudice and wishful thinking.

Human nature, in which the laws of politics have their roots, has not changed since the classical philosophies of China, India, and Greece endeavored to discover these laws. Hence, novelty is not necessarily a virtue in political theory, nor is old age a defect. The fact that a theory of politics, if there be such a theory, has never been heard of before tends to create a presumption against, rather than in favor of, its soundness. Conversely, the fact that a theory of politics was developed hundreds or even thousands of years ago—as was the theory of balance of power—does not create a presumption that it must be outmoded and obsolete. A theory of politics must be subjected to the dual test of reason and experience. To dismiss such a theory because it had its flowering in centuries past is to present not a rational argument but a modernistic prejudice that takes for granted the superiority of the present over the past. To dispose of the revival of such a theory as a "fashion" or a "fad" is tantamount to assuming that in matters political we can have opinions but no truths.

For realism, theory consists in ascertaining facts and giving them meaning through reason. It assumes that the character of a foreign policy can be ascertained only through the examination of the political acts performed and of the foreseeable consequences of these acts. Thus, we can find out what statesmen have actually done, and from the foreseeable consequences of their acts we can surmise what their objectives might have been.

Yet examination of the facts is not enough. To give meaning to the factual raw material of foreign policy, we must approach political reality with a kind of rational outline, a map that suggests to us the possible meanings of foreign policy. In other words, we put ourselves in the position of a statesman who must meet a certain problem of foreign policy under certain circumstances, and we ask ourselves what the rational alternatives are from which a statesman may choose who must meet this problem under these circumstances (presuming always that he acts in a rational manner), and which of these rational alternatives this particular statesman, acting under these circumstances, is likely to choose. It is the testing of this rational hypothesis against the actual facts and their consequences that gives meaning to the facts of international politics and makes a theory of politics possible.

2. The main signpost that helps political realism to find its way through the landscape of international politics is the concept of interest defined in terms of power. This concept provides the link between reason trying to understand international politics and the facts to be understood. It sets politics as an independent sphere of action and understanding apart from other spheres, such as economics, ethics, aesthetics, or religion. Without such a concept a theory of politics, international or domestic, would be altogether impossible, for without it we could not distinguish between political and non-political facts, nor could we bring at least a measure of systematic order to the political sphere.

We assume that statesmen think and act in terms of interest defined as power, and the evidence of history bears that assumption out. That assumption allows us to retrace and anticipate, as it were, the steps a statesman—past, present, or future—has taken or will take on the political scene. We look over his shoulder when he writes his dispatches; we listen in on his conversation with other statesmen; we read and anticipate his very thoughts. Thinking in terms of interest defined as power, we think as he does, and as disinterested observers we understand his thoughts and actions perhaps better than he, the actor on the political scene, does himself.

The concept of interest defined as power imposes intellectual discipline upon the observer, infuses rational order into the subject matter of politics, and thus makes the theoretical understanding of politics possible. On the side of the actor, it provides for rational discipline in action and creates that astounding continuity in foreign policy which makes American, British, or Russian foreign policy appear as an intelligible, rational continuum, by and large consistent within itself, regardless of the different motives, preferences, and intellectual and moral qualities of successive statesmen. A realist theory of international politics, then, will guard against two popular fallacies: the concern with motives and the concern with ideological preferences.

To search for the clue to foreign policy exclusively in the motives of statesmen is both futile and deceptive. It is futile because motives are the most illusive of psychological data, distorted as they are, frequently beyond recognition, by the interests and emotions of actor and observer alike. Do we really know what our own motives are? And what do we know of the motives of others?

Yet even if we had access to the real motives of statesmen, that knowledge would help us little in understanding foreign policies and might well lead us astray. It is true that the knowledge of the statesman's motives may give us one among many clues as to what the direction of his foreign policy might be. It cannot give us, however, the one clue by which to predict his foreign policies. History shows no exact and necessary correlation between the quality of motives and the quality of foreign policy. This is true both of moral and of political qualities.

We cannot conclude from the good intentions of a statesman that his foreign policies will be either morally praiseworthy or politically successful. Judging his motives, we can say that he will not intentionally pursue policies that are morally wrong, but we can say nothing about the probability of their success. If we want to know the moral and political qualities of his actions, we must know them, not his motives. How often have statesmen been motivated by the desire to improve the world, and ended by making it worse? And how often have they sought one goal, and ended by achieving something that they neither expected nor desired?

. . . Good motives give assurance against deliberately bad policies; they do not guarantee that the policies they inspire will be in fact morally good and politically successful. What it is important to know, if one wants to understand foreign policy, is not primarily the motives of a statesman, but his intellectual ability to comprehend the essentials of foreign policy, as well as his political ability to translate what he has comprehended into successful political action. It follows that while ethics in the abstract judges the moral qualities of motives, political theory must judge the political qualities of intellect, will, and action.

A realist theory of international politics will also avoid the other popular fallacy of equating the foreign policies of a statesman with his philosophic or political sympathies, and of deducing the former from the latter. Statesmen, especially under contemporary conditions, may well make it a habit of presenting their foreign policies in terms of their philosophic and political sympathies in order to gain popular support for them. Yet they will distinguish with Lincoln between their "*official* duty," which is to think and act in terms of the national interest, and their "*personal* wish," which is to see their own moral values and political principles realized throughout the world. Political realism does not require, nor does it condone, indifference to political ideals and moral principles, but it requires indeed a sharp distinction between the desirable and the possible, between what is desirable everywhere and at all times and what is possible under the concrete circumstances of time and place.

It stands to reason that not all foreign policies have always followed so rational, objective, and unemotional a course. The contingent elements of personality, prejudice, and subjective preference, and of all the weaknesses of intellect and will which flesh is heir to, are bound to deflect foreign policies from their rational course. Especially where foreign policy is conducted under the conditions of democratic control, the need to marshal popular emotions to the support of foreign policy cannot fail to impair the rationality of foreign policy itself. Yet a theory of foreign policy which aims at rationality must for the time being, as it were, abstract from these irrational elements and seek to paint a picture of foreign policy which presents the rational essence to be found in experience, without the contingent deviations from rationality which are also found in experience.

The difference between international politics as it actually is and a rational theory derived from it is like the difference between a photograph and a painted portrait. The photograph shows everything that can be seen by the naked eye; the painted portrait does not show everything that can be seen by the naked eye, but it shows, or at least seeks to show, one thing that the naked eye cannot see: the human essence of the person portrayed.

Political realism contains not only a theoretical but also a normative element. It knows that political reality is replete with contingencies and points to the typical influences they exert upon foreign policy. Yet it shares with all social theory the need, for the sake of theoretical understanding, to stress the rational elements of political reality; for it is these rational elements that make reality intelligible for theory. Political realism presents the theoretical construct of a rational foreign policy which experience can never completely achieve.

At the same time political realism considers a rational foreign policy to be good foreign policy; for only a rational foreign policy minimizes risks and maximizes benefits and, hence, complies both with the moral precept of prudence and the political requirement of success. Political realism wants the photographic picture of the political world to resemble as much as possible its painted portrait. Aware of the inevitable gap between good—that is, rational—foreign policy and foreign policy as it actually is, political realism maintains not only that theory must focus upon the rational elements of political reality, but also that foreign policy ought to be rational in view of its own moral and practical purposes.

Hence, it is no argument against the theory here presented that actual foreign policy does not or cannot live up to it. The argument misunderstands the intention of this book, which is to present not an indiscriminate description of political reality, but a rational theory of international politics. As such it cannot help being selective. Far from being invalidated by the fact that, for instance, a perfect balance of power policy will scarcely be found in reality, it starts with the assumption that reality is deficient in this respect.

3. Realism does not endow its key concept of interest defined as power with a meaning that is fixed once and for all. The idea of interest is indeed of the essence of politics and is unaffected by the circumstances of time and place. Thucydides' statement, born of the experiences of ancient Greece, that "identity of interest is the surest of bonds whether between states or individuals" was taken up in the nineteenth century by Lord Salisbury's remark that "the only bond of union that endures" among nations is "the absence of all clashing interests." It was echoed and enlarged upon in our century by Max Weber's observation:

> Interests (material and ideal), not ideas, dominate directly the actions of men. Yet the "images of the world" created by these ideas have very often served as switches determining the tracks on which the dynamism of interests kept the actions moving.[1]

Yet the kind of interest determining political action in a particular period of history depends upon the political and cultural context within which foreign policy is formulated. The goals that might be pursued by nations in their foreign policy can run the whole gamut of objectives any nation has ever pursued or might possibly pursue.

The same observations apply to the concept of power. Its context and the manner of its use are determined by the political and cultural environment. Power may comprise anything that establishes and maintains the control of man over man. Thus power covers all social relationships which serve that end, from physical violence to the most subtle psychological ties by which one mind controls another. Power covers the domination of man by man, both when it is disciplined by moral ends and controlled by constitutional safeguards as in Western democracies, and when it is that un-

[1] Marianne Weber, *Max Weber,* Tübingen: J. C. B. Mohr, 1926, pp. 347-8.

tamed and barbaric force which finds its laws in nothing but its own strength and its sole justification in its aggrandizement.

Political realism does not assume that the contemporary conditions under which foreign policy operates, with their extreme instability and the ever present threat of large-scale violence, cannot be changed. The balance of power, for instance, is indeed a perennial element of all pluralistic societies, as the authors of *The Federalist* papers well knew; yet it is capable of operating, as it does in the United States, under the conditions of relative stability and peaceful conflict. If the factors that have given rise to these conditions can be duplicated on the international scene, similar conditions of stability and peace will then prevail there, as they have over long stretches of history among certain nations.

What is true of the general character of international relations is also true of the nation state as the ultimate point of reference of foreign policy at the present time. While the realist indeed believes that interest is the perennial standard by which political action must be judged and directed, the contemporary connection between interest and the national state is a product of history, and is therefore bound to disappear in the course of history. Nothing in the realist position militates against the assumption that the present division of the political world into nation states will be replaced by larger units of a quite different character, more in keeping with the technical circumstances and the moral requirements of the contemporary world.

The realist parts company with other schools of thought before the all-important question of how the contemporary world is to be transformed. The realist is persuaded that this transformation can be achieved only through the workmanlike manipulation of the perennial forces that have shaped the past as they will the future. The realist cannot be persuaded that we can bring about that transformation by confronting a political reality that has its own laws with an abstract ideal that refuses to take those laws into account.

4. Political realism is aware of the moral significance of political action. It is also aware of the ineluctable tension between the moral command and the requirements of successful political action. And it is unwilling to gloss over and obliterate that tension and thus to obfuscate both the moral and the political issue by making it appear as though the stark facts of politics were morally more satisfying than they actually are, and the moral law less exacting than it actually is.

Realism maintains that universal moral principles cannot be applied to the actions of states in their abstract universal formulation, but that they must be filtered through the concrete circumstances of time and place. The individual may say for himself: "*Fiat justitia, pereat mundus* (Let justice be done, even if the world perish)," but the state has no right to say so in the name of those who are in its care. Both individual and state must judge political action by universal moral principles, such as that of liberty.

Yet while the individual has a moral right to sacrifice himself in defense of such a moral principle, the state has no right to let its moral disapprobation of the infringement of liberty get in the way of successful political action, itself inspired by the moral principle of national survival. There can be no political morality without prudence; that is, without consideration of the political consequences of seemingly moral action. Realism, then, considers prudence—the weighing of the consequences of alternative political actions—to be the supreme virtue in politics. Ethics in the abstract judges action by its conformity with the moral law; political ethics judges action by its political consequences. Classical and medieval philosophy knew this and so did Lincoln when he said:

> I do the very best I know how, the very best I can, and I mean to keep doing so until the end. If the end brings me out all right, what is said against me won't amount to anything. If the end brings me out wrong, ten angels swearing I was right would make no difference.

5. Political realism refuses to identify the moral aspirations of a particular nation with the moral laws that govern the universe. As it distinguishes between truth and opinion, so it distinguishes between truth and idolatry. All nations are tempted—and few have been able to resist the temptation for long—to clothe their own particular aspirations and actions in the moral purposes of the universe. To know that nations are subject to the moral law is one thing, while to pretend to know with certainty what is good and evil in the relations among nations is quite another. There is a world of difference between the belief that all nations stand under the judgment of God, inscrutable to the human mind, and the blasphemous conviction that God is always on one's side and that what one wills oneself cannot fail to be willed by God also.

The light-hearted equation between a particular nationalism and the counsels of Providence is morally indefensible, for it is that very sin of pride against which the Greek tragedians and the Biblical prophets have warned rulers and ruled. That equation is also politically pernicious, for it is liable to engender the distortion in judgment which, in the blindness of crusading frenzy, destroys nations and civilizations—in the name of moral principle, ideal, or God himself.

On the other hand, it is exactly the concept of interest defined in terms of power that saves us from both that moral excess and that political folly. For if we look at all nations, our own included, as political entities pursuing their respective interests defined in terms of power, we are able to do justice to all of them. And we are able to do justice to all of them in a dual sense: We are able to judge other nations as we judge our own and, having judged them in this fashion, we are then capable of pursuing policies that respect the interests of other nations, while protecting and promoting those of our own. Moderation in policy cannot fail to reflect the moderation of moral judgment.

6. The difference, then, between political realism and other schools of thought is real and it is profound. However much the theory of political realism may have been misunderstood and misinterpreted, there is no gainsaying its distinctive intellectual and moral attitude to matters political.

Intellectually, the political realist maintains the autonomy of the political sphere, as the economist, the lawyer, the moralist maintain theirs. He thinks in terms of interest defined as power, as the economist thinks in terms of utility; the lawyer, of the conformity of action with legal rules; the moralist, of conformity of action with moral principles. The economist asks: "How does this policy affect the welfare of society, or a segment of it?" The lawyer asks: "Is this policy in accord with the rules of law?" The moralist asks: "Is this policy in accord with moral principles?" And the political realist asks: "How does this policy affect the power of the nation?" (Or of the federal government, of Congress, of the party, of agriculture, as the case may be.)

The political realist is not unaware of the existence and relevance of standards of thought other than the political one. As political realist, he cannot but subordinate these other standards to the political one. And he parts company with other schools when they impose standards of thought appropriate to other spheres upon the political one. It is here that political realism takes issue with the "legalistic-moralistic approach" to international politics. That this issue is not, as has been contended, a mere figment of the imagination, but goes to the very core of the controversy, can be shown from many historical examples. Two will suffice to make the point.[2]

In 1939 the Soviet Union attacked Finland. This action confronted France and Great Britain with two issues, one legal, the other political. Did that action violate the Covenant of the League of Nations and, if it did, what counter measures should France and Great Britain take? The legal question could easily be answered in the affirmative, for obviously the Soviet Union had done what was prohibited by the Covenant. The answer to the political question depended, first, upon the manner in which the Russian action affected the interests of France and Great Britain; second, upon the existing distribution of power between France and Great Britain, on the one hand, and the Soviet Union and other potentially hostile nations, especially Germany, on the other; and, third, upon the influence that the counter measures were likely to have upon the interests of France and Great Britain and the future distribution of power. France and Great Britain, as the leading members of the League of Nations, saw to it that the Soviet Union was expelled from the League, and they were prevented from joining Finland in the war against the Soviet Union only by Sweden's refusal to allow their troops to pass through Swedish terri-

[2] See the other examples discussed in Hans J. Morgenthau, "Another 'Great Debate': The National Interest of the United States," *The American Political Science Review,* Vol. XLVI, No. 4 (December 1952), pp. 979 ff.

tory on their way to Finland. If this refusal by Sweden had not saved them, France and Great Britain would shortly have found themselves at war with the Soviet Union and Germany at the same time.

The policy of France and Great Britain was a classic example of legalism in that they allowed the answer to the legal question, legitimate within its sphere, to determine their political actions. Instead of asking both questions, that of law and that of power, they asked only the question of law; and the answer they received could have no bearing on the issue that their very existence might have depended upon.

The other example illustrates the "moralistic approach" to international politics. It concerns the international status of the Communist government of China. The rise of that government confronted the Western world with two issues; one moral, the other political. Were the nature and policies of that government in accord with the moral principles of the Western world? Should the Western world deal with such a government? The answer to the first question could not fail to be in the negative. Yet it did not follow with necessity that the answer to the second question should also be in the negative. The standard or thought applied to the first—the moral—question was simply to test the nature and the policies of the Communist government of China by the principles of Western morality. On the other hand, the second—the political—question had to be subjected to the complicated test of the interests involved and the power available on either side, and of the bearing of one or the other course of action upon these interests and power. The application of this test could well have led to the conclusion that it would be wiser not to deal with the Communist government of China. To arrive at this conclusion by neglecting this test altogether and answering the political question in terms of the moral issue was indeed a classic example of the "moralistic approach" to international politics.

This realist defense of the autonomy of the political sphere against its subversion by other modes of thought does not imply disregard for the existence and importance of these other modes of thought. It rather implies that each be assigned their proper sphere and function. Political realism is based upon a pluralistic conception of human nature. Real man is a composite of "economic man," "political man," "moral man," "religious man," et cetera. A man who was nothing but "political man" would be a beast, for he would be completely lacking in moral restraints. A man who was nothing but "moral man" would be a fool, for he would be completely lacking in prudence. A man who was nothing but "religious man" would be a saint, for he would be completely lacking in worldly desires.

Recognizing that these different facets of human nature exist, political realism also recognizes that in order to understand one of them one has to deal with it on its own terms. That is to say, if I want to understand "religious man" I must for the time being abstract from the other aspects of human nature and deal with its religious aspect as if it were the only one. Furthermore, I must apply to the religious sphere the standards of thought appropriate to it, always remaining aware of the existence of other standards and their actual influence upon the religious qualities of man. What is true of this facet of human nature is true of all the others. No modern economist, for instance, would conceive of his science and its relations to other sciences of man in any other way. It is exactly through such a process of emancipation from other standards of thought, and the development of one appropriate to its subject matter, that economics has developed as an autonomous theory of the economic activities of man. To contribute to similar development in the field of politics is indeed the purpose of political realism. . . .

Political Power

1. *What is political power?*

A. *Its relation to the nation as a whole.* International politics, like all politics, is a struggle for power. Whatever the ultimate aims of international politics, power is always the immediate aim. Statesmen and peoples may ultimately seek freedom, security, prosperity, or power itself. They may define their goals in terms of a religious, philosophic, economic, or social ideal. They may hope that this ideal will materialize through its own inner force, through divine intervention, or through the natural development of human affairs. They may also try to further its realization through nonpolitical means, such as technical co-operation with other nations or international organizations. But whenever they strive to realize their goal by means of international politics, they do so by striving for power. The Crusaders wanted to free the holy places from domination by the Infidels; Woodrow Wilson wanted to make the world safe for democracy; the National Socialists wanted to open Eastern Europe to German colonization, to dominate Europe, and to conquer the world. Since they all chose power to achieve these ends, they were actors on the scene of international politics.[3]

Two conclusions follow from this concept of international politics. First, not every action that a nation performs with respect to another nation is of a political nature. Many such activities are normally undertaken without any consideration of power, nor do they normally affect the power of the nation undertaking them. Many legal, economic, humanitarian, and cultural activities are of this kind. Thus a nation is not normally engaged in international politics when it concludes an extradition treaty with another nation, when it exchanges goods and services with other nations, when it co-operates with other nations in providing relief from natural catastrophes, and when it promotes the distribution of cultural achievements throughout the world. In other words, the involvement of a nation

[3] For some significant remarks on power in relation to international politics, see Lionel Robbins, *The Economic Causes of War,* London, Jonathan Cape, 1939, pp. 63 ff.

in international politics is but one among many types of activities in which a nation can participate on the international scene.

Second, not all nations are at all times to the same extent involved in international politics. The degree of their involvement may run all the way from the maximum involvement that at present has been attained by the United States and the Soviet Union, through the minimum involvement of such countries as Switzerland, Luxembourg, or Venezuela, to the noninvolvement of Liechtenstein and Monaco. Similar extremes can be noticed in the history of particular countries. Spain in the sixteenth and seventeenth centuries was one of the main active participants in the struggle for power on the international scene, but plays today only a marginal role in it. The same is true of such countries as Austria, Sweden, and Switzerland. On the other hand, nations like the United States, the Soviet Union, and China are today much more deeply involved in international politics than they were fifty or even twenty years ago. In short, the relation of nations to international politics has a dynamic quality. It changes with the vicissitudes of power, which may push a nation into the forefront of the power struggle, or may deprive a nation of the ability to participate actively in it. It may also change under the impact of cultural transformations, which may make a nation prefer other pursuits, for instance commerce, to those of power.

B. *Its nature.* When we speak of power in the context of this book, we have in mind not man's power over nature, or over an artistic medium, such as language, speech, sound, or color, or over the means of production or consumption, or over himself in the sense of self-control. When we speak of power, we mean man's control over the minds and actions of other men. By political power we refer to the mutual relations of control among the holders of public authority and between the latter and the people at large.

Political power, however, must be distinguished from force in the sense of the actual exercise of physical violence. The threat of physical violence in the form of police action, imprisonment, capital punishment, or war is an intrinsic element of politics. When violence becomes an actuality, it signifies the abdication of political power in favor of military or pseudo-military power. In international politics in particular, armed strength as a threat or a potentiality is the most important material factor making for the political power of a nation. If it becomes an actuality in war, it signifies the substitution of military for political power. The actual exercise of physical violence substitutes for the psychological relation between two minds, which is of the essence of political power, the physical relation between two bodies, one of which is strong enough to dominate the other's movements. It is for this reason that in the exercise of physical violence the psychological element of the political relationship is lost, and that we must distinguish between military and political power.

Political power is a psychological relation between those who exercise it and those over whom it is exercised. It gives the former control over certain actions of the latter through the influence which the former exert over the latter's minds. That influence may be exerted through orders, threats, persuasion, or a combination of any of these. The President of the United States, for instance, exerts political power over the executive branch of the government so long as his orders are obeyed by the members of that branch. The leader of a party has political power so long as he is able to mold the actions of the members of the party according to his will. We refer to the political power of an industrialist, labor leader, or lobbyist in so far as his preferences influence the actions of other men. The United States exerts political power over Puerto Rico so long as the laws of the United States are observed by the citizens of that island. When we speak of the political power of the United States in Central America, we have in mind the conformity of the actions of Central American governments with the wishes of the government of the United States.[4] Thus the statement that *A* has or wants political power over *B* signifies always that *A* is able, or wants to be able, to control certain actions of *B* through influencing *B*'s mind.

Whatever the material objectives of a foreign policy, such as the acquisition of sources of raw materials, the control of sea lanes, or territorial changes, they always entail control of the actions of others through influence over their minds. The Rhine frontier as a century-old objective of French foreign policy points to the political objective to destroy the desire of Germany to attack France by making it physically difficult or impossible for Germany to do so. Great Britain owed its predominant position in world politics throughout the nineteenth century to the calculated policy of making it either too dangerous (because Great Britain was too strong) or unnecessary (because its strength was used with moderation) for other nations to oppose it.

The political objective of military preparations of any kind is to deter other nations from using military force by making it too risky for them to do so. The political aim of military preparations is, in other words, to make the actual application of military force unnecessary by inducing the prospective enemy to desist from the use of military force. The political objective of war itself is not *per se* the conquest of territory and the annihilation of enemy armies, but a change in the mind of the enemy which will make him yield to the will of the victor.

Therefore, whenever economic, financial, territorial, or military policies are under discussion in international affairs, it is necessary to distinguish between, say, economic policies that are undertaken for their own sake and

---

[4] The examples in the text illustrate also the distinction between political power as mere social fact, as in the case of the lobbyist, and political power in the sense of legitimate authority; *i.e.*, of the President of the United States. Both the President of the United States and the lobbyist exercise political power, however different its source and nature may be.

economic policies that are the instruments of a political policy—a policy, that is, whose economic purpose is but the means to the end of controlling the policies of another nation. The export policy of Switzerland with regard to the United States falls into the first category. The economic policies of the Soviet Union with regard to the nations of Eastern Europe fall into the latter category. So do many economic policies of the United States in Latin America, Asia, and Europe. The distinction is of great practical importance, and the failure to make it has led to much confusion in policy and public opinion.

An economic, financial, territorial, or military policy undertaken for its own sake is subject to evaluation in its own terms. Is it economically or financially advantageous? What effects has acquisition of territory upon the population and economy of the nation acquiring it? What are the consequences of a change in a military policy for education, population, and the domestic political system? The decisions with respect to these policies are made exclusively in terms of such intrinsic considerations.

When, however, the objectives of these policies serve to increase the power of the nation pursuing them with regard to other nations, these policies and their objectives must be judged primarily from the point of view of their contribution to national power. An economic policy that cannot be justified in purely economic terms might nevertheless be undertaken in view of the political policy pursued. The insecure and unprofitable character of a loan to a foreign nation may be a valid argument against it on purely financial grounds. But the argument is irrelevant if the loan, however unwise it may be from a banker's point of view, serves the political policies of a nation. It may of course be that the economic or financial losses involved in such policies will weaken the nation in its international position to such an extent as to outweigh the political advantages to be expected. On these grounds such policies might be rejected. In such a case, what decides the issue is not purely economic and financial considerations but a comparison of the political changes and risks involved; that is, the probable effect of these policies upon the power of the nation.

2. *The depreciation of political power*

The aspiration for power being the distinguishing element of international politics, as of all politics, international politics is of necessity power politics. While this fact is generally recognized in the practice of international affairs, it is frequently denied in the pronouncements of scholars, publicists, and even statesmen. Since the end of the Napoleonic Wars, ever larger groups in the Western world have been persuaded that the struggle for power on the international scene is a temporary phenomenon, a historical accident that is bound to disappear once the peculiar historic conditions that have given rise to it have been eliminated. Thus Jeremy Bentham believed that the competition for colonies was at the root of all international conflicts. "Emancipate your colonies!" was his advice to the governments, and international conflict and war would of necessity disappear.[5] Adherents of free trade, such as Cobden[6] and Proudhon,[7] were convinced that the removal of trade barriers was the only condition for the establishment of permanent harmony among nations, and might even lead to the disappearance of international politics altogether. "At some future election," said Cobden, "we may probably see the test 'no foreign politics' applied to those who offer to become the representatives of free constituencies." [8] For Marx and his followers, capitalism is at the root of international discord and war. They maintain that international socialism will do away with the struggle for power on the international scene and will bring about permanent peace. During the nineteenth century, liberals everywhere shared the conviction that power politics and war were residues of an obsolete system of government, and that with the victory of democracy and constitutional government over absolutism and autocracy international harmony and permanent peace would win out over power politics and war. Of this liberal school of thought, Woodrow Wilson was the most eloquent and most influential spokesman.

In recent times, the conviction that the struggle for power can be eliminated from the international scene has been connected with the great attempts at organizing the world, such as the League of Nations and the United Nations. Thus Cordell Hull, then U.S. Secretary of State, declared in 1943 on his return from the Moscow Conference, which laid the groundwork for the United Nations, that the new international organization would mean the end of power politics and usher in a new era of international collaboration.[9] Mr. Philip Noel-Baker, then British Minister of State, declared in 1946 in the House of Commons that the British government was "determined to use the institutions of the United Nations to kill power politics, in order that, by the methods of democracy, the will of the people shall prevail." [10]

While we shall have more to say later about these theories and the expectations derived from them, it is sufficient to state that the struggle for power is universal in time and space and is an undeniable fact of experi-

[5] Jeremy Bentham, *Emancipate Your Colonies,* London, Robert Heward, 1830.

[6] "Free Trade! What is it? Why, breaking down the barriers that separate nations; those barriers, behind which nestle the feelings of pride, revenge, hatred, and jealousy, which every now and then burst their bounds, and deluge whole countries with blood." "Free trade is the international law of the Almighty," and free trade and peace seem to be "one and the same cause." See *Speeches by Richard Cobden,* London, The Macmillan Company, 1870, I, 79; *Political Writings,* New York, D. Appleton and Co., 1867, II, 110; letter of April 12, 1842, to Henry Ashworth quoted in John Morley, *Life of Richard Cobden,* Boston, Roberts Brothers, 1881, p. 154.

[7] "Let us suppress the tariffs, and the alliance of the peoples will thus be declared, their solidarity recognized, their equality proclaimed." *Oeuvres complètes,* Paris, 1867, I, 248.

[8] Quoted in A. C. F. Beales, *A Short History of English Liberalism,* p. 195.

[9] *New York Times,* November 19, 1943, p. 1.

[10] *House of Commons Debates,* Fifth Series, 1946, Vol. 419, p. 1262.

ence. It cannot be denied that throughout historic time, regardless of social, economic, and political conditions, states have met each other in contests for power. Even though anthropologists have shown that certain primitive peoples seem to be free from the desire for power, nobody has yet shown how their state of mind and the conditions under which they live can be recreated on a worldwide scale so as to eliminate the struggle for power from the international scene.[11] It would be useless and even self-destructive to free one or the other of the peoples of the earth from the desire for power while leaving it extant in others. If the desire for power cannot be abolished everywhere in the world, those who might be cured would simply fall victims to the power of others.

The position taken here might be criticized on the ground that conclusions drawn from the past are unconvincing, and that to draw such conclusions has always been the main stock in trade of the enemies of progress and reform. Though it is true that certain social arrangements and institutions have always existed in the past, it does not necessarily follow that they must always exist in the future. The situation is, however, different when we deal not with social arrangements and institutions created by man but with those elemental biopsychological drives by which in turn society is created. The drives to live, to propagate, and to dominate are common to all men.[12] Their relative strength is dependent upon social conditions that may favor one drive and tend to repress another, or that may withhold social approval from certain manifestations of these drives, while they encourage others. Thus, to take examples on from the sphere of power, most societies condemn killing as a means of attaining power within the society, but all societies encourage the killing of enemies in that struggle for power which is called war. Dictators look askance at the aspirations for political power among their fellow citizens, but democracies consider active participation in the competition for political power a civic duty. Where a monopolistic organization of economic activity exists, competition for economic power is absent, and in competitive economic systems certain manifestations of the struggle for economic power are outlawed, while others are encouraged.

Regardless of particular social conditions, the decisive argument against the opinion that the struggle for power on the international scene is a mere historic accident must be derived from the nature of domestic politics. The essence of international politics is identical with its domestic counterpart. Both domestic and international politics are a struggle for power, modified

---

[11] For an illuminating discussion of this problem, see Malcolm Sharp, "Aggression: A Study of Values and Law," *Ethics,* Vol. 57, No. 4, Part II (July 1947).

[12] Zoologists have tried to show that the drive to dominate is found even in animals, such as chickens and monkeys, who create social hierarchies on the basis of the will and the ability to dominate. See, *e.g.,* Warder Allee, *Animal Life and Social Growth,* Baltimore, The Williams and Wilkins Company, 1932, and *The Social Life of Animals,* New York, W. W. Norton and Company, Inc., 1938.

only by the different conditions under which this struggle takes place in the domestic and in the international spheres.

The tendency to dominate, in particular, is an element of all human associations, from the family through fraternal and professional associations and local political organizations, to the state. On the family level, the typical conflict between the mother-in-law and her child's spouse is in its essence a struggle for power, the defense of an established power position against the attempt to establish a new one. As such it foreshadows the conflict on the international scene between the policies of the status quo and the policies of imperialism. Social clubs, fraternities, faculties, and business organizations are scenes of continuous struggles for power between groups that either want to keep what power they already have or seek to attain greater power. Competitive contests between business enterprises as well as labor disputes between employers and employees are frequently fought not only, and sometimes not even primarily, for economic advantages, but for influence over each other and over others; that is, for power. Finally, the whole political life of a nation, particularly of a democratic nation, from the local to the national level, is a continuous struggle for power. In periodic elections, in voting in legislative assemblies, in lawsuits before courts, in administrative decisions and executive measures—in all these activities men try to maintain or to establish their power over other men. The processes by which legislative, judicial, executive, and administrative decisions are reached are subject to pressures and counter-pressures by "pressure groups" trying to defend and expand their positions of power. In the words of John of Salisbury:

> Though it is not given to all men to seize princely or royal power, yet the man who is wholly untainted by tyranny is rare or nonexistent. In common speech the tyrant is one who oppresses a whole people by a rulership based on force; and yet it is not over a people as a whole that a man can play the tyrant, but he can do so if he will even in the meanest station. For if not over the whole body of the people, still each man will lord it as far as his power extends.[13]

In view of this ubiquity of the struggle for power in all social relations and on all levels of social organization, is it surprising that international politics is of necessity power politics? And would it not be rather surprising if the struggle for power were but an accidental and ephemeral attribute of international politics when it is a permanent and necessary element of all branches of domestic politics?

3. *Two roots of the depreciation of political power*

The depreciation of the role power plays on the international scene grows from two roots. One is the philosophy of international relations which dominated the better part of the nineteenth century and still holds sway

[13] John of Salisbury, *Policraticus,* trans. John Dickinson, New York, Alfred A. Knopf, 1927, VII, 17.

over much of our thinking on international affairs. The other is the particular political and intellectual circumstances that have determined the relations of the United States of America to the rest of the world.

A. *Nineteenth-century philosophy*. The nineteenth century was led to its depreciation of power politics by its domestic experience. The distinctive characteristic of this experience was the domination of the middle classes by the aristocracy. By identifying this domination with political domination of any kind, the political philosophy of the nineteenth century came to identify the opposition to aristocratic politics with hostility to any kind of politics. After the defeat of the aristocratic government, the middle classes developed a system of indirect domination. They replaced the traditional division into the governing and the governed classes, and the military method of open violence, characteristic of aristocratic rule, with the invisible chains of economic dependence. This economic system operated through a network of seemingly equalitarian legal rules which concealed the very existence of power relations. The nineteenth century was unable to see the political nature of these legalized relations. They seemed to be essentially different from what had gone, so far, under the name of politics. Therefore, politics in its aristocratic—that is, open and violent—form was identified with politics as such. The struggle, then, for political power—in domestic as well as in international affairs—appeared to be only a historic accident, coincident with autocratic government and bound to disappear with the disappearance of autocratic government.

B. *The American experience*. This identification of power politics with aristocratic government found support in the American experience. It can be traced to three elements in that experience: the uniqueness of the American experiment, the actual isolation of the American continent from the centers of world conflict during the nineteenth century, and the humanitarian pacifism and anti-imperialism of American political ideology.

That the severance of constitutional ties with the British crown was meant to signify the initiation of an American foreign policy distinct from what went under the name of foreign policy in Europe is clearly stated in Washington's Farewell Address. "Europe has a set of primary interests, which to us have none, or a very remote relation. Hence she must be engaged in frequent controversies, the causes of which are essentially foreign to our concerns. Hence, therefore, it must be unwise in us to implicate ourselves, by artificial ties, in the ordinary vicissitudes of her politics, or the ordinary combinations and collisions of her friendships or enmities." In 1796, European politics and power politics were identical; there was no other power politics but the one engaged in by the princes of Europe. "The toils of European ambition, rivalship, interest, humor or caprice" were the only manifestations of the international struggle for power before the American eye. The retreat from European politics, as proclaimed by Washington, could, therefore, be taken to mean retreat from power politics as such.

Yet American aloofness from the European tradition of power politics was more than a political program. Certain sporadic exceptions notwithstanding, it was an established political fact until the end of the nineteenth century. This fact was a result of deliberate choice as well as of the objective conditions of geography. Popular writers might see in the uniqueness of America's geographic position the hand of God which had unalterably prescribed the course of American expansion as well as isolation. But more responsible observers, from Washington on, have been careful to emphasize the conjunction of geographic conditions and of a foreign policy choosing its ends in the light of geography, using geographic conditions to attain those ends. Washington referred to "our detached and distant situation" and asked: "Why forego the advantages of so peculiar a situation?" When this period of American foreign policy drew to a close, John Bright wrote to Alfred Love: "On your continent we may hope your growing millions may henceforth know nothing of war. None can assail you; and you are anxious to abstain from mingling with the quarrels of other nations." [14]

From the shores of the North American continent, the citizens of the new world watched the strange spectacle of the international struggle for power unfolding on the distant shores of Europe, Africa, and Asia. Since for the better part of the nineteenth century their foreign policy enabled them to retain the role of spectators, what was actually the result of a passing historic constellation appeared to Americans as a permanent condition, self-chosen as well as naturally ordained. At worst they could continue to watch the game of power politics played by others. At best the time was close at hand when, with democracy established everywhere, the final curtain would fall and the game of power politics would no longer be played.

To aid in the achievement of this goal was conceived to be part of America's mission. Throughout the nation's history, the national destiny of the United States has been understood in anti-militaristic, libertarian terms. Where that national mission finds a nonaggressive, abstentionist formulation, as in the political philosophy of John C. Calhoun, it is conceived as the promotion of domestic liberty. Thus we may "do more to extend liberty by our example over this continent and the world generally, than would be done by a thousand victories." When the United States, in the wake of the Spanish-American War, seemed to desert this anti-imperialist and democratic ideal, William Graham Sumner restated its essence: "Expansion and imperialism are a grand onslaught on democracy . . . expansion and imperialism are at war with the best traditions, principles, and interests of the American people." [15] Comparing the tendencies of

---

[14] Merle Curti, *Peace and War: The American Struggle 1636-1936,* New York: W. W. Norton and Company, 1936, p. 122.

[15] "The Conquest of the United States by Spain," *Essays of William Graham Sumner,* New Haven: Yale University Press, 1940, II, 295.

European power politics with the ideals of the American tradition, Sumner thought with George Washington that they were incompatible. Yet, as a prophet of things to come, he saw that with the conclusion of the Spanish-American War America was irrevocably committed to the same course that was engulfing Europe in revolution and war.

Thus the general conception the nineteenth century had formed of the nature of foreign affairs combined with specific elements in the American experience to create the belief that the involvement in power politics is not inevitable but only a historic accident, and that nations have a choice between power politics and other kinds of foreign policy not tainted by the desire for power.

2. Hans J. Morgenthau

Another "Great Debate": The National Interest of the United States

. . . What is the national interest? How can we define it and give it the content which will make it a guide for action? This is one of the relevant questions to which the current debate has given rise.

It has been frequently argued against the realist conception of foreign policy that its key concept, the national interest, does not provide an acceptable standard for political action. This argument is in the main based upon two grounds: the elusiveness of the concept and its susceptibility to interpretations, such as limitless imperialism and narrow nationalism, which are not in keeping with the American tradition in foreign policy. The argument has substance as far as it goes, but it does not invalidate the usefulness of the concept.

The concept of the national interest is similar in two respects to the "great generalities" of the Constitution, such as the general welfare and due process. It contains a residual meaning which is inherent in the concept itself, but beyond these minimum requirements its content can run the whole gamut of meanings which are logically compatible with it. That content is determined by the political traditions and the total cultural context within which a nation formulates its foreign policy. The concept of the national interest, then, contains two elements, one that is logically required and in that sense necessary, and one that is variable and determined by circumstances.

Published in the *American Political Science Review,* Vol. LXVI, No. 4 (December 1952), pp. 961-98.

Any foreign policy which operates under the standard of the national interest must obviously have some reference to the physical, political, and cultural entity which we call a nation. In a world where a number of sovereign nations compete with and oppose each other for power, the foreign policies of all nations must necessarily refer to their survival as their minimum requirements. Thus all nations do what they cannot help but do: protect their physical, political, and cultural identity against encroachments by other nations.

It has been suggested that this reasoning erects the national state into the last word in politics and the national interest into an absolute standard for political action. This, however, is not quite the case. The idea of interest is indeed of the essence of politics and, as such, unaffected by the circumstances of time and place. Thucydides' statement, born of the experiences of ancient Greece, that "identity of interest is the surest of bonds whether between states or individuals" was taken up in the nineteenth century by Lord Salisbury's remark that "the only bond of union that endures" among nations is "the absence of all clashing interests." The perennial issue between the realist and utopian schools of thought over the nature of politics, to which we have referred before, might well be formulated in terms of concrete interests vs. abstract principles. Yet while the concern of politics with interest is perennial, the connection between interest and the national state is a product of history.

The national state itself is obviously a product of history and as such destined to yield in time to different modes of political organization. As long as the world is politically organized into nations, the national interest is indeed the last word in world politics. When the national state will have been replaced by another mode of organization, foreign policy must then protect the interest in survival of that new organization. For the benefit of those who insist upon discarding the national state and constructing supranational organizations by constitutional fiat, it must be pointed out that these new organizational forms will either come into being through conquest or else through consent based upon the mutual recognition of the national interests of the nations concerned; for no nation will forego its freedom of action if it has no reason to expect proportionate benefits in compensation for that loss. This is true of treaties concerning commerce or fisheries as it is true of the great compacts, such as the European Coal and Steel Community, through which nations try to create supranational forms of organization. Thus, by an apparent paradox, what is historically relative in the idea of the national interest can be overcome only through the promotion in concert of the national interest of a number of nations.

The survival of a political unit, such as a nation, in its identity is the irreducible minimum, the necessary element of its interests vis-à-vis other units. Taken in isolation, the determination of its content in a concrete situation is relatively simple; for it encompasses the integrity of the nation's territory, of its political institutions, and of its culture. Thus bipartisanship in foreign policy, especially in times of war, has been most easily achieved in the promotion of these minimum requirements of the national interest. The situation is different with respect to the variable elements of the national interest. All the cross currents of personalities, public opinion, sectional interests, partisan politics, and political and moral folkways are brought to bear upon their determination. In consequence, the contribution which science can make to this field, as to all fields of policy formation, is limited. It can identify the different agencies of the government which contribute to the determination of the variable elements of the national interest and assess their relative weight. It can separate the long-range objectives of foreign policy from the short-term ones which are the means for the achievement of the former and can tentatively establish their rational relations. Finally, it can analyze the variable elements of the national interest in terms of their legitimacy and their compatibility with other national values and with the national interest of other nations. We shall address ourselves briefly to the typical problems with which this analysis must deal.

The legitimacy of the national interest must be determined in the face of possible usurpation by subnational, other-national, and supranational interests. On the subnational level we find group interests, represented particularly by ethnic and economic groups, who tend to identify themselves with the national interest. Charles A. Beard has emphasized, however one-sidedly, the extent to which the economic interests of certain groups have been presented as those of the United States.[1] Group interests exert, of course, constant pressure upon the conduct of our foreign policy, claiming their identity with the national interest. It is, however, doubtful that, with the exception of a few spectacular cases, they have been successful in determining the course of American foreign policy. It is much more likely, given the nature of American domestic politics, that American foreign policy, insofar as it is the object of pressures by sectional interests, will normally be a compromise between divergent sectional interests. The concept of the national interest, as it emerges from this contest as the actual guide for foreign policy, may well fall short of what would be rationally required by the overall interests of the United States. Yet the concept of the national interest which emerges from this contest of conflicting sectional interests is also more than any particular sectional interest or their sum total. It is, as it were, the lowest common denominator where sectional interests and the national interest meet in an uneasy compromise which may leave much to be desired in view of all the interests concerned.

The national interest can be usurped by other-national interests in two typical ways. The case of treason by individuals, either out of conviction or for pay, needs only to be mentioned here; for insofar as treason is committed on behalf of a foreign government rather than a supranational prin-

[1] Charles A. Beard, *The Idea of National Interest: An Analytical Study in American Foreign Policy,* New York, 1934.

ciple, it is significant for psychology, sociology, and criminology, but not for the theory of politics. The other case, however, is important not only for the theory of politics but also for its practice, especially in the United States.

National minorities in European countries, ethnic groups in the United States, ideological minorities anywhere may identify themselves, either spontaneously or under the direction of the agents of a foreign government, with the interests of that foreign government and may promote these interests under the guise of the national interest of the country whose citizens they happen to be. The activities of the German-American Bund in the United States in the 'thirties and of Communists everywhere are cases in point. Yet the issue of the national interest vs. other-national interests masquerading as the national interest has arisen constantly in the United States in a less clear-cut fashion.

A country which had been settled by consecutive waves of "foreigners" was bound to find it particularly difficult to identify its own national interest against alleged, seeming, or actual other-national interests represented by certain groups among its own citizens. Since virtually all citizens of the United States are, as it were, "more or less" foreign-born, those who were "less" so have frequently not resisted the temptation to use this distinction as a polemic weapon against late-comers who happened to differ from them in their conception of the national interest of the United States. Frequently, this rationalization has been dispensed with and a conception of foreign policy with which a writer happened to disagree has been attributed outright to foreign sympathy or influence or worse. British influence and interests have served as standard arguments in debates on American foreign policy. Madison, in his polemic against Hamilton on the occasion of Washington's Neutrality Proclamation of 1793, identified the Federalist position with that of "the foreigners and degenerate citizens among us, who hate our republican government, and the French revolution,"[2] and the accusation met with a favorable response in a majority of Congress and of public opinion. However, these traditional attempts to discredit dissenting opinion as being influenced by foreign interests should not obscure the real issue, which is the peculiar vulnerability of the national interest of the United States to usurpation by the interests of other nations.

The usurpation of the national interest by supranational interests can derive in our time from two sources: religious bodies and international organizations. The competition between church and state for determination of certain interests and policies, domestic and international, has been an intermittent issue throughout the history of the national state. Here, too, the legitimate defense of the national interest against usurpation has fre-

[2] "Helvidius, in Answer to Pacificus, on President Washington's Proclamation of Neutrality," in *Letters and other Writings of James Madison*, Philadelphia, 1867, Vol. 1, p. 611.

quently, especially in the United States, degenerated into the demagogic stigmatization of dissenting views as being inspired by Rome and, hence, being incompatible with the national interest. Yet here, too, the misuse of the issue for demagogic purposes must be considered apart from the legitimacy of the issue itself.

The more acute problem arises at the present time from the importance which the public and government officials, at least in their public utterances, attribute to the values represented and the policies pursued by international organizations either as alternatives or supplements to the values and policies for which the national government stands. It is frequently asserted that the foreign policy of the United States pursues no objectives apart from those of the United Nations, that, in other words, the foreign policy of the United States is actually identical with the policy of the United Nations. This assertion cannot refer to anything real in actual politics to support it. For the constitutional structure of international organizations, such as the United Nations, and their procedural practices make it impossible for them to pursue interests apart from those of the member-states which dominate their policy-forming bodies. The identity between the interests of the United Nations and the United States can only refer to the successful policies of the United States within the United Nations through which the support of the United Nations is being secured for the policies of the United States.[3] The assertion, then, is mere polemic, different from the one discussed previously in that the identification of a certain policy with a supranational interest does not seek to reflect discredit upon the former, but to bestow upon it a dignity which the national interest pure and simple is supposed to lack.

The real issue in view of the problem that concerns us here is not whether the so-called interests of the United Nations, which do not exist apart from the interests of its most influential members, have superseded the national interest of the United States, but for what kind of interests the United States has secured United Nations support. While these interests cannot be United Nations interests, they do not need to be national interests either. Here we are in the presence of that modern phenomenon which has been variously described as "utopianism," "sentimentalism," "moralism," the "legalistic-moralistic approach." The common denominator of all these tendencies in modern political thought is the substitution for the national interest of a supranational standard of action which is generally identified with an international organization, such as the United Nations. The national interest is here not being usurped by sub- or supranational interests which, however inferior in worth to the national interest,

---

[3] See, on this point, Hans J. Morgenthau, 'International Organizations and Foreign Policy," in *Foundations of World Organization: A Political and Cultural Appraisal,* Eleventh Symposium of the Conference on Science, Philosophy and Religion, edited by Lyman Bryson, Louis Finkelstein, Harold D. Lasswell, R. M. MacIver, New York, 1952, pp. 377-383.

are nevertheless real and worthy of consideration within their proper sphere. What challenges the national interest here is a mere figment of the imagination, a product of wishful thinking, which is postulated as a valid norm for international conduct, without being valid either there or anywhere else. At this point we touch the core of the present controversy between utopianism and realism in international affairs; we shall return to it later in this paper.

The national interest as such must be defended against usurpation by non-national interests. Yet once that task is accomplished, a rational order must be established among the values which make up the national interest and among the resources to be committed to them. While the interests which a nation may pursue in its relation with other nations are of infinite variety and magnitude, the resources which are available for the pursuit of such interests are necessarily limited in quantity and kind. No nation has the resources to promote all desirable objectives with equal vigor; all nations must therefore allocate their scarce resources as rationally as possible. The indispensable precondition of such rational allocation is a clear understanding of the distinction between the necessary and variable elements of the national interest. Given the contentious manner in which in democracies the variable elements of the national interest are generally determined, the advocates of an extensive conception of the national interest will inevitably present certain variable elements of the national interest as though their attainment were necessary for the nation's survival. In other words, the necessary elements of the national interest have a tendency to swallow up the variable elements so that in the end all kinds of objectives, actual or potential, are justified in terms of national survival. Such arguments have been advanced, for instance, in support of the rearmament of Western Germany and of the defense of Formosa. They must be subjected to rational scrutiny which will determine, however tentatively, their approximate place in the scale of national values.

The same problem presents itself in its extreme form when a nation pursues, or is asked to pursue, objectives which are not only unnecessary for its survival but tend to jeopardize it. Second-rate nations which dream of playing the role of great powers, such as Italy and Poland in the interwar period, illustrate this point. So do great powers which dream of remaking the world in their own image and embark upon world-wide crusades, thus straining their resources to exhaustion. Here scientific analysis has the urgent task of pruning down national objectives to the measure of available resources in order to make their pursuit compatible with national survival.

Finally, the national interest of a nation which is conscious not only of its own interests but also of that of other nations must be defined in terms compatible with the latter. In a multinational world this is a requirement of political morality; in an age of total war it is also one of the conditions for survival.

In connection with this problem two mutually exclusive arguments have been advanced. On the one hand, it has been argued against the theory of international politics here presented that the concept of the national interest revives the eighteenth-century concept of enlightened self-interest, presuming that the uniformly enlightened pursuit of their self-interest by all individuals, as by all nations, will of itself be conducive to a peaceful and harmonious society. On the other hand, the point has been made that the pursuit of their national interest by all nations makes war the permanent arbiter of conflicts among them. Neither argument is well taken.

The concept of the national interest presupposes neither a naturally harmonious, peaceful world nor the inevitability of war as a consequence of the pursuit by all nations of their national interest. Quite to the contrary, it assumes continuous conflict and threat of war, to be minimized through the continuous adjustment of conflicting interests by diplomatic action. No such assumption would be warranted if all nations at all times conceived of their national interest only in terms of their survival and, in turn, defined their interest in survival in restrictive and rational terms. As it is, their conception of the national interest is subject to all the hazards of misinterpretation, usurpation, and misjudgment to which reference has been made above. To minimize these hazards is the first task of a foreign policy which seeks the defense of the national interest by peaceful means. Its second task is the defense of the national interest, restrictively and rationally defined, against the national interests of other nations which may or may not be thus defined. If they are not, it becomes the task of armed diplomacy to convince the nations concerned that their legitimate interests have nothing to fear from a restrictive and rational foreign policy and that their illegitimate interests have nothing to gain in the face of armed might rationally employed. . . .

3. Raymond Aron

The Quest for a Philosophy of Foreign Affairs

The great debate on foreign policy which followed General MacArthur's recall by President Truman has been much discussed in Europe. . . . By contrast, Europeans have not been much concerned with another debate

Published in *Revue Française de Science Politique,* Vol. III (January-March 1953), pp. 69-91.

which deserves far more to be called the great debate, for it deals with the very bases of any foreign policy, with the nature of states, of their relations, of their contests, and with the approach to which the study, both empirical and philosophical, of diplomacy should lead.

As is well known, two philosophies have been clashing. One belongs to the tradition of *Realpolitik*. Professor Morgenthau is its theoretician, and Mr. G. F. Kennan is said to be one of its defenders. The struggle between states is seen as permanent, as dictated by the very essence of politics and as unlikely to disappear as long as man and society do not change most radically. This struggle is a corollary of power. Power is a means which each state uses in order to reach its objectives. Power is sometimes also an end, since power for power's sake represents one of the characteristic aspirations of communities throughout history. No legal system nor any court whose decisions would be accepted by the contending parties could put an end to this struggle. The rule of law presupposes a recognized authority capable of imposing its decisions. However, in order to impose the decisions of an international court to a rebellious great power, war would be necessary—the very evil which the ideal of an international rule of law wants to eliminate.

Therefore one is inevitably led to the conclusion that the defense of national interests is the essence of any foreign policy, and that foreign policy cannot be subordinated to any principle other than the defense of the national interest. . . . Vague slogans such as "to make the world safe for democracy" or "to insure collective security" often tend to make wars bigger and worse. Selfishness is not obnoxious in the case of nations; it is reasonable; indeed only selfishness is moral. So-called idealistic policies always amount to an attempt to impose a certain conception of social or international organization. Political idealism ends by degenerating into imperialism.

Maybe G. F. Kennan would not subscribe to all these statements, but the trend of his thought is similar. He too deplores the legalistic approach that has characterized American diplomacy in the last half-century, the crusading spirit which has led to all-out war and total victory, the tyranny of meaningless formulas such as "the open door in China," the oscillation from isolationism between wars to senseless fury once the war has started, because of American opinion's moralistic inclination to paint its enemies black, to idealize its allies and to expect that victory will eliminate once and forever the source of evil responsible for so many disasters. . . .

I

Let us begin our discussion by referring to the past. Do the crusading spirit and legalistic idealism appear in retrospect to be responsible for the mistakes made during or just after World War I, and during or just after World War II?

There are some realists who blame Wilsonian idealism for the "weaknesses" of the Treaty of Versailles, just as some idealists blame Clemenceau for the "injustices" of this very same treaty. I think that both groups are wrong.

The crucial fact which now appears to be at the root of Europe's misfortunes is the hyperbolic protraction of World War I, which favored the Bolsheviks' seizure of power and accelerated the disintegration of the Austrian-Hungarian Empire. The Europe of nation-states to which the Paris Conference gave its blessing had been created by the events much more than by the preferences of the negotiators in Paris. . . . No one has ever said what kind of a Europe of nation-states would have been absolutely fair. Nor could anyone say what a Europe based on Clemenceau's realism would have been like, for the annexation by France of the Germans on the left bank of the Rhine was unfeasible and democracies grow tired of having forces of occupation stationed in other states.

The two powers which were potentially the strongest in Europe were unfortunately absent from the peace conference: . . . the temporary absence of Germany and Russia was in itself a good reason for the fragility of the Versailles peace, but this weakness was bound to get inexorably worse if the Western allies failed to remain united. Now, this is where the other main blow fell: America's withdrawal into isolationism, an event as serious as the Russian or German grievances. . . . It may be that abstract idealism was partly responsible for isolationism. But isolationism was also defended in terms of the national interest. World War I had not been enough to persuade American opinion that the United States would, willingly or not, be drawn into a second World War. World War I had not taught American opinion that it is better to intervene in time of peace so as to prevent war, than to intervene during the last phase of a war in order to bring it to a winning close. Thus American isolationism, with the addition of British indecision and France's internal crisis, made hopeless the condition of Europe which the absence of Russia and Germany from Versailles had already weakened.

Was the crusading spirit responsible for the political defeat which followed World War II in spite of total military victory? One could present an indictment in such terms. Since the enemy is the incarnation of evil, one is duty bound to crush him. The Allies are transfigured by their participation in the crusade, etc . . . This way of thinking is perhaps partly responsible. But the responsibility of events seems much greater to me. One can't fight modern wars without propaganda and one doesn't dare to tell one's people that the regime of one's ally is not necessarily better than the enemy's. Roosevelt and Churchill were not necessarily as naive as the programs of the Voice of America or the BBC, but they were afraid of a separate peace between Stalin and Hitler (maybe Moscow also knew how to entertain such a fear through secret or pseudo-secret negotiations). Altogether, the war-time relations between the Western allies and the Soviet Union belong to the realm of realism rather than to that of political idealism. In 1915, the traditional diplomacy of His British Majesty had promised Constantinople to Tsarist Russia as a reward for Russian participation in the war against Germany. Similarly, Churchill took at Yalta the initiative of accepting a settlement of the Polish question which satisfied Stalin's desires.

If one goes beyond those circumstantial reasons, I think that what one finds is not so much the idealistic illusion, but rather a misinterpretation of reality. Roosevelt may have believed in the friendship of the Big Three. Churchill, at the end of the war at least, was worried by the Russian army's advance into the center of the continent. But neither Roosevelt nor Churchill were convinced that a country liberated by the Red army was sooner or later going to be a Soviet satellite. They were not convinced because they were not informed. And they had some good excuses for not knowing it, since those men whose profession should have obliged them to know it: the journalists and the professors, did not know it any better. The Soviet Union and Stalinism seemed like a distant and, after all, a rather uninteresting reality. . . . Both the idealism of the propaganda that celebrated Soviet democracy and the realism of the agreement on Poland have one common root: ignorance.

. . . In Asia as well as in Europe, we find errors due to mistaken idealism intermingled with errors due to mistaken realism. The mistaken idealism of inapplicable abstractions, the mistaken realism which makes one sacrifice lasting interests to superficially shrewd deals, both result from a common error: intellectual error. This can be either an error on the circumstances such as misunderstanding the true nature of a situation, or a theoretical error such as forgetting an eternal principle—for instance the subordination of strategy to policy—or forgetting historical regularities—for instance the long-term incompatibility between a system of independent states and unlimited wars and the necessary link between unconditional surrender and a will to create or restore a world acceptable to the victors and to the vanquished alike.

II

Mr. Kennan's name is linked in world opinion to the diplomatic conception called containment. Mr. Kennan has never taken his article, signed "X" in *Foreign Affairs,* for the statement of a doctrine. The purpose of his article was to explain the way of thinking and the probable behavior of the Soviet leaders to a public composed of officers and civil servants. As for the word containment, it does not define a policy: it indicates an objective. The real problem was, and still is, how to determine the ways in which the Soviet Union will be prevented from advancing beyond her borders.

. . . .

Professor Morgenthau's fundamental thesis is that there are two solutions, and only two: negotiations or war; the third one—the cold war, which is neither war nor peace—will necessarily lead to war if it does not end with negotiations. But negotiations suppose that we give at least as much as we receive. Thus they imply, in a way, appeasement of the Soviets. Hence, we come to the most serious question raised before American and even Western opinion: does the determination to avoid World War III necessarily entail the duty to negotiate with the Soviets, and consequently to make concessions big enough for them in turn to accept dealing with us?

It is, I believe, easy to show that this theory, whether it be right or wrong when put into practice (I think that it is wrong) is originally based on an intellectual error. Let us assume that the Soviets do not want any general settlement which would put an end to the cold war, and that they do not want an unlimited war either. If this is the case, there will be neither negotiations nor war, in the traditional meaning of this word. Professor Morgenthau would answer that the criticism which he aims at the West would then apply to the Soviet Union, for it is the Soviet leaders who would be making the mistake of believing that there is a third possibility outside of negotiated settlement or of war. But if both sides make the same mistake, if both the White House and the Kremlin agree on rejecting unlimited war as well as on rejecting a negotiated settlement, it would be most risky to pretend that unlimited war must break out even though the two leading powers do not want it. I think that the error lies in the confusion between an eternal but formal truth and a historical proposition.

Whenever there is a contest between two states, two wills to power, it is true that there are only two solutions: war or compromise. But it is wrong to believe that compromise must take the form of a negotiated settlement. Usually, in the history of the world or at least of the Western world the opposing states have negotiated agreements whenever they did not want to fight at all or to fight any longer. But states can reach compromises other than negotiated deals. Between the Parthians and the Romans, at the borders of Empires, semi-permanent wars did take place without any formal peace treaties putting an end to these wars, or without a death struggle evolving from them.

When the opposing states belong to the same civilization, when they apply the same conception of international relations, when both resort to diplomats who are committed to the same professional code of ethics and to the same reasonable Machiavellianism, compromises are negotiated, confirmed, ratified. During their first contacts with China or Japan, Western diplomats discovered or should have discovered the diversity of diplomatic practices. Later, the West had the strength to impose its own practices. It no longer has this strength. The Russian or the Chinese Communists use traditional diplomatic methods whenever it serves their interests, but they do not believe in these methods nor do they interpret them as the necessary expression of political realism. The same philosophy of permanent warfare between Socialist and capitalist states induced the

Communists at times to negotiate with the enemy and at times not to negotiate with him.

One current example will illustrate what I mean by compromises between rival wills to power, without negotiated deals. . . . It concerns the situation in Germany. Some time ago I shocked German journalists when I wrote that East and West were agreed on maintaining the present partition of Germany, although they could not state their agreement publicly. The West would of course prefer that the whole of Germany be provided with a liberal democratic regime which would lean toward the Atlantic community. The Soviets would of course prefer that the people's democracy extend all the way to France's border. But each camp is ready to accept the present partition; each camp secretly tends to believe that the other camp's conditions for reunification are unacceptable. The result is a continued division of Germany, combined with moral protests and with an effort to change the status quo through non-violent means. In other words, this non-negotiated agreement goes along with the cold war.

When Professor Morgenthau proclaims that the only alternative to World War III is the division of the world into spheres of influence, he is right, on condition that it be added that this division already exists and might never be written into any formal agreement. . . . Realism does not imply the quest for negotiated settlements, nor does it provide grounds for justifying or for condemning isolated decisions. It would have been wrong to believe that the UN intervention in Korea was the beginning of an era of collective security, but there were excellent realistic arguments in favor of such an intervention. . . . It would be wrong to describe Chiang Kai Shek as carrying the torch of freedom or crusading for Christianity against Communism, but there are many reasons (good and bad) for supporting him in Formosa as long as all of Asia's future is uncertain.

With respect either to the future or to the past, my conclusion would be just about the same. The critique presented by the realists is useful and often justified. It invites us to keep our heads cool, to be suspicious of abstractions, to look at the world as it is instead of imagining it to be what we would like it to be. Unfortunately, starting from such reasonable but vague generalities, the realists often tend to make an error as serious as the idealists': they mistake traditional diplomacy—the diplomacy of European cabinets—for eternal diplomacy.

Kennan's sudden faith in the actions of diplomats is hard to reconcile with his interpretation of Soviet psychology. Morgenthau confuses an agreement on spheres of influence, which can be implicit and bellicose, with a negotiated settlement, although nothing proves that the Soviets want or are ready to accept one. It would be fatal to fall prey to the characteristic illusions of certain misguided realists: seeing the other side under such a light that the method one advocates could indeed not fail to be successful. If the Soviet leaders thought about foreign affairs with the same concepts as 19th century Czars or Western diplomats, a negotiated settlement would undoubtedly be the accessible goal, the necessary and sufficient condition for avoiding the transformation of the present crisis into World War III. But Soviet realism, which is cynical when it comes to tactics and methods, is subordinated to a philosophy which assumes fundamental hostility between Socialist and capitalist states. Is it enough for us to oppose a revolutionary strategy or a strategy of world conquest with a diplomacy guided by national interests?

III

So far we have mainly discussed the problem of means. When we deal with the past, this problem is indistinguishable from the problem of causes. When we deal with the future, the question of means involves finding efficient methods toward such or such a purpose. We have not met true realism yet—realism capable of discriminating between historical aspects and permanent features of foreign policy, or of understanding that the search for values is part and parcel of human reality, be it individual or collective.

When we come around to discuss purposes, the controversy becomes more difficult. On the one hand the realists seem to possess a simple and convincing conception. The national interest must be the criterion of statesmen's actions, the national interest is the only purpose nations can set for themselves. Experience shows that human societies are permanently involved in a struggle for power. Idealists foolishly imagine that they can put an end to this struggle or change its timeless features. When a major power is determined to obtain certain advantages in spite of the rules or the laws of the world community, there is only one way of stopping it: the use of force or readiness to use force.

This type of reasoning is convincing when it is aimed at a naive interpretation of collective security (a subtle interpretation being the one which emphasizes that in the present world, if one takes into account the role of propaganda and of ideological convictions—or illusions—international organization is indeed capable of reducing the chances of aggression.) But if one pushes realism to its limits and if one eliminates any moral notions, is the idea of the national interest clear enough to serve as a guide to men's actions? Can the national interest be defined in strictly realistic terms?

Psychologists and philosophers have abundantly analyzed the concept of interest and have easily agreed that it is an ambiguous one. If one deals with the individual's pleasures, it is obvious that an ambitious person does not have the same interest as someone who is afraid of the public and of publicity. A sensual man will not find his interest in the kind of life that would be a scholar's ideal. Economists know that decisions can be called rational only by reference to a system of preferences, and that the system of preferences varies from person to person and from situation to situation. All our students have learned about the variations in the value of water, depending on the climate. Does interest become clear, certain and obvious when we deal with those collective persons which we call nations or states? I am afraid that the national interest is as ambiguous as the individuals' interest, and that the realists ignore this ambiguity either because they consider special cases or because they mistakenly identify the national interest with the peculiar meaning that a certain political philosophy gives to it.

Let us imagine two countries at opposite ends of the scale: a small one, caught in the middle of the big powers' pressures, and a big one which is the leader of a coalition. What is the national interest of a country such as Yugoslavia, Finland or Burma? A first answer would be: survival. The primary interest of any living body, be it individual or collective, is to exist. But for a community survival can have two meanings: one may call survival either the fact that the individuals who are the members of that community do not perish (survival in this first sense is the avoidance of genocide) or else the preservation of the community's language, culture or independence. These two objectives are very different. The desire to reach the second has often condemned communities to physical death. The Gauls did not survive Roman conquest in the second sense of the word survival, but they did in the first sense. The Carthaginians were destroyed as a people the day they lost their autonomy. The Finns survived their defeat and were not physically decimated but the other Baltic nations have been decimated without having had the possibility of fighting for their independence. Thus even from a realistic viewpoint it is difficult to make general statements as to whether the sacrifice of independence or culture is a good or bad way to avoid genocide. There are experiences on both sides. One can lose one's life because one has lost one's reason to live. In other cases, on the contrary, resignation to servitude is a way of saving one's life.

Even if this ambiguity were dispelled and if collective servitude were always a means of physical salvation, it would take a moral decision to grant precedence to physical salvation. Such a decision, which may be legitimate in certain cases, generally does not fail to corrode the collective will without which a political community disintegrates. A nation may often be excused or justified for having preferred life to liberty. But if it proclaimed this preference in advance and forever, it would be dead as a nation even before a conqueror had struck the fatal blow.

Let us jump now to the other extreme. What is the national interest of the United States? Let us begin again with the notion of physical survival. Such survival would be threatened by unlimited war and even more by defeat. The leader of a coalition sometimes runs greater risks than its allies in case of defeat. Carthage's satellites were spared the fate of the metropolis. It is therefore possible, should World War III break out, that the United States too, this time, would have to fight for their existence. Now, even if they were concerned with their own existence only, the United States could not lose interest in the marginal areas of Europe and

Asia all around the Soviet Empire. Let us leave aside the grave risks which the loss of the reserves of raw materials in the Middle East, in South East Asia and particularly in Africa would inflict on the American economy. Politically and militarily, the integration of Western Europe into the Russian empire would oblige the United States to live as a beleaguered camp, and to sacrifice a part of their culture and of their way of life to the necessity of defense.

But this is not all. A great power does not limit its ambitions to the desire to live; it wants a world which provides it with the maximum of security, or influence, or prestige. I use these different terms because doubt about the relative implications of different objectives sets in as soon as one goes beyond the elementary objective of survival. To want the maximum of security means to want the maximum of power, which in turn means the greatest number of allies, the fewest possible enemies. Now in certain situations it is the internal regime of states which determines their diplomatic alignment. Thus the great power is incited to intervene in the domestic affairs of other nations, and to favor its ideological allies. Realistic motives bring back that very crusading spirit which one had intended to exorcize. Furthermore even the maximum of security is not an obvious objective for a big power. The desire to influence other countries, to spread certain ideas or a way of life is not more absurd in the case of communities than in the case of individuals. Power is usually less an end than a means; glory or an idea justify power, which otherwise would be either the instrument of security or the instrument of tyranny. A great power always wants something else and something more than security and power, it wants an Idea, in the broadest meaning of this term. A great power would arouse surprise if it confessed that it did not see anything beyond its security or its power. Individuals do not divorce ideas from interests. A great power, however reluctant it may be, is condemned to the ambition of greatness.

It is true that communities are selfish, cannot help being selfish, and cannot be blamed for being selfish, since the human world is what it is. This selfishness expresses itself spontaneously in the desire of communities to stay out of conflicts if they have a chance. Even if the victory of one side would be fatally dangerous for it, a small nation tends to prefer the immediate interest of keeping out of war to the more distant danger of contributing to the victory of the side which threatens everyone including that small nation. Selfish abstention does not by itself appear to deserve blame, since the opposite attitude—idealistic participation—would not have better effects: it would tend to make all conflicts general.

Reference to the national interest is also helpful as a criticism of the simplifications or illusions of abstract idealism. There is a real danger of dividing the world into aggressors and victims through the use of formal criteria. It is good to recall the selfish reasons hidden behind all diplomacies; it is good not to accept too lightly the idea that there is a difference in essence between certain states and other nations. A country can be responsible for the incidents which immediately preceded a war, without having to take upon itself total historical responsibility. The selfishness of the national interest is sometimes more moral than the crusading spirit, for it teaches us to respect others, to control our passions, to try to settle conflicts at minimum costs and to appreciate national and ideological differences.

One therefore understands why the theory of the national interest might appear to be a meaningful philosophy of policy. For if one postulates a system of states of comparable power, belonging to the same civilization, and tacitly agreed on limiting the profits of victory to the transfer of a province or the payment of an indemnity—in short if one thinks about a system such as the system of European cabinets between the end of the religious wars and the beginning of the ideological wars, then the philosophy of the national interest is indeed a satisfactory formulation of a special kind of practice. This practice shines retrospectively like an ideal, when one looks back at it from the age of total wars, total victories, clashes of faith and creation of empires. But the very circumstances which make one regret the wisdom of moderately Machiavellian diplomats also make it impossible to apply such wisdom to periods of turmoil.

For most of the nations of the world, the national interest can no longer be defined apart from ideological preferences; the primacy of foreign policy without any connection with the domestic contests of political parties—such was the theory of 19th century German historians—is no longer a valid postulate when the very principles on which political units are based are at stake. The leading power cannot choose to ignore the ideologies on which the number of its allies depends and which serve as weapons in the struggle. When a coalition appeals to a certain ideology, the opposite coalition must have at its disposal at least a counter-ideology consisting of a critique of the ideology which tries to win over the whole world. One may have an interest in creating distinctions between Communism and Stalinism, between the expansion of Russian might and the broadening of the area ruled by Marxism-Leninism (especially in Asia). In order to stop Russian expansion, one must spread a minimum of ideas common to the coalition which opposes the joint imperialism of a secular religion and of a conquering Empire.

In other words, the theoreticians of the national interest are right in warning us against a tendency to let ourselves be carried away by blind ideological fury. But they make the radical error of mistaking for the essence of world politics a set of practices and a theory characteristic of those happy eras when within a stabilized civilization an unwritten code of legitimacy and illegitimacy sets limits to the contests of states—both to the means states use and to the consequences of their contests. When such a code is missing we are back in a state of nature where freedom and existence are at stake, where the clashing communities mobilize all their resources because they stake all their goods and their very life in the struggle. In these troubled eras no great power ever limits its objectives to the national interest, in the sense a Mazarin or a Bismarck would have given to this expression. In such periods a great power is defined by its capacity to show to humanity a perspective of stabilization and peace. When humanity is racked by the devastations of war and revolutions, the idea of a great power is not so much a certain conception of social relationships or of a better economic and social system, as it is the promise of order before and above anything else. The Soviet idea, at least in the West, is the idea of a power which puts an end at any price to wars among nations and wars among classes. The West passionately wants the end of the revolutionary period, whereas certain Asian countries are just beginning to enter into that period. The West does not have and does not need to have an equivalent of the Soviet's secular religion, with its church, its theology, and its interpreter (both pope and emperor) of the prophets. But the West must stand for an idea of an international order. The national interest of the United States, or even the collective interest of the Anglo-Saxon minority, will not win over any country nor will it cause any loyalties if it does not appear to be tied to an international order—the order of power as well as the order of law.

It must be a new order, for the old order based on independent nation-states does not exist in Europe any more and does not exist yet on the other continents. The constant rivalries, the shifting alliances and the cabinet diplomacy of European nations have disappeared, and moderate Machiavellianism is inadequate in our situation, although some of its counsels remain useful when they are codified. The system itself has become impossible, mainly for military reasons. National wars are incompatible with the total character of 20th century wars and with weapons of mass destruction. The disproportion between the costs and the profits of victory scandalizes the mind and revolts the conscience and the feelings of peoples. . . .

The Soviet Union offers the peace of Empires—a traditional way out of the struggles of nation-states or Greek city-states, when these struggles have become inexpiable. Our intellectual reply should not be limited to showing what such an Empire costs: the destruction of freedoms and the enslavement of cultures. Indeed, the Communist Empire promises peace only on condition that the central power keep absolute authority. If the capitalist enemy were to disappear the system of planned economies and totalitarian states would be likely to lead to wars of schisms and heresies. The order which the West proposes is not an imperial or totalitarian order, it would be based on a mixture of hegemony of the strongest and genuine consent of the weaker members. By transferring to international organizations effective supervision (or even the property) of the industries which produce weapons of mass destruction, by multiplying agencies for mediation and conciliation, the West announces, if not the certainty of peace (which does not go without servitude), at least gradual pacification, linked with the limitation of means and the moderating action of the dominant power.

Such pacification can hardly progress as long as the battle of the two worlds goes on. The West must therefore, in addition to the idea of an international order for the future, have a conception of strategy which fits the present crisis. It should be a double conception. On the one hand, within the free world the West must prove through experience its capacity to create communities bigger than the nation-states without any dictation by an Emperor-Pope. Among allies, traditional diplomacy must continue. On the other hand, in its relations with the Soviet Zone the West should shun both passiveness and aggressiveness. We should not dream up any sudden and radical solution, which only World War III could enforce. The refusal of World War III is not only a justified rejection of the horrors which are henceforth inseparable from wars, it also expresses the positive and reasonable conviction that pacification of the world without a third war is the common interest of all nations.

. . . .

We have followed so far an inductive order, as we went from controversies dealing with the recent past and from a discussion of policies to be followed, to general ideas. Let us sum up our conclusion in reverse order. Life and liberty are the stakes of war when war is total. The winner has the power to decide whether the vanquished will be annihilated or enslaved. . . . Therefore limited wars fought according to rules, respectful of prisoners and civilians, and leading only to the displacement of borderlines are partial conquests over the state of nature. They presuppose a legal community among the enemies. Nevertheless, foreign policy in such favorable periods keeps certain features of the state of nature: the games of alliances, the diplomatic maneuvers which have free play. Realists present with a good conscience such apparent immorality as a model. For it is true that when power relations are not transfigured by religious passions, when neither the existence nor the organization of states are threatened, the realism without illusions of the professionals does bring about, not peace, but the limitation of violence.

It is not surprising that one should regret those relatively quiet periods when one lives in the age of religious wars and Empires. But these regrets are not very meaningful or fruitful. It takes two to negotiate a settlement; both sides must speak the same language and follow the same principles. To suggest that one should behave toward an Empire animated by a secular religion in the same way as one behaved toward Czarist Russia, to ignore how different Nazi Germany was from Wilhelm's Germany is very much the opposite of realism and could lead to the disaster one seeks to avoid. It is legitimate that one should lament the passing of those centuries when diplomacy, divorced from ideas and morality, limited itself to a subtle game of influence and power. But in the twentieth century, a great power weakens itself if it refuses to serve an idea.

4. Kenneth W. Thompson

Toynbee and the Theory of International Politics

. . . The historian Arnold J. Toynbee . . . is of course a theorist in the more general sense of the history of civilizations. He has erected a theory of international politics, however, which is less well known and must be extracted from occasional writings such as his contributions to the Royal Institute's annual *Survey of International Affairs*. His concern with large historical ideas and suggestive comparisons makes this analysis more than the mere chronological account of events, and of course his major historical work is replete with philosophic insights.

If Toynbee contributes to a theory bearing on the relations between national political units, he eschews the more extravagant claims of political behaviorists who maintain that theorists are scientists and may confidently look forward to much the same progression characterizing the evolution of any of the natural sciences. The historian Huizinga once observed that if the scientific character of history were emphasized, the greatest historians of former times would have to be excluded.[1] Despite Mr. Toynbee's dedication to the empirical method, he too would probably be dismissed as a member of this group. There are three limitations inherent in the nature of history which restrict any science of politics and apply to Mr. Toynbee's attempt to construct a more rational theory.

The first is the limitation of materials. At first glance it would appear that this obstacle has here been surmounted. The screen upon which *A Study of History* is reflected is large enough to permit the illumination of from twenty to thirty civilizations over the time-span of 6,000 years. But this amplitude of material is more apparent than real, for on numerous occasions it becomes clear that Mr. Toynbee has proceeded from shreds of evidence and data which only imagination and guesswork could recon-

Published in the *Political Science Quarterly*, Vol. LXXI, No. 3 (September 1956), pp. 365-386.

[1] Raymond Klibansky and others, *Philosophy and History*, London, 1936, pp. 3-4.

struct. Minoan Civilization is the key to several of his principles but he admits he is "hampered by having no access to written records." [2]

Another handicap which confronts any historian is the limitation of his own energy and knowledge. In the *Study,* the architectural design is often much better than a good deal of the building material. The fund of available knowledge for the study of man is today so massive that no one can presume to speak authoritatively on all phases and periods of history. An isolated scholar, regardless of how enormous his learning, must draw heavily upon secondary sources. The problem here is to distinguish with reliability between good and inferior examples, and the strong and weak points, of those sources. In his dependence upon Bergson and Huntington, for example, Mr. Toynbee falls victim to this limitation. Perhaps only through cooperative efforts by teams of scholars can we expect any amelioration of this problem.

The third limitation is the paradox that historians must be both researchers and artists. History can be comprehended only through its narration. Here the observer stands not outside but curiously within the network of events he describes. The collection and ordering of data may be scientific up to a point; their recording and analysis require gifts of imagination and artistry of another order.

1. *"Laws" and Principles of History and Politics*

Despite Mr. Toynbee's defection from some of the tenets of modern social science, he must be considered a theorist. One of his foremost objectives has been to erect "laws" and principles which would demonstrate recurrence and regularity in history. An American scholar has argued on this point: "The absolutely unique, that which has no element in common with anything else is indescribable, since all description and all analysis are in terms of predicates, class concepts, or repeatable relations." [3] These predicates and relations are the keys to Mr. Toynbee's concept of history. He has asserted unequivocally that he conceives this to be both a necessary and manageable task. In a letter to this writer he notes: "As to the issue between recurrence and uniqueness, I think both elements are present in history as in everything else, and the logical difficulty of reconciling them is neither greater nor smaller in history than in other fields of thought." [4] He finds there is a compelling urgency to the job of formulating these principles of recurrence: "May not it mean that we ought all of us to give far more time and far more serious and strenuous thought than many of us have ever given to this job of forming one's general ideas?" [5]

Mr. Toynbee's "general ideas" in international politics as distinct from

---

[2] Arnold J. Toynbee, *A Study of History,* London, 1934, vol. I, p. 93.

[3] Morris Cohen, *The Meaning of Human History,* LaSalle, Ill., 1947, p. 84.

[4] Letter from Mr. Toynbee to this writer dated April 19, 1950.

[5] Arnold Toynbee, Pieter Geyl, and Pitirim A. Sorokin, *The Pattern of the Past,* Boston, 1949, pp. 90-91.

his "laws" of history spring from the soil of inter-state relations. For example, he posits as a principle of political dynamics the balance of power which "comes into play whenever society articulates itself into a number of mutually independent local states." [6] He appears to maintain, subject to certain qualifications, that this principle characterizes all political constellations in which multiple units seek to relate their actions to one another. The aversion of modern intellectuals to this concept ought not to obscure the fact that the greatest of English-speaking philosophers have greater affinity for Toynbee's views than for those of his more utopian peers. Specifically, Edmund Burke declared: "The balance of power had been ever assumed as the common law of Europe at all times and by all powers." [7] Since 1930 Mr. Toynbee has been fascinated particularly by one aspect of this "common law." He notes that, throughout most of history, the balance of power ineluctably has shifted from the center of a political system to its periphery. In contemporary history following World War I, Europe's declining position in world politics can be comprehended in terms of this law:

> . . . in the third century B.C., we see the city-states of Greece—an Athens, a Sparta, a Sicyon, a Megalopolis, a Rhodes—encircled and dwarfed by a ring of outer Powers which owed their own vitality to the elixir of Hellenism—a Macedon, a Syria, an Egypt, a Carthage, a Rome . . . [in] the Far Eastern extremity of the Old World, we shall similarly perceive the little states in the centre—a Song, a Chou, a Lu—which had been the seedbeds of Chinese culture, on the point of succumbing to the contending Great Powers on the Periphery: a Ts'i, a Ch'u, a Ts'in.
>
> From these analogies, it would appear that the plight in which . . . Europe found . . . [itself] was not after all an unprecedented departure from the ordinary course of history. . . .[8]

With similar illustrations from ancient and contemporary history Mr. Toynbee endeavors to prove that states which occupy the homeland of any civilization sooner or later are dwarfed and dominated by a new order of emerging "Great Powers" which inevitably spring up on the fringe.

No less pertinent for international politics is the "law" Mr. Toynbee evokes to account for the pattern in the recovery of great nations following major wars. The eventual recovery of Germany following World War I could have been forecast in at least a rough-and-ready reckoning, he believes, based on France's recovery following the Napoleonic Wars.

> The post-war recuperation of France after the General War of 1792-1815 declared itself when the Bourbon Restoration was supplanted by the Orleanist Regime of Louis Philippe through the Revolution of July, 1830, in the fifteenth year after the decisive military defeat of Napoleon at

[6] Toynbee, *A Study of History,* Vol. III, p. 301.

[7] Edmund Burke, "Third Letter on the Proposals for Peace with the Regicide Directory of France," *Works and Correspondence,* Vol. V, London, 1852, p. 381.

[8] *Survey of International Affairs, 1930,* Royal Institute of International Affairs, Oxford, 1931, p. 133.

> Waterloo. The post-war recuperation of Germany after the General War of 1914-1918 declared itself in the fifteenth year after the capitulation of the Prussian General Staff. . . .[9]

A final illustration of this type of "law" may be found in Mr. Toynbee's thesis that in a conflict between more and less civilized antagonists, the latter enjoys decisive advantages in any protracted struggle.[10] It is the reasoning supporting this "law" which is of primary interest in this connection. The civilized Power has greater ability to mobilize moral and material energy in peace and war. In peace, this fact accounts for its remarkable progress; in war, it condemns it to expend its whole blood and treasure to the point of self-destruction. After the First World War in 1918, Germany lay prostrate for over a decade but Russia and Turkey were enabled to retrieve their previous losses in the space of a few years. A backward country is less likely to consume its full strength in war and thus retains a margin of power for bold adventures and new programs. One might wonder how truly this applied to the United States or even Great Britain after World War II. These principles are plainly as stimulating and suggestive as they are lacking in precision and verifiability. Nor do they provide more than the most general indication of the essential qualities of Toynbee's theory of international relations. Before we seek to identify the basic ingredients of his theory, however, it may be useful to point to the main features of his conception of international relations.

2. *The Nature of International Relations for Mr. Toynbee*

From the beginning there has been no unanimity among scholars in the field as to a proper definition of international relations. In the same way, Mr. Toynbee has moved uneasily through three separate definitions at three different stages in his thinking. In the nineteen twenties, he conceived of the field as limited narrowly "to the relations between sovereign independent states." [11] There was only a faint indication of any consciousness of the kind of problem which would be presented by the Spanish Civil War more than a decade and a half later. In a preface to the first *Survey* he made one prophetic addition to his theory: "Not states but relations between states have been chosen as the units, except in the few cases . . . in which the status or internal condition of a country was itself an international affair." [12]

In the nineteen thirties, however, Mr. Toynbee altered this definition and abandoned the sharp distinction between internal and foreign affairs. An American scholar made this same point with great persuasiveness by

[9] *Survey of International Affairs, 1933,* Royal Institute of International Affairs, Oxford, 1934, p. 112.

[10] Toynbee, *A Study of History,* Vol. IV, pp. 303-94.

[11] *Survey of International Affairs, 1929,* Royal Institute of International Affairs, Oxford, 1930, p. 202.

[12] *Survey of International Affairs, 1920-1923,* Royal Institute of International Affairs, Oxford, Preface.

emphasizing that "there is no clear dichotomy between internal and foreign affairs." [13] Mr. Toynbee pointed out that this distinction was really little more than a convention which in most cases confused the individual who was seeking a proper understanding of the international drama.

More specifically in 1933 he was impressed that the two most outstanding events in international relations were the American depression and the German political revolution neither of which would have been properly defined under his first classification. Whenever the internal affairs of any one of the sixty or seventy countries affected the potential world distribution of power, but only then, they became a *bona fide* topic within international relations. He was arguing at this point that the mutual interpenetration of domestic and international affairs had become the rule rather than the exception. The historical episode which most emphatically confirmed this belief was the Spanish Civil War in the summer of 1936. . . .

A third conception of the scope of international relations which has occupied the attention of Mr. Toynbee down to the present day is a conception which is Janus-headed in character. One type of international relations is that among communities within a civilization; another is among the civilizations themselves. These two conceptions influence and affect one another and it is therefore incumbent upon scholars that they explore the latter form of international relations as carefully and as thoroughly as they have the former.

In recent years the foremost practical concern in international relations has been the analysis of power politics. On numerous occasions, Mr. Toynbee has made it plain that contemporary international society is one in which the precepts of Machiavelli have been more appropriate for action than those of Grotius. Our international politics is an expression of the fundamental and unceasing drives for power among individuals. Mr. Toynbee has remarked: "I certainly believe that anarchic power politics are simply the reflection of the power drives of a number of individuals." [14] On the level of individuals, power is manifested in numerous ways. In the Far East, the prestige of the Confucian scholars enabled them to dominate and ruthlessly exploit the peasants. In other civilizations, the peculiar positions of priests, philosophers, or warriors have permitted them to dominate. This underlying force of human conduct which is often concealed or disguised within a nation is obvious, fundamental and universal on the contemporary international scene.

Our surest guide for international politics as it is practiced is Machiavelli. If his exposition of the nature of politics "seemed shocking to Western minds for several centuries after the date of the publication of *The Prince,* it offended through being innocent of both obtuseness and hypocrisy, and not through being guilty of any misrepresentation of the principles on which

[13] Edward M. Earle, "National Security," *Yale Review,* Vol. XXIX (Spring, 1940), p. 452.

[14] Letter from Mr. Toynbee to this writer dated April 19, 1950.

the philosopher's contemporaries and successors were acting in real life." [15]

There are ample illustrations of the workings of power politics which may be taken from Hellenic history. These include, for example, the curious shift in alliances among Greek city-states culminating in the policy of the Aetolian Confederacy of aligning itself with Rome against Macedon which ultimately involved Greece in the Hannibalic War. But power politics as such attains its present character only with the passing of the *Republica Christianum*. Significantly, in Toynbee's discussion of the handling of the Crusades and relations with the House of Hohenstaufen, the papacy is criticized not for engaging in power politics but for making such poor guesses regarding the causes and leaders which should be encouraged. Some of the strongest passages in Mr. Toynbee's writings concern the radical discrepancy between the pretenses and ideological rationalizations of statecraft and the political principles on which action is really based.

One event which vividly illuminates the nature of international relations concerns the meeting of British and Persian statesmen following the Versailles Peace Conference of 1919. The Persian statesman repeatedly mentioned his great disappointment at the cynical sacrifice of his nation upon the altar of the Anglo-Russian entente. British policy, he acknowledged, had been honorable and fair before 1907 but to sacrifice Persia now in this way was an act of moral degeneracy and timidity. The Englishman sought to explain by discussing Britain's strategic interests and the threat of a Russo-German Alliance. He asked his Persian friend to put himself in the British position and choose between the probable sacrifice of Persia to Russia and the possible destruction of Western Civilization. At this, the Persian lost his temper and declared that such cynicism was beyond all imagination. To speak with complacency of the sacrifice of Persia, "the priceless jewel of civilization," on the off-chance of saving a worthless Western society was sheer impudence. He concluded: "What should I have cared and what do I care now, if Europe perishes so long as Persia lives!" [16] Mr. Toynbee concludes with enviable candor that those views reflect more often than we might prefer the present standards of international society and the primacy of loyalty to the state in power politics.

It may serve to help us identify further Mr. Toynbee's approach if we note that two philosophies of international relations have coexisted in Western society for at least a century and a half. The one has been idealistic and moralistic in character and crusading in spirit. Rivalry and conflict among nations has been viewed as a mere temporary distortion of the normal pattern of international life. The second philosophy interprets politics as an unending struggle for power. It focuses attention on practical choices in diplomacy, on permanent aspects of foreign policies,

[15] *Survey of International Affairs, 1933*, pp. 116-17.
[16] Toynbee, *A Study of History*, Vol. I, pp. 162-63.

and on techniques of accomodation and adjustment. The question it asks is what techniques are necessary and essential for international peace and order when there is no world state in existence nor any binding system of world law. In a most striking and revealing fashion, Mr. Toynbee combines these two philosophies in his own theory and emphasizes first one and then the other.

In the nineteen twenties and well into the nineteen thirties, he was a prominent spokesman of the idealist school. He appeared to agree with Lord Curzon that a new alliance between England and France would be inconsistent with the League of Nations. He noted with displeasure that the Franco-Polish military alliance "introduced an unfortunate element of *raison d'état*" into French policy respecting the sanctity of the European Peace Treaties. In appraising the work of the Temporary Mixed Commission on Armaments of the League of Nations, Mr. Toynbee emphasized the overweening influence of the munitions makers. At times he verged on the "devil" theory of politics, looking for individual scapegoats accountable for the sorry state of the world.

At the same time, his faith in the League of Nations was often extravagant. He criticized Austria for turning to Italy at the time of the Ethiopian crisis. It seemed inconceivable that nations would depend upon traditional alliances now that a collective system was available. He spoke of the "sinister play of 'power politics' " within the League of Nations. "The League of Nations represented an attempt to reconcile peace with growth . . . treaty law with international equity. A relapse [from the League] . . . would signify . . . the problems of postwar Europe would not or could not, after all, be settled by the new method or reason, debate and a conciliation." [17] The underlying cause of these lapses was human wickedness and sin. He spoke of British and French foreign policy as "negative, weak-willed, cowardly egotism which . . . the reigning politicians . . . in deference to what they believed to be the will of their constituents—to stop short of an effective fulfillment of their own covenants." [18] The foreign policy of the United States was "captious and perverse . . . in the sight of a neutral observer." [19] All during this period, British interests, international law, and universal morality were equated. What served British interests was unabashedly said to further law and morality —in all cases. This is the Toynbee with whom students of power politics like E. H. Carr were especially impatient at the time.

There is a second Toynbee, however, who sets forth a philosophy of international politics which goes back to what some have called political realism. This is the Toynbee who emphasizes underlying political issues and the problem of conflicting foreign policies. In the mid-thirties he began

[17] *Survey of International Affairs, 1930,* p. 10.

[18] *Survey of International Affairs, 1935,* Royal Institute of International Affairs, Oxford, 1936, p. 2.

[19] *Ibid.,* p. 96.

to wonder whether a settlement between Germany and France was not more important than the perfecting of new machinery of international organization. At this point, we shall cite only two references from Mr. Toynbee's writings which illustrate the second philosophy.

> A definitive territorial settlement between Germany and France would assuredly do more than any other single international transaction . . . to assure . . . the peace of Europe. It could not, perhaps, absolutely ensure that France and Germany should live, henceforth, in perpetual peace with one another; for the territorial question was not, unfortunately, the sole question . . . but if once the territorial conflict between the two principal Powers of Continental Europe were removed from the arena the whole international situation in Europe was likely to improve almost beyond the range of imagination.[20]

The second illustration represents Mr. Toynbee's outlook toward the United Nations and can well be contrasted with his earlier view of the League.

> The United Nations organization may fairly be described as a political machine for putting into effect the maximum possible amount of cooperation between the United States and the Soviet Union—the two great powers who would be the principal antagonists in a final round of naked power politics. The present constitution of the U. N. represents the closest degree of cooperation that the United States and the Soviet Union can reach at the present.[21]

The final step in Mr. Toynbee's disenchantment with the idealistic philosophy of international relations appears to have been reached as we moved into the deepening Soviet-American crisis called the "cold war." In 1949 he declared: "anything that would enable us to buy time seems worth thinking about; and, therefore, I suggest a provisional partition of the world into a Russian and an American sphere by agreement between the two." [22] In the nineteen thirties Mr. Toynbee was critical of those so-called cynical views which were contrived merely to gain time. His more recent statement, however, places him alongside other students of diplomacy who have recognized the need for techniques appropriate to the unregulated character of international politics.

Finally, one observes an interesting correlation between Mr. Toynbee's general historical method at a given period and his philosophy of international affairs. There is at least a rough correspondence between his exclusively nation-centered historical method of the nineteen twenties and the exceedingly strong emphasis upon the idealistic philosophy of international relations. As the focus of his history shifts from nation to civilization to higher religion, there is a perceptible change from idealism to realism

---

[20] *Survey of International Affairs, 1934,* p. 627.
[21] A. J. Toynbee, *Civilization on Trial,* New York, 1948, p. 204.
[22] A. J. Toynbee, *The Prospects of Western Civilization,* New York, 1949, p. 46.

in international politics. Cautious and hesitating at first, this change becomes clear as his thinking reflects the mounting crisis between East and West. It may be worthy of note that this same combination of theological absolutism and political relativism can be found in Niebuhrian Protestantism and the proclamations of the Vatican on the "cold war."

3. *The Balance of Power as Law or Alternative*

Mr. Toynbee's ambivalence between idealism and realism, the two prevailing ways of thinking about international politics, can be tested by examining his approach to one of the fundamental problems of international society. The balance of power is discussed in almost every treatise on international politics, but the place and significance it is given depend upon which of two philosophies the writer or publicist has accepted. A popular and widely held view assumes that statesmen have a choice between policies based upon the balance of power and more desirable policies based on morality and justice. A second and less popular view has served as the common law of diplomats and statesmen for at least the past four centuries. It maintains that "any given system is perpetually subject to that play of political forces which is known as the Balance of Power." [23] There is a social principle underlying the relations of independent units which provides that stability can be achieved through a tendency of the separate units to establish and reestablish some kind of equilibrium. This equilibrium is at best uncertain, precarious and temporary, for life can never be kept in a static balance but is subject to unceasing change and variation. A rough stability is achieved from time to time, however, through forces which combine to reestablish the lost equilibrium. This social law can be formulated in terms that are broader than international politics:

> If one species happens to vary in the direction of greater independence, the interrelated equilibrium is upset and cannot be restored until a number of competing species have either given way to the increased pressure and become extinct, or else have answered pressure with pressure and kept the first species in its place, by themselves too discovering means of adding to their independence.[24]

Mr. Toynbee never leaves any doubt as to which of these positions has greater relevance for the present. For him, as we have seen, "the Balance of Power is a system of political dynamics that comes into play whenever a society articulates itself into a number of mutually independent local states." [25] The balance of power manifested itself during the second chapter in the history of our own Western Civilization which extended in duration from 1075 to 1475. Then the structure of our contemporary

[23] *Survey of International Affairs, 1930,* p. 134.

[24] Julian S. Huxley, *The Individual in the Animal Kingdom,* London, 1912, pp. 115-16.

[25] Toynbee, *A Study of History,* Vol. III, p. 301.

multiple state system was being foreshadowed among the little North Italian city-states. The same system of pressures and balances operated to preserve the independence of individual states and prevent their domination by any would-be conqueror. Moreover, one can extract from this episode in history principles and "laws" which will be manifested again in other political constellations.

One "law" which comes into play when balance-of-power policies are successfully pursued provides that "the Balance of Power operates in a general way to keep the average calibre of states low in terms of every criterion for the measurement of political power: in extent of territory and in head of population and in aggregate of wealth." [26] When conditions are most favorable for the operation of balance of power, this condition obtains. Thus Quincy Wright asserts that "stability will increase as the parity in the power of states increases." [27] Much of the anxiety over contemporary problems has been produced by an awareness that this condition has been destroyed by the emergence of the two "Super-Powers" since World War II.

In another "law," Toynbee asserts that a balance-of-power policy can be most effectively applied and executed at the fringe or periphery rather than at the center of a political system. The pressures which resist the necessary adjustment and accomodation are intensified at the center of a system. The job of a diplomat is, therefore, compounded when he deals with resentments and jealousies over small plots of territory at the heart and core of an established state system. A corollary of this theory which the political scientist finds more immediately significant is the principle of international politics that conflicts of power are most effectively composed in political "open spaces" away from the territories of the dominant Powers. What is of interest here is the political and diplomatic significance of Mr. Toynbee's thesis. Africa has traditionally performed the function of "open space" for the European Powers, as have Afghanistan, Siam, and sometimes America. Within Europe a similar role has been played by buffer states "which precariously protected by the equilibrium of the vast masses around them . . . preserve their poise by maintaining a rigid neutrality." [28] Such was the pattern of European power politics in the half-century between 1871 and the First World War.

A third "law" takes as its text the theme that in practice the purpose of the balance of power is to maintain order and safeguard the independence of member states within a political system. If this is taken as our guide in evaluating the balance of power, then its record has been quite successful. Especially until the Partitions of Poland at the end of the eighteenth century this principle was useful and effective. "In all the warfare be-

---

[26] *Ibid.*, p. 302.
[27] Quincy Wright, *A Study of War,* Chicago, 1942, Vol. II, p. 755.
[28] *Survey of International Affairs, 1926,* Royal Institute of International Affairs, Oxford, 1927, pp. 18-19.

tween French and Spanish armies, and French and Austrian armies, that met in battle on Italian soil in the course of nearly four centuries of European contests from the days of Charles VIII to the days of Napoleon III, no combatant, from first to last, ever dealt his adversary a mortal blow." [29] These achievements were possible because of a moral and political climate which has since disappeared. The moral consensus to which Gibbon pointed in 1781 was primarily responsible for the nature of European politics during the four centuries of "temperate and undecisive" warfare. The balance of power was ideally suited for its principal task under these conditions; for, as Gibbon observed, it would "continue to fluctuate, and the prosperity of our own or the neighbouring kingdoms may be alternately exalted or depressed; but these partial events cannot essentially injure our general state of happiness, the system of arts and laws and manners." [30] If international peace instead of order is made the yardstick for the balance of power, then its history becomes a far more melancholy one.

A final "law" is a summary of the others. It contends that the balance of power is a universal instrument of foreign policy for any nation seeking to preserve its independence. From Henry VIII to Winston Churchill it has been the first principle of British foreign policy. Its ubiquitous character is revealed in Greek politics where leagues were formed against Athens, Sparta, or Thebes when one or the other represented the dominant thrust. Moreover, the Phoenician and Etruscan foes of the Greeks themselves combined to defend their vital interests. In the religious sphere the universality of this force emerged in the contests between Christians and non-Christians in the Roman Empire. Under Christian emperors and under pagans such as Julian there was mutual toleration based on an equilibrium of power rather than on common moral principles. ". . . during those years, the material strength of the Christians and non-Christians in the Roman empire was approximately equal, so that, for the time being, neither party could attempt to suppress the other with any hope of success." [31] When this equilibrium was superseded by a superiority of power for the Christians, the policy of toleration was abandoned with alacrity.

. . . .

During most of the history of the modern state system the main weights of the balance of power were predominantly in Europe. Expansion of any major political importance was conducted by Western European countries which bounded the Atlantic Ocean or the North Sea. Indeed,

> . . . for several centuries this particular balance did not transcend the limits of Western and Central Europe. For example, no Islamic countries

[29] Toynbee, *A Study of History,* Vol. III, p. 311.
[30] Quoted, *ibid.*
[31] Toynbee, *A Study of History,* Vol. IV, p. 226.

> entered into it until the General War of 1792-1815, and no Far Eastern countries until the conclusion of the Anglo-Japanese Alliance a dozen years before the outbreak of the General War of 1914-1918.[32]

Since the beginning of World War II, however, the principal weights in the balance of power have become non-European. Similarly, the scales of the balance have been transplanted from Europe to the United States and the Soviet Union. All other local or "inferior" balances have become mere functions of the dominant world system.

It is possible to estimate the approximate weights already in opposite scales of the balance of power. Most of the nations which appreciably affect the world-wide distribution of power are committed to either the Soviet or American bloc and so there is less uncertainty about the strength of the major protagonists. The chances of fresh reserves of power being thrown in at the "eleventh hour" have been greatly diminished. At least this is true for the immediate future. What interested Mr. Toynbee in 1948 was that on this basis the United States and the West were "so much stronger than the Soviet Union that, short of attempting to wrench out of her rival's grip some country upon which the Soviet Union had already fastened its hold, it is apparently possible today for the United States to assert her own protectorate over any country she chooses in the no-man's-land between the Soviet Union and herself." [33] Turkey and Greece lie on the very threshold to the chief granary of the Russians in the Ukraine and the Caucasus. Yet we have had sufficient power to extend our influence to the boundaries of the Soviet sphere. This factor coupled with an immense superiority in technology appeared in 1948 to give us a preponderance in the world balance of power. One word of caution offered by Mr. Toynbee then was that the dynamic and simple communist ideology might whittle away this advantage through a process of missionary appeals and political penetration. Only a program of social transformation could compete with this revolutionary ideology and on this point there was some question as to how far the world could be attracted "by the present rather conservative American gospel of out-and-out individualism." An estimate today would be less favorable to the West than when Mr. Toynbee made his earlier comparison, and it is noteworthy that the bipolar world has already tended to fragment into local and regional centers of power to an extent he had not anticipated.

Finally, Mr. Toynbee, as his approach has matured, has maintained that there are probably no clear and distinct alternatives to the balance of power. Even his conception of the world state has been revised and "politicized" so that one "Great Power" or combination of Powers would serve as its cornerstone. In the "idealist" period of his writing, Mr. Toynbee gave the impression of sharing the misconception that statesmen

---

[32] Toynbee, *A Study of History,* Vol. I, p. 28.
[33] Toynbee, *Civilization on Trial,* p. 144.

and politicians have a choice between balance-of-power policies and a better kind of international relations. Of Mr. Neville Chamberlain's "Munich" policy he wrote that it was an attempt "to make the perilous passage from a newfangled British foreign policy based on a collective system of international security within the framework of the League of Nations to an old-fashioned policy based on the Balance of Power." [34] Again, in his study of the history of Islam he depreciates the policy of the twelfth- and thirteenth-century Caliph Nasir who sought to check the imperialist adventures of any of the "successor states" which threatened to become too strong. "This hazardous play with an unstable Balance of Power was less statesmanlike than the simultaneous efforts that Nasir made to rehabilitate the Caliphate by peaceful means." [35]

On the surface, this appears to be a thoroughgoing repudiation of political principles which are basic to the balance of power. In fact, however, there is some evidence that these statements may not be fully representative even of Mr. Toynbee's "idealist" thinking. At the time of Munich, he refers to the argument that the balance of power is unreal and thus cannot have been affected by German expansionism. He observed then: "That is comforting; I can go to sleep again. All the same, I rather mistrust this argument that such a thing as 'the balance of power' does not exist." [36]

He goes on to show, in a way reminiscent of the famous memorandum of Sir Eyre Crowe, that Great Britain has always taken steps to prevent the aggravation of any political situation where there was a threat to the European balance of power. Was Munich this kind of a situation? One school of thought insisted that no threat existed since Germany had for centuries dominated Central Europe. This point is unacceptable to Mr. Toynbee, for he properly distinguishes domination by a unified Germany from that by a disunited Germany, as in the past. An imperialist state which has united eighty million people is a different kind of threat than a loose confederation of princes and petty rulers. Against the former, the same policy which had been used against Louis XIV, Napoleon, and the Kaiser must be employed. ". . . we have generally resisted the domination of Europe by a single Power when there seemed a possibility that the Power would use its domination of the Continent to threaten the independence of the British Isles and the interests of Great Britain overseas." [37] This is surely an outlook which leaves little room for a conception of foreign policy based on alternatives to the balance of power.

The source of confusion between these contradictory statements about the balance of power is probably a deep conviction born of the times that the new system of collective security was a step beyond the previous

[34] *Survey of International Affairs, 1935,* Vol. II, p. 479.

[35] Toynbee, *A Study of History,* Vol. III, p. 212, n. 3.

[36] Toynbee, "After Munich: The World Outlook," *International Affairs,* Vol. XVIII (January-February 1939), p. 9.

[37] *Ibid.,* p. 10.

techniques for preventing wars. If Mr. Toynbee's fervor was extravagant, so were the sentiments of most fellow interpreters at that time. Obviously the last statement we have quoted more nearly reflects his permanent views on the balance of power, made just as he was crossing the chasm which separates the "idealist" from the "realist" school of thought. Within or outside a collective security system, the balance of power is plainly one of the paramount forces in international politics.

5. Morton Kaplan

System and Process in International Politics

This book represents an attempt to analyze international politics systematically and theoretically. This book therefore is part of a series of recent academic efforts to reduce a vast amount of data to a set of relatively orderly propositions.

In a strict sense, a theory includes a set of primitive terms, definitions, and axioms. From this base, systematic theorems are derived. These theorems should be logically consistent. The terminal theorems or propositions should be interpreted in such a way that the terms of the theorems can be given unequivocal empirical references. Finally, the theorems should be capable of refutation or confirmation by means of controlled experiment or systematic observation. If "theory" is interpreted in this strict sense, this book does not constitute a theory.

A framework for a theory specifies the variables which a theory will employ. It constitutes a conceptual scheme within which it may be possible to organize a theory. It does not relate variables to form a body of systematic propositions. This book is not a framework for a theory—although it includes such a framework—because it does state a body of systematic propositions.

If some of the requirements for a theory are loosened: if systematic completeness is not required; if proof of logical consistency is not required; if unambiguous interpretation of terms and laboratory methods of confirmation are not required; then this book is, or at least contains, a theory. This theory may be viewed as an initial or introductory theory of international politics.

One question in particular may arise in the minds of readers. Why should there be a theoretical treatment of international politics, particularly

---

Reprinted from *System and Process in International Politics,* pp. xi-xviii and 3-20, by permission of John Wiley and Sons, Inc. Copyright, 1957, by John Wiley and Sons, Inc., New York.

when a theoretical treatment involves a new language or set of terms which the reader must learn?

Theory has a number of distinct uses. In the first place, it permits an explicit statement of the set of variables about which various propositions are enunciated. A history, for instance, continually brings in "facts" which are believed relevant as a story is told. But histories are never explicit concerning the variable categories within which "facts" should be placed nor with respect to how a "fact" as a variable is related to other variables. Thus the system of reference of the historical exposition is continually shifting although this is not done clearly and explicitly.

In the second place, theory—in particular, systems theory—permits the integration of variables from different disciplines. One may consider the economic, political, and other aspects of a particular organization. However, only a theoretical treatment of the organization will permit the synthesis of distinct types of variables within a common framework. For instance, the political behavior of an organization under conditions of economic scarcity involves a theory of organization which is not solely economic or political. Moreover, the theory of this organization or of this type of organization must be so structured that it permits all relevant variables, regardless of the discipline within which they are normally included, to be built into the models employed. I believe that the systems theory[1] employed in the body of this work is best suited to this task.

In the third place, it is important for the research worker to direct his attention to all relevant variables. An explicit statement of the variables employed and of their interrelationships necessitates an organized examination of the completeness of a set of variables. Although theory is no more a guarantee of completeness than it is of creative insight, it does provide a convenient, explicit method for eliminating or detecting deficiencies in the treatment of a subject.

In the fourth place, theory provides a method for "fitting" structural similarities from one type of subject matter to another. In particular, systems theory permits a rapid study both of similarities and differences between otherwise completely different kinds of structures.[2]

---

[1] See pages 110-23 for a treatment of systems theory.

[2] Similarities between systems theory as employed in this volume and information theory as developed by such writers as Wiener and Shannon, particularly with respect to some aspects of vocabulary, may be noted by the reader. These similarities should not be overstressed. Information theory is a mathematical theory dealing with highly precise aspects of the communication of information in terms of bits through well-defined channels. The theory of international politics developed in this volume is non-mathematical and non-precise. Technically, it does not—except perhaps rarely—deal with information flows even through poorly defined channels.

Nevertheless, technical information theory does have its value for such studies as the present one. Particularly in structural aspects of the international system which seem somewhat like more precise communication systems, the consideration of the similarities may generate a number of important hypotheses. It would be a serious mistake to assume more than a superficial similarity or to assume that hypotheses

Theory is not a thesis. Thus a theorist is not committed to a particular proposition—perhaps that wars can be traced to economic causes or that imperialism is a product of capitalism or that considerations of national power motivate states. The theorist, in particular the systems theorist, is interested in studying the behavior of a system under various conditions. He will use the tools available to him. In some cases it may be necessary to grapple with the subject matter of the study by approaching it from more than one point of view.

The four parts of this book, to be described below, represent four methods for studying behavior in the international system. Although interrelated—as they must be—there is no natural ordering in terms of which one section is a development of the others. The justification of each section is, first, that it helps to illuminate one aspect of international behavior and, second, that it will permit the generation of empirical research projects which will either confirm or lead to a revision of the propositions which have been asserted.

The volume therefore represents a systematic effort to cope with the many aspects of international politics from an abstract, theoretical, and semiformal point of view. In the absence of the evidence necessary to sustain the propositions of the theory in other than a heuristic sense, it is desirable to maintain some reserve with respect to them.

Theory, regardless of its heuristic value, should be directed toward empirical problems. If it is, the question of testing and verification arises. The theory employed in this book gives rise to distinct empirical research problems and necessitates the systematic collection of evidence according to criteria of relevance embedded in the theory. It would not be useful to clutter the body of the book with research designs intended to test the theory, particularly since many of the designs would be experimental and subject to change in the process of experimentation.

Nevertheless, it may be useful in this preface to illustrate the kinds of research projects which may be indicated by the theory. The reader will observe that some are straightforward and can be attempted without great difficulty, if not without great effort. Others involve grave theoretical and methodological problems.

In the first part of the book an attempt will be made to describe alternative possible international systems and to specify the environmental circumstances under which each system is likely to persist or the conditions under which it is likely to be transformed into one of the other systems. The mere statement of the alternative models necessitates the collection of information relevant with the patterns of national interactions. It is

---

working in one area will work elsewhere unless one knows that the structural aspects are genuinely isomorphic. But there is never any substitute for intelligence! The use of a common language permits the transference of hypotheses from discipline to discipline and is a particular boon for the inexact and somewhat ambiguous disciplines, in which problems of variable criteria and measurement are most pressing.

significant that the simple task of counting various kinds of interactions has never seriously been attempted in the literature and that this information is essential to the description of the states of the international system.

Some consequences of the theory which can be empirically tested are fairly obvious. For instance, the rules of the "balance of power" system specify a great fluidity in the formation of alliances and of groupings with respect to particular issues. The analysis of national interactions during the "balance of power" period should test this consequence and should also permit a more detailed specification of the characteristics of the "balance of power" system.

If the theory is correct, there should be a difference between the "balance of power" and bipolar systems with respect to the frequencies of certain groupings. For instance, in the "balance of power" system, groupings will depend primarily upon the interests of nations in particular situations. Therefore, they will tend to break up as soon as the interests are satisfied or as soon as it becomes clear that they cannot be satisfied in this way. New groupings should continue to depend upon particular short-term interests. Therefore, there should be great variety in the groupings.

In the loose bipolar system, on the other hand, groupings will depend upon long-range rather than upon short-term interests. Therefore, some alignments will have an extremely high probability, and others an extremely low probability. The study of interaction patterns in the two systems should serve both to test these propositions and to permit a greater specification of the characteristics of the two systems.

To be more specific, the "balance of power" system postulates that any alignment is as probable as any other alignment prior to a consideration of the specific interests which divide nations. Moreover, any particular alignment should not predispose the same nations to align themselves with each other at the next opportunity. Therefore, was there any period of the "balance of power" system during which the fluctuations in alignments did not shift as the theory predicts? If there was, some other factors must be located to account for the pattern of preferences.

It is also possible that the systems of alignments became more rigid over time. In other words, it is possible that any one alignment increased the probability with which that alignment would reoccur in the future. If so, an element of instability has been found within the system.

Of course, the frequency of interactions is not identical with the predisposition to interact. Other variables complicate the picture. Nevertheless, if it is true historically that the frequency of interactions changed in some systematic manner, this in itself would have great importance.

If some important patterns of behavior are discovered, an effort should then be made to discover whether they are linked to internal system characteristics, for example, increasing probability of previous patterns of alignment; or whether they are linked to external factors, for example, technological change; or to some combination of the two.

Still additional consequences may be derived from the rules of the various international systems. Although the problems involved in testing these propositions may prove difficult, the problems nevertheless arise in the area of empirical theory and are brought to attention by abstract theoretical considerations.

In the second part of the book, a number of regulatory and integrative propositions will be stated. The easiest to test will be the eight specific propositions enunciated in Chapter 5,* although it is questionable whether the propositions may best be studied through the use of small group experiments or by means of comparative case studies of various international agencies or by more direct methods.

For instance, is it true that a decision-making unit in which the role holders represent diverse interests or organizations will consider more alternatives for action than one in which the role holders come from a homogenous population? A small group experiment may be able to test this. Do memberships in some outside groupings or rotations of role holders function as insulating devices within decision-making units? A small group experiment may be able to test this. If decision-making units are linked through the personality systems of role holders, does the set of units reduce its alternatives over time? Again, a small group experiment may be able to test this.

The set of eight hypotheses accounts for a socialization process and the development of a political system. It is possible that each hypothesis may be tested by a small group experiment unrelated to the problems of international politics. Although not sufficient to predict the integrative strength of supranational agencies, the hypotheses may provide at least one measurable key to this problem. In this way, some test of the integrative strength of organizations like NATO and the Communist bloc may become available. Moreover, it may be possible to locate the areas of greatest integrative strength and weakness within such organizations and to know why these areas are a source of strength or weakness.

The small group study has the advantage that the factor of interest can be controlled, and therefore the difficult problem of measuring an inferred variable in an uncontrolled situation can be avoided. It has the disadvantage that some differences between it and the international political setting may be overlooked by the experimenter.

On the other hand, if comparative case studies are employed, many experiments will prove necessary in order to get satisfactory criteria for the variables employed in the research design. Whether reliable criteria can be found must remain an open question at present. If independent measures of interest can be found, a third research method, which directly tests the specific propositions, may be employed.

---

* [Editor's note: Chapter 5 deals with "the integrative and disintegrative processes."]

The third part of the book, on value theory, will entail propositions concerning the relationship between values, value change, information, and social structure. This area of study is so large that the theory only indicates the relevance of the variables rather than specifying the relationships between them. However, many of the propositions employed in Part One, on systems theory, actually are propositions about the valuational dispositions of various kinds of national structures. These propositions are still too general to be highly useful. However, they do indicate the directions in which research may prove useful.

Specific areas of attention may be indicated. For instance, national actors are classified within the theory as system or subsystem dominant and as directive or non-directive. This system of classification is possibly too crude for long-run purposes, but initially it provides four boxes for the classification of national actors.

Can systematic differences in choice patterns be discovered between actors falling into different classifications, or does one have to look to cultural factors not directly related to the classification? Possible test situations include the conditions under which war is preferred to peaceful compromises or to judicial procedures, the extent to which the acquisition of material capabilities is preferred to conservatism in such things as the expenditure of human lives. In this way, it may be possible to relate aspects of political structure to types of actions which are important within the international system.

The problems arising in the fourth part, which deals with game theoretic concepts, will involve primarily the fitting of various models to the social structure of the international system. In the process some strong constraints upon behavior may emerge from the normative models. In this case, empirical tests can be developed although it would not be useful to attempt greater specificity until the problems arising in this area have been treated in considerably greater detail.

Perhaps one last word about the problem of prediction is in order. It is my belief that many social scientists attempt the wrong kind of prediction and therefore demand too much of theory. At the same time, as a consequence of an unreasonable demand, they underestimate the true potential power of a theory of international politics.

For instance, can a theory of international politics be used to predict a specific event or action like the Hungarian revolution of October 1956? The answer probably must be negative. Yet why make such a demand of theory?

There are two basic limitations upon prediction in the physical sciences which are relevant to this problem. In the first place, the mathematics of complicated interaction problems has not been worked out. For instance, the physical scientist can make accurate predictions with respect to the two-body problem, rough guesses with respect to the three-body problem, and only very incomplete guesses concerning larger numbers of bodies. The scientist cannot predict the path of a single molecule of gas in a tank of gas.

In the second place, the predictions of the physical scientist are predictions concerning an isolated system. The scientist does not predict that so much gas will be in a tank, that the temperature or pressure of the tank will not be changed by someone, or even that the tank will remain in the experimental room. He predicts what the characteristic behavior of the mass of gas molecules will be if stated conditions of temperature, pressure, and so on hold.

The engineer deals with non-isolate systems in which many free parameters play a role. If he acts wisely—for instance, in designing aircraft—he works within certain constraints imposed by the laws of physics. But many aspects of exact design stem from experiments in wind tunnels or practical applications of past experiences rather than directly from the laws of physical science.

The theory of international politics normally cannot be expected to predict individual actions because the interaction problem is too complex, and because there are too many free parameters. It can be expected, however, to predict characteristic or model behavior within a particular kind of international system. Non-conforming individual actions would constitute deviations from this mode rather than mere random responses. Moreover, the theory should be able to predict the conditions under which the characteristic behavior of the international system will remain stable, the conditions under which it will be transformed, and the kind of transformation that will take place.

The book which follows attempts to chart the equilibrium conditions for six different models of international systems, the characteristic behavior of such systems, and the transformations which such systems undergo when the equilibrium conditions no longer hold. Although the hypotheses of this book must be viewed as tentative rather than as representative of a finished theory, it is my hope that at least the proper path has been chosen.

The Analysis of Systems of Action

Systems analysis

There is one respect in which a science of international politics must always be indebted to history. History is the great laboratory within which international action occurs. Experiments in this field cannot be performed under controlled conditions, a difficulty not without precedent in science, however. Although the astronomers cannot control the movements of the stars, they have discovered systematic regularities in their movements. The crux of the matter is whether regularities can be discovered which permit the organization of the materials of international politics within a simple framework of reasonable explanatory or predictive power.

If such an endeavor is to succeed, analytical tools are required in order to abstract systematically the materials of international behavior from their biographical or historical setting and to organize them into a coherent body of timeless propositions. This statement, however, demands qualification. To begin with, one must not expect propositions to hold true throughout recorded history regardless of the entities to which they are applied or of the conditions which provide the setting for those entities.

It is legitimate to demand that propositions be independent of labeling. The laws governing the relationship of heavenly bodies should apply regardless of the names of the stars. But one does not expect these laws to apply to heavenly bodies regardless of their weight, size, distance from each other, or the presence of other heavenly bodies. In the same way, the propositions of international politics should apply to international actors regardless of the labeling of the actors, but not regardless of factors which differentiate actors in other ways. The actors of international politics have changed during recorded history in ways which give rise to legitimate expectations that their characteristic behavior also will change.

Whereas heavenly bodies undergo little change in their relative locations during time periods of interest to mortal men, social groupings change more rapidly. The number of nation states changes; the relative importance of such actors changes; war, conquest, revolution, peaceful change, population growth, and technological developments continually weave new threads in a complex woof of interrelationships.

It is the thesis of this volume that a scientific politics can develop only if the materials of politics are treated in terms of systems of action. A system of action is a set of variables so related, in contradistinction to its environment, that describable behavioral regularities characterize the internal relationships of the variables to each other and the external relationships of the set of individual variables to combinations of external variables. Technically, this definition is faulty, for any set of specified variables may be considered a system. Napoleon, the Columbia River, and a dinosaur may be considered a system. However, it would be most difficult to find a relationship between the variables, and also that relationship would be uninteresting or useless.

Since a system has an identity over time, it is necessary to be able to describe it at various times, that is, to describe its successive states. It is also necessary to be able to locate the variable changes which give rise to different succeeding states.

The "state of a system" designates a description of the variables of a system. The doctor's description of such things as pulse, temperature, and respiration constitutes a partial state description of the physiological system. The political scientist's description of such things as the political machinery, the characteristics of various candidates for office, and the temper of the electorate constitutes a partial state description of a political system.

The invasion of the organism by a virus may be regarded as an input to the physiological system, and a fever as the output of the system. A declaration of war followed by mobilization may be regarded as political input and output respectively. An input may come from outside a system to the system or it may simply be a previous state of the system. Thus an election is an input, and an inauguration an output. These terms are relative, for the inauguration may be regarded as an input, and the policy of the new official as the output.

When an input leads to a radical change in the relationship of the variables of a system—or even in the identity of the variables—it is said to transform the characteristic behavior of the system. Such an input, for purposes of this volume, will be called a step-level function. A step-level function differs from other functions by virtue of the fact that it alters the characteristic behavior of a system. For instance, if a political system is democratic, the election of one candidate rather than another changes the state of the political system but does not change its characteristic behavior. In the same way, shining a light in a person's eye produces a contraction of the pupil, changing the state of the eye but not its characteristic behavior. However, morphine addiction or nerve deterioration may change both the state and the behavior of the eye. The eye may no longer exhibit the same characteristic responses to the same stimuli. For instance, light may no longer cause the pupil of the eye to contract.

Revolution may perform a step-level function for a political system by changing the characteristic behavior of the system, for instance, legal procedures, modes of selecting officials, and the rights of citizens. Parameter values which act as step-level functions are of great importance in the analysis of action or behavioral systems.

Systems are said to be coupled when the output of one system acts as an input for the other system. Thus the personality of the secretary of State is an input for American foreign policy, and the foreign policy of the United States is an input for the international system.

It is possible to think of systems which are coupled as elements in a larger system. However, it is convenient to treat coupled systems separately. The United States and Great Britain constitute coupled systems. They are members of NATO and of the United Nations; economic developments in one country affect the economy of the other; the policy of each serves as an input for the other. Consider, however, the difficulty in attempting to study the operation of the American political system with respect to foreign policy if one were to make a detailed study of every system to which the United States is coupled, for instance, a study of all external systems and all internal subsystems.

It is simpler from an analytic point of view to consider what the United States will do if Great Britain does *x*, *y*, or *z*. If one wants to know what in fact the United States will do, detailed information concerning British politics—or at least a probability distribution over the possible states of the British political system—becomes essential. If one is interested not in a specific prediction but in knowing the characteristic behavior of the United States in the area of foreign policy, it is convenient to consider how it will behave if the inputs from other systems take given arbitrary values.

Unless the problem is considered in this fashion, it will be difficult to make progress. It makes good sense, for instance, to ask how prices vary with the supply of money or goods, even if one does not know how to account for the supply of money or goods. Scientific laws state only what will happen if something else happens. For instance, if one body strikes another, x will happen. Whether one body will strike another is a separate problem.

When systems, whether on the same or different levels, are coupled in two directions, feedback takes place. The foreign policy of the United States affects that of the Soviet Union and is, in turn, affected or influenced by the foreign policy of the Soviet Union. Negative feedback operates in the direction opposite from that of the input. Automatic pilots that counteract deviations from level flight exhibit negative feedback. Positive feedback operates in the same direction as the input. The printing of money during inflation leads to still higher prices and the printing of still more money and so on.

Rate of change is important in the feedback process. Negative feedback may fail in its functions if a given process begins to accelerate at a rate beyond some given rate, for example, the feeding process in the uranium pile. An increase in the capabilities of a national actor, if great enough and if at a fast enough rate, may prevent other national actors from taking compensating action. In this fashion, a system may be transformed, or it may even perish if the rate of increase or decrease of some important factor is great enough to prevent compensation.

Equilibrium and dynamic change

Equilibrium must always be defined with respect to arbitrarily chosen variables which remain within arbitrarily chosen limits for an arbitrarily chosen length of time when subject to a specified set of disturbances. Equilibrium and stability are not the same concepts, for an equilibrium may be unstable. The stable equilibrium is the equilibrium that fluctuates within given limits. A more precise definition will be offered toward the end of this section.

The stable system remains within specified limits for arbitrarily defined variables. Such stability may be mechanical as in the case of the seesaw, which returns to a position of rest after a disturbance. Or it may represent some form of "steady-state" or homeostatic process, in which some variables continually readjust to keep other variables within given limits. Consider the action of the thermostat or the way in which the temperature of human blood is maintained by the process of perspiring in hot weather and by such means as shivering in cold weather. Such stability may be maintained by negative feedback, exemplified by the automatic pilot. Political systems represent homeostatic or steady-state stability.

Political equilibriums may be dynamic in the sense that the system keeps changing its internal arrangements in order to maintain its stability. Ashby distinguishes between stability and ultrastability.[3] Consider again the automatic pilot. If the connections of the automatic pilot to the ailerons of the plane are reversed, a shift of the plane from level flight will result in positive feedback, and the plane will go into a spin. In theory, however, an ultrastable homeostat could be constructed which would adjust its own behavior and maintain level flight.

Ultrastable systems "search" for stable patterns of behavior. They may make internal changes or may attempt to change the environment. They reject unstable patterns of behavior. Periods of transitional adjustments, either in the behavior of individuals or in social systems, may represent attempts to find new patterns of stable behavior after the old patterns have proved unstable for some reason. Such processes are those of an ultrastable system, and if in the future the shorter term stability is used for convenience, the distinction should be kept in mind.

In considering the stability of a political system, it is important to distinguish between the stability of a given state of equilibrium and the stability of the system, that is, the ability of the system to find a stable equilibrium. . . .

It is obvious that stability can be used to refer to a state of a system, that is, to its state of equilibrium, as well as to the system itself. For many purposes, the stability of a given state of equilibrium is very important. For instance, how stable are democratic rules of government?

It is also important whether a particular sequence of changes in the states of equilibrium of a system introduces irreversible changes in the system and, if so, what kind of changes. The following definitions are offered:

1. A system in equilibrium will remain in equilibrium unless a parameter value changes, that is, unless the system is disturbed. If there does not exist a type of disturbance which is reasonably likely to move the system from its state of equilibrium to a new one, the equilibrium has stability. If such a type of disturbance exists but its effect depends upon its strength, the equilibrium has local stability.

2. If a system with a locally stable equilibrium is subjected to a disturbance of sufficient critical strength, it will either change to a new state of equilibrium or it will cease to exist as an identifiable system with boundaries distinguishing it from its environment. If the system continues, this

[3] W. Ross Ashby, *Design for a Brain*, Wiley, 1952, p. 99. In Chapter 15, Ashby introduces the concept of multistability, and thereby adds a new dimension to the theory of stability. This concept is too complex, however, to be discussed in these pages.

change will be called "equilibrium change." This system is ultrastable.

3. If the parameter value, that is, the disturbance, which is responsible for the changed state of equilibrium has returned to its previous value and no other critical change has occurred, and if the system does not then return to its original state of equilibrium, the change is called "system change" to distinguish it from "equilibrium change." This system is ultrastable but irreversibly altered.

Specification of the variables

If the study of systems involves the study of relationships between variables, it is necessary to specify explicitly the variables employed in any particular study. Physicists use variables like mass, energy, temperature, and pressure. The importance of a variable stems from its utility in the formulation of significant generalizations.

The choice of variables is, in effect, a choice of subject matter. The variables chosen not only permit or prevent generalization but also focus attention on specific aspects of a problem. Although reasons will be given for the particular choices made, the only proper criterion is the success of the set of variables in permitting the investigation of the subject matter of the inquiry.

The state of an international system or of its subsystems will be described when values are assigned to the following variables: the essential rules of the system, the transformation rules, the actor classificatory variables, the capability variables, and the information variables.

The essential rules of a system are those rules which describe general relationships between the actors of a system or which assign definite systemic role functions to actors independently of the labeling of the actors. In a monogamous family system the essential rule would specify that one man is married to one woman. This does not mean that no exceptions occur. The rule is not a law in the sense of physical laws; it merely specifies characteristic behavior.

The inclusion of the set of essential rules in the state description of political or social action systems reflects the belief that the most important descriptive aspects of these systems are represented in those general relationships which are independent of the specific role occupants. No matter how important labeling was to the Tarquins, sociological or political analysis of the Roman Kingdom must be directed to the social and political relationships between rulers and led rather than to the fact that a particular family, the Tarquins, was incumbent in that role. Political theory aspires to discover why such a system arose, how it operated, and why it declined. Political theory assumes that had any other family the same attributes and opportunities, the same kind of system would have arisen. Essential rules permit the investigation of types rather than of particulars.

The transformation rules of a system are those rules which relate given sets of essential rules to given parameter values or step-level functions. They are the laws of change of the dynamic system.

. . . .

Given knowledge of the present state of a system and of the value of its parameters, the future states of the system are, in principle, predictable—whether with certainty or with some degree of probability is not at issue—if the changes in parameter values are given.

The transformation rules may be viewed as programming rules for the entities which manifest behavior corresponding to sets of essential rules. When environmental conditions are such that changes in characteristic behavior, that is, in the essential rules, are induced, the transformation rules specify the transformations in that behavior. Thus transformation rules imply that behavior is a product of internal system influences as well as of external influences. Different kinds of systems will respond or change in different ways. . . .

The actor classificatory variables specify the structural characteristics of actors. These characteristics modify behavior. For instance, "nation state," "alliance," and "international organization" name actors whose behavior will differ as a consequence of structural characteristics. If nation states were to be divided into authoritarian and democratic, this would also have consequences for their behavior. The structure of an actor system produces needs which are peculiar to that structural form of organization and which therefore distinguish its behavior from that of other kinds of actors.

The capability variables specify the physical capability of an actor to carry out given classes of actions in specified settings. They do not express a general power to act but are relative to type of action and the conditions under which the action is taken. Various factors enter into the determination of capability: among others, territory, population, industrial capacity, skills of various kinds, military forces, transportation and communication facilities, the willingness to use physical capabilities for given objectives, and the capacity to draw upon the aid of others.

Information variables enter into capabilities but are not identical with them. An actor may fail to do something he has the capability to do if he is unaware of his capabilities. He may attempt something he is unable to do if he overestimates his capabilities.

Information includes knowledge of long-range aspirations as well as of immediate needs. It includes estimates of capabilities. It includes knowledge of the means by which objectives may be achieved and of the ways in which other actors may behave in response to one's actions or in pursuit of their own independent objectives.

Information, whether accurate or inaccurate, is an important determinant of action in any political or social system. If accurate, information aids in the achievement of objectives; if inaccurate, it interferes. In either case, knowledge of the information which an actor has is important in predicting what that actor is likely to do.

However, knowledge of information is not sufficient for this purpose if the desire is to predict more than one step into the future. A discrepancy between the information of an actor and the objective character of the states of the world will affect the future information states of the actor. The ways in which it may do so are quite complex, however, since the present information state will also influence the future capability states. Feedback is involved in the information factor.

Information also has a peculiar relation to the past. History creates a predisposition to aim at certain objectives although other objectives might satisfy needs just as well. More specifically, past promises, actions, goals, etc., exercise restraints on future actions, even in situations in which objective analysis would indicate equally valuable objectives that are easier to attain.

The same variables will be used at different system levels. The international system is the most inclusive system treated by this book. National and supranational systems are subsystems of the international system. They may, however, be treated separately as systems, in which case inputs from the international system would function as parameters. This holds also for subsystems of nation states and even for personality systems. The system consists of the variables under investigation. It has no absolute status.

Political systems

. . . .

A completely satisfactory definition of politics is most difficult to find. A satisfactory definition would have to include most of those things which common parlance calls political and would have to be restricted sufficiently to limit the subject matter to what is ordinarily considered political.

Yet there must be some reason why family affairs are not regarded as political. Surely power is involved in some sense, just as power is involved in politics. However, it would seem just as surely that power is not the individuating or distinguishing element of the political; otherwise family relations either would be political or would not involve power or influence relations.

In every social system there is some set of rules which describes system levels and relations between those levels. In France, for instance, municipalities are subordinate to the central government. Imperative communications from the Minister of the Interior to a municipal official are both obeyed and regarded as obligatory with a very high degree of statistical frequency.

In any organization, there is some method for deciding not only what should be done, but also where the decision to do it should be made and who is qualified to make it.

A political system is the largest or most inclusive system which has recognizable interests which are not identical—though not necessarily opposed and perhaps complementary—with those of the members of the system and within which there are regularized agencies and methods for making decisions concerning those interests. These rules for decision making, including the specification of the decision-making roles, are independent of the labeling of the actors who fill the decision-making roles of the system.

The political system is distinguished by the fact that its rules specify the areas of jurisdiction for other decision-making units and provide methods for settling conflicts of jurisdiction. It is hierarchical in character and territorial in domain. The existence of a government is an unambiguous sign of a political system since governments are hierarchical in organization and since they arbitrate jurisdictional disputes between other subsystems of the society.

If a religious institution also performs governmental functions, it becomes a political as well as a religious institution. If it shares these functions with a separate institution and no institution has the recognized right to settle jurisdictional disputes, quasi-political systems coexist in the same territory. They regulate those functional areas in which the jurisdiction of each is not challenged. No political system exists in the functional area which is subject to jurisdictional dispute. Since no arbiter is available to keep jurisdictional disputes within any given bounds, the system lacks full political status. In the present international system, the nation states have political systems, but the international system itself lacks one. Alternatively, the international system may be characterized as a null political system.

Law is the consequence of past political decisions. Constitutions are laws which specify hierarchical relationships within the political system and methods for changing these relationships. Political objects are objects which are instrumental in maintaining a political system. Politics is the contest to fill decision-making roles, to choose alternate political objects, or to change the essential rules of the political system. A political system exists when its constitution and laws are communicated successfully within a social system.

Should the political system channel only the request for action toward the attainment of political goal objects without at the same time communicating the imperative character of the communication, the communication is incomplete and partially ineffective. Systems which communicate very ineffectively cease to exist, although revolutionary systems may require time before they communicate with full effectiveness. The object of a revolutionary group is to eliminate one set of essential rules and to substitute another.

Although physical force may be employed, unless communication is effective, that is, has persuasiveness, without the employment of force, the political system may have difficulty in operating and in time may collapse. In any large system, it is imperative to communicate "oughtness" as well as the specific demand for action. Those to whom information is channeled must consider it authoritative. Such "oughtness" must be an integral part of the message. In this respect, "oughtness" does not signify merely that the recipient of the message is aware that the sender of the message intends the message as a command to him. It is necessary also that the message be received as a command; this may, in fact, be quite independent of the intention of the sender in some cases.

It is not important at this stage of the analysis—although with respect to certain propositions concerning the political process it would be a most important factor—why the message is received as a command, whether, for instance, because the recipient of the message expects the external authority to punish him if he does not obey or because the recipient has an internalized sense of obligation. The message must in fact command with respect to political action regardless of the reason it does so if it is to constitute a political message.

International actors communicate externally information concerning the desires of national or supranational actors with respect to the essential rules of the international system and the choice of political goal objects instrumental either to the maintenance of the essential rules of the international system or instrumental to the essential rules of a national or supranational system.

If American-Soviet differences over Korea are examined, the various messages can be analyzed in this fashion. American objections to the government of North Korea can be formulated in terms of an objection to a government not based on the existing will of the Korean people, that is, a demand that certain principles of political organization apply to all actors in the international system. The American response to North Korean aggression can be viewed as a demand that force not be used to change existing political situations, a demand related to the rules the United States wants to govern the international polity. The specific actions taken by the United States are designed either to facilitate an international system obeying desirable rules of order or to protect the American system by preventing the expansion of the Communist system.

Soviet support of North Korea can be viewed as a communication that governments should be based upon the "real" will of the people, that is, the self-conscious vanguard of the proletariat. Its use of force can be viewed as a communication that the keeping of agreements with "reactionary" governments is not required by the international rules of action it desires to enforce. The specific actions taken by the Communists may be viewed as designed to improve the chances for a Communist world order and to give increasing protection to the existing Soviet system. The political contest between the Soviet Union and the United States may be viewed in part as a contest to control or dominate the channels for communicating the essential rules of world organization.

The communication process is considered analytically. There is no assumption of a hierarchy of persons with a descending chain of communications, although this may occur in certain kinds of systems, for instance, some kingdoms.

But the hierarchy may also be a system hierarchy. A person may communicate an order as a consequence of his role in the system hierarchy and receive an order as a consequence of a different role. For instance, the federal government administrator may issue an order requiring cities to engage in air raid drill but himself receive an order from a city official to cease keeping a goat in his back yard. The right of the city in this case may stem from a higher system, or it may be a functionally coordinate exercise of authority.

A political system may be either system dominant or subsystem dominant. Dominance has an explicit meaning. For instance, in the perfectly competitive market, although prices are determined by the activities of all, they function as parametric givens for any single buyer or seller. The political system is dominant over its subsystems to the extent that the essential rules of the political system act as parametric "givens" for any single subsystem. A subsystem becomes dominant to the extent that the essential rules of the system cannot be treated as parametric givens for that subsystem.

A system may be dominant over individuals, although specific associations of individuals may be dominant over the system. Collective leadership in the Communist Party of the Soviet Union would be an example of this.

A system may be subsystem dominant. Yet it may be in relatively stable equilibrium. Suppose that one economic concern produces more or raises prices. If other concerns can take countervailing actions which force the first concern to return to the old prices, the first concern is in fact unable to change or to modify the prices.

The criterion for dominance depends upon the degree of influence. In the perfect market, the withdrawal or addition of any single individual would not affect prices or production. In the oligopolistic market if, for any reasons, one of the oligopolistic concerns ceases to function, the state of equilibrium of the market will change. In terms of such a criterion, the modern totalitarian party exercises greater subsystem dominance than the nineteenth century monarchy.

In these terms, the international system—as it has been known for the past several hundred years—tends toward the subsystem dominant pole. However, there are a number of major or essential subsystems, namely the major national states, which enter into an equilibrium somewhat like that of the oligopolistic market. This point will be explored in the next chapter during the discussion of the "balance of power" international system.

If a single subsystem has dominance over the system and does not share this dominance with other subsystems, the essential rules of the system may be subject to rapid change. For instance, the Presidium of the Communist Party of the Soviet Union can institute changes in political structure, economic policy, the distribution of rewards within the system, and the structure of the family almost at will.

If a few subsystems share dominance, the equilibrium of the system will tend toward greater stability. It will be more difficult to change the essential rules of the political system. For instance, the farm bloc in the United States could not succeed in changing the democratic rules of the American political system, but changes in other political rules and the distribution of price supports are related to its degree of dominance.

In many respects, changes in the character of American political life over the last half century are directly related to changes in the number, influence, and representative character of subsystems having some degree of influence upon American political life. In game theoretic terms these subsystems are actors in a cooperative game and succeed in gaining for their members a share of the rewards of the system greater than they could gain individually but at a cost that transforms the character of the political system.

If the system is so constructed that the subsystems have influence over the system but the members of the subsystem—expect perhaps for its elite group—lack influence or dominance over the subsystem, the rewards may go almost entirely to the subsystem(s) and only negligibly to the members of the subsystem(s).

Political systems rarely are system or subsystem dominant in any absolute sense. For political purposes these terms should be viewed as scalar. Reference to directive political systems as system or subsystem dominant represents an attempt to scale such systems with reference to relative degrees of this characteristic rather than with reference to non-directive systems. A similar rule will be followed with respect to non-directive systems. Therefore, a system dominant directive system may have a greater degree of subsystem dominance than a subsystem dominant non-directive system. . . .

Non-directive and directive correspond for rough purposes to democratic and dictatorial. Their explicit definitions, however, are somewhat more technical. A system tends toward the directive end of the scale to the extent that (a) it is hierarchical in character; (b) directives flow from the top of the hierarchy downward and not in the reverse direction; and (c) the higher in the hierarchy one proceeds, the fewer role holders there are.

The American democratic system, for instance, has hierarchical elements. However, there are coordinate branches in the government and many role holders in the legislative branch. Moreover, at elections rather general but effective directives travel from the base to the summit of the system.

It is obvious that the same tests can be applied within subsystems of a political system. The armed forces are directive subsystems of the political system. However, the Joint Chiefs participate directly in a non-directive subsystem operating at the next to the highest executive level in the government. The executive branch or subsystem of the American government is more directive than the legislative or the judicial.

These scalar terms will be applied crudely in Chapter 3. It is obvious, however, that any analysis aspiring to high predictive power cannot be based upon such simplified applications.

The system dominant and subsystem dominant and the directive and non-directive variables seem to be partly interdependent but, at least tentatively, they seem to measure different aspects of system organization.

The use of role analysis

A system is an anlytical entity. The same individuals may be members of a labor organization; employees of business; citizens of cities, states, and nations; and humans in a world community. The steel industry has a role in the American economy, which has a role in the American society, which has a role in NATO, and so forth. Each role has certain requirements that may, under some conditions, conflict with the requirements of other roles.

A man may have a role as head of a family and as a bookkeeper in a business. This is a relatively simple situation with only two roles directly involved. Yet even here conflicting requirements may arise. Each one of these systems is subject to diverse influences arising from parameter changes. The baby becomes ill and more money is needed. The father has made a fool of himself before his friends and feels a need to increase his prestige, perhaps by being able to spend large sums of money. The business suffers reverses and may not be able to meet the pay roll, or the supervisor of the bookkeepers may be engaging in some private graft. The equilibrium is delicate and can only maintain itself as a dynamic, never as a static, process since each role responds to distinct needs in the particular system in which it functions, and since each system is subject to a different set of parameters, many of which undergo continual or rapid change. Deviancy of the individual who holds these roles from the requirements of the role in one of the systems—perhaps he peculates or fails to report the graft of the supervisor or cuts himself in on the graft—occurs in terms of the needs of the system that happens to have dominance under the existing parameter values.

Systems and subsystems in the international systems have roles, and these roles have different functions depending on whether they couple activity within the subsystems of a larger system or between system levels.

Deviancy, accommodation, assimilation, conflict, and other forms of change occur as the functions of the roles change in the various systematic topological economies. These, moreover, can best be studied in terms of the essential rules of the various systems and subsystems. The Communist Party, for instance, has a role function in maintaining the internal Soviet political structure, a different role function in spreading the Communist system externally, a third role function in safeguarding the Soviet Union against external assault, and a fourth role function in maintaining itself as a going organization. The possible inconsistencies of these role functions under changing parameter values lead to restructuring of some of the role functions in order to maintain others. If the dominant system can be found and its essential rules and transformation rules formulated, a long stride will be taken toward predicting the changes that the party will attempt to make in the systems to which it is coupled and also within its own internal structure in order to maintain itself under changing boundary conditions.

One reason the international system is not a political system[4] stems from the fact that, within the personality systems of decision makers, their role in the international system is subordinate to their role in the national actor system. Moreover, to the extent that this is not true of a particular decision maker, he is likely to be replaced in office. The question of role dominance is one of the more important in political science.

Primitive concepts of the international system

The international system has among its subsystems a set of actors. These actors will be called international actors and will remain undefined. The set of international actors will be divided into the subsets "national actors" and "supranational actors." These also will be undefined. An extensional or "pointing" reference, however, will be offered. The United States, France, and Italy are examples of national actors. The subset of supranational actors will itself be broken into subsets of bloc actors and universal actors. NATO and the Cominform are examples of bloc actors. The United Nations is an example of a universal actor.

International action is action taking place between international actors. International actors will be treated as elements of the international system. Their internal systems will be parameters for the international system; their outputs will be variables of the international system. However, in the chapter on the international actors, the systems of the international actors will be treated as differentiated systems; the international system will then be treated as a parameter for these systems of action.

Thus, it is important to examine both what happens to the international system as changes occur inside the systems of the international actors and to examine how the behavior of the international actors is modified as the international system undergoes change.

[4] It can be considered a null political system.

6. Jessie Bernard

The Sociological Study of Conflict

Research Based on a Systematic Orientation Toward Conflict

Research on conflict which is based on a systematic orientation assumes that all social life consists of interaction within and between social systems. The system may be a small group, even a pair, or it may be a nation or an empire, or anything in between. It may be a political party; it may be a denomination. It may be a work group; it may be a factory. The sociology of conflict attempts to describe, analyse, and explain how such systems fall apart or how they are built up, but only when there is some cost involved in the process. . . .

Mathematical studies in the sociology of conflict

The first work to be reported is among the most general. It is offered by its author, Walter Firey, as a theory of schism, a theoretical model for measuring the conditions under which a system of accommodated groups may fall apart and the conditions necessary for its reintegration. He carries through his analysis in terms of fairly small, informal groups, especially in industry, but this is only incidental; for his conceptual framework is general enough to include all kinds of systems, even a world system.[1]

On the basis of a set of premises and the deductions he makes from them, Firey evolves the formula

$$U = -k(u - x)^{2m} + C,$$

where U stands for utility, u the attainment of a given end, k and m constants for any particular system, and C the point of maximized utility. By setting up differing conditions, he arrives at models in which separate curves tend to emerge out of the original single curve. If the distance between the two curves remains within certain limits, the sub-system will remain within the super-system. But if the curves diverge too greatly, the sub-system will

Reprinted from Jessie Bernard, "The Sociological Study of Conflict," in International Sociological Association, *The Nature of Conflict, (Studies on the Sociological Aspects of International Tensions)*, Chapter I, pp. 64-73, and 100-102, by permission of the United Nations Educational, Scientific, and Cultural Organization. Copyright, 1957, by UNESCO, Paris. *The Nature of Conflict* is distributed in the United States through UNESCO Publications Center, 801 Third Avenue, New York 22, New York.

[1] W. Firey, "Informal organization and the theory of schism," *Amer. Sociol. Rev.*, 1948, vol. 13, no. 1, p. 15-24.

tend to break off; the disadvantages or costs of remaining within the system will be greater than the costs of schism. Sometimes the cost of alliance, or remaining within the system, is borne by one system, sometimes by the other. Firey is not interested in the methods used in schism. That is, violence or war is not essential. Either may or may not be involved. Nor need hate or hostility be involved. Firey's statement is independent of the content of the behaviour.

Firey applies his model to several kinds of real-life situations in industrial plants in order to illustrate its applicability, with intriguing and stimulating results. The model could, as he says, be equally well applied to the relationship of a colony to an empire, of a sect to a denomination, of a minority group to a nation, or to any other set of systems. Firey believes his model could be of practical value to administrators or policy makers. The implication is that if they recognize the signs of schism in time, concessions will be made to reduce the costs of the sub-system's continued relationship, or, if this is impossible and schism is inevitable, at least the break might be made without violence.

The great theoretical roadblock to the acceptance of Firey's theory—as to the acceptance of so many other mathematical models—is the psychological basis—in this case the concept of "utility"—on which it rests. Like "effort" or "satisfaction functions" to be referred to presently, it offers enormous difficulties of both a theoretical and practical nature. What, exactly, is it? And how can it be measured? Is it the opposite to "cost"? Can it be objectively assessed?

Also in terms of costs, but from a somewhat different angle, is the approach of George Kingsley Zipf through his "principle of least effort" (Chapter 10).[2] This principle states that individuals govern their behaviour in such a way as to minimize the probable average rate of work. In the course of developing this theory over a wide range of data, Zipf applies it to the size and location of communities, finding that his "minimum equation"

$$P.Sn = \frac{P}{1^p} + \frac{P}{2^p} + \frac{P}{3^p} + \ldots + \frac{P}{n^p}$$

adequately describes rank-population distributions, where P.Sn equals the total C population of the terrain, and where P is the population of the largest community . . . , and where the exponent p equals $1/q$ (p. 366). The equation says that in an integrated and stable social system, the second largest community will be half as large as the largest, the third largest will be one third as large, and so on. When the equation does not hold, as in the United States from 1820 to 1860, according to Zipf, this is an indication that the social system is splitting into separate systems. After the Civil War, the reintegration of the South into the Union shows up in

[2] G. K. Zipf, *Human Behavior and the Principle of Least Effort: an Introduction to Human Ecology* (Boston: Addison-Wesley, 1949).

Zipf's equation "as an ever greater approximation to rectilinearity" (p. 422). Wars and revolutions, according to Zipf, are incidental to the process of achieving the rectilinearity in population distribution called for by the principles of least effort and as embodied in his equation.

Zipf applies his theoretical system to an analysis of class conflicts also. He believes that the tendency for men to exploit one another when they can is inevitable. The strength of a given class and hence its potential for rebellion is determined by its income. The incentive to remain in any given system is proportional to the income of the individual. The two magnitudes must be in an appropriate relationship in order to have equilibrium. If classes are ranked from the bottom up, the income of the individuals in each class should be proportional to the rank of his class; the number of individuals in a class should be inversely related to the square of its rank. Equilibrium, concludes Zipf, is reached under these conditions and rebellion is averted (Chapter 11).

Applying the same principle to international relations, Zipf finds the "least work centre" now to be in Germany rather than in England, where it formerly was. In effect, Zipf's theory states that conflict represents an effort to align production forces and factors in such a way as to minimize human effort. "We shall view wars and revolutions as potential equilibrating devices for effecting a more stable equilibrium" (p. 436).

So far as application is concerned, the implication of Zipf's work is that the rational policy-maker will work with his equations, rather than against them; if he works against them, he will lose out.

Aside from the substantive criticisms which might be levelled against Zipf's work—his theory of class conflict being far too simple, for example, in the light of recent research in this area—the following methodological criticism has been made by Kenneth J. Arrow[3] (pp. 149-50):

> Dr. Zipf's work does not constitute a properly developed mathematical model. The fundamental postulates are nowhere stated explicitly; though mathematical symbols and formulas are sprinkled rather freely through a long work, the derivations involved are chiefly figures of speech and analogies, rather than true mathematical deductions; in some cases, they are simply wrong. Thus, as an attempt at a systematic social theory, Zipf's work can only be regarded as a failure.
>
> However, two empirical regularities do emerge which are highly suggestive and may prove promising for further research. [The two regularities referred to are those discussed above.] . . .

[3] K. Arrow, "Mathematical models in the social sciences," in D. Lerner, H. D. Lasswell, *The Policy Sciences: Recent Developments in Scope and Method* (Palo Alto: Stanford University Press, 1951), p. 120-54.

Begins with a brief analysis of the utility of mathematical reasoning. The author examines, in turn, certain models; assessment of the individual interest as against the collective interest, where he defends a theory of relations between 'total quantities'; the principle of rationality, defined as a choice between possibilities logically deduced and compared with the tastes of the individual. A third section deals with the theory of games. An appendix is devoted to Rashevsky's theory and Zipf's reflections on the principle of the "least effort."

Still another deductive approach to the sociology of conflict has been made by Herbert A. Simon.[4] The system he is dealing with is a social group whose behaviour can be characterized by four variables, all functions of time, namely: (a) intensity of interaction as among members; (b) level of friendliness among the members (c) amount of activity carried on by members within the group; and (d) the amount of activity imposed by the external environment, that is, the external system. In addition, three sets of dynamic relationships among these variables are postulated: (a) the intensity of interaction depends upon, and increases with, the level of friendliness and the amount of activity carried on within the group; (b) the level of group friendliness will increase if the actual level of interaction is higher than that "appropriate" to the existing level of friendliness; and (c) the amount of activity carried on by the group will tend to increase if the actual level of friendliness is higher than that "appropriate" to the existing amount of activity, and if the amount of activity imposed externally is higher than the existing amount of activity. Simon presents equations for all of these postulates. He then derives the conditions of equilibrium, of stability, and then the method of what he calls comparative statics. From his equations he finds conditions which indicate positive and negative morale, the latter not unrelated to Durkheim's *anomie*. Under certain conditions, his equations indicate that groups will dissolve. He finds, further, that if a group has been dissolved by reducing one of the parameters of his equation, it cannot necessarily be restored by increasing the parameter once again.

Simon validates his work by reference to George Homans' study of *The Human Group*,[5] but in addition he applies his models to clique formation, to "conflict of loyalties," and to competition of groups. He feels that his model "offers an explanation for some of the commonly observed phenomena relating to the stability and dissolution of groups" (p. 211).

An empirical researcher might wish to question some of Simon's postulates. It may be true, for example, that intensity of interaction increases with the level of friendliness in a group; might it not also increase with the level of hostility in the group? Hostility is often, if not necessarily, a concomitant of competition; competition has been found greatly to accelerate the amount of activity, if not its quality.

A mathematical biologist, Nicolas Rashevsky,[6, 7] has been attempting in two books to build up a mathematical sociology, including a sociology of

---

[4] H. A. Simon, "A formal theory of interaction in social groups," *Amer. Sociol. Rev.*, 1952, vol. 17, no. 2, p. 202-11.

[5] G. C. Homans, *The Human Group* (New York: Harcourt Brace, 1950).

[6] N. Rashevsky, *Mathematical Biology of Social Behavior* (Chicago: Univ. of Chicago Press, 1951).

The author shows how the mathematical method can be applied to the structure of society and to the conduct of its members.

[7] N. Rashevsky, *Mathematical Theory and Human Relations, an Approach to a Mathematical Biology of Social Phenomena* (Bloomington, Indiana: Principia Press, 1947).

conflict and of war. His aim is to interpret neurobiological mechanisms of the central nervous system as revealed in group behaviour. In one sense his theory may be viewed as a theory of an élite. His theory is wholly general; it does not apply to any specific system. He posits two populations or systems, both made up of "actives"—élites, perhaps—and "passives." The two sets of actives, or the two élites, are in conflict, and each attempts to influence the other individuals in their respective populations or systems to engage in the conflict also. Or there may be in each population two active groups in conflict with one another, one wishing to carry on the conflict, the other not wishing to. For simplicity's sake Rashevsky assumes only one active set of individuals in each population. He derives the inequalities which must be satisfied if both populations are to engage in conflict. The length of the conflict is computed from the rate of destruction of the members of the populations, or of their removal from combat. If the rate of destruction of the active members of a population is more rapid than that of the passive members, a point is reached where "the active group can no more influence the passive individuals and make them continue to fight. The populations stop fighting, become demoralized. . . . We thus have a quantitative interpretation for the 'breakdown of morale,' which is usually a rather elusive notion" (pp. 185-6). The population whose morale breaks down first loses the conflict. As related to war, Rashevsky applies his formulas to describe the rate of retreat, including in his variables and constants such factors as amount of land involved, technical equipment and productivity, natural resources, and changes in the ratio of actives to passives. Differences in defensive capacity and in striking power are also involved. The offensive is taken by the population which is favoured in the mathematical inequality.

As an illustration of the kinds of situations which Rashevsky attempts to reduce to mathematical formulae we cite the following (pp. 218-19):

> What looms ahead as a result of such studies is the possibility of describing in mathematical terms the following situation: Let n social group with initial populations $N_0 1$, $N_0 2 \ldots$, $N_0 n$ settle at a given moment in n adjacent areas of sizes, S_1, $S_2 \ldots S_n$, characterized by coefficients k^1, $k^2 \ldots k^n$, which measures the fertility of soil and the mineral resources. Groups with initially small values of $N_0 i/S_i$ will develop technical abilities more slowly. Since those factors act to decrease a,[8] the value of a will be less in such groups after a time. If we consider warlike interactions between the various groups, we will find that the incidence of wars favours a special class of military rulers, who survive wars better than other individuals do. The ratio $p = N_{im}/N_i$ of the military people will vary with time. . . .
>
> Groups with small initial N_i/S will develop a higher a and a_f. If a change in behaviour pattern occurs, the new regime in such groups would be more

[8] The concept a refers to "actives" as contrasted with "passives," as described in the preceding paragraph.

> intolerant, according to equation 26. We may have here the clue to understanding the different results of revolutions in different countries. A smaller *a* at the moment of a revolution results in greater tolerance and more freedom.
>
> In principle, all these relations can be described mathematically by developing further the theory outlined here. The different parameters may be estimated by comparison with historical data.

Basically Rashevsky's system rests on a cost theory of conflict, although it is not identical to those already referred to. In pleading for objectivity in analysing the conflict of systems—in this particular instance capitalism versus socialism, but equally relevant for any other conflict between systems—he points out that although the group which profits from any particular social form tends to evaluate it as superior and any other as inferior, actually such subjective evaluations do not hold. It is always a question of superior for whom, inferior for whom. "Fundamentally . . . any advantage to a group of individuals results in some disadvantage to others" (p. 235).

Since Rashevsky's models are perfectly general, wholly independent of empirical data, it is impossible to make any substantive critique. So far as method is concerned, he is, apparently, rigorously correct. His "standards of mathematical rigour are high. The methods used are drawn from the calculus and the theory of ordinary linear differential equations, with a few tentative steps toward the use of integral equations" (p. 149). The test of this work will come in the stimulus it offers to others and in whatever application can be made of it.

Another mathematically oriented approach is that of Anatol Rappaport who, in a series of articles dealing mathematically with what he calls "satisfaction functions" has explored the rewards of co-operation between two individuals under given conditions of sharing, of need, of output, and of initiative. In the course of his analyses he derives an equation which he interprets as follows[9] (pp. 118-19):

> The logarithmic terms of S_1 and S_2 represent the satisfaction of two "states" arising from "security" which each believes results from armaments. Hence the satisfaction depends not only on the absolute amount of armaments possessed but also on the excess of armaments over those of the neighbour. Here, of course, the increased efforts of Y detract from the satisfaction of X. The linear terms represent the detraction from satisfaction due to the burden of taxation, etc., that is, the "effort" in producing the armaments. The amount of armaments produced under these circumstances will be given by equation 16, and the resulting satisfactions will be less than they would be if the "competitive term" were not present, in spite of the fact that this term vanishes at $x = y$, where "balance of power" is achieved. It is interesting to note that both competitors are losers.

[9] A. Rappaport, "Forms of output distribution between two individuals motivated by a satisfaction function," *Bulletin of Mathematical Biophysics,* 1947, vol. 9, p. 109-22.

This would seem to be a mathematical statement of the invidious nature of all status phenomena; no matter how high one stands absolutely, one still remains low as compared to another. Perhaps Rappaport's work applies more specifically to competitive situations than to conflict, but it may be useful for both. An exploration of his theory in relation to reference group theory would seem to be in order. As in the case of other mathematical models, the perfectly general nature of Rappaport's models renders them independent of empirical tests. The mathematical procedures seem rigorous and correct.

Karl W. Deutsch[10] has contributed an interesting theory of national assimilation and conflict based on the currently popular cybernetic concepts of information and communication. He suggests that on the basis of numbers in nine population groups and six rates of change, "the probable developments towards either national assimilation or national conflict in a given area" can be calculated (p. 102). The nine population groups are as follows. The total population, P; the public, or socially mobilized population, M; the unmobilized or underlying population, U; the assimilated population, A; the differentiated population, D; the mobilized and assimilated population, N; the mobilized but differentiated population, W; the underlying assimilated population, Q; (for quiescent); and the underlying differentiated population, R. The six rates of change needed are: the natural rate of growth of the total population; the rate of natural increase of the mobilized part of the population M; the rate of entry of outsiders into M; the rate of natural population increase for the assimilated population; the rate at which outsiders are entering the assimilated group; and the rate of natural increase of the differentiated population. He documents his conclusions with data dealing with Finland, Bohemia-Moravia-Silesia, India-Pakistan, and Scotland.

The last of the mathematically oriented approaches to the sociology of conflict to be presented here is that of the British student of inter-group relations, L. F. Richardson, who has classified and illustrated from international behaviour, the probable reactions of one group to a threat by another as: contempt, submission, negotiation followed by submission, negotiation followed by a bargain, and retaliation. He is particularly interested in the last-named, which usually takes the form of an arms race toward war. Richardson begins with a concept borrowed from Gregory Bateson's study of the Iatmul tribe in New Guinea, called "schismogenesis," which means "the manner of formation of cleavages." Schismogenesis

[10] K. W. Deutsch, *Nationalism and Social Communication* (New York: Published jointly by The Technology Press of the Massachusetts Institute of Technology and J. Wiley and Sons, Inc.; and London, Chapman & Hall, Ltd., 292 p.

Attempt at an application of the mathematical methods of cybernetics to sociology, and particularly to the problem of nationalism, in view of the fact that the automata of cybernetics provide a high-grade model of dynamic equilibrium. The basic concepts of cybernetics (information, transmission, complementariness, efficiency) are applied to socio-psychological processes.

may be symmetrical or complementary, according as the behaviour developed by the two sides is the same or complementary. An arms race is a case of symmetrical schismogenesis. Basing his analysis on the defence budgets of leading nations from 1909 to 1914, Richardson evolves a set of equations for the rate of increase in arms expenditures, namely:

$$\frac{dx}{dt} = ky \text{ and } \frac{dy}{dt} = lx.$$

He then continues[11] (pp. 229-30):

> This is a mathematical expression of the idea of permanent peace by all-round total disarmament. Criticism of that idea will follow, but for the present let us continue to study the meaning of equations 1 and 2. Suppose that x and y being zero, the tranquility were disturbed by one of the nations making some very slightly threatening gesture, so that y became slightly positive. According to equation 1, x would then begin to grow. According to equation 2 as soon as x had become positive, y would begin to grow further. The larger x and y had become the faster would they increase. Thus the system defined by equations 1 and 2 represents a possible equilibrium at the point where x and y are both zero, but this equilibrium is unstable, because any slight deviation from it tends to increase. Stability is not the same as equilibrium; for on the contrary stable and unstable are adjectives qualifying equilibrium. Thus an equilibrium is said to be stable, or to have stability, if a small disturbance tends to die away; whereas an equilibrium is said to be unstable, or to have instability, if a small disturbance tends to increase.

Richardson develops his statements to include a formula for disarmament by a victor—a formula used by physicists to describe "fading away" phenomena, or by accountants to describe depreciation.[12] To take account of these phenomena, Richardson amends his equations to include another constant which gives a "fatigue and expense coefficient" or a "restraint coefficient." These restraining influences may be sufficient to render the equilibrium stable, or they may not. Richardson concludes that there is a theoretical possibility of permanent peace by universal total disarmament, but to meet the argument that "grievances and ambitions would cause various groups to acquire arms in order to assert their rights, or to domineer over their unarmed neighbours," he again amends his formulae by

---

[11] L. F. Richardson, "Threats and security," in: T. H. Pear, ed. *Psychological Factors of Peace and War*. Contributions by G. W. Allport, J. Cohen, H. V. Dicks, H. J. Eysenck, J. C. Flugel, H. Himmelweit, M. Kerr, T. H. Pear, L. F. Richardson (London, Hutchinson and Co.), 1950, p. 219-35.

The phenomenology of "arms races" in the past. The phenomenon of so-called "schismogenesis," expressed as an equation to assess, mathematically, the close relationship between fear and threat, and vice versa in arms races. Armaments budgets from 1910 to 1914 as an additional test confirming the algebraic theory.

[12] S. C. Dodd reports a similar fading away phenomenon in connexion with "tension" in a housing project: "A measured wave of interracial tension," *Social Forces,* 1951, vol. 29, no. 3, p. 281-9.

adding another set of constants so that the formulae no longer indicate a permanent condition. He now has two straight lines in two planes; if they intersect, a condition of equilibrium—stable or unstable—is indicated at the point of intersection. This set of equations, the author points out, does not take into account other than retaliatory reactions to threats, that is: contempt, submission, negotiation, or avoidance, since his theory "is restricted to the interaction of groups which style themselves powers, which are proud of their so-called sovereignty and independence, are proud of their armed might, and are not exhausted by combat. This theory is not about victory and defeat. In different circumstances k or l might be negative" (p. 233).[13] Richardson proposes the concept "warfinpersal" (war-finance-per-salary) as the best measure of a nation's warlike preparations. On its subjective side —moods, friendly or unfriendly, before a war—he finds that the best equation to describe the way such moods behave is one used in the theory of epidemics of disease, so that, he argues, "eagerness for war can be regarded analogously as a mental disease infected into those in a susceptible mood by those who already have the disease in the opposing country" (p. 235).[14]

The work of Deutsch and Richardson differs from that of some of the other mathematical work here reported in that it is based on empirical data; it is intended to be descriptive of the behaviour of nations internally and externally. There is little attempt to ferret out new relationships; nor is the mathematical basis in any way new.

The mathematical models of social conflict so far presented are based on conventional, if difficult, mathematics, mainly on systems of linear equations enlisted for *ad hoc* analyses. There is in process of developing at the present time a radically different kind of mathematical model, dependent more on combinatories[15] and matrix algebra, but evolving its own mathematics as it proceeds. It may be viewed as a method for measuring the costs of differing policies or plans or strategies and thereby helping in selecting the best one. It is called the theory of games of strategy.[16, 17]

[13] Richardson refers to his theory of submissiveness, which appeared in the following publications: L. F. Richardson, J. Griffin, *Alternatives to Rearmament* (London: Macmillan, 1936) and in *Psychometrika,* 1948, 13, pp. 147-74, 197-232.

[14] J. F. Scott, R. F. Lynton, *The Community Factor in Modern Technology* (Paris: UNESCO, 1952) (*Tensions and technology* series, no. 2).

[15] Or combinatorial analysis, which deals with combinations, permutations, arrangements and distributions.

[16] J. von Neumann, O. Morgenstern, *Theory of Games and Economic Behaviour* (Princeton: Princeton Univ. Press, 1947).

The aim of this book is twofold: first, to give an exact definition of what can constitute "rational" behaviour by an individual who encounters a "hostile" force on his route; second, to study the special problem of a coalition in cases where there are more than two belligerents. The authors are particularly concerned to establish how far the parallel between the strategy of games and that of social behaviour is justified. They therefore proceed to a series of sociological studies, from which they finally deduce that the parallel is not necessarily valid.

[17] G. Morgenstern, *Pearl Harbor: the Story of the Secret War* (New York: Devin-Adair, 1947).

Since we shall discuss it at some length in a later chapter, we mention it here merely for the sake of completeness.

Most of the mathematical models for the study of conflict derive directly or indirectly from physics. In this sense they often seem rigid and mechanical, even when they do fit life situations. Thus, for example, when Simon went over his equations with Homans, on whose work he was basing his model, Homans concluded "that the mathematical treatment does not do violence to the meanings of his verbal statements, but that the equations do not capture all of the inter-relations he postulates—that they tell the truth, but not the whole truth." [18] This will probably always be true of any equation.

Nevertheless, equations and especially formulas of inequalities seem to constitute an appropriate language for conflict situations. Inequalities may, by varying parameters, pass through equalities and then reverse themselves. This oscillation of position seems to constitute a reasonable model for many conflict situations, especially in those where bargaining is involved.

To some students, especially to those who come to research by way of empirical work, the currently increasingly popular postulational approach seems vaguely unsatisfying. It seems to begin without sufficient empirical basis; it seems, in effect, to beg the question. The postulates assume given conditions; the empirical researcher would like proof that such conditions actually exist generally. The deductive approach, however, aims at finding conditions which the empirical approach cannot locate with its method. And ultimately the deductive approach tests itself by its ability to "explain" real-life situations. Still it must be granted that the deductive approach seems to assume that we know more on the simple descriptive level than perhaps we really do know. The relationships assumed among given variables, again, strike some students as unrealistic, or at any rate, as requiring more validation.

Perhaps most troubling is the assumption in mathematical models that all the variables involved can be precisely measured and that in the case of those referring to subjective phenomena—e.g., cost, utility, satisfaction, "effort," etc.—they are additive in nature. This last-named difficulty haunts researchers in all the social sciences. Perhaps the chief contribution of mathematical models may turn out to be the stimulus they offer for the invention of techniques for measuring the parameters involved. The measures needed may far transcend those now available. Perhaps a totally new attack on the problems of measurement is needed. It may be that we are in a rut in our thinking, that present approaches—in terms of attitude scales, "utils" [19] and the like—are inhibiting the emergence of better ones.

---

[18] Simon, "A Formal Theory of Interaction in Social Groups," p. 204 fn.

[19] "Utils" are statistical constructs devised for the measurement of "utility" or "subjective value." Since the chapter was originally written, there has developed a new approach to the measurement of "utility" or "subjective" value which goes under the name of Decision Theory. See: I. Bross, *Design for Decision* (New York, Macmillan,

It has become so easy for good technicians to whip up new instruments based on current assumptions that the invention of better instruments may be prevented. Here as in so many other fields, the good may be the enemy of the better. The problem is especially acute in the sociology of conflict because here "cost" is so often in terms of phenomena as yet unmeasurable. In this area the work of the social-psychological school of conflict and that of the sociological school can find a common problem to attack, requiring all the skills and insights both can muster.

. . . .

The theory of games of strategy as the basis for a modern sociology of conflict

The theory of games of strategy is both a theoretical system throwing light on the nature of social organization and social conflict and a technique for solving concrete and specific problems of a technical nature. It is based on a theorem first worked out by John von Neumann in 1928 and since then elaborated by other mathematicians. As a theoretical system, it has been applied most thoroughly to economic behaviour, especially by Oskar Morgenstern. As a technical tool it has been applied to a great many kinds of specific problems, especially military ones, such, for example, as the optimal behaviour in an air duel. What is now needed is some solid work by sociologists to render their data amenable to game theory analysis. The present statement is about the theory rather than a statement of the theory itself.[20]

The theory of games of strategy is a theory of rational behaviour; in this respect it differentiates itself markedly from social-psychological theories which view conflict as non-rational behaviour. It deals with people in interaction, that is, with people who must plan their behaviour with reference to the behaviour of other people. Every strategy, or rule of behaviour, must be evaluated in terms of the expected behaviour of others. The theory of games does not assume that one's opponents are necessarily attempting to injure one—that would be a theory of paranoia—but only that they are attempting to do the best they can, even at your expense.

A fundamental concept in the theory of games of strategy is that of the payoff function. If player A does this and player B does that, what will

---

1953); Ward Edwards, "The Theory of Decision Making," *Psychological Bulletin*, July 1954, XLI, pp. 380-417; L. J. Savage, *Foundations of Statistics* (New York, Wiley, 1954); S. A. Siegel, "A Method for Obtaining an Ordered Metric Scale," *Psychometrika*, in press; and R. M. Thrall, C. H. Coombs, and R. L. Davis, *Decision Processes* (New York, Wiley, 1954).

[20] For a fuller statement about the theory see J. Bernard, "The Theory of Games of Strategy As a Modern Sociology of Conflict," *Amer. J. Sociol.*, 1954, vol. 59, no. 5, p. 411-24.

The theory of games of strategy explained by six fundamental concepts: rational behaviour, strategy, the pay-off matrix or function, rules of the game, coalitions, alliances and imputations, and, lastly, the solution.

be the consequences for each one? The theory of games of strategy is worked out best for two-person zero-sum games, which means that what player A wins, player B loses, and vice versa. In parlour games the payoff function is specified by the rules of the game or by the players themselves; they decide what it will be. But for sociological "games" the payoff function is determined by the "laws" of nature, including "human nature." The "rules of the game" are not human creations, but natural phenomena. If Nation A does this and Nation B does that, what will be the consequences? What will be the payoff? Which combination of strategies or rules of behaviour will favour Nation A? which, Nation B? The determination of the payoff function for sociological "games" is, of course, a monumental research task. Until we know what the payoff function for every combination of strategies of the players is, we cannot apply the theory of games.

But once the payoff function is known, it is tabulated in a payoff matrix, as follows:

Player A	*Player B*	
	Strategy B-1	Strategy B-2
Strategy A-1	−8	4
Strategy A-2	0	−10

Note. Such a matrix is to be read as follows: If player A uses strategy A-1 and player B uses strategy B-1, player A will lose 8 points; if player A uses strategy A-1 and player B uses strategy B-2, player A gains 4 points; if player A uses strategy A-2 and player B uses strategy B-1, player A gains nothing; if player A uses strategy A-2 and player B uses strategy B-2, player A loses 10 points.

By convention, the matrix is read in terms of player A; player B's gains and losses are the same as player A's, but with the signs reversed. The number of strategies—here limited to two—may be infinite. For non-zero-sum games—in which gains and losses do not cancel one another—dummy players are introduced to absorb gains and losses.

The problem for each player now is to select the strategy which over the long run will net him the most, regardless of what his opponent does. This is done by the so-called minimax and maximin procedure. Player A finds the minimum gain he can make with any strategy; he then selects the strategy which nets him the largest of these minimum gains. Player B finds the minimum gains he can hold Player A down to, and then selects the strategy which results in the lowest of these minimums.

When a third player is introduced new theoretical problems emerge. Now coalitions or alliances tend to be formed. And the distribution of gains among the members of the coalitions—imputations, so-called—looms up as a problem. Presumably players will coalesce in a manner to make their gains optimal, since they are rational. The distribution of gains—the imputation—must conform to accepted standards of behaviour. Attempts to pay any one member of a coalition less than he could get in another coalition will mean that he will desert the coalition, producing loss to the other player in the coalition.

The application of game theory will probably come first in combination with statistics in problems of statistical inference. It may take some time before it can be applied to sociological data. But it is probably important for sociologists to work with the mathematicians who are developing the theory, since the direction of mathematical research will doubtless be determined by the nature of the models presented for its consideration.

In the meanwhile, all the dependable research that sociologists and social psychologists can do may have to be harnessed. Just what are the "laws" of social life? Of "human nature"? Just what is the payoff function of certain combinations of strategy or behaviour or policy? A great deal more will have to be known about the way groups function before we can supply the data necessary for application of the theory. The tension studies which Unesco has sponsored may be part of the indispensable foundation for determining the rules of the game and for computing payoff functions.

The chief criticisms of the theory of games of strategy as a basis for a sociology of conflict, aside from those invoked in connexion with our presentation of other mathematical models above, may be summarized under three headings: (a) conceptual-technical difficulties; (b) practical difficulties; and (c) ethical difficulties.[21] The conceptual-technical difficulties centre about the problems of determining and assessing costs, or payoffs. This is a psychological as well as a sociological problem. The practical difficulties inhere in the overwhelming volume of computations necessary to apply the theory even in relatively simple practical situations—running into the millions and even billions and trillions. The ethical difficulties lie in the apparently Machiavellian conception of human nature implicit in the theory. The theory does, however, leave room for ethical considerations. For it assumes that when several solutions in a strategic game are possible and equally good, the one will be selected which conforms most closely to accepted standards of conduct.

---

[21] For a more extended discussion of these points see Bernard, "The Theory of Games of Strategy as a Modern Sociology of Conflict," pp. 422-4.

7. GEORGE LISKA

International Equilibrium

The Outlines of a Theory

. . . In his *Study of the Principles of Politics,* George Catlin places at the center of his analysis the basic element of individual will, rather than interest, and the act of control. He conceives the political process as a more or less stabilized interaction of individual and collective wills in different control relationships within a material and social environment. Catlin professes theoretical indifference to ends; yet the end of political action implicit in his analysis is individual freedom in an integrated society balancing liberty with authority. The many writings of Harold D. Lasswell, in turn, are concerned with the value and policy-oriented approach. Lasswell is interested chiefly in revolutionary changes in the shape and composition of value, symbol, and élite patterns in national and international society. Power is merely the means toward the integration of central values such as safety, well-being, and respect. Individual personality—organized in groups within a cultural and technological environment—is central, while the theoretical ideal is a model, or speculative construct, which would isolate social trends by means of a developmental and equilibrium analysis. In the elaborate structural-functional scheme of Talcott Parsons, finally, the more "static" aspect bears on the structure of legitimately expected action of individual personalities as actors in an interacting social system and culture. The more "dynamic" aspect concerns the allocation and integration of social roles and cultural values by means of suitable institutional mechanisms. All these factors are functional in the degree to which they promote the maintenance of an integrated system of action as a going concern within the given human and nonhuman environment. A major part in the integrative function falls to organized authority, which depends for compliance on the shared values and interlocking expectations of the members of a society rather than on coercive sanctions.

Merely to touch upon a related effort, David Easton has recently suggested "authoritative allocation of values as it is influenced by the distribution and use of power" to be the most fruitful organizing formula for

---

Reprinted from *International Equilibrium: A Theoretical Essay on the Politics and Organization of Security,* pp. 10-17, and 193-201, by permission of the Harvard University Press, Cambridge, Massachusetts.

a systematic theory of politics. And finally, Quincy Wright has attacked the problem with special reference to international relations by way of a capability and value field theory, which would make use of the measurement of social communications.[1]

Though different in many respects, Catlin, Lasswell, and Parsons converge in their general orientation and use of certain organizing categories. They all center their analyses in the human personality, or will, and in the action and interaction of individuals and groups within a social and material environment. The interaction constitutes a process which is somehow related to structure. These writers are all concerned with the distribution and integration of chosen values by means of an authoritative institutional mechanism, seeing coercive control through power as a more or less latent and sublimated technique. With varied emphasis they try to encompass the conditions of both social stability and change. They are, lastly, more concerned with a fundamental analysis than with an inquiry into the means of implementing the values postulated or implied in the analysis.

It is not at all simple and obvious how to apply to international relations the findings of these theoretical efforts. Notably concepts developed to analyze a relatively integrated society will not automatically fit a state system that is far from constituting an integrated system of action and a community; there is moreover the increasing relevance of the ideas of Thomas Hobbes, as we pass from the dynamics of primary social groups to the dynamics of armed states. Yet a series of attempts to formulate a substantive theory will show what can and what cannot be done more conclusively than an endless debate over methodology with its diminishing returns.

One possibility is a systematic equilibrium theory. The concept of equilibrium is, of course, widely used in a number of theoretical disciplines, its application in economic theory being especially suggestive. Joseph Schumpeter saw in equilibrium a tool which, ideally, might assemble into one model the causes, mechanisms, and effects of economic phenomena, provided one can postulate equilibrium as both an existing tendency and a theoretical norm against which to assess actual dynamics. Economic theory has generated or taken over from mechanics a whole typology of the equilibrium family in order to include in the concept developments that do not conform to the ideal of a self-maintaining system. It distinguishes between general and partial; unique and multiple; stable, neutral and unstable; long- and short-term; perfect and imperfect equilibrium; between equili-

---

[1] In addition to G. E. G. Catlin, *A Study of the Principles of Politics* (1930), the discussion draws chiefly on Lasswell's *World Politics and Personal Insecurity* (1935); Lasswell and Kaplan, *Power and Society;* Daniel Lerner and H. D. Lasswell, *The Policy Sciences: Recent Developments in Scope and Method* (1951); Talcott Parsons and Edward Shils, *Toward a General Theory of Action* (2nd ed., 1949); David Easton, *The Political System* (1953); Quincy Wright, *The Study of International Relations* (1955); and Karl W. Deutsch, *Nationalism and Social Communication* (1953).

brium at a low and at a high level of employment, and the like. This variety is the product of theoretical difficulty and calls for caution in defining the kind of equilibrium one is prepared to defend as operative in the investigated realm.

Fairly extreme is the maximalist idea of a "static" equilibrium as a self-maintaining system of automatic compensatory reactions to disturbances, restoring the original state. If such an unfailing equilibrium operates anywhere, it is certainly not in the social realm. More realistic and at the same time "dynamic" is the view of the equilibrium mechanism as a state of relative temporary stability, uniquely or recurrently upset by factors precipitating change and replaced eventually by a new temporary equilibrium. When applied to intelligent and purposive actors, such an idea of equilibrium may be supplemented by that of equilibration or balancing as a deliberate policy. Together with the qualifications implied in the typology of equilibrium, this lessens the austere simplicity of the maximalist equilibrium concept, but saves the general idea for use in the social sciences.[2]

George Catlin—perhaps more explicitly than any other systematic theorist of society and politics—regards the equilibrium and equilibration of wills as the fundamental condition of social order and integration. In sympathy with Spencer's law of equilibration, he assumes the tendency of progressively integrated society to realize an equilibrium of wills in variously stabilized control relationships. Harold Lasswell, apart from advocating cross-reference between developmental and equilibrium analysis as the most promising method in political analysis, uses amply the idea of the balancing process with regard to problems of power and security. Talcott Parsons, too, draws on the idea of equilibrium as a state or an ordered process of change in an interdependent social system, maintained by a variety of mechanisms of social control. It seems that all three theorists would agree to treat the equilibrium of a political society in terms of the interaction of human actors in an environment, stabilized by the existence of some kind of authoritative social control with a moral, legal, and sentimental basis. None of them, to my knowledge, defines his idea of equilibrium as a norm and as actual dynamics with sufficient rigor. And the anthropologists have not fared any better in conceiving of equilibrium in terms of countervailing tensions between groups in a pluralistic society, or of compensatory rates and frequencies of interaction between individuals and groups in response to situations of stress.[3] Although such

---

[2] Cf. Joseph A. Schumpeter, *Business Cycles* (1939), Vol. I, ch. 2; A. C. Pigou, *Economics of Welfare* (4th ed., 1932), pp. 794-795; George J. Stigler, *The Theory of Price* (1946), pp. 26 ff., on the idea of equilibrium in economics; and Robert W. MacIver, *Social Causation* (1942), p. 169, for the concept of the "precipitant."

[3] See Catlin, pp. 114, 197, and *passim;* Lasswell, *World Politics and Personal Insecurity,* pp. 52 ff.; Lasswell and Kaplan, pp. xiv ff., 250 ff.; Parsons and Shils, pp. 107-108, 230. Also see M. Fortes and E. E. Evans Pritchard, eds., *African Political Systems* (1940) pp. xxii-iii, 14, 16-18, 271; and Eliot D. Chapple and Carleton S. Coon, *Principles of Anthropology* (1942), pp. 44 ff., 362, 462.

shortcomings are largely due to the nature of the subject-matter itself, they diminish the value of the imaginative equilibrium analyses by students of literate and preliterate societies for a theory aspiring to some specificity of statement.

There is, finally, the use of the equilibrium concept in the study of public administration by Chester I. Barnard and his followers, and—a path-breaking precedent for my own efforts—Carl J. Friedrich's early discussion of the balance of power within the framework of the League of Nations.[4] My chief inspiration came, however, from the idea of the economic firm in equilibrium; it helped mightily in systematizing an until then disjointed analysis.

Drawing selectively on the surveyed ideas, I shall now present the barest outline of an equilibrium theory of international organization of security and international relations in general, merely suggesting what will be refined and elaborated upon in the course of the discussion. I shall be using the concept of equilibrium in both of the accepted ways—first, as a theoretical norm or point of reference; second, as denoting an actual tendency toward changing states of temporary equilibrium in political institutions. In qualifying the tendency, I shall rely mainly on the ideas of progressive, stable, and unstable equilibrium. My central concept is that of *institutional equilibrium,* applied primarily to international organization with respect to its structure, the commitment of its members, and its functional and geographic scope.

A composite organization is in structural equilibrium if there is an over-all correspondence between the margins of restraints it imposes on members and their willingness to tolerate them; if the ratios between the influence exercised by individual members and their actual power are not too unequal; and if the respective powers of the different organs correspond to the composition of their membership. At best, the several organs should reinforce each other in a progressive equilibrium movement; at worst, their efficiency and that of the entire organization will decrease as a result of an unstable equilibrium. More important than structure is the commitment of states participating in an international organization—in our case mainly that for mutual assistance against threats to security. What matters is that the actual readiness of members to perform correspond to their formal obligations. A disequilibrium between readiness and obligations results in pressure on the commitment toward its reduction, decentralization, or evasion, which tends to be cumulative. And, lastly, an international organization is in equilibrium with respect to its functional scope when the functions and jurisdiction which it actually exercises correspond to the extent of the needs relevant to its purpose. Depending on the adequacy of

[4] Cf. Carl J. Friedrich, *Foreign Policy in the Making: The Search for a New Balance of Power* (1938); and Chester I. Barnard, *The Functions of the Executive* (1940).

the area covered by the organization, its geographic scope can be analyzed in analogous terms.

International organization is thus related to crucial features of international relations and their environment. This is least obvious in the case of structure, concerning such matters as the relation of formal equality, representation, and influence to a hierarchically ordered society of unequally powerful states. It is more readily apparent with respect to a mutual security commitment which cannot but influence the state of the military-political equilibrium, traditionally known as the balance of power. If the balance of power is a persistent feature of international politics, it is not—as Canning among others realized—a fixed and unalterable standard. It is rather a standard perpetually varying as new materials of compensation arise.[5] These derive, however, not only from political geography, but also from newly relevant spheres of reality, now especially institutional and socio-economic. It is the latter sphere which is most directly affected by the functional scope of international organization.

Individual personalities, organized social groups, economies, and cultures are all involved in the international equilibrium. The psychological balance of individuals and groups is influenced by feelings of security and insecurity; it is stabilized to the extent that routine fulfillment of expectations relieves the contest for control among subjects of more or less complementary roles, shared values, and recognized authority. Equilibrium within and between economies is promoted or inhibited by the exchange of economic goods; the inner resiliency of cultures depends largely on the efficacy of their moral and material components in meeting the needs of both stability and change.[6] If the ideal is cultural diversity within the bounds of political and economic interdependence, unilateral abuses of power will tend to aggravate cultural antagonisms and induce the threatened party to compensate for its weakness by stressing its distinctive peculiarities. In any event, the absence of mutually responsive, cooperative, or peacefully competitive communication of values and satisfaction of needs among cultural, ideological, ethnic, and economic groups is certain to be reflected in social maladjustments and to aggravate the operation of both the military-political and the institutional equilibrium.

In view of such ramifications, international organization may be treated as part of a dynamic interplay of institutional, military-political, and socio-economic factors and pressures, constituting a *multiple equilibrium.*

An analysis of international relations can shift emphases among at least three complementary standpoints. First, it may stress individual states as collective actors in the international political process, animated by a

---

[5] Cf. H. W. V. Temperley, *The Foreign Policy of Canning: 1822-1827* (1925), p. 466. Canning had in mind the enlargement of the balance of power to include the newly arising Latin American states.

[6] Cf. Melville J. Herskovitz, *Man and his Works: The Science of Cultural Anthropology* (1948), pp. 522 ff.

more or less unified will under the guidance of their respective elites, and pursuing a measure of security, welfare, and prestige which would exceed —whenever possible—their share as determined by their relative power. Once the balance of power among states is controlled by means of effective international organization, the distribution of security, welfare, and prestige (within the existing conditions of the military-political, socio-economic, and institutional equilibrium) ceases to be the result of conflict and competition only, or even primarily. It is then at least supplemented by an authoritative distribution of the coveted values, governed by the norms and sanctions of the organization's security commitment, functional scope, and institutional structure. Whatever the means to it, however, when individual states feel that the existing distribution of security, welfare, and prestige is the best possible one relative to their power positions, and could not be substantially improved by unilateral efforts at redistribution, the state system as such is in an ideal state of equilibrium.

This leads to the second emphasis, from the viewpoint of the state system, or developing international community, as a going concern. Here, a theory will examine and evaluate the policies of states as being "functional" or "dysfunctional," depending on whether or not they promote the objectives and conform to the rules of a system. Criteria will vary for different systems, among which most relevant for our purpose are the international hierarchy of great and small states, the balance of power, collective security, and the more advanced forms of international integration. Among matters to consider are the sanctions attached to different forms of behavior, the conditions of stability and organized change, the functional requirements and alternatives for the attainment of postulated values, and the functionality of a course of action for the entire state system or for only one of its segments in a disunited world.[7]

Such a "functional" analysis would relate the activities of states to the third standpoint of possible theoretical emphasis, the social and material environment in which states seek to maintain and improve their position individually and in combination. The main analytical components of the environment are: first, the plurality of nations with a "personality" influenced by physical and cultural factors; second, the strictly material configuration of territorial bases of states in a geopolitical pattern conditioned by the state of technology; and third, the international and supranational processes and institutions which cannot be readily subsumed under either of the two other components.

For all these viewpoints the idea of equilibrium is a convenient unifying concept. In the first place, all states seek to secure for themselves by all kinds of policies the best attainable position in the international equilibrium. Second, the majority of states must behave so as to promote the equilibrium of the state system surviving and evolving by no other than peaceful means into higher forms of community. Third, many important

[7] Cf. Robert K. Merton, *Social Theory and Social Structure* (1949), pp. 21 ff.

aspects of the environment of international relations can be interpreted in equilibrium terms. And, finally, the dual character of the equilibrium concept as a theoretical construct and a desirable policy for safe-guarding humane values brings together the analytical and the normative perspectives, as well as some causal implications, of the investigated dynamics.

Faced with the occurrence of a possibly oppressive disequilibrium, this theory sees in the institutional and the multiple equilibrium a legitimate minimum objective of national and international action. It has been said that a healthy democracy balances all social forces in a contrived harmony of power.[8] International politics, too, revolves in large part around attempts —admittedly less consistent and successful—to control the oscillations of a dynamic balance. The theory here submitted holds that a workable organization on national, regional, or global scale required that institutional, military-political, and socio-economic factors and pressures for and against stability be deliberately equilibrated. The task is complicated by the forces generated by industrialism, nationalism, and mass democracy; cabinet diplomacy can no longer be isolated from total relationships among peoples. A measure of rational adjustment is thus both harder to attain and more necessary, in order to approximate an equilibrium which would be more than an accidental deadlock of opposites.

. . . .

The prospects of an equilibrium theory

One fact emerges clearly from the analysis: it is the persistent reassertion of the balance or equilibrium of power as the irreducible if changing central dynamics of international relations. It changes internally as developing technology subordinates balance or preponderance of conventional military forces to relative offensive and defensive strength in nuclear weapons, long-range ballistic missiles, and strategic aircraft; and it changes externally as balancing of vertically organized and territorially based national military power structures is ever more intertwined with, and seeks vainly to override, larger socio-economic and political needs and aspirations, cultural idiosyncrasies, and institutional norms and practices. Both major powers of today have experienced the consequences of obsolete policies as Soviet territorial encroachments and one-sided American emphases on military factors have provoked hostile reactions of a kind reserved for political behavior out of keeping with the mood of the day. Victory in the rising and falling global crisis, which has not been resolved in open war, will ultimately come to the power learning soonest and best how to manipulate to its advantage the compensatory, nonmilitary elements of the larger equilibrium that fluctuates uncertainly over the thermonuclear stalemate.

Such a state of things has theoretical implications which carry on the ideas put forward in the introductory chapter.

[8] Reinhold Niebuhr, *Christian Realism and Political Problems* (1953), p. 51.

It is now more than suggestive to represent schematically the full scope of power-normative international reality as consisting of an inner hard core, or central dynamics, of continually balanced military power, shading off into militarily and politically ever less directly relevant factors, processes, interests, and values. All influence in their multiple interaction the behavior of politically significant individuals on national and international plane; but different, more or less forcible, components of the spectrum become relatively more efficacious depending on the degree of crisis, i.e., the extent to which the survival of one or more states as independent political societies is at stake. It is impossible to overemphasize the theoretical significance for all politics of the differentiation between a crisis situation—implying conflict over sheer physical or political survival as the minimum immediate objective of policy—and a noncrisis situation (in times and conditions of relaxed competition and tensions)—implying an often cooperative quest for additional goals, such as individual freedoms, general welfare, and justice, as the maximum and long-range political objectives. Failure to make the differentiation explicit has been responsible for much confusion in theoretical debate.

Some of it has concerned the problem of scope, symbolized in the terminological question of international "politics" versus "relations." The analyst confining himself self-consciously to the strictly political (meaning power) phenomena tends to reject all else as irrelevant to a realistic inquiry. His strength is a cogent doctrine of political dynamics reducible to a fairly simple and exciting formula, attractive to the student who is unwilling or unable to cope with the complex and changing inter-relationships in the social and political world. The success of this kind of analysis in the United States after the Second World War is due to an intellectual need at least as much as to the historic conditions of post-Wilsonian disenchantment and the Soviet threat. Conversely, the advocate of a broader scope for international relations, including the social, cultural, and institutional factors, will see in the narrowness of the strictly political approach a major weakness. He admits the centrality of the strictly political, however conceived, but wishes to include the other factors as a condition of genuine realism. He can insist that this is no innovation or sign of liberal fuzziness, but rather a return to Aristotle in a situation of total politics reminiscent of the Greek *polis*. The weakness of the more inclusive inquiry is an almost inevitable loss of cogency, as the great methodological difficulties confronting the social sciences and their integration threaten to cause a relapse into the diffuseness (now aggravated by jargon) afflicting the study of international relations in the interwar period.

A theoretical analysis need not choose sides. To deal with the hard core of military-power dynamics, the determining influence of which grows with the rising level of crisis, the analysis will seek to develop and refine a "pure" power and equilibrium model, positing rational weighing of alternative means for maximizing chosen values; and it will relate this hard core to the less tangible modifying outer phenomena, chiefly socio-economic and institutional, which have grown in importance over time and become relatively more significant in situations of lessened crisis. This book has essayed such an approach between the Scylla of traditional realism, mistakenly representing the dynamics of too broadly conceived national power as being the whole of international relations, and the Charybdis of apolitical sociologism and legalism, which would miss the distinctive features of international politics. An attempt to account for as much as possible in terms of institutional equilibrium in no way precludes and in many respects supplements other methods and concepts of the behaviorial sciences focusing attention on individual and group action, attitudes, ideologies, personality in culture, the role of elites, social communication, or decision-making. Pending further progress along these lines, the outline given in these pages may have some merits despite its own particular pitfalls and limitations.

It is anything but easy to analyze an equilibrium situation with respect to nonquantitative relationships and noncomparable, if related factors. The resulting statement is not conclusively verifiable. This may offend the uncompromising empiricist, prone to mistake illustrations for clinching verifications and loathe to accept a measure of inner consistency and over-all plausibility of a theory resting on sympathetic understanding of the subject-matter as a valuable feature in its favor. A necessarily simplified construct, however dynamic, can besides present only a lifeless approximation to the complex and changing interplay of real forces and events. Yet as a generalization stands for no specific instance, so an abstraction may correspond to nothing actual without ceasing therefore to denote something real. Impressive critics would make the scientific use of the equilibrium concept depend on the development of methods for measuring the power and other variables whose equilibrium makes for stability, and for defining operationally the conditions which produce them. The objection has force, but would be decisive only if measurements in social sciences were clearly established as possible and really fruitful in producing crucial insights into social processes. As it is, some precision can be introduced into an equilibrium analysis by the use of rough indices that point inferentially from qualitative and quantitative symptoms to underlying structures. For instance, abstention from war despite aggressive tendencies may serve as an index of military-political equilibrium; the frequency with which especially great powers act through international organization and the kind of business which they transact there are a possible index of the state of the institutional equilibrium, and, as regards socio-economic equilibrium, the well-developed economic measurements may be supplemented by quantifying the extent and evaluating the content of social communication within and between groups.

In mentioning economics, it is possible to derive some comfort (without ceasing to deplore the difference in possible accomplishment) from the continued use of the concept in economic theory despite its shortcomings, including a limited analytical and predictive value, and the loss of specificity when too many data are included in a "general equilibrium." Nor is the economic world at all immune to disequilibrium, approximating at best the "neighborhood of equilibrium," or unaffected by the existence of oligopoly—broadly comparable in the political world to the concentration of power in a few members of the international oligarchy—which mars the assumptions of the equilibrium theory, as much as those of the classical theory of collective security, by enabling a few players to change in their favor the terms of the game.[9]

To the extent that it focuses the resultants of individual behavior, our theory tends to reify such social processes and phenomena as the state, international institutions, and power. The drawback is minimized in approaches that put at the center individual human beings, their behavior and motives. Since the members of the general public are as a rule not sufficiently involved and articulate to have an identifiable direct influence on policy, it is both tempting and wise to seek meaningful statements of actual interrelations by the study of elites, i.e., politically crucial individuals. Yet, apart from the dangers of arbitrary selection, the elites which can be subjected to intensive inquiry are too few, their communications too largely inaccessible, and their behavior too variable to produce safe generalizations. Without at least a hypothesis (such as that of equilibrium) concerning the principles and dynamics of international relations and organization, which both govern and result from the interactive behavior of actors in the social and material environment, behavioral approaches will not do. A good instance is the approach from decision-making, which, though promising as a focus for the subjective-attitudinal and objective-environmental aspects, depends too much on an impossible historical reconstruction of situations, communications, and motives, often imperfectly known to the actors themselves.[10]

As an alternative, this essay has rooted the equilibrium analysis in a corresponding idea of rational decision-making: it posits as a guide to policy behavior the weighing of means, marginal and total costs and advantages, with the view toward maximizing chosen values like security, welfare, and prestige. Such a balancing procedure affects foreign policy not only when it is applied to relations with other states by the ideal detached foreign-policy maker, but also as it (ever less rationally) impinges on such policy from the interplay of particular, variously intensive and influential calculations and decisions within and between the different specialized

---

[9] Cf. Schumpeter, *Business Cycles,* Vol. I, pp. 66 ff., and Stigler, *The Theory of Price,* p. 28. The concept of equilibrium is criticized by Easton, *The Political System,* pp. 266 ff., and Wright, *The Study of International Relations,* pp. 515 ff.

[10] Cf. Richard C. Snyder et al., *Decision Making as an Approach to the Study of International Politics,* Foreign Policy Analysis Series No. 3, Organizational Behavior Section, Princeton University (June 1954).

publics, interest-groups, and branches and agencies of government. A rational, utilitarian pattern of decision-making may be of limited significance in modern international relations, yet it does gain ground whenever there is a weakening of the ideological, mass psychological, and other "irrational" modifiers of the fairly rational rules of traditional diplomatic statecraft.

Moreover, reification, rationalism, and relative deemphasis of the domestic political process of the states-actors are less grievous shortcomings in a study concentrating on the over-all process of international relations resulting from the interaction of foreign policies of the members of the state system, rather than on the foreign policy of one or several nations. Not only would the opposite procedure multiply variables to the point where they defy any but a taxonomic theoretical statement; but also, quite apart from the question of feasibility, the new fashionable treatment of the domestic political process as the major determinant of foreign policy and international relations can be vastly overdone.

No one will deny that there is a relationship between domestic and international politics with regard to their principles and actual practice. And where there is a relationship, there is a problem; in this case the problem of conceptual and functional unity or disparity between the two branches of politics.

The liberal idealist and the conservative realist are superficially agreed upon the conceptual identity of all politics, domestic and international. However, the realist will castigate the liberal's tendency to transfer mechanically the principles of domestic, constitutional politics to the international sphere. He will deride liberal ideas about the feasible scope and function of law as an instrument of social control among states. The critique will rightly point out the confusion of cause and effect implicit in the attempts to extend the ideal of an unaided "rule of law" to interstate relations. It will emphasize the differences in the nature of the actors and their relations, and the lack of a firm supporting fabric of shared convictions in a primitive international community. The realist will, therefore, reject as fallacious and naive the tendency to set up constitutional principles as an easily reproducible model for international politics, and to attribute to domestic politics legitimate priority over foreign affairs. Instead, the realist will see the unity of political phenomena in the pervasive role of power and will incline to assert the primacy of external over internal politics in a situation of chronic international crisis. Yet his tendency to treat nations as homogeneous units with a definable national interest will be rejected in turn as unrealistic by students who emphasize the determining influence on foreign policy of heterogeneous interest-groups in a pluralistic political community.

There is room for an intermediate position. As regards the conceptual identity or else disparity of domestic and international politics, an inquiry may attempt to isolate relevant principles and other variables common to all politics, and to differentiate their respective place, weight, and manifestation in the different types of the two major areas of politics. In a general way, such an inquiry is facilitated if one assumes a continuum in the forms of possible control relationships, passing from coercive or competitive application of physical power to a complex interaction of normatively ordered competitive and cooperative responses, regulated by a fundamental consensus and a generally recognized authority. Any actual political system, democratic or totalitarian, domestic or international, will approximate in an imperfect fashion the one or the other extreme type of control. Or, more specifically, a theory can assume the operation in all politics of an essentially identical principle, for instance that of equilibrium. The difference between various political systems ceases then to appear as one of basic principle and becomes one of the principle's implementation: while interstate and preconstitutional domestic politics revolve around a relatively unregulated balance of power in inchoate institutions for the coordination of interests, constitutional domestic politics rests on an equilibrium of interest groups within an elaborate system of institutional and other checks and balances.

As for the question of functional interdependence, few will deny that the predominant values of a political society influence foreign-policy attitudes. Nor is there any doubt about the growing interrelation of practical domestic and foreign politics. But, on the latter score, it is necessary to avoid extremes. A sound theoretical outlook will not worship at the altar of an irresistibly self-evident and morally absolute national interest. Neither will it see foreign policy as a mechanical resultant of the interplay of domestic political forces. To the extent that the slogan is true, foreign-policy analysis may and often has to start where domestic politics ends, that is to say, at the watershed. There are two major reasons. First, international politics of the state system has its conventions, techniques, and requirements which, embedded in tradition and existing conditions, are relatively independent of the internal political system of any one participant nation. These are the international equivalents of the generally supported "rules of the game" which even the most determined special-interest-group analyst must introduce as a vitiating exception into his scheme of the domestic political process. At the very least, an informed interpretation of the conventions and requirements of the international game will rule out certain foreign-policy ideas of special interest-groups as patently absurd and weight others as more plausible. This will affect decisively the balance of domestic pressures on foreign policy-making—notably when these pressures cancel themselves out into a deadlock or are overwhelmed by the impact of international crisis—and ensure considerable continuity in the foreign affairs of a plural society within the broad framework of majority consensus, strikingly demonstrated whenever political parties abandon or substantially modify their foreign-policy nostrums once they have attained the responsibilities of executive office.

The second and related reason for drawing a line, however thin, between domestic and foreign politics is the persistence of national "self-preservation" and "survival" as the necessary and in themselves sufficient goals of foreign policy. To say that they are teleologically ambiguous since they beg the question of the values to be preserved is to miss the point. The irreducible minimum objective of foreign policy is precisely to safeguard the integrity of the state so that the values of the surviving society can be determined by domestic political processes independently of external pressures. Where this objective is realized, the diminished role of domestic politics in foreign policy-making is compensated by an enlarged autonomy in all other matters. The deeper the crisis and more difficult sheer survival, the greater will be the predominance of foreign over domestic politics. According to their security position and, secondarily, their domestic political system, countries have thus to work out their individual compromises between the two extremes of domestic determinism of foreign policies on the one hand, and international determinism of domestic policies on the other.

In such a situation, policy-makers may profit by theories that place in a unifying focus the factors and processes to be taken into account in the pursuit of security and welfare; and a policy-oriented bias puts high premium on a theory organized around a basic principle which the makers of policy are familiar with and actually apply in daily decisions. As the empty boxes of conceptual frameworks are piled up and move in the opposite direction, the gap between theory and foreign policy-formulation widens to the detriment of maker and student alike.

If, finally, one makes the most of the institutional aspect, such an approach has its merits provided it remains in close touch with international realities. First, the norms of international law and organization constitute one scientifically ascertainable variable and one of the elements in the definition of the institutional equilibrium. Second, and more important, the various actors in, factors for, and relations of international politics are subjected to analysis while they pass through an organized framework, and the produced effects can be translated into qualitative and quantitative indices. In addition, a theory emphasizing institutions supplements otherwise focused theories with the inquiry into some of the means, other than national power, of implementing desired values. It is not impossible that well-chosen instrumentalities might enlarge the "quantity" of security and welfare to be distributed, relieving thus the mercantilistic mentality which continues to pervade much of international politics.

There are many approaches and intermediate objectives under different names and symbols; the ultimate goal remains the good life of individual men in free communities, great or small.

8. Richard C. Snyder, H. W. Bruck, and Burton Sapin

Decision-Making as an Approach to the Study of International Politics

"The State As Actor in a Situation"

This diagram (*see page opposite*) will serve as a partial indication of the fundamental approach adopted in this essay.

Commentary 1. The first aspect of this diagrammatic presentation of an analytical scheme is the *assumption* that the most effective way to gain perspective on international politics and to find ways of grasping the complex determinants of state behavior is to pitch the analysis on the level of *any state*. An understanding of *all* states is to be founded on an understanding of *any one* state through the use of a scheme which will permit the analytical construction of properties of action which will be shared in common by all specific states. That is, the model is a fictional state whose characteristics are such as to enable us to say certain things about all real states regardless of how different they may appear to be in some ways. Therefore if the scheme is moderately successful, we should be able to lay the foundation for analyzing the impact of cultural values on British foreign policy and on Soviet foreign policy even though the values are different in each case and produce quite different consequences. "State X," then, stands for all states or for any one state. We have rejected the assumption that two different analytical schemes are required because two states behave differently.

It should be added immediately that theoretical progress in the study of international politics will require eventually a *typology*[1] of states based on: basic political organization, range of decision-making systems, strengths and weaknesses of decision-making systems, and types of foreign policy

---

Reprinted from *Decision-Making as an Approach to the Study of International Politics* (Monograph No. 3 of the Foreign Policy Analysis Project Series), pp. 34-9, 57-8, 60-66, and 118-120, by permission of the authors. The publication series and the research of the Foreign Policy Analysis Project (formerly at Princeton University) are now being carried on by the Graduate Program of Research and Training in International Relations, Department of Political Science, Northwestern University.

[1] We shall have occasion later on to suggest the necessity for other typologies.

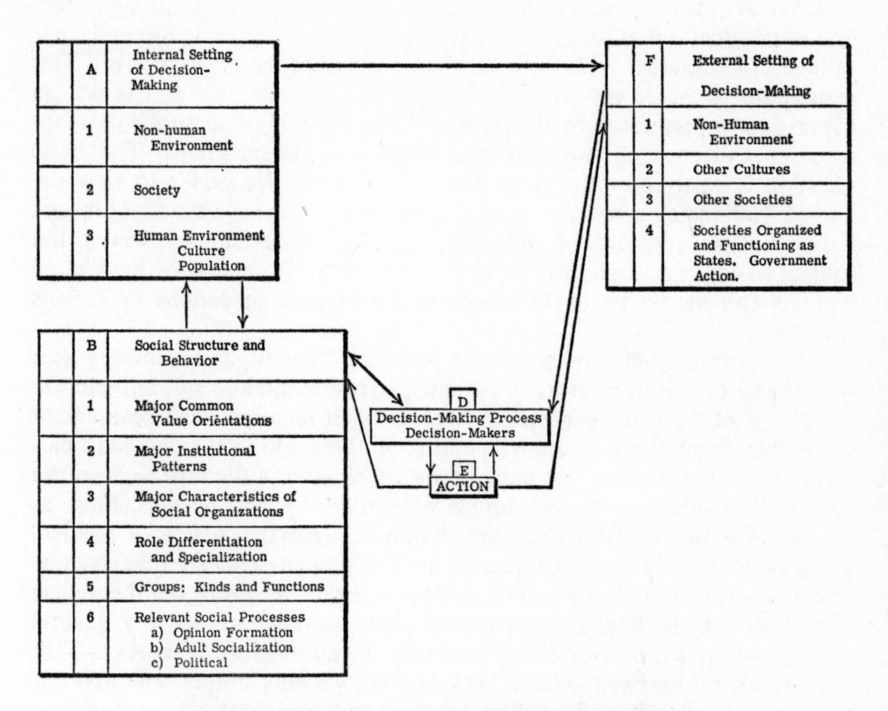

STATE "X" AS ACTION IN A SITUATION

(Situation is comprised of a combination of selectively relevant factors in the external and internal setting as interpreted by the decision-makers.)

NOTE: *This diagram is designed only to be crudely suggestive. Detailed explanation must be deferred. The term non-human environment is construed to mean all physical factors (including those which result from human behavior) but not relationships between human beings or relationships between human beings and these physical factors. The latter relationships belong under society and culture.*

strategies employed. This will facilitate comparison, of course, but it will also make it possible to take into account certain significant differences among states while at the same time analyzing the behavior of all states in essentially the same way.

2. We are also assuming that the nation-state is going to be the significant unit of political action for many years to come. Strategies of action and commitment of resources will continue to be decided at the national level. This assumption is made on grounds of analytical convenience and is not an expression of preference by the authors. Nor does it blind us to the development or existence of supranational forces and organizations. The basic question is solely how the latter are to be treated. We prefer to view the United Nations as a special mode of interaction in which the identity and policy-making capacity of individual national states are preserved but subject to different conditioning factors. The collective action of the United Nations can hardly be explained without reference to actions in various capitals.

3. The phrase "state as actor in a situation" is designed primarily as a short hand device to alert us to certain perspectives while still adhering to the notion of the state as a collectivity.[2] Explicit mention must be made of our employment of action analysis and (both here and in the detailed treatment of decision-making) *of some of the vocabulary* of the now well-known Parson-Shils scheme.[3] We emphasize vocabulary for two reasons. First, as new schemes of social analysis are developed (mostly outside of political science) there is a great temptation to apply such schemes quickly, one result being the use of new words without comprehension of the theoretical system of which they are a part. Second, we have rejected a general application of the Parson-Shils approach as an organizing concept—for reasons which will emerge later. At this point we may simply note that our intellectual borrowings regarding fundamental questions of method owe much more to the works of Alfred Schuetz.[4]

Basically, action exists (analytically) when the following components can be ascertained: actor (or actors), goals, means, and situation. The situation is defined by the actor (or actors) in terms of the way the actor (or actors) relates himself to other actors, to possible goals, to possible means and in terms of the way means and ends are formed into strategies of action subject to relevant factors in the situation. These ways of relating

---

[2] Some social scientists argue that a collectivity cannot properly be regarded as an actor as the term is used in the analysis of social action. However, see Talcott Parsons and Edward Shils, *Toward a General Theory of Action,* pp. 192-195.

[3] The vocabulary of action analysis has become fairly common, yet there are several kinds of action theories (for example, note the differences between Levy and Parsons and Shils, *op. cit.*).

[4] In particular, "Choosing Among Projects of Action," *Philosophy and Phenomenological Research,* 12:161-184 (December 1951) and "Common-Sense and Scientific Interpretation of Human Action," *Philosophy and Phenomenological Research,* 14: 1-37 (September 1953).

himself to the situation (and thus of defining it) will depend on the nature of the actor—or his orientations. Thus "state X" mentioned above may be regarded as a participant in an action system comprising other actors; state X is the focus of the observer's attention. State X orients to action according to the manner in which the particular situation is viewed by certain officials and according to what they want. The actions of other actors, the actor's goals and means, and the other components of the situation are related meaningfully by the actor. His action flows from his definition of the situation.

4. We need to carry the actor-situation scheme one step further in an effort to rid ourselves of the troublesome abstraction "state." It is one of our basic methodological choices to define the state as its official decision-makers—those whose authoritative acts are, to all intents and purposes, the acts of the state. *State action is the action taken by those acting in the name of the state*. Hence, the state is its decision-makers. State X as *actor* is translated into its decision-makers as actors. It is also one of our basic choices to take as our prime analytical objective the re-creation of the "world" of the decision-makers as *they* view it. . . . This is a quite different approach from trying to re-create the situation and interpretation of it *objectively,* i.e., by the observer's judgment rather than that of the actors themselves.

To focus on the individual actors who are the state's decision-makers and to reconstruct the situation as defined by the decision-makers requires of course that a central place be given to the analysis of the behavior of these officials. One major significance of the diagram is that it calls attention to the sources of state action and to the essentially subjective (i.e., from the standpoint of the decision-makers) nature of our perspective.

5. Now let us try to clarify a little further. We have said that the key to the explanation of why the state behaves the way it does lies in the way its decision-makers as actors define their situation. The *definition of the situation*[5] is built around the projected action as well as the reasons for the action. Therefore, it is necessary to analyze the actors (the official decision-makers) in the following terms:

(a) their *discrimination* and *relating* of objects, conditions and other actors—various things are perceived or expected in a relational context;
(b) the existence, establishment or definition of *goals*—various things are wanted from the situation;
(c) attachment of *significance* to various courses of action suggested by the situation according to some criteria of estimation.
(d) application of *"standards of acceptability"* which
  (1) narrow the range of perceptions;
  (2) narrow the range of objects wanted; and
  (3) narrow the number of alternatives.

---

[5] Compare this concept with Arthur Macmahon, *Administration in Foreign Affairs* (1953), Chapter I, entitled "The Concert of Judgment."

Three features of all orientations emerge: *perception, choice,* and *expectation.*

Perhaps a translation of the vocabulary of action theory will be useful. We are saying that the actors' orientations to action are reconstructed when the following kinds of questions are answered: what did the decision-makers think was relevant in a particular situation? how did they determine this? how were the relevant factors related to each other—what connections did the decision-makers see between diverse elements in the situation? how did they establish the connections? what wants or needs were deemed involved in or affected by the situation? what were the sources of these wants and needs? how were they related to the situation? what specific or general goals were considered and selected? what courses of action were deemed fitting and effective? how were fitness and effectiveness decided?

6. We have defined international politics as processes of interaction at the government level. However, there are non-governmental factors and relationships which must be taken into account by any system of analysis, and there are obviously non-governmental effects of state action. Domestic politics, the non-human environment, cross-cultural and social relationships are important in this connection. We have chosen to group such factors under the concept of *setting*. This is an analytic term which reminds us that the decision-makers act upon and respond to conditions and factors which exist outside themselves and the governmental organization of which they are a part. Setting has two aspects: *external* and *internal*. We have deliberately chosen setting instead of environment because the latter term is either too inclusive or has a technical meaning in other sciences. Setting is really a set of categories of *potentially relevant factors and conditions* which may affect the action of any state.

External setting refers, in general, to such factors and conditions beyond the territorial boundaries of the state—the actions and reactions of other states (their decision-makers) and the societies for which they act and the physical world. Relevance of particular factors and conditions *in general* and *in particular situations* will depend on the attitudes, perceptions, judgments and purposes of State X's decision-makers, i.e., on how they react to various stimuli. It should be noted that our conception of setting does *not* exclude certain so-called environmental limitations such as the state of technology, morbidity ratio and so on, which *may* limit the achievement of objectives or which *may* otherwise become part of the conditions of action *irrespective of whether* and *how* the decision-makers perceive them.[6] However—and this is important—this does not in our scheme imply the substitution of an omniscient observer's judgment for that of the decision-maker. Setting is an analytical device to suggest certain enduring

[6] We are indebted to Professor Harold Sprout for calling our attention to this point. See our more detailed discussion of limitations below.

kinds of relevances and to limit the number of non-governmental factors with which the student of international politics must be concerned. The external setting is constantly changing and will be composed of *what the decision-makers decide is important.* This "deciding" can mean simply that certain lacks—such as minerals or guns—not imposed on them, i.e., must be *accepted.* A serious native revolt in South Africa in 1900 was not a feature of the external setting of U. S. decision-makers; it would be in 1954. Compare, too, the relatively minor impact of Soviet foreign activities on the U. S. decision-makers in the period 1927 to 1933 with the present impact.

Usually the factors and conditions referred to by the term *internal setting* are loosely labeled "domestic politics," "public opinion" or "geographical position." A somewhat more adequate formulation might be: some clues to the way any state behaves toward the world must be sought in the way its society is organized and functions, in the character and behavior of its people and in its physical habitat. The list of categories under B (Social Organization) may be somewhat unfamiliar. There are two reasons for insisting that the analysis of the society for which State X acts be pushed to this fundamental level. First, the list invites attention to a much wider range of potentially relevant factors than the more familiar terms like morale, attitudes, national power, party politics, and so on. For example, the problem of vulnerability to subversive attack is rarely discussed by political scientists in terms of the basic social structure of a particular nation, i.e., in terms of B3. Nor is recruitment of manpower often connected up with the way the roles of the sexes are differentiated in a society. Second, if one is interested in the fundamental "why" of state behavior, the search for reliable answers must go beyond the *derived* conditions and factors (morale, pressure groups, production, attitudes, and so on) which are normally the focus of attention.

. . . .

The Decision-Making Approach

We shall not review existing definitions of decision-making but shall present our own and comment on it.

A definition. Decision-making is a process which results in the selection from a socially defined, limited number of problematical, alternative projects[7] *of one project intended to bring about the particular future state of affairs envisaged by the decision-makers.*

Explanation and assumptions. 1. Decision-making leads to a *course of action* based on the project. The term *project* is employed here to include both objectives and techniques. The course of action moves along a path . . . toward the outcome envisaged. Adoption of the project signifies that

[7] We employ the term "projects" here because of the nature of our definition of decision-making and because more than a synonym for "objective" is needed.

the decision-makers were motivated by an intention to accomplish something. The means included in the project are also socially defined.

2. Organizational decision-making is a *sequence of activities*. The particular sequence is an *event*[8] which for purposes of analysis may be isolated. The event chosen determines in good part what is or is not relevant for the observer's analytical purposes.

To illustrate, if the event in which the observer is interested is American policy-making on the Japanese Peace Treaty, then the focus of attention is the system within the American government which was concerned with this problem and the various factors influencing the decision-makers in that system. NATO, EDC, ERP, the Technical Assistance Program, etc., were not immediately relevant. If, on the other hand, the overall cluster of decisions with respect to the policy of containment of Soviet power is the focus, the Japanese Peace Treaty and NATO, EDC, ERP, the Technical Assistance Program and a number of other factors all become a part of the strategies of implementation.

3. The event can be considered a unified whole, or it can be separated into its constituent elements. A suggested breakdown might be in terms of the sequence of activities: (a) pre-decisional activities; (b) choice; and (c) implementation. These need not necessarily occur in chronological order but in all probability they will. Nor are these sealed compartments within the total process.

4. Some choices are made at every stage of the decision-making process. The *point of final decision* is that stage in the sequence at which decision-makers having the authority choose a specific course of action to be implemented and assume or are assigned responsibility for it. At this point the decision becomes official and thus binding on all decision-makers whether they participated or not.

The weeding out of information, condensation of memoranda, etc., all involve decisions which must be recognized by the observer.

5. Choice involves *valuation* and *evaluation* in terms of a *frame of reference*.[9] *Weights and priorities* are then assigned to alternative projects.

6. The *occasion for decision* arises from uncertainty. In other words, some aspect of the situation is no longer taken for granted, becomes problematical, in terms of the decision-makers' frame of reference.

7. The problem requiring decision or the stimulus to action may originate within the decisional system or it may originate in a change in the internal [10] or external setting.

---

[8] "Event" here refers to a unit-act in effect performed by many actors and corresponds to the definition of situation.

[9] The term is used in its social-psychological sense. . . .

[10] In an earlier section we did not define the term *internal setting* beyond saying it referred in general to the *society or to the total social structure* in which the decision-makers function. Now we must note that internal setting really has two components: the total social structure *and the total governmental institutional structure* which is discussed immediately below.

8. The *range of alternative* projects which the decision-makers consider is limited. Limitations exist both as to means and ends. Limitations of the range of alternative projects are due in large part to the following factors: the individual decision-makers' past experience and values; the amount of available and utilized information; situational elements; the characteristics of the organizational system and the *known,*[11] available resources.

. . . .

The organizational unit. Since the *organizational or decisional unit* is at the very heart of the kind of analysis we are suggesting, its constituent elements will be discussed at length below. Here we shall confine ourselves to some fairly general observations. The unit, as we have indicated above, is an observer's analytical device to allow identification and isolation of those actions and activities which are of concern to him. . . . In our view all decisional units are organizational systems and by organization we mean the system of activities and the structure of relationships. That is, the activities and relationships will be the outcome of the operation of formal rules governing the allocation of power and responsibility, motivation, communication, performance of functions, problem-solving and so on. Each unit will have its own organization in this sense. Naturally the particular organizational form which a unit takes will depend on how and why the unit was established, who the members are, and what its specific task is.

It should be apparent that for the observer one and only one organizational unit can act with respect to any one objective. That is, for example, there can be only one set of American decision-makers who were concerned with the Japanese Peace Treaty since the Japanese Peace Treaty was a unique historical event. This holds true whether the primary institutional affiliation of these decision-makers was the Department of State, the Department of Defense, the Congress or whatever. Here we must once again point to the importance of typification of objectives and units. An initial and tentative listing of some of the criteria by which units may be typified is the following:[12]

1. *Size.* Number of participants, ranging from a single member to large bodies such as legislatures. In addition to sheer size the number of participants at any one level would have to be considered.
2. *Structure.* Some of the factors that may be relevant here are whether or not the unit is hierarchical, whether the relationships of authority and the communications net are clearly defined or are ambiguous, and the degree of explicitness and conventionalization of the competences.

[11] This is consistent with our earlier formulation of the concept of setting which alerts the observer to factors which may become conditions of action for the decision-makers without their directly perceiving such factors in the usual sense.

[12] A number of terms introduced in this classification will be defined and discussed below.

3. *Location in the institutional setting.* Two factors are pointed to here. First, the primary institutional affiliation of the members. Secondly, the level in the institutional setting at which the unit operates.
4. *Relation to other organizational units.* Here the relative dependence or independence, isolation or involvement, would be indicated.
5. *Duration of the unit.* The relative permanence or impermanence of units would be the guiding consideration here.
6. *Type of objective.* This is probably one of the most important criteria, and further exposition of the factors involved will have to await the development of a typology of objectives.

We might indicate at this point that it does not appear likely that all decisional units which can be distinguished are representatives of particular types. Some, and perhaps a substantial number, may be more unique than typical. Perhaps future research will provide us not only with useful typologies of objectives, but will also discover important differences between continuing units and those existing only briefly.

We have tried to indicate here that there are essentially three ways of looking at decisional units. (1) *An actual system existing with respect to a particular concrete objective.* We might call this the historical point of view since it involves the reconstruction by the researcher of a particular past event. (2) *A typical unit existing with respect to a typical objective.* Here the kinds of typologies discussed above come into play and types of units would be matched with types of objectives. Typification such as that indicated should ultimately permit predictions of the "If . . . then . . ." kind. (3) *Any unit in general.* This is the manner in which we shall discuss the characteristics of decisional units under various headings below. Furthermore, this very general level is also the one of greatest usefulness to the teacher of foreign policy, since, in the absence of complete and specific data, it allows him to characterize the foreign policy decision-making process in various states in general terms. Sufficient information for such general characterizations exists for almost every state.

The institutional setting. We have thus far not discussed at all those institutions of government which are the traditional subject matter of the student of foreign policy. We have not done this for two reasons. Firstly, as noted immediately above, the approach to foreign policy analysis we are presenting in tentative form cuts across the departments and agencies of government that constitute the traditional units of study. Secondly, the regulation of foreign policy has come to involve so many of the activities in the total national governmental structure that it is difficult indeed to locate precisely the foreign policy function within this structure.

How, then, are the various governmental institutions to be treated? It seems most profitable to consider this institutional setting as a great pool of personnel and information for the decisional units. Within this pool, some important kinds of activities and services, notably the collection and analysis of information, are of course carried on continuously. Also, some of the agencies are primarily concerned with the execution of policy and with the carrying out of routine duties.

We do not mean to imply by any means that it is not highly important that systematic studies be made of institutions like the Department of State or the Department of Defense. Indeed it is vitally important that more and more thorough analyses of these agencies be available, since the behavior of the decision-maker in the decisional unit is largely conditioned by the directives, rules, precedents and ideologies of these governmental institutions or their subdivisions.

The origins of units. We have said that the unit is an analytical tool—a guide to the way the observer reconstitutes the decision-making universe and how its boundaries are to be established. The empirical questions underlying the concept of unit are: *who becomes involved in a decision, how* and *why?* How does the group of officials (actors or decision-makers) whose deliberations result in decision become assembled? Often the answer to this question is essential to an explanation of why the decision-makers decided the way they did.

This is a major point in the analysis of decision-making, but we shall have to postpone detailed treatment. For the moment we may note two methods of unit construction: *automatic assignment* and *negotiation.* That is, the personnel and activities which we analytically call the unit are specified and established within the total decision-making structure by these two methods. Often the selection of decision-makers from the total number who might become involved is based on a simple classification of problems or decisions. The formal roles of the actors provide the clue as to whether they will be part of the unit. Also there are standing units, i.e., committees or groups who are expected to act on given matters. A quite different method of selection is *negotiation* in cases where no routine procedures exist or where new conditions require a special procedure. Some of the great struggles within the total foreign policy-making structure are over *who will decide.* Negotiation may be simply a matter of "springing loose" the right officials for a particular task, or it may represent basic disagreement over the location of authority and power.

The decision-makers. One of the most important methodological assumptions we have made is that *only* those who are government officials are to be viewed as decision-makers or actors. In other words, no private citizen—no matter how powerful—can be a member of the analytical unit *unless* he temporarily holds a federal office. It will be argued by some that this is a step backward, a denial of the progress made by a distinguished group of scholars in freeing the study of politics from its narrow, formal institutional focus. There is no doubt that we have clear differences with some of our colleagues on this point. Suffice to say here, we do *not* differ with others on the significance of social factors in the internal setting, particularly opinion leaders and organized group leaders. The issue is whether it is methodologically feasible or advantageous to put non-governmental personnel in the same action system with the governmental personnel. It appears to us more difficult to isolate the decision-making process (or system or unit) and to relate officials and non-officials when there is no way of assigning recognized roles to *all actors*. Actually there is no state action until *some* officials act and, no matter how powerful, there is no way of imputing official status to private citizens. Usually the argument is that regardless of the *official locus* of decision-making authority it is where the decision is *really made* which counts. But fundamentally this is a matter of the cruciality of certain determinants, not of the location of authority. Furthermore, if interest groups *really make* decisions, the behavior of officials who must translate these into official action must still be accounted for. Except for cases where a private group "owns" a decision-maker, the latter's conduct must also be explained in terms of the other (i.e., organizational) factors at work. *Access*[13] brings us right to the decision-maker's door, yet doesn't tell us why he succumbs. Our scheme does not, to repeat, ignore so-called "informal" [14] factors; it does imply a different way of handling them analytically.

Limitations on decision-making. The concept of *limitations* constitutes a set of assumptions about *any* decisional system. The assumptions concern the factors or conditions which limit: (a) alternative objectives; (b) alternative techniques; (c) the combination of (a) plus (b) into strategies or projects; (d) decision-making resources such as time, energy, skills, information; and (e) degree of control of external setting. In accordance with our general phenomenological approach, we feel that the range and impact of limitations should be considered from the decision-maker's point of view, although many such assessments will be objectively verifiable. The main categories of limitations in terms of their sources are: those arising from *outside* the decisional system, those arising from the nature and functioning of the decisional system and those arising from a combination of both of these. It is only necessary here to suggest briefly the possible kinds of limitations under each heading.

External to the system. Although it might seem as though limitations in the setting, i.e., internal and external, are "objective" to the decision-makers, it cannot be over-emphasized that the estimates of such limitations by the observer and by actors may not be identical. In other words, it cannot—or, rather should not—be assumed that the observer and the actor will agree.[15] Presumably—by some criteria of rational behavior—it is

[13] Our notion of "access" is discussed below under *communication and information* and *motivation*.

[14] We have referred to this concept in connection with organizational theory but here we refer to the fact that many students also call non-specified relationships between any organization and its social setting informal.

[15] This touches on the concept of rationality, discussion of which must also be deferred.

irrational for a state to select objectives for which it has inadequate means of achievement or to select techniques which are less conducive to the achievement of feasible objectives than others. By implication, these judgments are made from a vantage point *not shared necessarily* by the actor. The latter may have less knowledge than the observer *or* the actor may also know what the observer knows but be—*in his view*—unable to behave differently.

Once again, what our scheme requires is a classification of *potential* limitations—factors which may restrict the way the decision-makers deliberate and the results of their deliberations. The important point here is that these factors are mediated—or gain their significance—from the perceptions and judgments of the decision-makers. It is also important to remember that for the most part the decision-makers do not confront external limitations directly on a personal, face-to-face basis so to speak. Rather, their perceptions and judgments result from their participation in a decision-making system.

Judgments of external conditions, objects, events, and other actors as limitations on the action of any particular state may be of two types. First, those in which there is relatively little room for doubt or error and in which fewer qualitative appraisals are required. The phenomena being perceived are susceptible to identification and measurement by agreed standards. Such would be quantitative, concrete data. Second—and probably constituting the opposite end of a continuum—are those phenomena which are less measurable by agreed standards and which require qualitative appraisal. In these cases, there is more room for individual judgments which cannot be either proved or disproved merely by an appeal to logical or other criteria. One would expect, accordingly, more possible disagreement between an observer and an actor with respect to the latter category.

Internal to the system. Limitations external to the system are by far the best known and most dramatic. We have tried to suggest that decision-making in a complex organizational context is a complicated process requiring the performance of a number of functions and many skills. The limitations traceable to bureaucratic pathology are of course familiar but they are by no means the only ones. However, aside from these there are less obvious yet extremely significant limitations having their sources within the system.

1. *Information*—the decision-makers may lack information or may act on inaccurate information; in either case the range of alternatives considered may be affected. It would appear to be a permanent liability of the decision-making process that pertinent information is almost never complete and information which is available, i.e., present within the system, is rarely completely testable. Furthermore, information within the system may not be "available" to the decision-makers. The necessity to adopt and employ interpretative schemes and compensatory devices such as

simplification of phenomena provides a related source of limitation in decision-making.

2. *Communications failures*—reasonably full information may be present in the decisional unit but not circulate to all the decision-makers who need it to perform their roles satisfactorily. A decisional unit may be resistant to *new* information or the significance of new information may be lost because of the way messages are labeled and stored.

3. *Precedent*—previous actions and policy rules (the givens for any unit) may automatically narrow the deliberations of the decision-makers. Previous action may prohibit serious consideration of a whole range of projects. Reversal of policies is difficult in a vast organization.

4. *Perception*—the selective discrimination of the setting may effectively limit action. What the decision-makers "see" is what they act upon. Through perception—and judgment—external limitations gain their significance. Factors objectively identifiable by an observer may be ignored by decision-makers or over-weighted.

5. *Scarce resources*—the fact that any unit is limited in the time, energy, and skills (and sometimes money) at its disposal also tends to limit the thoroughness of deliberation and the effectiveness with which certain related functions are performed. Time pressures may seriously restrict the number of possible courses of action which can be explored.

The combination of external and internal limitations. Obviously, the two sets of potential limitations are related and may be combined. While the external limitations have an independent existence, their significance depends on the judgments of the decision-makers, who may be operating under internal limitations as well. One of the crucial questions in the analysis of foreign policy decision-making is whether particular external limitations are assumed or calculated. Another question concerns the degree to which the decision-makers regard certain limitations as subject to their control. Since internal limitations may either reinforce external ones or minimize them, the extent to which internal limitations are known and allowed for in decision-making may be crucial.

. . . .

Recapitulation

We began our brief exposition of our frame of reference by stating our conviction that the analysis of international politics should be centered, in part, on the behavior of those whose action is the action of the state, namely, the decision-makers. We insisted, further, that state action grew out of and was embodied in the "definition of the situation" by the decision-makers. Finally, we have attempted to demonstrate that the definition of the situation resulted from a decision-making process which took place within a decisional unit. In our scheme, decision-making is accounted for in terms of the activities and relationships of the unit members. The unit is viewed as functioning in an internal and external setting.

We then attempted to define the concept of decision-making and to specify what we meant by treating decision-making as "organizational behavior." To explain the actions of decision-makers we employed three basic determinants: spheres of competence; communication and information; and motivation.

We shall suggest certain obvious connections among the three sets of variables leaving for a later time a more systematic joining of the concepts:

First, the knowledge and information which comprise some of the ingredients of perception are *communicated* through a decisional system or are usually available for communication other than by individual memories. Second, motives, i.e., attitudes and frames of reference—must be *communicated* throughout a decisional system in order that an agreed range of objectives, integration of perspectives, and hence a common definition of the situation on the part of decision-makers is possible and likely. Third, *motives* are linked to *spheres of competence* because the latter provide cues as to the decision-maker's value (location in the total hierarchy and organizational membership), his actual range of choice (responsibilities and power relationships), and his skills and training (specific functions). Fourth, the communication network helps him to carry rules and commands and also confirms or supports the *structure of competence.*

About the decision-makers in any decisional system concerned with any particular problem we want to know: What are the characteristics and relationships of the spheres of competence? What are the motivational influences at work? What is the nature of the communication network? What is the nature, amount and distribution of information? And, finally, what is the reciprocal impact of these on each other? Answers to these questions should provide a basis for adequately describing and explaining state action. It should be remembered that any one of the three fundamental concepts to which these questions point can serve as a separate tool of analysis independent of the other two.

We shall have to postpone consideration of two concepts which can be derived from our analysis, namely, *intellectual process* and *policy attention.* Both can be used to probe certain behavioral patterns and conditions without elaborate organizational analysis in the structural sense. The first points to the patterns of thought or problem-solving which may be typical of certain decisional systems or issues. The second points to the distribution of the total organization's resources with respect to policy problems.

The essence of decision-making analysis: the nature of choice. We shall terminate our essay with an attempt to characterize our central focus. We have thus far discussed a variety of factors relevant to the formulation of a scheme for analysis of foreign policy decision-making. We have sought to stress the interaction of the decision-maker with the various elements of his situation and to point to some of the consequences of this interaction. But we have not said much about what precisely it is that the decision-maker does when he decides. In the following paragraphs we shall try to deal briefly with this matter.

In another context we have alluded to some contemporary work in economics, philosophy and psychology dealing with the Theory of Choice. A number of these suggested models show extensive agreement in certain of the assumptions made by their proponents.[16] First the actor or decision-maker is generally represented by a *scale of preferences,* that is, the values of the decision-maker are assumed to be ordered from the most to the least highly regarded. Some of the writers presenting somewhat more complex models assume further that, let us say, decision-maker A will take into account the reaction of decision-maker B to his (A's) suggestion. Secondly, it is usually assumed that a *set of rules* governs the actions of the decision-makers. These rules determine the manner in which the alternative choices shall be presented, the procedure of voting and so forth. It should be remembered that most of the models are logical and mathematical in character and that the scales of preference and rules are logical devices. They are not intended to be relevant to every empirical choice situation.

These models, to which we have probably not done justice in our all too brief characterization, do provide a convenient point of departure for a discussion of choice. No matter how much certain situational elements are stressed, and we have of course stressed these considerably and (we believe) justifiably so, choices are in the final analysis made by the decision-makers. Decision-makers have preferences, they value one alternative more highly than another. Though the scales of preference may not be as highly ordered as the logical ones referred to above, decision-makers may be assumed to act in terms of clear-cut preferences.

The key questions, then, are: what is the nature of these preferences? what are the factors influencing them? The first statement that may be made in very general terms is that these preferences do not appear to be entirely individual. In other words, we would propose the hypothesis that one element of the scales of preference derives from the rules of the organizational system within which the decision-makers operate. Here we might mention both prescribed rules and conventions and precedents.

A second element might be a shared organizational experience over a period of time. A third has been treated under the general heading of biography, the decision-makers past experiences. Here the expectation would be that similarities and divergences of class background, education

---

[16] See Duncan Black and R. E. Newing, *Committee Decisions with Complementary Valuation,* (1951); Duncan Black, "On the Rationale of Group Decision-Making," *Journal of Political Economy,* 56: 23-24 (February 1948); Kenneth J. Arrow, *Social Choice and Individual Values,* (1951); Felix E. Oppenheim, "Rational Choice," *The Journal of Philosophy,* 50: 341-350 (June, 1953).

and so forth would make for similarities and divergences in preferences.

An additional factor that must be considered together with the various elements of the decision-maker's preferences is the information the decision-maker has. We have spoken earlier of a process of deliberation in connection with the making of choices. This would presumably involve taking into account, in selecting one of several alternatives, the information available. The information, as we have tried to indicate, is assessed selectively in terms of the decision-maker's frame of reference.

It has probably been apparent to the reader that there is considerable difference between what we have called rules and the kinds of rules discussed in connection with the models of choice. We would assert at least initially that the rules governing the decision-maker's behavior are expressed directly through a component of the scale of preferences. The rules which relate to such factors as the presentation of alternatives, the order of voting and so on are considerably more difficult to deal with since in the empirical situation there is a great variety of forms that these rules take. For example, in some choice situations, a vote is avoided at all costs and in others a vote may be used as a punitive measure against some member of the system. In the face of very little evidence, it seems difficult indeed to generalize about the effects of the various procedures that may actually be found. Suffice it to suggest here then that on the basis of various elements of the scales of preference we would expect considerable similarity in these preferences to the extent that the elements are similar.

In conclusion, we might summarize our comments on the nature of choice as follows: information is selectively perceived and evaluated in terms of the decision-maker's frame of reference. Choices are made on the basis of preferences which are in part situationally and in part biographically determined.

C. SELECTED BIBLIOGRAPHY

1. On "power politics" and its critics

Butterfield, Herbert, "The Scientific vs. the Moralistic Approach," International Affairs, Vol. XXVII, No. 4 (October 1951), pp. 411-22.

Carr, E. H., *The Twenty Years' Crisis* (London: Macmillan, 1939).

Cook, Thomas I., and Malcolm Moos, "Foreign policy: the realism of idealism," *American Political Science Review,* Vol. LXVI, No. 2 (June 1952), pp. 343-356.

———, *Power through Purpose* (Baltimore: The Johns Hopkins Press, 1954).

Furniss, Edgar S., Jr., "The Contribution of Nicholas John Spykman to the Study of International Politics," *World Politics,* Vol. IV, No. 3 (April 1952), pp. 382-401.

Grosser, Alfred, "L'étude des relations internationales, spécialité américaine?" *Revue Française de Science Politique,* Vol. VI, No. 3 (July-September 1956), pp. 634-651.

Herz, John, *Political Realism and Political Idealism* (Chicago: University of Chicago Press, 1951).

Kennan, George, *American Diplomacy, 1900-1950* (Chicago: University of Chicago Press, 1951).

———, *Realities of American Foreign Policy* (Princeton: Princeton University Press, 1955).

Morgenthau, Hans J., *Politics Among Nations,* 2nd Edition (New York: Alfred A. Knopf, 1954).

Organski, A. F. K., *World Politics* (New York: Alfred A. Knopf, 1958).

Shelling, Warner R., "The Clarification of Ends, or, Which Interest is the National?" *World Politics,* Vol. VIII, No. 4 (July 1956), pp. 566-78.

Snyder, Richard C., "Toward Greater Order in the Study of International Politics," *World Politics,* Vol. VII, No. 3 (April, 1955), pp. 461-78.

Sprout, Harold, "In Defense of Diplomacy," *World Politics,* Vol. 1, No. 3 (April 1949), pp. 404-13.

Spykman, Nicholas, *America's Strategy in World Politics* (New York: Harcourt, Brace and Co., 1942).

Thomson, Kenneth W., "Theories and Problems of Foreign Policy," in: Roy C. Macridis (ed.), *Foreign Policy in World Politics* (Englewood Cliffs, N. J.: Prentice-Hall, Inc., 1958).

Tucker, Robert W., "Professor Morgenthau's Theory of Political Realism," *American Political Science Review,* Vol. LXVI, No. 1 (March 1952), pp. 214-224.

———, "The Study of International Politics," *World Politics,* Vol. X, No. 4 (July 1958), pp. 639-47.

Wolfers, Arnold, "The Pole of Power and the Pole of Indifference," *World Politics,* Vol. IV, No. 1 (Oct. 1951), pp. 39-63.

2. On philosophies of history

Ashley-Montagu, M. F. (ed.), *Toynbee and History* (Boston: Porter Sargent, 1956). "The Contribution of Arnold Toynbee," *Diogenes,* No. 13 (September 1956).

Geyl, P., A. J. Toynbee, and P. Sorokin, *The Pattern of the Past* (Boston: Beacon Press, 1949).

Hughes, H. Stuart, *Oswald Spengler: A Critical Estimate* (New York: Charles Scribners' Sons, 1952).

Kissinger, Henry A., *The Meaning of History* (Unpublished dissertation, Harvard University, 1950).

Schuman, Frederick L., *The Commonwealth of Man* (New York: Alfred A. Knopf, 1952).

Spengler, Oswald, *The Decline of the West* (New York: Alfred A. Knopf, 1926-8).

Toynbee, Arnold, *Civilization on Trial* and *The World and The West* (New York: Meridian Books, 1958).

Thompson, Kenneth W., "Mr. Toynbee and World Politics," *World Politics,* Vol. VIII, No. 3 (April 1956), pp. 374-91.

———, "Toynbee and the Theory of International Politics," *Political Science Quarterly,* Vol. LXXI, No. 3 (September 1956), pp. 365-86.

3. On methodology in the social sciences (Works useful or suggestive for the study of international politics)

Apter, D., A. Rogow, and D. Smith, "A Symposium," *American Political Science Review,* Vol. LI, No. 3 (September 1957), pp. 734-5.

Aron, Raymond, *German Sociology* (London: William Heinemann, Ltd., 1957).

———, *La théorie de l'histoire dans l'Allemagne contemporaine* (Paris: Vrin, 1938).

Beschers, J. M., "Models and Theory Construction," *American Sociological Review,* Vol. 22, No. 1 (February 1957), p. 32.

Catlin, George, *The Science and Method of Politics* (New York: Alfred A. Knopf, 1927).

Cohen, Morris, *Reason and Nature* (New York: Harcourt, Brace and Co., 1931).

Dahrendorf, Ralf, "Out of Utopia: Toward a Reorientation of Sociological Analysis," *American Journal of Sociology,* Vol. LXIV, No. 2 (September 1958), pp. 115-127.

Deutsch, Karl, "Mechanism, Organism and Society: Some Models in Natural and Social Science," *Philosophy of Science,* Vol. 18, No. 3 (July 1951), pp. 230-52.

Easton, David, "Limits of the Equilibrium Model in Social Research," *Behavioral Science,* Vol. I., No. 2 (April 1956), pp. 96-104.

Gouldner, A. W., "Theoretical Requirements of the applied Social Sciences," *American Sociological Review,* Vol. 12, No. 1 (February 1957), pp. 92-102.

Hayek, Friedrich, *The Counter-Revolution of Science* (Glencoe: The Free Press, 1952).

Kaufmann, Felix, *The Methodology of the Social Sciences* (New York: The Humanities Press, 1958).

Lasswell, H., and A. Kaplan, *Power and Society* (New Haven: Yale University Press, 1950).

Lazarsfeld, P., and M. Rosenberg (eds.), *The Language of Social Research* (Glencoe: The Free Press, 1955).

Lévi-Strauss, Claude, *Anthropologie structurale* (Paris: Plon, 1957).

Leoni, Bruno, "The Meaning of 'Political' in Political Decisions," *Political Studies,* Vol. V, No. 3 (October 1957), pp. 225-239.

MacIver, Robert, *Social Causation* (Boston: Ginn and Co., 1942).

Meadows, P., J. M. Beschers, and A. W. Gouldner, "Models Systems and Science," *American Sociological Review,* Vol. 22, No. 1 (February 1957), pp. 3-8.

Meyer, J., and A. Conrad, "Economic Theory, Statistical Inference and Economic History," *Journal of Economic History,* Vol. 17, No. 4 (December 1957), pp. 524-44.

Meynaud, Jean, *Introduction à la Science Politique* (Paris: Armand Colin, 1959).

Mill, John Stuart, *A System of Logic* (New York: Longmans, Green and Co., 1930).

Myrdal, Gunnar, *An American Dilemma* (New York: Harper and Brothers, 1944).

Moore, Barrington, *Political Power and Social Theory* (Cambridge: Harvard University Press, 1958).

Parsons, Talcott, *The Structure of Social Action* (New York: McGraw Hill, 1937).

———, *The Social System* (Glencoe: The Free Press, 1951).

———, *Essays in Sociological Theory,* revised edition, (Glencoe: The Free Press, 1954).

Pooper, Karl, *The Poverty of Historicism* (Boston: Beacon Press, 1957).

Rostow, W., "Toward a General Theory of Action," *World Politics,* Vol. V., No. 4 (July 1953), pp. 530-54.

Shils, E. A., and H. A. Finch (eds.), *Max Weber on the Methodology of the Social Sciences* (Glencoe: The Free Press, 1949).

Simon, Herbert, *Models of Man* (New York: John Wiley and Sons, 1957).

White, Leonard (ed.), *The State of the Social Sciences* (Chicago: University of Chicago Press, 1956).

Young, Roland (ed.), *Approaches to the Study of Politics* (Chicago: Northwestern University Press, 1958).

4. On systems theory, equilibrium theory and decision-making in international relations

Deutsch, Karl, *Nationalism and Social Communication* (New York: John Wiley and Sons, 1953).

———, "Game Theory and Politics: Some Problems of Application," *Canadian Journal of Economics and Political Science,* Vol. XX, No. 1 (February 1954), pp. 76-83.

Guetzkow, Harold, "Isolation and Collaboration: A Partial Theory of Inter-nation Relations," *Conflict Resolution,* Vol. I, No. 1 (1957), pp. 48-68.

International Sociological Association, *The Nature of Conflict* (Paris: UNESCO, 1957).

Kaplan, Morton, *System and Process in International Politics* (New York: John Wiley and Sons, 1957).

———, "An Introduction of the Strategy of Statecraft," *World Politics,* Vol. IV, No. 4 (July 1952), pp. 549-76.

Lerner, D., and H. Lasswell (eds.), *The Policy Sciences* (Stanford: Stanford University Press, 1951).

Lipsky, George, "The Theory of International Relations of Harold D. Lasswell," *Journal of Politics,* Vol. 17, No. 1 (February 1955), pp. 43-58.

Liska, George, *International Equilibrium* (Cambridge: Harvard University Press, 1957).

———, "The multiple equilibrium and the American national interest in international organization," *Harvard Studies in International Affairs* (February 1954).

McClosky, Herbert, "Concerning Strategies for a Science of International Politics," *World Politics,* Vol. VIII, No. 2 (January 1956), pp. 281-95.

Schelling, Thomas C., "Bargaining, Communication and Limited War," *Conflict Resolution,* Vol. I, No. 1 (1957), pp. 19-36.

Snyder, Richard, H. W. Bruck, and Burton Sapin, *Decision-Making as an Approach to the Study of International Politics* (Princeton: Princeton University Press, 1954).

Wheeler, Henry, "The Political Limitations of Game Theory," *Western Political Quarterly,* Vol. X, No. 3 (September 1957), pp. 669-74.

Part III

Suggestions for the Study of International Relations

A. COMMENTARY

We have been engaged in a wrecking operation. Nevertheless, the need for conceptualization and theory remains. I would like to offer some suggestions for a far more modest and slow way of proceeding toward theory. They are based on postulates which are certainly as debatable as those I have discussed. But there is one difference: I do not claim that it is possible to squeeze the whole camel of international relations through the eye of one needle.

1. Three postulates

Indeed, my first assumption is one of relativism and pluralism. Each one of the approaches I have reviewed has something to contribute; none is the only right way of phrasing the question, or the only right answer. In every social science, and quite obviously here, the facts we can gather are too numerous, too open to conflicting interpretations, too "unstructured" to fit only one scheme of analysis.

On the one hand, the social scientist's selection of facts is always subjective, and the broader the area he wants to understand, the more he is guided by his own values. There is no approach, no "typology" which does not reveal somehow the author's postulates. They may be shown either by the kind of hierarchy he establishes among variables (for instance by a higher ranking given to certain "permanent" factors in a state's material environment, than to human and social variables),[1] or by his refusal, in the name of "system," to establish a hierarchy. I do not understand why social scientists sometimes try to act as if reality contained one true order, and as if the inevitable subjectivity of their minds—potentially as useful as an entrepreneur's inventiveness—were some sort of bias to be ashamed of.

[1] See for instance Mr. Kenneth Thompson's "concentric circles" in Roy Macridis (ed.), *Foreign Policy in World Politics,* Englewood Cliffs, 1957, pp. 355 ff.

As many writers have pleaded in recent years, social scientists should state openly their own values in the works they publish.[2] This would help them considerably to classify and refine their assumptions. Anyhow, their only alternative is "the characteristic positivistic suppression of these problems under a new disguise." [3] It is this very suppression which allows the dominant values of the community to infiltrate into the theory behind the façade of objectivity, and then to cripple the theory with the static bias which I have mentioned before. The scientific methods of verification and validation of hypotheses can and should be free of any value other than scientific truth; but the selection of facts and the choice of hypotheses cannot. "There must always be some reason why from the infinity of true propositions about the behavior of man we choose to present so-and-so as evidence for such-and-such." [4]

On the other hand, we never first approach a whole field merely with the desire to "understand it." What we originally want to understand is a set of problems, and very often we mistake an understanding of certain problems for a definitive theory of the whole field. The analytical models we use are influenced both by each age's view of human nature and by the most pressing contemporary problems. This is true even of the schemes that claim to be most "scientific," although here again the effort to appear detached all too often succeeds only in giving to the scheme a quality of abstraction tantamount to irrelevance. Thus utopianism corresponded to an impulse to solve the problems of war and world order in an international-democratic way. Similarly, the systems of today are keyed to the problems of statecraft and strategy raised by a bipolar world and by the spread of nationalism. The new image of man as one living organism among many, conditioned by environment, and to be best understood in terms of adjustment or maladjustment, underlies much of modern social science, including international relations.

Second, when one tries to understand a field, there is no sounder method than that of drawing one's questions and concepts, as Antaeus' strength was drawn, from contact with the earth. This means, on the one hand, that the tools of analysis to be used should not be taken from other disciplines, except in so far as they deal with factors or units relevant to international relations. It is as unwise to impose on an area which has "a rich and old history" concepts derived from the experience of other sciences, as it is to apply to one society concepts derived from the experience of a very different one.[5] It may be that too many of our traditional concepts, such

[2] For an example of such a statement, see H. Stuart Hughes, *Consciousness and Society* (Cambridge, 1958), Ch. 1.

[3] C. J. Friedrich, "Some Observations on Weber's Analysis of Bureaucracy," in Robert K. Merton et al., *Reader in Bureaucracy*, Glencoe, Ill., 1952, p. 63.

[4] Bernard Crick, "The Science of Politics in the United States," *Canadian Journal of Economics and Political Science*, Vol. XX, No. 3 (August 1954), p. 317.

[5] See Richard Pipes, "Max Weber and Russia," *World Politics*, Vol. VII, No. 1 (April 1955), pp. 371-401.

as the balance of power, or aggression, or imperialism, are soaked by conflicting value judgments. But the use of such terms as "explanatory categories" can never be avoided, and it can be useful when these terms express, not the values of the writer who refers to them, but the values of the individuals, groups, or communities with whom he is concerned. Furthermore, if we decide that it is politics, rather than economics or law, which should provide the core of our discipline around which the contributions of the other fields will be organized, and the set of questions which will be asked from those various fields, then we should stick to the concepts without which no study of politics can be undertaken.

On the other hand, international relations, like other social relations, involve not mere impersonal forces, but men. It is through men's values and institutions, through the thoughts and acts of their leaders, that the basic factors of the material environment affect international politics. Particularly in the area which has been at the origin of so much nonsense: the geographical milieu, the "compelling" character of the environment has been much too easily assumed. The relationship between man and milieu is not one-way. Different human groups in similar environments behave differently; they differentiate space, they can shape the vegetation, the soils, the hydrographical network according to their political and economic aims. World politics in this century have proven that geography can be exploited by a policy, at least as much as policies are "dictated" by geography. What counts in policy-making is how the policy-maker views the environment, and to what use he wants to put it. "The most stubborn facts are those of the spirit, not those of the physical world." [6] Therefore the consideration of men's values, beliefs, and emotions, of their purposes and ideas, is indispensable. It is always preferable to phrase and check one's hypotheses by referring to commonly accepted notions of human behavior, than by turning to the conduct of gases or pistons.

Third, because of the inevitable subjectivity and 'problem-orientation' of the social scientist, and because of the presence of human beings in all the processes we want to study, the strict distinction between "purely scientific" and "normative" theory should be dropped. We evaluate as we breathe, and if we don't do it in terms of ethical norms, we do in terms of "integration," "eufunction," and "dysfunction." Politics is a purposeful activity; foreign policy involves questions of right or wrong. To deal only with "objective behavior," and resort only to strictly scientific investigations, is like trying to explain man after we had merely seen him move his hands and lips in a phone booth. Furthermore, "pure science" is a myth; science has its own philosophical postulates. Ivory-tower science, which refuses to pronounce on value problems and thus condemns itself, as we have seen, either to irrelevance or to an unacknowledged bias toward the status quo, leads to a policy scientism which endorses the values set by the policy-

[6] Jean Gottmann, "Geography and International Relations," *World Politics*, Vol. III, No. 2 (January 1951), p. 163.

makers—for pure empirical science cannot tell us what we should do—then proceeds in the name of science to a task of engineering based on truncated premises. As Mill stated, good policy advice presupposes both science and a teleology. Conversely, discussions of value problems in world affairs, divorced from a consideration of the special milieu and the special rules of the game, will produce only stale moralizing.

On the basis of the preceding postulates, I would like to suggest two kinds of systematic research. The first is turned toward the past; it is predominantly, but far from exclusively, empirical. The second is turned toward the future, and it is more normative. Both are efforts to provide us with a reliable map, simplifying the landscape so as to emphasize its most important features. We should remember that some schematization is inevitable. We should avoid the distortions criticized in Part II, but we should keep on our map all the features rightly and adequately represented on the maps previously reviewed.

2. Two directions of research

(1) The past: historical sociology. The first road I want to suggest is the road to what Raymond Aron has called "historical sociology." It is not a general theory in the sense of a global explanation or of a set of global hypotheses—at this stage, as I have stated in part I, there can be no more such general theory here than in, let us say, sociology. It is a general approach based on the following ideas. The search for timeless propositions, and the deductive method, are, at present, disappointing. We must proceed inductively; before we reach any conclusions about general trends manifest throughout history, we should resort to systematic historical research, not in order to turn our discipline into history, but in order to accomplish the tasks to be suggested here in general terms.

Our starting point would be an analysis of what Raymond Aron calls "diplomatic constellations," or historical situations.[7] This analysis should try to answer a set of questions which will be examined later in this chapter. By comparing the results of our analysis of various situations separated by fairly even time intervals we would be able to delimit and describe historical systems of international relations; we would try to identify the main variables of each such system, and to discover the dynamics of change from one system to another. This stage would be similar to the description of domestic political systems.

A second stage would be the comparison of historical systems. Here one aspect of our task would be the equivalent of Montesquieu's typology of regimes or Weber's typology of economic action or of authority: we should define types of international systems, each type being characterized by a feature or combination of features which determines its originality. One might be the type of international systems of revolutionary periods—periods when the old rules of the game are challenged, and totally new problems appear, which the processes and institutions available during the previous period are powerless to handle. Ours is not the first such period. The

[7] See the selection below, pp. 191-208.

problem which outer space poses for us is comparable to the problems raised by the great discoveries in the 16th century (new rules needed for the acquisition of territory, for the sea, and so on). The only radically new problems of today are those raised by nuclear weapons and those of economic development in a post-colonial phase. The rest—the break-up of empires, the clash of super-states, ideological warfare, and so on—is not at all unprecedented.[8] Another sort of comparison between systems would lead us, at last, to some meaningful generalizations about aspects common to many systems. Thus one could study types of relations between the basic units, that appear in almost every system: for instance, armed conflict, or the balancing process, or international law, or relations between units of a different nature (an Empire and a city state, or a multinational state and a nation state). One could also, by comparing systems, study types of foreign policies, such as: the foreign policies of nations in periods in which they lose their influence; the foreign policies of newly created nations; the problems faced and the reactions adopted by powerful states which, in trying to preserve a balance of power in the world and to prevent world hegemony by a rival, are constantly faced with the need to find ways of mitigating disputes between their own associates, or between one of their allies and an uncommitted party, or between two uncommitted states. The role of selected factors which influence foreign policy could also be examined in various systems; for instance, the channels and the weight of public opinion, or the role of "objective" economic factors and of pressure groups.

Finally, we could proceed to comparisons between domestic political systems and international ones, and between types of domestic and international systems. For there are many similar problems: the organization of, and restraints on, power, the balancing of interests, the development of consensus and legitimacy, the availability of procedures of change. I have stated before both the autonomy of each "milieu" and the unity of politics. Since many writers in our field have tended either to assume a rigid difference between domestic and international forms of political organization, or to treat the latter as if they were deviations from the former, such a comparative effort would be interesting.[9]

---

[8] On this point, see John H. Herz, *International Politics in the Atomic Age,* New York, 1959, pp. 12 ff.

[9] It might be useful to indicate the relationship of my position to that of Robert Merton, (*Social Theory and Social Structure,* revised edition, Glencoe, 1957), who distinguishes between general and middle range theories. Like Mr. Merton I consider general theories, defined as "all-inclusive speculations," to be "premature and apocalyptic." Like Mr. Merton, I think that "a total system of theory" can only emerge from the efforts to consolidate "groups of special theories." Thus the research I suggest could be called middle range. However, as I have said in Part I, such middle range theories will make most sense, and such consolidation will be most possible if we take international systems as our starting points and if we are guided in our research by a general conceptual framework defined as a set of questions covering the field (see above, pp. 9-10, and also my remarks below, pp. 179 ff.).

Behind the program I suggest, there is one assumption which should be spelled out. An understanding of world politics, or of any aspect thereof, supposes an understanding of the characteristics of the international system. The behavior of a given variable depends on the kinds of situations or constellations in which it figures, and these situations in turn are largely a function of the international system in which they occur. In particular, the basic units' freedom of action is limited, and their choices conditioned, by the nature of the system. This assumption carries three implications.

The first is that it is a mistake to limit the study of international relations to contemporary problems. Our incurable tendency to generalize is particularly misleading when our generalizations are based on a very small segment of the field. Each concept we use has a different meaning in different contexts of time and space. This is true in comparative government too—but we rarely discuss it without historical perspective. Writers frequently stress as essential for the realization of world harmony certain instrumentalities of foreign policy—for instance, diplomacy as in the case of Hans Morgenthau, or international organization as was the case for so many authors in the interwar period. But the effectiveness of these instruments varies with the nature of the international system in which they are employed; only a historical approach can help us avoid the error of generalizing from the experience of one system. A return to history would cure us of our tendency to treat international relations as a predominantly Western activity, begun at the end of the Middle Ages; we must include in our research the international relations of non-Western civilizations, and world politics of periods other than those of the city-state or nation-state. The relations between Empires, the complex hierarchies within Empires, the relations between Empires and peoples at their borders, are worth a study.

Also, as we have emphasized before, the study of international relations is a study of change; forces of change cannot be treated as external or deviants: they are fundamental, and internal; furthermore, the lack of a supreme straitjacket comparable to the state in domestic politics turns world affairs into the pure dynamics of "open" systems. This does not mean that there are no regularities or cycles; but those who are most interested in such patterns should be particularly urged to look at history, for it is from history, and not through deduction from abstract hypotheses, that theory might obtain "laws" of the field. "Seeing the general in the historically unique is a method of abstraction different from that of omitting more and more of the characteristics of what we are studying until the residue is something approaching pure form without content" [10]—different and far superior. A return to history would also discourage us from producing explanations in which a determining role is given to a specific

---

[10] Barrington Moore, Jr., *Political Power and Social Theory*, Cambridge, 1958, p. 151.

variable which happens to play such a role in the present, but did not do it to the same extent at all times; for instance, economic development. Finally, an exploration of history will allow us to discriminate between the new problems thrown up by contemporary developments, and the old and recurring ones.

A second implication is that we must avoid both the danger of presenting a static scheme of "interrelated" variables without indication as to their relative importance, and the danger of stressing exclusive causes or certain trends or variables in isolation. "Studies on the causative influence of a given set of circumstances cannot be divorced from an analysis of the various components of the diplomatic complex." [11] We will avoid this double peril if we begin with the analysis and comparison of concrete situations. We will thus be able, on the one hand, to determine what factors and correlations were indeed relevant (and in what circumstances) and, on the other hand, to test the hypotheses derived from specialized studies in our disciplines or in others. Such studies are often based on assumptions concerning international relations which cannot be accepted at the outset (such as the postulate of many psychologists that individual and group tensions are similar).[12]

The approach I suggest might be a way out of the social scientist's dilemma: a "social whole" such as a total field can never be grasped scientifically, and we can only deal with selected aspects. But if we do not start with at least an approximation of the whole, and concentrate either on single trends or on small empirical research, those fragments of the whole cannot be assessed correctly. We will, for instance, make the mistake of discussing the problems and effects of foreign economic aid without taking into account the political and social conditions which largely determine what the effects of such aid on the recipients will be. Or else we will treat historical complexes as if they were daisies to strip. We will generalize for instance about the role of a certain background condition for national or regional integration without remembering that this factor's effect in different instances of integration cannot be easily separated from the effects of other background conditions which operated in conjunction with the factor which we arbitrarily try to isolate.[13] We should certainly not assume that the nature of the international system fully determines the conduct of its components, but we should not analyze the latter apart from the former.

The third implication might be more controversial. There are three tasks at least as necessary as the search for regularities and generalizations. First

---

[11] Raymond Aron, "Conflict and War from the Viewpoint of Historical Sociology," in *The Nature of Conflict,* Paris, 1957, p. 180.

[12] See a critique by Jessie Bernard, "The Sociological Study of Conflict," in *The Nature of Conflict,* Paris, 1957, pp. 46 ff.

[13] This is one of the flaws of the analysis by Karl Deutsch et al., *Political Community and the North Atlantic Area,* Princeton, 1957.

there is a task of classification: for "description of the anatomical sort" [14] and categorization may be as important as, and are a prerequisite to, recurrencies and prediction. We must give far more attention to the tools of analysis we use every day. Each of the expressions in the textbooks conceals, more than it reveals, a number of different situations. There are different classes of conflicts, different types of accomodation techniques, of integrative processes. Such sub-categories as war, the balance of power,[15] negotiation, federalism, and imperialism also need to be broken down. Second, there is a need for a systematic analysis of differences—not similarities—between patterns of international relations, for only in this way will we be able to identify the dominant variables operating at different times and places, and to distinguish types. (Similarly, the ideal-type analysis practiced by Max Weber and by many contemporary social scientists seeks to account for social phenomena by emphasizing their unique features, not their common ones.)[16]

A third and related task is to determine the role of contingent factors, as opposed to regular ones—a role which political and social scientists tend to brush aside too easily, as if in particular the acts of individuals in history could always be either eliminated or reduced to general trends or laws. To relegate them to the position of "random variables" encourages such a mistake. The present century, which at first sight seems to be dominated by the "revolt of the masses" or the action of huge collective movements might well remain in history as the century of powerful individual leaders. We should not disregard the acid comments of Tocqueville, who worried almost one hundred and twenty years ago about the tendency of "those who write in democratic ages" to neglect the role of individual behavior, to stress the inevitability of past events and to be more concerned with general theories of action than with the actors. Thus, he said, they tend to subject the people whom they discuss "either to an inflexible Providence or to some blind necessity. . . . To their minds it is not enough to show what events have occurred; they wish to show that events could not have occurred otherwise," [17] a tendency all too common among modern system builders.

For all these purposes, and for the quest of regularities as well, the comparative method is indispensable. Without it, we would fall from the extreme of totally uprooted abstractions into the extreme of considering only individual events without sufficient conceptualization. The techniques which remain the most appropriate for any branch of politics are what Mill called the historical method and what Robert MacIver calls imagina-

---

[14] C. J. Friedrich, "Policy—A Science?" *Public Policy,* Vol. IV (1953), p. 274.

[15] See Ernst B. Haas' excellent analysis, "The Balance of Power: Prescription, Concept or Propaganda?" *World Politics,* Vol. V, No. 4 (July 1953), pp. 442-77.

[16] Raymond Aron, *German Sociology,* London, 1957, pp. 71 ff.

[17] Alexis de Tocqueville, *Democracy in America,* Vol. II, Book I, ch. xx. (A. Knopf, New York, 1945, p. 88).

tive reconstruction; i.e., either generalizations about "uniformities of co-existence between the states of the various phenomena" and about uniformities of succession, derived from history under the check of "general laws of human nature," or mental experiments designed to discover what events would have happened if a certain factor had been missing, or what factors would be necessary for certain events to occur.[18] These techniques are based on comparisons of historical complexes.

The reader might object that what I suggest is exactly what is being done both by theorists and by textbooks. However, my point is, on the one hand, that we have to proceed methodically and gradually, and that the weakness of many theories comes from their attempt to skip stages. As for the texts, they are often both unsystematic and limited to the description of the contemporary international system, with a sprinkling of memories from nineteenth century European diplomacy.

This point brings me back to the first stage of our program—the only one which, at present, can and should be planned in some detail: the description of historical systems of international relations. We must remember that "the application of the comparative method to historical material is not possible if it is confined to a comparison of chains of events, since these are essentially unique in character." We need "variables which are capable of general treatment."[19] They are to be provided by a general framework defined as a set of interrelated questions, or, as it is sometimes called, a "box," but, if I may say so, a flexible one, and one whose main role is to be put to use. For the social sciences are littered with unused boxes that have taken on a morose, pointless life of their own, like the fascinating bones scattered on the shores painted by de Chirico.

The most fruitful approach to building such a box is, as Quincy Wright has suggested, to consider the world as a field in which individuals, groups, nations, international organizations, and so on, compete, clash and co-operate, rather than as a plan designed by God, by history, or by nature, or as an equilibrium, or as an organization, or as a community: at any given moment the world might present certain aspects of one of the latter models, but never of all of them, whereas the idea of a field is always a more accurate approximation.[20] Within this field we must study in correlation four sets of data, for each international system can be defined in terms of these four series.

(a) The first series concerns the particular structure of the world in the period considered. What are the basic units (or actors), how many are they, how is power distributed, and what is the hierarchy among them (a

[18] See: J. S. Mill, *An Essay on Logic,* pp. 594 ff.; Robert MacIver, *Social Causation,* Boston, 1942, pp. 259 ff.

[19] Bert F. Hoselitz, "On Comparative History," *World Politics,* Vol. II, No. 2 (January 1957), p. 274.

[20] See Quincy Wright, *The Study of International Relations,* New York, 1955, especially pp. 481 ff.

crucial problem, for it seems that one of the few constants of world politics is a sharp difference in role and attitude between major powers and lesser ones). Can one distinguish in the world separate diplomatic fields, each one corresponding, for instance, to a civilization, a continent, a certain racial or cultural solidarity? Since when have these units operated as independent actors within one of the fields? What is the "relationship of major tension" [21] i.e., the nature and the location of the major competition for power at the moment, a relationship which tends to set the tone and pace of world politics and to determine the degree of expectation of violence in the world? This series is the basis of any investigation—and it is one which is frequently neglected. Some of the major differences between the international system of 1815-1914 and the present one are to be found here: for instance, the disappearance of the frontier which backward areas provided for the major powers, the multiplication of the number of states, the reduction of the number of great powers, and the appearance in world politics of a supreme tension—the Cold War—which dominates and affects all the other issues.

(b) The second series is composed of all the forces that cut across, or operate within many of the units. From the perspective of a historical system of international relations, these forces are factors of change. But at any point in time, for a decision-maker, they represent "givens": they can be used, or fought, but cannot be ignored. The more numerous the forces are, the more the units are, so to speak, caught in a transnational net: they may still preserve a large measure of freedom, but the forces are like railways which determine the directions in which the actors may go, and they limit the actors' capacity for unpredictable action. The number and nature of these forces is thus an index of the intensity of international relations.

Among them, there are "objective" factors such as technological, military, or economic developments (for instance the industrial revolution and the nuclear revolution). There are also transnational movements, organized (the Internationales, the Church, international pressure groups), or not (such as internationally shared values or philosophies: for instance anticolonialism today, or revisionism aimed at the 1919 peace treaties during the inter-war period). We know little about how such movements, especially the unorganized ones, become active forces in world politics. Ideological drives, their appeal, and their propagation should also be examined here. Similarly, ruling concepts of legitimacy, the ways in which legitimacy is acquired or lost, the ways in which such concepts rule out or depreciate certain methods of conducting international affairs (such as the use of force in colonial situations today) should be studied. We must trace the origins, the strength, the scope and the directions of these forces.

[21] Arnold Wolfers, "The Pole of Power and the Pole of Indifference," *World Politics*, Vol. IV, No. 1 (October 1951), pp. 39-63.

(c) The third series of data concerns the relations between the domestic and the foreign policy of the basic units. These data have been analyzed only fragmentarily by the "realist" theory, although their importance can hardly be exaggerated. Three groups of problems should be studied here.

First, what are the "objective factors" for the unit considered (geography, technological level, economic resources, population, military potential)? Secondly, how does the unit's pattern of power affect the making of foreign policy? By pattern of power, I mean the internal constitution, in an Aristotelian sense: the political institutions, but also the social and economic structure (including the system of distribution of property), the channels of information leading to the government (a vital category, for no executive is better than its awareness of domestic and foreign problems), and the amount of independence of the policy-makers from the rest of society. The extent to which the system of international relations reflects the pattern of relations between government and society in economic affairs has been underemphasized. For instance, the moderation of world politics and the successful development of international law (particularly the law of war and neutrality) in the nineteenth century resulted very largely from the Liberal divorce between government and economic enterprise, whereas today's extension of the world power struggle to the whole economic sphere corresponds to the decline of private enterprise and to the growth of state interventionism everywhere. Similarly, the relative isolation of the policy-makers from the electorate and the relative indifference of the voters' representatives, who were on the whole willing to entrust a professional elite and a largely autonomous foreign minister with the responsibility of foreign affairs, contributed to the moderation of nineteenth century world politics and to the formation of a horizontal "international elite," one of the prerequisites for a successful balance of power system.

Thirdly, how does the unit's political culture affect the making of foreign policy? Here I refer both to the judgments, beliefs, and emotions toward outside units held by those domestic groups which try to influence foreign policy, and to the origin, training and ideas of the decision-makers themselves: what are their views about the ends of their policy, and about the means to be employed? Is there a "national style" of foreign policy—a mixture of traditions, impulses, and habits created by history, by the system of government, by manipulators of public opinion, which conditions foreign policy to a large extent? [22] It is in this series that the contributions from sociology and social psychology are likely to be most useful.

(d) The fourth series of data deals with the outcome of the interrelationship between the various series mentioned before: international relations in the more narrow or precise meaning of the term. Here, some important distinctions must be made. Many theories (and texts) look at these relations from one angle only: the foreign policies of the units; the perspective

[22] On an "American style," see Robert S. Osgood, *Ideals and Self-interest in America's Foreign Relations*, Chicago, 1953, and *Limited War*, Chicago, 1957.

is from below (the units), looking up. This is indispensable, but it is not enough. The situations created by the interaction of the units, whether their occurrence was expected by the units or not, have a logic of their own; the types of "power configurations" that result not only from the conflict, or convergence, of foreign policies, but also from the very structure of the world and from the operation of transnational forces, in turn reshape, condition, and often command foreign policies. For instance, a country such as France which is in the Western camp and a country such as Egypt which finds itself among the leaders of the anticolonial revolution and among the champions of neutralism, are almost inevitably condemned to clash, because of the distribution of power in the world and because of the ideological movements in which they are caught, even though there might not be any necessary direct antagonism between these states, and even though attempts at a rapprochement might be made from time to time. Thus we also need another kind of perspective: from the top, looking down.

Excessive emphasis on one perspective produces optical illusions. The illusion produced by the second distorts contemporary theories of international law, which as a rule underestimate the wrecking power of the separate states and overstress the factors of world-wide or regional unification. The illusion produced by the first perspective leads, for instance, the 'realists' to exaggerate the weakness or voluntary character of international restraints, or to examine only one kind of balance of power: the balancing which is a deliberate policy of states, rather than the balancing that is an automatic device.[23] It is dangerous to study international organizations as if they were exclusively agencies of world order; they are also instruments of foreign policies. It is equally dangerous to see in states only forces serving national interests, for they are also the agents of varying types of international order.

A suitable approach to the study of this series of data might be the following. Within each international system, international relations can be defined as the combination of two kinds of activities. On the one hand, the units into which the world is divided try to reach certain goals; we can start with a general classification of these ends, as Arnold Wolfers has suggested, and adopt his threefold division: self-preservation, self-extension, self-abnegation.[24] On the other hand, from the perspective of the system as a whole, a number of basic tasks are being performed by the processes of international relations. These tasks result from the fragmented structure of the world, and from the unevenness of political, economic, and military development,[25] coupled with the units' inability to remain completely

---

[23] See Fred A. Sondermann, "The Study of International Relations; 1956 Version," *World Politics*, Vol. X, No. 1 (October 1957), pp. 102-12.

[24] Wolfers, "The Pole of Power and the Pole of Indifference," pp. 39-63.

[25] The role of unevenness in development as one of the main "dynamics" of international relations has not received sufficient attention since Lenin's classical observations in his *Imperialism* (1916). There are useful indications in A. F. K.

isolated: we can list conflict; political accommodation; political diffusion; economic transformation. We must of course remember that there is no world "society" or "community" which sets its own goals, defines these tasks, and allocates roles; also, the system of international relations is rarely "total and global": there are almost always "sub-systems" which operate with a logic of their own in various parts of the world, and which are only slightly affected by the "relationship of major tension." [26] However, if the purpose of all sociological research is to discover "constant themes and multiple concrete realizations," and if the field of politics can be seen as the code of answers to a small number of permanent problems,[27] then it might be interesting to start with the identification of the "unit goals" and "world tasks" which can be found in *any* system, and to continue with a systematic study of their evolution, interaction, and realization in *each* system.

For what distinguishes the international relations of the system from those of another, is the answer to two questions. First, the question of *scope:* what is, in this system, the range of the goals which units try to reach, and of the tasks which are being performed among them? The transformation of the subject-matter of international relations is a crucial aspect of the field. Thus an important change is the contemporary politization of a huge range of "functional" activities which, in the century of the liberal state and of cabinet diplomacy, were largely beyond the pale of world politics and safely within the realm of private transnational relations.

Second, there is the question of *means:* what processes, techniques, or institutions are being used by the units in order to achieve their respective goals and to perform their collective tasks, as well as in the mutual relations that develop from the units' efforts to reach their goals and accomplish their tasks? This question is equally important, since the nature of world politics depends largely on the choices made by the actors among available techniques of war or negotiations, among conceivable types of law, groupings and organizations, or among possible methods of economic transformation.

The reasons for those choices must be studied. Such decisions are conditioned by the place of the actor in the international hierarchy: E. H. Carr has observed that reliance on economic rather than on naked military strength is a sign of the great powers.[28] They are also influenced by the domestic balance of forces within the actor's unit, and by "trans-unit" factors such as the development of technology and the concept of legitimacy:

Organski, *World Politics,* New York, 1958, with reference to economic unevenness, and in Herz, *International Politics in the Atomic Age,* Part I, with reference to military unevenness.

[26] See Leonard Binder, "The Middle East as a Subordinate International System," *World Politics,* Vol. X, No. 3 (April 1958), pp. 408-29.

[27] Raymond Aron, *Le développement de la société industrielle,* Paris, 1956, (mimeographed).

[28] E. H. Carr, *The Twenty Years' Crisis,* London, 1951, p. 129.

thus today military means tend to be a last resort and—if we may borrow, for once, a term from economics—a substitution effect seems to be taking place; other means of action—economic and ideological methods, and even the weapon of collective pressure through parliamentary diplomacy—are developed instead. The way in which the methods selected by the actors contribute (or not) to the attainment of the units' goals and to the fulfillment of the basic tasks performed in world affairs, must also be studied carefully. It would for instance be most interesting to know how regional and functional organizations have actually affected their members, and whether these bodies have created among the participants purely utilitarian ties that could be broken easily, or whether they have contributed to a "devaluation of borders" and to a gradual development of a real (not merely an assumed and rhetorical) community.

Among the materials to be used for such research, none have been more neglected than the writings of philosophers, theorists, and statesmen. We are still able to gain as many insights into the American political system, or into the politics of liberalism, from Locke or Rousseau or Tocqueville as we get from the analysis of institutions and political behavior. In the same way, the writings I refer to would provide us with "models" of international politics that would help us understand the problems I have tried to list, both by reference and by contrast. Modern sociology of knowledge may have exaggerated the degree of dependence of ideas on the social environment; but no one can deny the correlation, and it should be studied in our discipline too. There have been some path-breaking efforts, which study theories and writings of statesmen as distorted mirrors of the world around them, but much more could be done, if we used such works not for new chapters in histories of political thought but as tools for the analysis of actual systems and situations. Our present rather contemptuous approach to the body of theories of international law—theories that are far less narrow than one often believes—is particularly regrettable. Also, one of the key sources of tension and change in any political system is the contrast between the values and beliefs of some of the leaders, and the underlying realities of politics; only a study of the ideas expressed by the leaders, and by writers who spell out the generally accepted assumptions which inspire the leaders, can allow us to locate and analyze intelligently this source of tension.

(2) The future: relevant utopias

In addition to such systematic research, there is a need for a different kind of task. I have mentioned earlier some of the permanent reasons for a political philosophy of world affairs. More contemporary reasons are equally important. What Kant stressed almost two centuries ago has become irrefutable in the world of "total" international relations or "international civil war." The problems of peace and of a world order command all the others. No citizen will enjoy autonomy in a world whose fragmentation produces imperatives of national survival and differentiation fatal to such autonomy.

The two traditional tasks of political philosophy: the search for the proper relation between the individual, the communities in which he lives, and the world, on the one hand, and concern for the best method with which a desirable relation could be realized, have not been well performed in world politics. There have been too many assumptions—conflicting ones, to be sure—which converge toward the conclusion that such a search and such a concern are unnecessary in our field. We have been listening to too many counsels of laziness or of despair.

First, the belief in the inefficacy of ethical considerations in world affairs or in the evil qualities of all political actions, the raising of prudence to the position of a supreme value, the tendency to see in political conflicts an inevitable clash between national values and international ones, which must therefore be prudently sacrificed to the preservation of the former—this is one counsel of despair. It has been admirably criticized by Arnold Wolfers, in particular in his essay on "Statesmanship" which is reproduced below. The emphasis on the imperative of survival as an absolute which must inevitably limit or even prevent ethical considerations from playing in world affairs a role comparable to the part they have in domestic affairs, raises a host of troublesome questions which "realism" rarely discusses, such as survival *of* what (a specific political form, such as the nation-state? an ideology? moral values? men?) and survival *for* what? In other words, the discussion of survival as an end of foreign policy, far from ruling out the examination of other ends in international affairs, should be subordinated to a previous definition of purposes.

Second, the tendency to advocate as a solution for world problems theories proposed for problems that have arisen within nations, is a counsel of laziness. For what is assumed is that such an extension to the world raises no bigger problem than the elimination of "bad men," obscurantists, reactionaries, ammunition-makers, corrupt politicians, and so on, who block the way to the millennium; or that the division of the world in jealously separate units is an accidental and temporary factor; or that universal values can be promoted at little cost of national values. Those are the mistakes made by the Liberal theory of politics as applied to world affairs, either in its nineteenth century variety (best represented by Woodrow Wilson) or in one of its contemporary varieties—the advocacy of world government. The nineteenth century doctrine was looking forward to "a universal society of nations above power politics," [29]—a society in which each nationality would have its state, and in which the triumph of democracy in each state would remove the main causes of power conflicts among states; ordinary clashes of interests could thus be solved by

[29] Robert E. Osgood, *Limited War,* Chicago, 1957, p. 89.

democratic and (increasingly) legal methods without any need for superior temporal power over the various states. The harmonization of nations' interests would be assured by two forces operating throughout the world: the objective force of free trade, and the subjective force of public opinion.

Such "depreciation of political power" at the level of world affairs has disappeared; and the very division of the world into nation-states has to be recognized as a potential source of chaos; hence the advocacy of world government as a new version of liberalism for a world in which multiple sovereignties have led to two total wars within twenty-five years. Once again the solution of world problems is sought in a formula which proves effective within nations—this time however it is thought that this formula must be applied at the level of the world as a whole, whereas it had been the hope of liberals before 1914 that its application within each of the world's units would constitute all by itself the solution for the world. This theory suffers, as Wolfers shows, from an excessive faith in the virtues and powers of government. It suffers from a philosophical contradiction: "world governmentalists describe the world's situation in Hobbesian terms, but they depict the resultant government in Lockian terms, with a view to making the social contract palatable. It would be better to recognize that in so far as this is a Hobbesian world, it is likely to require a Hobbesian government." [30] Finally, this theory is too much concerned with the achievement of a single value (such as peace) and of a simple institutional panacea.

Third, there is one approach which is both a counsel of laziness and a counsel of despair: the "scientific" attempt at building purely "empirical" or "causal" theories without discussion of the problems of values and purposes in world affairs, except in so far as values and purposes too are either taken to be determined by the "system" or treated as ordinary data. In contemporary sociological theory a similar approach has led to the conservatism of complacency, since the scholar's detachment from such problems under the pretext of objectivity reinforces in fact, or at least refrains from any challenge to, the status quo. We have seen that the same cause produces the same effect in the study of international relations: at best, the outcome is that the ethical problems are altogether left to others—to the "non-scientists"; at worst the outcome is the kind of policy advice which consists of a scientific coat of paint on classical Machiavellianism: advice on strategy, i.e., on how the present units of the world (or one of them, usually the one to which the scientist belongs) should keep what they have, or get more at least cost. "The political scientist, in so far as he wishes to remain a scientist, is limited to the study of techniques." [31]

Thus, we cannot assume that the problem of what the world ought to be and how states should morally behave is irrelevant, and that all we can

[30] I. L. Claude, *Swords into Plowshares,* New York, 1956, p. 429.

[31] Alfred Cobban, "The Decline of Political Theory," *Political Science Quarterly,* Vol. LXVIII, No. 3 (September 1953), p. 335.

do is to cultivate the best values in our domestic system. World politics raise moral questions, and they have to be examined, just as moral questions have traditionally been the concern of "domestic" political theory; otherwise the neglect of problems which are burning and unavoidable will continue both to drive the political "scientist" into generalized irrelevance and to turn the political "philosopher" into a guide in the academic cemetery of bygone ideas. Nor can we assume that the world arena offers, in Wolfers' phrase, the same "moral opportunity" to political action as a domestic arena, and that all we need to do is to transpose into the world the procedures that promote the best values at home. For the setting of world politics puts moral questions in a light which differs from the light of domestic politics; hence the need, in this area also, for a distinct and careful examination.

Two tasks can be distinguished analytically. Our first problem is the clarification of values we would like to see promoted in the world—and, as I have suggested, we cannot do so if we do not start with a view of man as, at least in part, a community-building animal, making moral decisions among alternative courses of action which all involve the presence of some values and the sacrifice of others.

Second, we must relate these values to the world as it is, far more closely than we usually do. A total separation of "empirical science" and "moral philosophy" would be disastrous. To go on repeating that only the latter can discuss what ought to be, and that the former has neither the function nor the possibility of passing ethical judgments, since one cannot deduce an "ought" from an "is"—this cannot be our last word. For the statement is accurate but incomplete. "Empirical science" helps us, indeed not to decide what we should want, but to see how we could get what we want, what would be the implications of what we want, and even what we should not want. A systematic empirical analysis can reveal that the achievement of certain ends is totally impossible and, as Kant has shown, there is no moral duty where there is a total material impossibility. Such an analysis can also reveal that certain of our moral objectives are contradictory and mutually exclusive in their application. Thus, in our field as in others, commitment cannot be separated from investigation, unless one is satisfied with a most un-political moralism. The range of value conflicts and the degree to which values are shared, in world politics, are not necessarily different from what they are in domestic affairs; but the fundamental differences in structure and institutions, justly emphasized by "realism," oblige us to be very precise about the ways in which such conflicts can be reduced and such sharing promoted, if these are our objectives. For the burden of proving that the present pattern of power politics is compatible with the realization of an "international morality" remains on us, although or rather precisely because we do not accept the view that the divorce is inevitable. There are many advocates of courses of action which obviously clash with the characteristic features of the present international system—either because the course belongs to a bygone system judged more satisfactory by the writer,[32] or because the course would put on the road to a new and more progressive system a world obviously unable or unwilling until now to travel such a road.[33] These advocates should not only plead for the destination, they should tell us in detail how we can reach it. Kant, in his essay on "Perpetual Peace," did the former but (in his enumeration of preliminary conditions of peace) only part of the latter; his hypothesis of a "hidden plan of nature" which would bring about "a perfect civil association of mankind" may explain why the steps to the millenium were not too carefully traced. Such confidence in an inevitably benevolent history is gone, and we must compensate in empirical precision for the faith in progress which we have lost.

Indeed if one wants to revive a political philosophy of international relations the two tasks I have just tried to sketch should be undertaken and continued *together*. For if one starts by positing certain values totally a priori and in the abstract, one risks either getting stuck with well-meaning platitudes or proceeding to purely "perfectionist" ethics, which brush aside the problem of the difficult and dirty means to utopia. If one starts with a purely empirical study of contemporary world politics, one is in danger of becoming an addict of the kind of policy scientism which believes that what ought to be emerges from what is, or implies that one can decide what policy should be pursued without any previous decision as to what moral objectives should be pursued—and thus forgets that one's expressed pragmatic choices result in good measure from one's repressed ethical choices. If, as other policy scientists do, one does indeed *start* both with certain abstract values one wants to promote, and with an empirical study of the "policy alternatives by means of which goal values can be maximized," [34] but one *then* stops paying attention to these values and proceeds to focus one's interest entirely on policy, one falls into the worst of all possible worlds. For it is a world in which values remain disembodied rituals, in which the means which are advocated because of their efficiency may contradict the values originally stated, and in which those values are finally turned into mere pawns of national strategies. (". . . each participant has at his disposal values that he employs as bases for the influencing of outcomes. . . . Base values are made effective by the strategies used to affect outcomes"; [35] but they can also be perverted by

[32] Proposals for the neutralization of various states (such as Germany) as one way of improving East-West relations seem to me to mistake the present pattern of world politics for a system such as the nineteenth century's, of which neutralization (of certain *small* states) was an integral part; the classical conception of neutrality in international law has collapsed along with the world of 1914.

[33] See for instance Grenville Clark and Louis B. Sohn, *World Peace through World Law,* Cambridge, 1958.

[34] Harold D. Lasswell, "The Political Science of Science," *American Political Science Review,* Vol. L, No. 4 (December 1956), p. 978.

[35] Myres S. McDougal and Harold D. Lasswell, "The Identification and Appraisal of Diverse Systems of Public Order," *American Journal of International Law,* Vol. 53, No. 1 (January 1959), p. 8.

those strategies in the process). Thus perfectionism and Machiavellianism, irrelevance and manipulation can be avoided only if we do not separate our two tasks and do not neglect either one for the other.

I would therefore like to suggest a task in which systematic empirical analysis and a philosophy of international relations would merge, just as the empirical and the normative elements did coalesce in the great theories of politics and economics of the past—for instance in political liberalism, in classical economics, and in Marxism. We must try to build relevant Utopias. By spelling out our views on the purposes, the prerequisites, the possibilities and the procedures of an ideal international order, we would accomplish a triple task. We would meet the requirement of clarifying our personal value positions. We would avoid the piecemeal engineering approach of policy scientism. We would avoid the twin escapisms of "realism," which gloomily assumes the inevitability of the customary, and of "idealism," which postulates an easy road to world progress. In such an effort, we should take into account all the aspects of world politics which I have suggested; see what obstacles or opportunities are provided by the lasting "political styles" of nations and of their leaders, show what role is played and can be played by the forces that cut across nations, and examine what kinds of situations are most likely to favor or to hinder the objectives we advocate; discuss to what extent reliance on existing processes and institutions is enough, to what extent the creation of new ones is required and possible for bold political innovation, to what extent on the contrary weight should rather be put on material and spiritual factors which operate within the nations and peoples of the world.

We are beginning to have at our disposal the tools which would make such a task possible; thus, should our ideal be the creation of communities bigger than the nation-states, we could use the important empirical studies in community-formation recently completed by Karl Deutsch and his associates of the Princeton Center for the Study of World Political Institutions, and by Ernst Haas (whose article reproduced below summarizes both his and their main findings).[36] These studies confirm, for instance, the point I made above concerning the importance of available techniques and processes in world affairs. A partial transfer of loyalty to institutions other than the state can be achieved when new bodies and channels are created, so that interests which previously depended on the state for their satisfaction can now address themselves to these newly available procedures; this result can be obtained even though the initial motive of statesmen in creating these new organs was a selfish one—the promotion of the nation's own interest. There is another, more general range of problems into which we should look: the devising of new peaceful substitutes for the use of force, since force today seems less and less admissible and practical as a method of change. Here again, objectives

[36] See also S. Hoffmann, "Vers l'étude systématique des mouvements d'intégration internationale," *Revue Française de Science Politique,* Vol. IX, No. 2 (June 1959), pp. 474-85.

should be set according to the values we want to serve and to the empirical lessons we can draw from a systematic analysis of world politics.

It is not, and cannot be, our task to guarantee that Utopia will be reached. Nor should we confine ourselves to proposals which are timid enough to be uncontroversial. Our task is to say what goals we want for the world, to explain what our Utopia implies, to suggest methods for building it, and to show how such methods might appear and work in the world as it is. Whether these goals and methods are adopted or not does not depend on us. It is the task of politics. Except when we accept to participate formally in policy-making, either as advisers or as civil servants, as scholars do from time to time, we should not gear our research, our findings, our goals to the limitations of the office-holders and the requirements of the mighty. But precisely because it is the scholars' duty to dominate routine, to assess and to challenge the existing order, to suggest purposes and directions, we should not encourage by our silence, our subservience, or our scholasticism the politicians' all-too-frequent inclination to believe that the future is merely the sum of habits from the past and survival in the present.

It is a difficult task. I do not see how we can avoid it, if we believe that "the mechanisms of nature, working through the selfish inclinations, which in their external relations naturally work against one another, can be employed by reason as a means of realizing . . . the reign of law." [37]

B. READINGS

Of the two groups of selections here, the first is intended to illustrate my suggestions for a "historical sociology" of international relations. Raymond Aron's essay is a brilliant demonstration of the advantages of such an approach with particular reference to the study of conflict. Herbert C. Kelman's article (which follows a series of articles on research approaches to the problem of war and peace all published in the same issue of the *Journal of Social Issues*) represents a sociologist's attempt to build a "box" which could supplement the broad framework suggested by Aron, and be used particularly well in the study of a nation's foreign policy and attitudes toward other nations: i.e., what I called the third series of data in the scheme I suggested above. In both those essays I have cut brief passages which were more relevant to the study of war itself than to a theory of international relations. Ernst B. Haas' article summarizes scholarly findings in the one area in which systematic analysis along the lines of historical sociology has been undertaken in recent years: regional integration. Those conclusions, it seems to me, would be most helpful to whomever would want to think about the future, and to try to build "relevant utopias" for the future.

[37] Kant, *Perpetual Peace.* Boston, American Peace Society (1897), pp. 27-8.

The second group of readings deals with the relations between political philosophy and international politics. Arnold Wolfers' introduction to a book of readings on "international political philosophy" is both a plea for a "remarriage" between philosophy and the study of world politics, and a searching examination (and criticism) of the reasons for their past divorce. E. H. Carr's chapter on morality in world politics shows that there are in fact standards of international morality, and that they are usually considered to differ from standards of individual morality—an illustration of my argument about the need to deal with problems of morality in our discipline, and to deal with them in a special way. Finally, Arnold Wolfers' essay on statesmanship and moral choice uses in a normative way the arguments stated factually by Carr. Wolfers shows why there *ought* to be standards of international morality (thus counter-attacking the modern followers of Machiavelli) and why these standards ought to be "non-perfectionist." Such a discussion of the role of ethics in world politics is a prerequisite to any effort at orienting political philosophy in the direction of world problems, rather than domestic problems exclusively.

1. RAYMOND ARON

Conflict and War from the Viewpoint of Historical Sociology

. . . When we turn from the tensions within the individual psyche to the tensions within groups or between groups, we have not merely to face the difficulty of giving exact definitions; we no longer know, even in broad general terms, what we are talking about. If we consider a simple group—such as a class in a secondary school, a company or section in the army—we may, at a pinch, trace out social tensions by observing the tensions (in the psychological sense) within the minds of the individuals making up the group. Failure in leadership on the part of the teacher or the lieutenant is externalized in his own anxiety and the dissatisfaction of the pupils or soldiers. But this method of diagnosing social tensions from individual tensions cannot be generally applied. Any form of organized life entails certain

---

Reprinted from International Sociological Association, *The Nature of Conflict* (*Studies on the Sociological Aspects of International Tensions*), pp. 177-203, by permission of the United Nations Educational, Scientific and Cultural Organization.

The Nature of Conflict is distributed in the United States through UNESCO Publications Center, 801 Third Avenue, New York 22, N. Y.

tensions in the minds of individuals. In order to discover what tensions there may be, in the sociological sense of the term, it would be necessary to determine which are inseparable from the institutional structure and which are due to the personalities inserted into that structure. It would be necessary to make a distinction between what is due to the individuals filling the various roles in society and what is due to those roles themselves. Institutional tensions show in individual tensions, but we cannot diagnose and define the former by studying the latter.

Tension between individuals is a quite different concept from the tension within the individual's mind brought to light by the psychoanalyst. The latter, no doubt, often tends to explain tensions between individuals by tensions within individuals. Aggressiveness is due to frustration. Whatever may be the value of this theory—which I am neither capable nor desirous of assessing—it would be difficult to say that competition, rivalry and conflict between individuals are not normal phenomena, either from the standpoint of psychology or from that of sociology. A psychologically normal individual is quite likely to be hostile to certain of his fellows, either because he disapproves of their conduct or because he finds himself in conflict with them for the possession of certain goods or the attainment of certain values. It would therefore still be necessary to distinguish, in psychological terms, conflict between normal individuals from conflict between individuals who are aggressive as a result of frustration. It is by no means certain that such a distinction is easy, even as a concept, but there can be no doubt that in the practical field it is quasi-impossible.

Even if it were feasible to make this distinction in the psychological sphere, it would not be possible to do so in the sociological sphere. What is normal or pathological in psychology does not correspond exactly with what is normal or pathological in sociology. A movement which is the symptom of a social crisis does not necessarily have neurotic subjects at its head or in its ranks. In a stable social structure, a normal protest movement may be led or supported by neurotics. One might almost be tempted to say that for most social rebels to be neurotic is evidence of sociological normality, while for "normal" individuals to support revolutionary extremism is evidence of social pathology. Speaking generally, I would simply reiterate that intra-individual tensions do not entirely explain the question of inter-individual tension.

Analysis of diplomatic complexes

Let us consider the definition of war formulated by Professor Malinowski . . . "Armed conflict between two independent political units, by means of organized military forces, in the pursuit of a tribal or national policy."

It would be easy to criticize such a definition by pointing out that the various features mentioned are not always found together and that as a result, the classification of certain cases may be difficult. A civil war is not conducted by two "independent political units," yet often involves clashes between two "organized military forces." Does it come under the heading of war? If we answer in the negative, it may be pointed out that two political units may be independent at the beginning but not at the end of a conflict. . . . Such objections seem to me to be, at one and the same time, legitimate and unimportant. In the actual life of societies there are always doubtful, marginal cases. The definition describes, so to speak, the "perfect" phenomenon. . . .

In other words, the marginal cases which may or may not involve independent political units or organized military forces do not invalidate the definition quoted, but are simply fresh evidence of the graduation always found in social phenomena. On the borderline, civil war and international war merge together, as do the clash of armies and guerrilla warfare. We must not overlook this area of doubt on the borderline—we shall take account of it in the course of the explanations that follow—but it does not make it impossible for us to begin by considering the phenomenon in the "perfect" state.

War so defined is an integral part of the relations between political units. These units are not, at various times, continually in a state of war, but those who are responsible for directing the affairs of states have the possibility of war constantly in their minds. Diplomacy and warfare are historically inseparable, since statesmen have always regarded war as the last resort of diplomacy. Starting from this obvious observation, we can begin to study the system of relations between States. Understanding of this system may not enable us to determine the reasons why diplomacy is accompanied by war and what changes would have to be made to see that diplomacy should not imply war, but it will at least help us to explain the machinery of the diplomatic system and the machinery of war by reference to one another.

As warfare is the last resort of diplomacy, the statesmen who take decisions or the sociologists who interpret those decisions must, when analysing a situation, begin by determining three factors: What is the area of diplomatic relations? What is the disposition of power within that area? What is the method of warfare which is more or less clearly in the minds of statesmen when they estimate the importance of positions or relations? These three factors together represent the aspect of international policy which, for certain statesmen, is the only consideration, or rather which is said by certain political scientists to be the sole consideration of statesmen.

In practice, three other factors come into play, which together represent the ideological aspect of international relations: To what extent do the contending States recognize one another, so that the issue at stake is the frontiers and not the very existence of the States themselves? What bearing does domestic policy have on the decisions of statesmen? How do statesmen understand peace, war and inter-State relations?

The six questions formulated above can easily be elucidated by historical examples. The area of diplomatic relations for Talleyrand or Bismarck, William II or Delcassé, scarcely extended beyond the boundaries of the old world. The European States reached out across the seas and might take up the Eastern or Far Eastern question, but they hardly expected non-European States to play an important part in the event of a general conflict in Europe. Japan and the United States of America had no place in the area of diplomatic relations in 1913; but they had in 1939 and, still more clearly, in 1954.

In 1913 the principal powers were associated by alliances which could be denounced, so as to preserve a sort of balance between them. Several of them belonged to the same category, so that alliances were concluded on a relatively equal footing. Today, the concentration of military power in the hands of two States has brought into being two camps, each of which has a leader. The present characteristic of the balance of power is that it is bipolar, instead of being a balance among several States of the same category.

The size of States and the size of the area of diplomatic relations are obviously influenced by the technique of warfare, which alters the value of distances and of so-called strategic positions. In this respect, the factor which is considered to be novel is the danger of total annihilation that would be involved in an atomic war. The novelty is not so great as it is said to be, since the wars of the past (in ancient Greek and Roman times, for example) in practice entailed the danger of total destruction for the vanquished. The only difference is that the trial might, almost simultaneously, wipe out both belligerents.

The connexion between these first three considerations is clear—they might be defined as the boundaries, the disposition and the resources of power—and the connexion between the next three is no less clear. In 1910 the great European powers recognized one another's right to existence and, until the first gun was fired, had no idea of overthrowing any particular form of government, or any individual government, as being unlawful or as being a danger to the European balance or to world peace. The 1914 war gradually became an ideological conflict as the Allies set themselves the object of "freeing" the national groups in the Austro-Hungarian Empire—and therefore of destroying the dual monarchy—and of instituting democracy in Germany on the ground that autocracy endangered peace. There are therefore many varieties of non-recognition: Prussia did not recognize the sovereignty of Hanover when Bismarck was striving to build up the German Empire; the Allies ceased to recognize William II when they no longer wished to treat with him; they ceased to recognize Austria-Hungary when they proclaimed that an independent Hungary and an independent Czechoslovakia were ideologically acceptable to them and in line with their war aims; the Europeans did not recognize the tribes or kingdoms of Africa when they made them into colonies or protectorates, the West does not accord legal recognition to the People's Republics of

North Korea or East Germany; they do not recognize the Communist régimes in Eastern Europe as legitimate and, if total war were to break out, they would inevitably be led to make the destruction of Communism one of their aims, just as the Soviet bloc would introduce a system of government modelled on its own into the countries that it conquered.

A State may thus be denied recognition in many different circumstances —when the population is considered by the conqueror to be unworthy of independence; when the conqueror aims at subjecting the conquered to his dominion; or finally when the belligerents each think that their respective systems of government and ideologies are incompatible and, in the name of world peace or the trend of history, seek to eradicate the enemy's system of government and ideology.

Light may be thrown on this question of non-recognition by two sorts of studies—that of the nature of communities and the influence of the various forces within each nation on the conduct of diplomacy, and that of the conception held by statesmen of the functions of foreign policy. The leaders of the Soviet Union might secretly negotiate the pact with Hitler and secure its acceptance by a docile public opinion but, in peacetime, the leaders of a parliamentary democracy could not do so. The leaders of the Soviet Union view conflicts with other States against the conceptual background of a particular doctrine, and their conduct is a compromise between the logic of the system and historical expediency. Talleyrand or Bismarck regarded alliances and breaches, hostilities and negotiations as the normal course of affairs, and sought to achieve certain objects by a combination of force and ruse, armed might and negotiation. Woodrow Wilson was against secret diplomacy and warfare on principle and thought that lasting peace, and possibly universal peace, could be achieved by spreading democracy throughout the world. The leaders of the Soviet Union probably believe that peace would be certain if all States were Communist States. There can scarcely be any doubt that they attribute imperialism to the inconsistencies of monopolistic capitalism and consider it to be inevitable at a certain stage of historical development.

If we wish to conceptualize the facts of international politics by reference to the situation-decision antithesis, the "situation" will cover not only the relations of forces within a certain diplomatic area with reference to a certain technique of warfare, but also the type of government, the forms of pressure to which the policy-makers are subjected, and the opposition or compatibility of the systems of government and ideologies involved. With regard to the policy-makers, it would be a mistake to regard their decisions as representing no more than calculations designed to secure a balance, or to suppose that such decisions do not change, as between different systems of government, because national interests remain the same. The outlook on the world, the system of values, and the strategical and tactical standards adopted by the ruling groups influence the conduct of statesmen.

Because of its effect on the psychology of rulers and people, and because of the inevitable clashes between régimes subscribing to opposing principles, ideology is a factor to be reckoned with in international relations. It may be desirable, as the "realist" school asserts, that diplomats should open their eyes to the facts and accept the enduring rivalry of States as the essence of the international system. In eras when the gods worshipped by the peoples cannot be set together in the same Pantheon, neither scholars nor politicians can do away with ideology and revert to the wisdom of realistic compromise. Ideological situations can no more be moulded at will than geographical formations or armaments. To ask the Soviet leaders to act as if they did not believe in Marxism, or to ask the Western leaders to regard the present occupants of the Kremlin simply as the spokesmen of eternal Russia, is to ask the former to deny their very selves and the latter to shut their eyes to some of the facts. This does not mean that realistic compromises between the two parties are impossible; it does mean that neither party can—and perhaps it is not desirable that either should—strive to forget the factors which have brought them into opposition.

The inter-disciplinary approach

The foregoing conceptual framework, which needs further analysis (under each of the six headings, subsidiary questions should be formulated to elucidate the various types of situations), is designed solely to give shape to the studies which are already being carried out, not so much by sociologists as by historians or political scientists. Some people refuse to see the connexion between this analysis of historical complexes and the psychological, psychoanalytical and sociological studies of tensions. It is my purpose, however, to show that no psychological, psycho-analytical or sociological study of international conflicts can produce really informative results until the examples considered are viewed against the background of a real political complex.

Take, for example, the attempts made to explain the foreign policy of a country by cultural anthropology's method of global community analysis. In an extreme, caricatured form, such attempts would lead to explaining the Russian attitude by the effects of a certain way of swaddling infants. Diplomatic aggressiveness, without military aggression, would be regarded as a consequence of the Russian mentality. This example, which is a rough-and-ready summary of a method of study which is rough-and-ready in itself, does not mean that the whole school must be condemned; that school is liable to base its work on false premises, even when it is cautious enough to make the error less immediately apparent.

The investigation of the cultural basis of a certain foreign policy in a given community comes under our headings five and six. The policy-makers do their thinking with reference to a certain system of values, a conception of their community and of the world which reflects the special individuality of the nation. It is perfectly legitimate—indeed it is necessary—to determine, in each set of circumstances and in each country, the ideological system to which the policy-makers subscribe and the influences, in the form of tradition and public opinion, to which they are subjected. But just as the exponents of the balance of power theory distort the facts of international politics when they regard all Heads of States as Talleyrands or Bismarcks, calculating the balance of strength anew each day, so the cultural anthropologist who proceeds more or less directly from the culture pattern and the psycho-analytical interpretation of that pattern to the conduct of diplomacy falls into error. Historical comparisons may enable us to discover certain features common to the foreign policy of a certain country at various periods, provided that the country in question preserves its own particular characteristics; such common features are probably matters of general approach and attitude and do not really determine the content of decisions, which latter are always, at least partially, dictated by the balance of power.

. . . .

All psychological, psycho-analytical and anthropological studies on the foreign-policy-determining factors rooted in communities themselves are, at least in complex civilizations and in modern times, complementary to political study proper. When divorced from the latter, they cannot provide material for any statement of cause and effect. In a certain sense, this assertion simply represents the application, to a concrete case, of Max Weber's idea that the historian begins by applying the *zweckrational* scheme and introduces other factors to account for the ends selected and for any deviations in the methods employed. To begin with, a certain policy is considered against the background of the whole complex of forces, and the methods, the objects and indeed the instruments of that policy are explained by reference to internal factors and to the general situation. Any study confined to one or other type of explanation is incomplete, but limitation to the first type (internal factors) is more dangerous than limitation to the second.

Explanation by reference to the general situation is superficial but not essentially false; it in fact links up an historical event with historical circumstances. Explanation by internal factors, on the other hand, is often liable to lead to the explanation of an event at a certain date by circumstances, also drawn from history, which were in existence before the phenomenon to be explained and which continued after it. The cultural pattern is more enduring than an aggressive or pacific, imperialistic or defensive, foreign policy.

Moreover, if we confine ourselves to psychological or psycho-analytical studies, we risk taking something which is simply an effect to be a cause. In order to discover whether national stereotypes are influential in determining the decisions of policy-makers or merely reflect those decisions after the lapse of a few months or years, it would be necessary to follow out the changes in such stereotypes as events, propaganda and diplomatic circumstances develop.

In the same way, it is extremely difficult for the psychologist to determine whether and to what extent the expectation of war is a factor liable to cause war. It is not impossible to investigate this question in a given case. It can be shown with some plausibility that, in a given country at a certain time, the conviction that war was inevitable has helped to bring it about (by inducing those responsible for affairs to take certain decisions). The expectation of war, however, was also brought into being by real and not imaginary facts. If we confine ourselves to the psychological approach, how can we avoid confusing cause and effect, taking the expectation of war for the cause when that expectation simply ensues from the existence of insoluble conflicts between States and from a well-founded feeling that the nations, or those who govern them, are preparing to settle these conflicts by a resort to arms? There is no evidence, incidentally, that "expectation of war," as a secondary cause, may not have been of only slight importance in certain circumstances (e.g. before 1939), though of considerable importance in 1910-14. From 1936-37 onwards, any intelligent observer could see that, for a number of objectively observable causes, a European war was likely in the coming years; events confirmed that expectation, and anyone who had attempted to safeguard peace by removing the expectation of war would have laboured in vain, for he would have done nothing to change either Hitler or the reactions of the French, the British and the Russians to Hitler's proceedings.

This second example brings us on to the second sort of conclusion which may be drawn from such analysis: any steps recommended for "improving international understanding" which are based on an abstract study of one of the many factors involved are liable, in a real historical situation, to produce results the opposite of those desired.

Let us suppose that the anthropologist regards the strict discipline of the drives inseparable from the Japanese culture-pattern as the source of the nations aggressiveness or of the sudden outbursts of violence on the part of individual Japanese. Let us suppose that the high regard accorded to obedience, and the cult of heroic values, are taken to be one of the causes of militarism and that this in its turn is held to be one of the main causes of the imperialism which led to the war against China in 1895, to Pearl Harbour, and to the surrender. The occupying Americans will seek to change the cultural pattern, to "emancipate" women, to reduce the constraints on spontaneous individual development, to do away with the "divine" character of the Emperor, to challenge heroic values, etc. Japan, having been more or less Americanized, will be appreciably less "military" or "militaristic" if the process of Americanization has been effective. Japan might not have provoked the 1939 war if it had previously undergone that same process (it is difficult to be sure that the situation would not have encouraged even a less militaristic people to aggression: the situation was enough, in 1940, to produce aggression on the part of the Italian people, who were very far from militaristic in spite of their form of government). But a people may be instrumental in causing a particular war by weakness as well as by strength, by passivity as well as by inordinate violence. So long as statesmen think in terms of power relations, a power vacuum is as dangerous to peace as overwhelming power. If Japan or Germany, having been "democratized," were to continue to assert that they would not defend themselves by armed force, would such absolute pacifism be conducive to peace or to war? The least that can be said is that the reply, either way, would be open to dispute among scientists.

We may accept as an hypothesis that the anthropologist is capable of drawing attention to those changes in the psychological and social structure of the community which would render it less hostile to the outside world, more ready for conciliation, and less convinced of the superiority of the military virtues over the civic virtues. Obviously the anthropologist cannot foresee the historical consequences of such a conversion: since the militarism of yesterday's aggressor was dangerous only in the context of a given past situation, the "civilization" of that aggressor may, in the circumstances of tomorrow, be either a good thing or a bad thing. Generally speaking, such conversions are more likely than not to be inopportune. Efforts are made to convert the vanquished when he is already at least temporarily harmless because of his defeat, while what is necessary is to "convert" one or other of the victors. It is easier to take effective steps against the war of yesterday than against that of tomorrow.[1]

The same idea might again be expressed as follows: in the course of history there have been few great powers who have been able or willing to call a halt. The attitudes of the peoples, the passions of the masses, the political system, and population pressure have exerted their influence on the conduct of foreign affairs. The phenomena of international relations are global phenomena reflecting both the body and the soul, the material equipment and the values of the community. But, at least in modern times,[2] the disposition of forces aspect is so obviously a significant factor in international politics that any attempt to influence intra-community factors without reference to the whole diplomatic complex would be bound to produce unforeseeable consequences.

---

[1] Needless to say, this observation also is not of general application. There are plenty of examples of "militaristic" countries which, having once failed, have, after a short interval, embarked anew on a course of aggression.

[2] In one sense, this aspect was more obvious in the past, as the whole community stood in danger of extermination in the event of defeat; but there were no complex calculations of relative strengths or of balance involved—only an elementary struggle for life.

Historical sociology

Political scientists have a tendency to simplify in two respects, both of which are dangerous. The first simplification is that of the historical school, which would end by describing the vicissitudes of international relations without explaining them; while the second is that of the "realist" school, which tends to hypostasize the States and their so-called national interests, to attribute to those interests a sort of patency or permanence, and to regard events as reflecting nothing but the calculation of power and the compromise necessary to achieve a balance.

The mere story of events teaches us nothing unless it is given form and meaning by reference to concepts; unless it entails an effort to distinguish the essential from the subsidiary, and deep-lying trends from accidents; and unless it seeks to compare the means, differing from age to age, by which international relations and wars are conducted. The realistic simplification is liable to distort the real psychology of the rulers, and to lead to neglect of certain factors which are sometimes of decisive importance, such as the influence of systems of government and ideologies on the conduct of diplomatic affairs and the character of conflicts or wars. The function of the system of headings I have sketched in above is to rule out such simplifications and to substitute for them the various forms of study which are actually being conducted or which are possible. Sociology, psychology, anthropology and psycho-analysis do not take the place of political science; they make it possible to fill in the skeleton outline drawn, but left partially blank, by the latter.

Let us for example consider the fifth and sixth headings—the influence of domestic policy on the foreign policy of States, and the view that the rulers take of foreign policy. All branches of social study can play their part in clarifying these questions. If, for instance, we were seeking to clarify the present situation, we should begin by investigating the question of how decisions concerning foreign policy are taken in a particular country and under a particular system of government (e.g. in the United States of America). Naturally we should not confine ourselves to elucidating the constitutional rules, but should seek to understand the real office and the real influence of the President, his advisers, the National Security Council, the armed forces, the press, public opinion—or at least what goes by that name—and so on. This type of study is within the sphere of political science (or political sociology, for the name matters little); it is obviously easier to carry out in a democratic country than in authoritarian or totalitarian countries (it was only afterwards that we learnt how decisions were taken in the Third Reich). The information it furnishes gives us only part of the picture and may not remain true indefinitely. The part played by the President in the United States of America changes with the individuals who hold that office. The more concrete and the more detailed the study, the more likelihood there is of arriving at the truth, but the truth arrived at may be made up of so many unrelated particles as to be useless for practical purposes.

When we consider the foreign policy of the Soviet Union, two types of investigation come to mind. An attempt might be made to analyse the process by which decisions are reached, the relations between the various authorities (what influence, if any, is exercised by the military? what individual influence is exercised by a particular member of the Politburo or the Praesidium?). This type of analysis, as applied to contemporary phenomena in the Soviet Union, is more or less useless because we have so little information to go on. On the other hand, we can make an analysis of the system of thought and action characteristic of the Communists since 1917. We can discover this system by studying the writings of Communists and their conduct and, as a result of this analysis, we can predict with a reasonable probability of accuracy how the leaders of the Soviet Union will act in given circumstances (specialists explained in advance, for instance, why the leaders of the Soviet Union would immediately reject the Marshall Plan offer, why they would not attempt an invasion of Western Europe at a time when that part of the continent was completely disarmed, etc.). As prediction has always been regarded as one of the tests of success in science, the studies which make such prediction possible must be admitted to have some scientific value.

Could similar studies be undertaken on other countries? The results would doubtless not be exactly similar, because American statesmen do not follow so rigid a doctrine as Soviet statesmen. There is no common doctrine to which the whole American political class subscribes; there are schools with different ideas about the part to be played by the United States (in the Soviet Union, the most that can be said is that there are "trends" within the Bolshevik party, but these trends are always subordinate to the same body of doctrine). The result is that the world is uncertain about the main lines of the United States' foreign policy. In 1914 the Americans were scarcely expected to intervene in 1917; in 1939, the Germans feared they might intervene, the French and the British hoped that they would, but neither side was sure. A less important decision, such as the American intervention in Korea, was probably a surprise to the members of governments most directly concerned.

The degree of predictability in a country's foreign policy is a matter of fact which can be objectively observed. This fact, in its turn, requires explanation. Investigations may follow two different lines: Is the fact attributable to the special characteristics of the nation or to its system of government? To what extent is it attributable to the nation and to what extent to democracy? It is impossible to answer these questions without having recourse to the most distinctive method of historical sociology—comparative study. A comparison may be made of the way in which foreign policy is determined in the United States of America or Great Britain, of the differing parts played by Congress and Parliament, and of the influence of the press. In the same way, we may show—or at least attempt to show—the special conditions imposed in the conduct of foreign policy by a democratic form of government (the policy-makers probably have less tactical freedom). Lastly, an investigation may be made, on the basis of past history, into the conceptions of national interest of which we hear so much. Is it true that national interest is always the same, however the form of government may change? To what extent is Soviet diplomacy, in the long run, similar to that conducted by Czarist Russia or to that which would have been conducted by a democratic Russia? The method of historical comparison can and must be used to test the correctness of the theories advanced to explain phenomena by reference to geography, population or economics.

There are diplomatic traditions in all countries, allegedly based upon the lessons of history. On analysis, these lessons turn out to represent no more than the relative permanence, or the repetition, of certain typical groupings of powers. On the assumption that we have a diplomatic field of given scope and that the same States remain in this field, certain situations are obviously bound to recur. France will seek the support of the power situated to the east of the neighbouring, rival power and so the tradition of the pincer alliance grows up. In a balance of power policy, this tradition is good only if several conditions are fulfilled. The diplomatic field must not be altered (when Europe becomes part of a world-wide field, the constants of yesterday cease to be applicable); the strength of the principal parties must remain approximately the same (if the eastern country becomes as strong, by itself, as all the others together, the pincer alliance is undesirable for the very reasons which previously commended it. Rules of caution based on experience are often dangerous, because they are formulated without any exact definition of the conditions in which they are applicable.

The same criticism applies to allegedly scientific general propositions. Most general statements about the factors determining foreign policy are mistaken for two reasons: they tend to establish "causes" where, at most, there are trends, and they do not take account of all the factors involved but exaggerate the influence of those that are considered.

Let us take, for example, the geographical determinants of foreign policy. The usual clichés about the "need for an outlet to the open seas" or the "mastery of the seas and the balance in Europe in relation to an insular position" sum up certain contingent factors. The importance that the Russian leaders attribute to free access to the sea depends on strategic considerations which alter with changes in the methods of warfare, and on the importance accorded to the problems of war as compared with those of peace. Czarist Russia was much more concerned about Constantinople and the Dardanelles than Soviet Russia (the former secured undertakings in 1915, the latter asked for no such undertakings during the hostilities of 1941-45).

There would be no difficulty in showing that the fact of being an island presents a country with various possibilities, among which the peoples make different choices for a variety of reasons; they may isolate themselves in their island and take no interest in the rest of the world; they may achieve supremacy by leaving the peoples of the continent to fight among themselves or to preserve a balance; they may seek to conquer positions on the continent, or they may embark on conquests beyond the seas; each of these four attitudes, in turn, has been adopted by Japan and Great Britain. The first was the attitude adopted by Japan under the Tokugawa Shogunate (there is no equivalent in British history since the formation of the United Kingdom); the second has been the attitude of Great Britain during modern times (the position in Asia made it impossible for Japan); the third was the attitude of England at the time of the Hundred Years War and of Japan after 1931; and the last, combined with the second, has been the attitude of Great Britain in modern times, and, combined with the third, that of Japan in the twentieth century.

In more abstract terms, it may be said that geographical factors explain certain relatively enduring features of each country's situation in the diplomatic field and, consequently, in the pattern of power relations and military might. The development of military technique brings about changes in this situation: by 1954, Great Britain was closer to the Continent than it had ever been before. Moreover, the geographical position indirectly influences a country's foreign policy to the extent that it is instrumental in determining ways of thought and political systems. The institutions of the Russian State, and the Russian mentality (whatever that term may mean exactly), are partly attributable to the influence of the enormous tract of country, without definite boundaries or visible lines of demarcation, which has gradually been conquered and organized by the Russian people. The influence of geographical circumstances also comes under our fifth heading.

Similarly, when we seek to determine the influence of the "economic factor," we shall find that it comes under our first set of headings, as one of the causes of change in the technique of warfare, the relative strength of the parties (since economic progress or decline entails an increase or a decrease in the strength of the nations), or change in the area of diplomatic relations, whose possible size is partly determined by the available means of transport. From another point of view, efforts can and should be made to discover how far the economic system and, more precisely, those in charge of the economy, influence the conduct of diplomacy. General propositions must therefore, at all events, be checked against experience.

The method of historical comparison is simple enough in theory but complicated in practice. In theory, it is a question of drawing attention to both similarities and differences between two given situations; this calls for a conceptual system by which to recognize the principal determinants. A strict comparison between the conduct of foreign policy in Great Britain and the United States of America, for example, presupposes a knowledge of the main factors exerting an influence in both countries. But such a knowledge must be based on study of the facts quite as much as on theory. We must therefore turn constantly from study of the facts to structural analysis or investigation of the principal determinants, and vice versa.

No comparison can cover the whole field: in other words, we always seek to determine the consequences of a particular phenomenon, such as the existence of a certain pattern in the relative strengths of countries. What are the effects of a bipolar structure? To what extent do we find the same developments in the Peloponnesian War and in the present conflict between the Soviet bloc and the free world? Or again, to what extent do we find similarities between periods in which the wars between States have been of a religious or ideological character?

The danger of such comparisons—and, still more, of the conclusions that we may claim to draw from them—is that the similarities are found only in certain features and the differences are so considerable that we cannot hope for more than a moderate prospect of being right in our forecasts or in the advice we give. There are cases in which two great coalitions have engaged in a war to the death, and others in which they have resigned themselves to coexistence on a more or less warlike footing. There have been centuries in which wars of religion have ended in compromise peaces, obliging men holding apparently incompatible convictions or fanatical beliefs to tolerate one another within the boundaries of the States, and at the same time defining the regions or nations in which one or other doctrine has triumphed. Analogies are ready to hand, but the question is whether the differences do not reduce the value of the analogies.

Apart from the reservations inseparable from the fact that comparisons are incomplete, there is another difficulty connected with the determination of the best level at which to conduct research. Let us suppose that we wish to discover the influence exercised by population pressure on the foreign policy of States. Historians are prone to say that Japanese imperialism was, if not caused, at least aggravated by the small space available and the growth of the population—an opinion which at first sight appears reasonable. But India is today suffering quite as much from over-population without displaying the slightest inclination for aggression or the least belligerency. This does not mean that it is false to say that there is a connexion between population stresses and aggressiveness (or warlike tendencies). The contrast between Japan and India suggests that we should investigate the circumstances in which the growth of the population, or the increase in the number of young men, helps to increase the aggressiveness of nations.

In 1931 unemployment led Germany to rearm but did not have the same effect in the United States of America where, at the same date, there were millions of unemployed workers. Japan seems to have been incited by the rapid growth of its population to seek markets or sources of supply beyond its borders, while India is not embarking on the same course. There are too many differences between India and Japan for us to be able to state precisely what has, in one case, caused bellicosity, and, in the other, pacifism. The first stage in the investigation must be to consider the differing conduct of the leaders: during this century, the Japanese leaders have encouraged the increase of the population, while the Indian leaders are seeking to spread birth control. The former were thinking in terms of numbers and power, the latter are primarily concerned—or claim to be primarily concerned—with the living conditions of the common people. Neither unemployment nor over-population leads directly to a policy of aggression; the essential intermediate term is a certain way of thinking or acting in the governing class.

Is this way of thinking in the small governing group itself an almost inevitable consequence of psycho-social phenomena attributable to over-population? I cannot give a dogmatic answer: in certain cases there are no signs of the sort of effervescence which seems to seize hold on the governing class, but a general review of the past would be necessary to confirm or refute the reality of the effects of over-population. Such a review should perhaps give a "bird's-eye picture" of the whole of a certain period. If too much attention is devoted to the detail of events, it is obvious that the effects of a continuing cause will escape the observer. Population phenomena are among those which generally escape the historian's grasp because they are not apparent to anyone who is following men's acts and deeds from day to day. Over-all comparisons between periods are possibly necessary to bring out the part played by such continuing factors.

What is the logical way to approach the problem of causality? In the first place, it seems to me, we may look for the immediate or sufficient cause of a particular war in population phenomena. In most cases, the demographic cause, assuming that there is such a cause, is not the only one, but is reinforced or weakened by the psychology of the leaders and the people, as expressed in a particular manner in a given historical situation. The wars which seem to be directly due to demographic factors are the variety in which colonies are founded by men who no longer have the necessary resources for life in their country of origin.

Secondly, we may compare the foreign policy of a nation at times when its population has been very large in relation to its resources with the foreign policy of that same nation at times when it is less so. This type of comparison will give us results which may be somewhat doubtful, for, on the assumption that over-populated countries pursue more aggressive policies than under-populated countries—which seems often to be the case—the state of affairs can be explained quite as well by reference to the general situation and calculations regarding the balance of power as by reference to the demographic position.

Again, we may consider a particular period of history as a whole—a given century in a given civilization—and gauge the frequency of wars and the mode of international relations by reference to population pressure. It is possible—indeed probable according to certain studies, though the truth of the conclusions drawn is not yet proved—that wars are more frequent in periods of over-population and less frequent in periods of relative depopulation but, in this case, it would seem that wars in the strict sense should be considered in conjunction with civil wars and manifestations of violence. It would appear that manifestations of violence increase in periods of over-population, and the increased frequency of war often coincides with increased frequency of civil conflict. If this is so, however, the periods when there have been great wars might coincide with periods of domestic upheaval, either moral or political. Such upheavals are sometimes, but not inevitably, a consequence of over-population. Over-population would therefore be one of the possible causes, but not the only possible cause, of a "high incidence of war."

Finally, we may wonder whether the removal of over-population may not be an essential (but not sufficient) condition for peace in international relations. So long as there is overpopulation in any part of the world, will not war have a function to fulfil, and will it not be found in the guise of civil war if international war becomes impossible through the establishment of a world State?

These, in summary outline, are the questions that history may be asked to answer about a cause such as the demographic cause. Beyond a doubt, it would be a good thing if we could avoid these manifold investigations and comparisons and bring to light relationships which would represent something more than mere trends. This complexity in investigation and uncertainty in results could be overcome only if there were enormous and comparatively independent units, in whose evolution we could find evidence of regularity in the repetition of phenomena at comparable periods of development. In other words, if there were entities, known as civilizations or cultures, which could be compared and which would display typical stages of development, comparison would be made simpler and would be more exact. As Spengler would say, civilization would be compared with civilization, the Rome of the Caesars with the Western world of the twentieth century, or the period of upheaval in ancient times with our own.

But are Toynbee's 23 civilizations intellectual concepts or real things? How far are they intellectual concepts and how far realities? It has not yet been proved that these comprehensive units are realities and, for the time being, political science cannot decree that there is one level, and one only, on which comparisons can be made.

. . . .

Peace and war

As all the civilizations known to us have had wars, the latter seem to be connected with certain characteristics, not necessarily of human nature as investigated by the psychologist, but of the nature of communities. Every specialist, after concentrating on particular aspects of the historical sequence leading up to a given war or to frequent wars, is naturally inclined to think that removal of the factor whose influence he has been studying would result in the prevention of war. But the fact that the sociologists have not yet made an exhaustive list of such factors, and still more that sociology has not arrived at a unanimously accepted theory of civilization without war, means that any advice given can be based, at best, only on probabilities, and must generally be ambiguous and doubtful.

Here again, historical sociology seems to me to offer the only middle course between moral platitudinizing ("if only the nations knew one another better, . . . if only education were developed and every people were taught to rid themselves of their prejudices and to see others as they really are," . . . etc.) and conservative cynicism ("there have always been wars, and so what else is to be expected").

Since the end of the last world war, there have been wars in the usual sense (between Israel and the Arab countries, and in Korea), and wars which were semi-civil and semi-international (in China and Indo-China). There is no reason to ask ourselves whether wars will occur in future; it is a fact that, at this moment of writing, wars are in progress. On the other hand, the idea of "cold war" introduces an element of confusion because it seems to suggest that the Soviet Union and the United States of America —or the Soviet camp and the camp of the so-called democratic or capitalistic nations—are at war, which is not in fact the case. There is conflict between these two powers or groups of powers. This conflict is more acute than the ordinary rivalry of nations in time of peace, and involves the use of certain methods which at other junctures in the past were used only in time of war; but it is by no means tantamount to a war in the traditional sense of the term. Nowhere are the American and Russian armies actually at strife.

The use of our six main headings would be helpful in an analysis of the present situation: the area of diplomatic relations covers at least the Americas, Europe, Asia, the Middle East and North Africa; there is a bipolar balance; military technique is undergoing rapid changes, and includes conventional armaments (those used in the last conflict), weapons of mass destruction and guerrilla warfare; a large number of peoples are gaining independence and setting up States which are internationally recognized, but the most powerful States deny the legitimacy of the ideological foundations of their respective régimes; the relations between domestic policy and diplomacy vary from country to country, but the two extremes are to be found in the Soviet Union, where the government has the maximum influence on public opinion, and in the United States of America, where the forces which help to shape public opinion are legion and often at variance; lastly, in both cases, foreign policy combines the pursuit of power and the espousal of an ideology, but the general lines of international relations are no easier to understand, because nationalistic slogans so often accompany imperialistic expansion, and the desire to spread an ideology is so often inconsistent with the use of the classic methods of diplomacy.

It would be possible to find precedents in the past for the greater number of these factors, the most novel of which is probably the existence of weapons of mass destruction. On the other hand, when we consider all the factors together, the present situation clearly stands alone. Historical comparisons might well provide suggestions for dealing with certain of its aspects (When and how have empires existed side by side? When and in what circumstances have ideological conflicts been smoothed over? etc.), but these suggestions would always involve the element of uncertainty inseparable from the fact that the combination of all the series of factors involved is unique.

The object, by this line of approach, would be not to do away with all war, but to seek to avoid a particular war which appears to be a possibility. I do not suggest that historical sociology could say with certainty what ought to be done in order to ensure that World War III does not break out in the next few years or decades. I simply say that only historical sociology—and not partial analyses or abstract theories—can state the problem in the form in which statesmen have to face it. Only a sociologist using the historical method could become the Adviser of the Prince.

If the Prince or his Adviser cherished loftier ambitions and dreamt of establishing peace in the world for ever, they would have first to diagnose the fundamental causes, bound up with the very structure of the known civilizations, which have made lasting and universal peace impossible. I do not believe that this task is scientifically hopeless, but I am less confident that, on this point, science is encouraging. I fear that the conversion which communities would have to undergo if they were never again to resort to organized violence is hardly regarded by science as imminent or indeed, in the long run, as likely.

2. HERBERT C. KELMAN

Societal, Attitudinal and Structural Factors in International Relations[1]

In classifying research approaches to the problems of war and peace, Angell distinguishes between those who do research in terms of governments and those who do research in terms of peoples.[2] It is possible to make another distinction which overlaps to some degree with that made by Angell. This is a distinction between those who approach the problem in terms of macroscopic units, such as the nation, and those who essentially use the individual as their unit of analysis. . . .

Along with this difference in terms of the units of analysis used in the two approaches, there appears also to be a difference in the assumption about the nature of the phenomenon of war.

War as a Deviation and War as an Instrument of Policy

Those who deal with the individual tend to conceive of war as a deviation: essentially, it occurs because of some failure in the mechanisms of maintaining peace. The extreme of this position is represented by the psychoanalytic approach, as described by Farber.[3] According to this approach, war is an aspect of irrational behavior, related to irrelevant, personal motivations, usually traceable to childhood experiences. According to the approach presented by Gladstone,[4] war is related to the typical ways in which individuals react to threat. It is assumed that certain kinds of attitudes in the face of provocation or perceived threat are likely to interfere with a peaceful settlement of conflict. For Angell, one of the determinants of war

Published in the *Journal of Social Issues,* Vol. XI, No. 1 (1955), pp. 42-56. Reprinted by permission of the author and the Society for Psychological Study of Social Issues.

[1] Many of the ideas presented in this article were originally developed at the 1953 summer workshop of the Research Exchange on the Prevention of War by William Barth, Arthur Gladstone, Dean Pruitt and the author (f).*

[2] Robert C. Angell, "Governments and Peoples as Foci for Peace-Oriented Research," *Journal of Social Issues,* Vol. XI, No. 1 (1955), 36-41.

[3] Maurice L. Farber, "Psychoanalytic Hypotheses in the Study of War," *ibid.,* 29-35.

[4] Arthur I. Gladstone, "The Possibility of Predicting Reactions to International Events," *ibid.,* 21-28.

* This letter, and others throughout the text, refer to References listed on p. 222 (Editor's note).

is a lack of adequate cultural bridges which would promote international understanding and prevent the outbreak of war when conflicts arise. It follows, from the conception of war as a phenomenon of deviant behavior, that war could be prevented by changing the people (their attitudes, motivations, understanding) and by placing individuals of a certain type into leadership positions.

. . . .

Those who deal with more macroscopic units tend to conceive of war as an instrument of policy. According to this view it is possible that war will occur even if the elite of a nation is not particularly subject to war-like motivations and attitudes and even if there is considerable understanding among the nations concerned. In fact, an elite may decide on war without any substantial provocation or threat. War in this view, is one of many means used by an elite in the pursuit of its ends. An elite may decide "cold-bloodedly" that war is necessary, or it may follow policies which are likely to result in war, in order that it may achieve certain ends that are important to it. Cottrell is quite explicit about this assumption.[5] He conceptualizes war as a consequence of human choice and an outcome of an elite's normal pursuit of its ends. War will be selected if the elite considers it the course of action most likely to maximize its values. It follows from this view, as Cottrell points out, that to prevent war it would be necessary to show to the elite in a convincing way that war is not the best way to maximize their particular values, that it is actually more costly than other means available to them.

The conception of war as an instrument of policy seems to rest on the further assumption that the choices made by the elite are essentially "rational." Cottrell indicates that these choices may be determined by myths, prejudices and hunches, but he implies that they would be rational if the elite had all the necessary facts. They would choose peace if it could be demonstrated convincingly that peace would make more likely the maximization of their values. This, however, is precisely one of the major difficulties in war prevention. How *can* it be made clear and convincing to an elite that war is not the best means available to them? There have certainly been occasions when, to the objective observer, it seemed clear that war was not a desirable course of action, and yet, the elite resisted this evidence. Their perceptions were distorted, either because of some particular investment in the method of war as such, unrelated to the rational, conscious ends that they were pursuing; or because of some strong resistance to the alternative means that were available. In such cases it would do little good to demonstrate that the elite's ends could be served best by peaceful means, because the real problem would be to persuade the elite to accept the diagnosis. . . . It is here that the kinds of variables discussed by Gladstone, Farber and Angell may become of primary importance. Per-

[5] W. Fred Cottrell, "Research to Establish the Conditions for Peace," *ibid.*, 13-20.

haps there is something in the basic values and character patterns of a nation and its elite or in their traditional attitudes towards the other nations concerned which predisposes them towards perceiving situations as requiring war and towards resisting alternative means.

In short, we have tried to point out that while personal attitudes and motivations may be of great importance in the conduct of international relations, "societal" factors set very stringent limits on their operation; and while war and peace may be instruments of policy, selected by the elite in line with their goals, "attitudinal" factors predispose them towards one or the other course of action. The study of war and peace inevitably, therefore—as recent writers are increasingly pointing out—requires us to pay attention to both societal and attitudinal factors and to the interaction between the two.

Societal Factors

It is probably clear from the preceding comments what we mean by societal factors. In the most general terms this refers to those variables which describe characteristics of the society as a whole. Societal factors relate to macroscopic units—usually nations, but sometimes also large segments of a nation, or certain groupings of nations. Some of these factors represent aggregations of actions on a part of a large number of individuals, or products of such actions. In these cases the individual behavior is abstracted via concepts which refer to the aggregations or the products as such.

There is a wide variety of societal factors that are likely to affect the probability of war and peace. For example, there are such "natural" factors as the geographic position of the country and the basic resources that it has available. Probably of great importance are the economic conditions of the country, including the kind of productive activities on which its economy is based, the point in the business cycle in which it finds itself, and the general standard of living of the population. Closely related are the technological conditions, whose relationship to war and peace is described in detail by Cottrell. (See especially b.) Population factors may be related to tendencies towards geographic or economic expansion, and also determine the manpower resources and hence the productive capacity and the military potential of a nation. Other military factors and strategic considerations are also likely to enter into the picture. And there are political conditions, such as the nature of the regime, the stability of the government, and the existence of internal political conflict. Finally, there are factors relating to international politics and diplomacy, such as the existence of power blocs and alliances, the maintenance of balance of power, and the many other factors which are the traditional domain of the students of international relations.

It can be assumed that societal factors determine to a great extent the policies followed by the decision-making elite, since they affect the goals towards which the decision-makers are striving and the means that are available to them. For example, if nation A has a poorly developed technology, it is likely that its elite will pursue a policy of peaceful cooperation vis-a-vis its more advanced neighbor B, both because the elite may desire technical and economic assistance from B and because it lacks the means for effective military resistance to B. Attitudinal factors may modify the effects of such societal factors, but the latter will surely set limits on the policies pursued by the elite. The decisions of the elite will be affected not only by the conditions in their own country, but also by the conditions in other countries and the resulting goals and means of these other elites. For example, if the conditions in nation C are such that the elite of C is bent on territorial expansion, and if C has the necessary resources to carry this program through, then the elite of A may decide to increase its own arms production and to enter into military alliances with other nations. Of course, here again, other factors enter into the picture: A's perception of the goals and resources of C may be distorted because of certain attitudes on the part of the elite of A, or because of certain flaws in the communication process.

The study of societal factors is important both in the analysis of a specific international situation, and in the derivation of general laws about international relations. In a specific situation, determination of such factors helps predict the probability of war or peace. It may also point to the specific conditions that would have to be changed in order to reduce the probability of war; and it may help to convince the elite—as Cottrell suggests—that war would not be the most effective means for maximizing their values. As far as general laws are concerned, it might be useful to establish two kinds of relationships. On the one hand, one could attempt to derive laws which link societal factors to certain broad social outcomes: in this type of law, in other words, both the independent and dependent variables would refer to macroscopic units (as they do in modern economic theory). On the other hand, one could attempt to derive laws which link societal factors to the decision-making processes. When we are dealing with laws of the first kind, it is possible to ignore the attitudes and motivations of the individuals who determine the final outcome, and to seek relationships completely on the macroscopic level. When dealing with laws of the second kind, however, the importance of the attitudes and motivations of the decision-makers, and of all those who influence their decisions, becomes particularly apparent.

Attitudinal Factors

When speaking of "attitudinal" factors we refer, in a general way, to those variables which describe characteristics of individuals. More specifically, we want to deal with attitudes, values and motivations which are part of the individual's general outlook on the world and which determine his reactions to important social events. The individual—whether he be a member of the elite or of the public-at-large—brings these attitudes and motivations into situations which require decision and action relevant to international affairs. We might also speak of these variables as "predispositional" factors, in that they tend to predispose the person towards one kind of perception, decision and action as over against another.

Attitudinal factors relevant to international relations may be unique to the individual involved, or (and these are probably more important in international relations) they may be typical for the culture as a whole. The source of these attitudes may be in the past history of the individual . . . , in the immediate social conditions of his society, or in previous interactions between his and other nations . . . . When their source is the life history of the individual, then we may speak of these attitudes as products of individual personality or national character—particularly if they are rooted in the process of socialization: we can then proceed . . . to relate attitudes to personality factors. When their source is interaction with the other nation, then they may take on the character of stereotypes and social distance scales (h). Regardless of the source, these factors constitute readinesses or tendencies to prefer certain kinds of goals over others, to choose or accept certain courses of action as over against others, to perceive and interpret the actions of other groups and nations in certain ways rather than in others.

Examples of attitudinal factors that might affect international relations are attitudes toward other nations (often based on traditions of long standing); attitudes towards internationalism in general . . . , international organization, specific international bodies; attitudes towards one's own nation, its destiny, its honor, its sovereignty; general attitudes relating to the perception of threat . . . ; values or ideologies regarding war and violence, regarding alternative ways of resolving conflicts; expectations about war and assumptions about its inevitability; images of war and military life (such as the glamorization of war as an exciting experience, or as a test of heroism). As far as the general public is concerned, the kinds of attitudes that are particularly important are those which determine the extent to which people will *accept* the policies of the elite and the enthusiasm with which they will help to carry them out. Included here, for example, would be attitudes towards the government in general and values regarding political action and individual responsibility. The acceptance and morale of the public is always a factor in foreign policy, although there are differences in the amount and kind of influence which public opinion exerts, depending on the political structure (e).

It would be possible to ignore attitudinal factors and to deal completely on the level of societal factors if we could make two assumptions: (1) that the goals of decision-makers (and opinion-makers) are, within broad limits, geared to some sort of "objective needs" of the society, and (2) that the actions of the decision-makers are, by and large, rational, in the sense that they are chosen so as to maximize their conscious goals. In the field of international relations, however, it seems hardly possible to make these assumptions. First of all, the decisions are made and influenced by a large number of individuals and groups, each of whom brings into the picture a wide variety and a complex constellation of goals, many of which are only indirectly related to the international situation as such. The relation of this complex array of goals to the needs of the society is certainly not a simple one. Secondly, even some of the goals and values relating to war and peace which are generally shared in the society are not produced by the needs of the society in any objective sense, but rather by the dominant ideology and ethos. Thirdly, there appear to be preferences, in every society, for certain kinds of policies and actions, even if these do not lead to a maximization of conscious goals; and aversions to certain alternative policies which might actually be more profitable. These preferences become especially important since the ambiguities faced by decision-makers in the area of international relations make "rational" choices extremely difficult: the goals towards which they are striving are often not clear-cut, particularly when they aim for goals which are incompatible with each other and when some important goals are not verbalized; and frequently they have little objective basis for evaluating the consequences of various courses of action, particularly when these evaluations depend on guesses about the goals, plans and reactions of other nations. For all these reasons, then, it seems to be necessary to supplement the study of societal factors with a study of attitudinal factors, and particularly to deal with the interaction between the two.

The study of attitudinal factors, just like the study of societal factors, is important both in the analysis of a specific international situation and in the derivation of general laws. It is necessary to establish the exact nature of the attitudes that underlie foreign policy, as well as public opinion on international affairs. Without this information, programs designed for attitude change may be ineffective since they may not be aimed at the relevant issues.

Structural Factors

The attempt to deal with the interaction between societal and attitudinal factors raises the question of *whose* attitudes have to be studied. One could arbitrarily limit oneself to the official decision-makers. In doing so, however, a great deal of information would be lost, since they are not the only ones who have a hand in formulating policy. Their decisions are influenced by various individuals and groups, official and unofficial, within their own nation as well as outside it. Within a given country, the list of influential groups would include, for example, governmental agencies, legislative bodies, military agencies, economic groupings, various pressure groups, and the communications industry. Outside of the nation it would include the elites of other nations with whom this particular nation is in alliance or who are co-members in certain regional groupings, international organizations (such as the U. N.) and less official international bodies (such as churches and labor organizations). To varying degrees, the actions of decision-makers are also determined by public opinion and public sentiment. If we want to take into account the effects of these different influences, we have to deal with the problem of how the attitudes and actions of the different groups and individuals are aggregated so as to produce national policy and action. In other words, we have to identify the individuals and groups who are able to exert influence, and to determine the degree to which they are influential, the issues over which they have some control, and the way in which they exert their influence.

The need for dealing with this problem of aggregation brings into focus a third set of factors that have to be studied: structural factors, including the power structure and the communication structure of the nations in question. Study of the power structure would reveal which groups have control over foreign policy decisions (or, more probably, over particular areas of foreign policy) and under what conditions and in what ways they can make their influence felt. Study of the communication structure would reveal which groups have access to the information enabling them to play a role in foreign policy and to communication channels enabling them to exert influence. The distinction between power structure and communication structure is, of course, only a formal one, since in actuality power depends on a central position in the communication structure, and vice versa.

Structural factors represent a level of analysis different from that of either societal or attitudinal factors. As we have seen, societal factors typically describe characteristics of nations; attitudinal factors refer to characteristics of individuals. In the study of structural factors, however, the units of analysis are formal or informal structures, or machineries for aggregating the values of a variety of individuals and groups (cf. a). Structural factors refer to the characteristics of such structures or machineries. These factors are of great importance since they determine the way in which societal and attitudinal factors are channelled into decisions and actions. The nature of this channelling process in itself may have decisive effects on the probability of war and peace. It is quite conceivable that two situations in which societal and attitudinal factors are alike will have different effects depending on the power and communication structures through which decisions are made.

Since decisions are affected by groups and individuals within and outside the nation, it is important to study both the national and international structures. The national structure will affect, among other things, the amount and kind of influence exerted by public opinion. On the one hand, it will determine the extent to which the public is able to make its "will" felt, i.e., how much information is available to the citizens, how much power they have to influence policy, and how much opportunity is given them to communicate their wishes to the decision-makers. One might assume, for example, that there would be considerable differences in this respect between democracies and dictatorships, although these differences are by no means simple, since in the area of foreign relations dictatorships also consider the public will in order to be sure of morale and support, and democracies also ignore and manipulate the public will in determining policy. On the other hand, structural factors will largely determine the actual content of public opinion, by affecting the kinds of information that will be communicated *to* the public. A totalitarian regime, for example, is in a better position to manipulate public opinion since it has almost sole control over the mass media of communication.

In studying the international structure, we would have to consider the alliances and groupings to which a nation belongs. Elites of allied nations will be in a position to exert influence on this nation's policies, depending on the degree to which it needs their support and the extent to which channels of communication are available. If two nations involved in a potential conflict are themselves allies or co-members of a group of nations, certain additional channels for mutual influence and resolution of the conflict would be available; and also, both would be more receptive to influence from other allies. An international organization would be in a position to exert influence on a given nation depending on its power, the place of the nation within the structure of the international organization, the availability of institutionalized ways of dealing with conflicts between nations, and the extent to which it provides open channels of communication among its member-nations. International communication structures, formal and informal, will be of decisive importance, since they will determine to a large extent the way in which one nation will interpret the intentions and estimate the capacities of other nations.

In the analysis of a specific international situation, one would want to identify the different positions in the power and communication structures and determine the amount and manner of influence exerted by each. While this appears to be a huge task, it may actually turn out that the number of people that have decisive influence on international relations is fairly small (cf. d). This kind of analysis would point to the groups that are influential and upon whom attempts at changing attitudes should be concentrated; and to possible changes in the structure (e.g., increasing the power or information of certain groups) which might produce changes in foreign policy. On the level of general laws, we would want to establish relationships between particular kinds of structures and the probability of war and peace. The derivation of such laws would be greatly facilitated if we had concepts that provide summary descriptions of complex structures (such as democratic vs. totalitarian). The development of such concepts is a difficult task, and it is here that a great deal of creative imagination is needed.

The Process of Interaction Between Nations

In our attempt to provide a preliminary kind of mapping or framework for research on international relations we have, so far, distinguished three types of variables which may affect the probability of war and peace. Up to this point this framework is essentially static. We have discussed relationships between these variables and the probability of war or peace at a given moment in time, but have not presented the variables in the context of continuing interactions between nations. The interaction between nations, of course, involves an ever-changing succession of events. An action on the part of one nation . . . will be communicated to another, and produce a reaction which in turn will be communicated to the first nation, and so on. It is very likely that the effects of our three types of factors will change in relation to this flow of events. For example, if nations A and B mutually distrust each other but are both disarmed, the chances of war are probably low; as these two nations become engaged, however, in the mutual stimulation of an armaments race (g), the effect of attitudes of distrust on the probability of war is likely to become more noticeable. To be sure, it may happen that there are forces so strong that they will determine war or peace almost regardless of particular events in the relations between two nations: for example, a nation may initiate war without provocation, or keep out of war no matter how extreme the provocation. In general, however, societal, attitudinal and structural factors will operate with reference to specific events in the process of interaction, and a useful framework must, therefore, include consideration of these events.

In line with this requirement, we would state the problem with which the framework deals as follows: when a particular event, or situation of interaction, occurs, what is the probability that its outcome will be peace or war, and how is this probability affected by societal, attitudinal and structural factors? By situation of interaction is meant any action on the part of A which is communicated to B and which B deems relevant to its own interests. Selecting a specific situation of interaction and trying to determine its outcome is, of course, an abstraction from the real situation made for purposes of exposition. In actuality, especially in present-day international relations, there are always a series of situations of interaction occurring simultaneously and it is impossible to trace the effects of one of them without taking into account the whole set of events that are occurring. Perhaps, eventually, this gulf will be bridged by the development of indices which stand for a whole set of simultaneous events, such as Richardson's index of arms expenditures (g).

A situation of interaction, or a series of such situations is, however, not the proper starting-point for our analysis. Each situation of interaction occurs in the context of the general *level of interaction* that exists between two nations. Level of interaction refers to the nature of the relationship as it extends over a period of time. Examples of such levels are all-out war, limited war, armed peace, stable compromise, peaceful cooperation, and federation. The level of interaction is, of course, never completely stable. There will always be fluctuations in it due to forces pushing it one way or the other. We can say, however, that a given level of interaction exists between two nations, as long as, despite minor fluctuations, the relationship will tend towards an equilibrium over a period of time. It is this level of interaction, then, that should be used as the starting-point for analysis, and the effects of a specific situation of interaction must be evaluated in relation to this general level. We might restate the problem with which the framework deals as follows: when a particular situation of interaction occurs, what is the probability that the sequence of events initiated by it will produce a change in a given level of interaction, or that—despite minor fluctuations—the level will remain stable and return to its equilibrium; and how is this probability affected by societal, attitudinal and structural factors? [6]

If we want to design research that will help us answer this question, it would be useful to have some way of spelling out the sequence of events that leads from a particular situation of interaction (or set of such situations) to a final outcome (i.e., change of or return to the initial level of interaction). This kind of detailed analysis of the sequence will give us a picture of exactly how a given outcome is produced. When we know this process we are in a much better position to evaluate the effects of different societal, attitudinal and structural factors on this outcome. The usefulness of a detailed analysis is particularly clear when we are interested in producing change: we may be unable to change a situation of interaction which initiates a sequence, but we might be able to change the final outcome by affecting one or another step in the sequence.

Steps in the Sequence of Events

We shall illustrate the kind of analysis we have in mind by suggesting a distinction among five steps in the sequence of events that is initiated by a given situation of interaction. These steps refer to the sequence of events within a single nation only. Actually, of course, a situation of interaction will initiate a sequence in every nation that is involved in the interaction. Moreover, events occurring in one nation will produce reactions in other nations, which in turn will initiate new sequences of events. The final outcome of a situation of interaction depends, therefore, on a number of sequences occurring simultaneously or successively in different nations. We shall restrict ourselves, however, to an analysis of a single sequence in one nation, keep-

[6] It is likely that the factors that determine changes in the level of interaction will turn out to be the most significant variables in this area. In general there seem to be forces, towards the maintenance of a stable equilibrium in international relations. If this equilibrium breaks down and a new level of interaction is achieved, such as the outbreak of war, then it must mean that some kind of turning-point has been reached which caused a reversal in the direction of the forces that usually maintain the equilibrium. The same would be true if the relationship between two nations has been one of intermittent war and armed peace for a period of time, and then it turns into one of friendly cooperation. An understanding of the characteristics of such turning-points and the factors that affect them would be a great advance in our knowledge

ing in mind that it represents only a small part of the flow of events. The steps are merely illustrative, and may not at all represent the best way of slicing the process.

(1) *Communication about the situation to the elite and other segments of the population:* What is the content of the information that is communicated? How much distortion has entered into it and what is the direction of the distortion?

(2) *Definition of the situation and perception of choices:* Is there a perception of threat or provocation? Is the situation defined as one of conflict or harmony? As a matter of central importance to the nation or one of peripheral interest? What courses of action are seen as available to the policy-makers and other influential groups? Do they see the choices as limited to the use of violent force or do they consider other alternatives?

(3) *Development of a climate or state of readiness for certain actions:* Is the general climate favorable to violence or to compromise? Is the atmosphere characterized by military preparations, threats, expectations of attack and war, anxiety and hysteria—or is it characterized by calm, confidence, faith in existing mechanisms for adjusting conflict, disarmament, and conciliatory gestures?

(4) *Commission of specific acts relevant to the interests of the other nation:* What specific actions are taken by the government or by other official or unofficial groups or individuals? Are actions of a hostile nature taken, such as border incidents, blockades, etc.? Actions of a friendly or conciliatory nature?

(5) *Achievement of a new level of interaction or return to the initial equilibrium:* Does the situation of interaction which initiated the sequence of steps represent only a temporary fluctuation in the level of interaction between the nations, or does it lead to a general change in the level of interaction? If a new level develops, what is its nature?

Research can be done on the relationships among these five steps, and particularly on the relationship between each step and the final outcome of the sequence. For example, we might study whether certain kinds of climate are conducive to certain kinds of specific actions; or whether certain definitions of the situation are more likely to result in war than others. In general, it can be assumed that the sequence of steps we have outlined represents a cumulative process, at least to some extent: a particular situation of interaction is likely to be communicated in a particular way; this communication, in turn, is likely to produce a particular definition of the situation, and so on.

The chain reaction which is implied here, however, is by no means inevitable—and that is precisely where societal, attitudinal and structural factors enter the picture. The way in which a given sequence develops towards a final outcome depends on a large number of factors of these three types. A given factor may affect any or all of the steps in the sequence, and in this way alter the probability of a given outcome: it may enhance the probability that the sequence will take its "natural course" or it may help to reverse the course of events. For example, let us say nation A has taken an action which appears threatening to nation B, but A and B are actually allies and very dependent on each other because of the existence of a common enemy. This fact is likely to affect the way in which the event is communicated, such that the threat will be minimized; even if it happens that the event is communicated with its full impact, it is likely that the situation will be redefined so as to reduce that impact. In every stage of the process it is likely that forces will be created in the direction of maintaining the existing level of interaction, and that the "natural" sequence will be reversed. On the other hand, let us say again that nation A has taken an action which appears threatening to nation B, but this time the elite of B is an oligarchy which is in danger of losing its power and therefore eager to create a climate of external threat. In this case, forces will be created to enhance the impact of the communication of the threatening event, the definition of the situation as one of imminent danger, and the creation of a climate of anxiety and hysteria.

Spelling out the steps in the sequence of events that lead to a final outcome is likely to suggest hypotheses about various societal, attitudinal and structural factors that may affect the probability of war or peace. There are many such factors which affect final outcomes by virtue of the fact that they influence particularly one or another of the steps in the sequence, e.g., the kinds of choices that are perceived or the kind of climate that is developed. Some of these factors are only indirectly related to the international situation as such. It is quite possible that factors of this sort would not come into consideration if we deal only with final outcomes, and not with the detailed processes whereby these outcomes are produced.

. . . .

Spelling out the steps in the sequence has another advantage in that it greatly increases the range of researchable problems. It is usually difficult to do research in which certain factors are related to final outcomes, but it is much simpler to relate these factors to some of the steps in the sequence that leads to the final outcome. For example, if we wanted to establish the relationship between attitudes of internationalism and the frequency of war, we would be restricted to historical research in which our indices of attitudes would not be very trustworthy. If, however, we wanted to relate attitudes of internationalism to the way in which situations of interaction are defined, then we could set up a wide variety of empirical researches and might even be able to design appropriate experimental models (c). Of course, we could also have to establish the kind of relationship that exists between the definition of a situation and the final outcome of a sequence of events that this situation initiates.

Summary and Conclusions

We have presented a framework for research on war and peace designed to answer the following question: Given a particular level of interaction between two nations, what is the probability that the sequence of events initiated by a given situation of interaction will produce war or peace, or some other final outcome? The framework suggests a breakdown of the sequence of events into five steps: communication of the event, definition of the situation, development of a climate, commission of specific actions, and achievement of a new level of interaction (or return to the initial equilibrium). It suggests, further, a distinction among three types of factors which are likely to affect each step in the sequence and hence the final outcome of the interaction: societal, attitudinal and structural factors. These three types of factors differ in terms of the units of analysis and levels of theorizing to which they refer: societal factors describe characteristics of nations, attitudinal factors characteristics of individuals, and structural factors characteristics of structures or aggregating machineries. Societal factors set limits on international relations; attitudinal factors determine predispositions towards certain decisions and actions and thus modify the effects of societal factors; and structural factors determine who influences decisions and how this influence is exerted and thus prescribe the way in which societal and attitudinal factors are channelled into action. It is assumed that factors of each of these three types are important in determining the final outcome of interactions between nations, and that their effects —and particularly the effects of interaction between them—should be explored.

The framework is applicable not only to *existing* societal, attitudinal and structural conditions, and the effects that they might have on one or more of the steps in the sequence of events, but also to *potential* conditions. In other words, we could ask the question: What sets of conditions would have to exist (or be created) in order that the sequence of events would have a particular desired outcome? This is, of course, the question with which most of us are really concerned, since we are afraid that the existing conditions in the world will lead to war, and want to discover conditions which would increase the chances for peace. Research oriented to this question would explore alternatives to the techniques used by the great powers today for the resolution of international conflicts; and ways of changing societal conditions, attitudes and social structure so that they would favor the chances for peace.

The framework can be visualized, essentially, as a matrix consisting of fifteen cells. Each of these cells poses special questions of its own, which need to be subjected to research. Similarly, relations among the cells have to be investigated. The framework is not intended to be a theory as such: it does not propose a set of concepts, definitions and propositions and does not postulate relationships between specific variables or derive hypotheses for research. It is intended to be preliminary to the steps of theorizing and hypothesis-testing. It is at best the scaffolding within which theories may be built. Essentially, it is designed to call attention to the types of variables that may be important and to help us determine relevant questions for research. In short, it is simply a more systematic way of asking questions which can then be subjected to empirical tests. As research is done on a given question, it is hoped that creative theories will be developed to deal with it. The kinds of research that are needed and the kinds of theoretical models that will prove useful will differ for the different questions. Eventually it may be possible to build a coordinated theory with a unified set of concepts to handle the entire framework, but for the present it will probably be most fruitful to use separate concepts and miniature theories for the different questions, which are most suited to their particular requirements.

. . . .

References

a. Arrow, K. J., *Social Choice and Individual Values.* New York: John Wiley and Sons, 1951.

b. Cottrell, W. F., "Men cry peace," *Research for Peace,* Essays by Q. Wright, W. F. Cottrell and Ch. Boasson. Published for the Institute for Social Research, Oslo. Amsterdam: North-Holland Publishing Company, 1954. Pp. 95-162.

c. Gladstone, A. I., "Can the prevention of war be studied experimentally?" *Bulletin of the Research Exchange on the Prevention of War,* Vol. 1, No. 2 (1953) pp. 1-3.

d. Hunter, F., *Community Power Structure.* Chapel Hill: University of North Carolina Press, 1953.

e. Kelman, H. C., "Public opinion and foreign policy decisions," *Bulletin of the Research Exchange on the Prevention of War,* Vol. 2, No. 4 (1954), pp. 2-8.

f. Kelman, H. C., "A proposed framework for the study of war and peace," *Bulletin of the Research Exchange on the Prevention of War,* Vol. 2, No. 6 (1954), pp. 3-13.

g. Richardson, L. F., "Threats and security," *Psychological Factors of Peace and War,* edited by T. H. Pear. London: Hutchinson, 1950. Ch. 10.

h. Sherif, M. and Carolyn W. Sherif, *Groups in Harmony and Tension.* New York: Harper, 1953.

3. Ernst B. Haas

The Challenge of Regionalism

. . . It is my contention that the most interesting challenge inherent in the study of regionalism lies in the potentialities of the field for insights into the process of community formation at the international level. Regional relations, meetings, decisions, administrative devices, bureaucracies, inter-ministerial, inter-expert and inter-parliamentary institutions provide a mass of data on the process of "denationalization" of normal government functions with their delegation to regional decision-making units. While it is true that universal institutions can be used for precisely the same kind of study, it is likely that the data will prove more instructive at the regional level, if only because of the greater bulk of activity. I propose to take advantage of the recently published pioneering work of the Princeton Center for the Study of World Political Institutions by stating its conclusions and the context to which they apply.[1] . . . I shall then proceed to discuss the possibility of generalizing these propositions by applying them to the study of supranational economic integration in contemporary Europe and to state the lessons to be derived from this regional experience.[2] Our examination will close with proposals for applying this type of analysis to other regional settings.

Published in *International Organization,* Vol. XII, No. 4 (Autumn 1958), pp. 440-458.

[1] Karl W. Deutsch, Sidney A. Burrell, Robert A. Kann, Maurice Lee, Jr., Martin Lichtermann, Raymond E. Lindgren, Francis L. Loewenheim, and Richard W. Van Wagenen, *Political Community and the North Atlantic Area: International Organization in the Light of Historical Experience* (Princeton, N. J.: Princeton University Press, 1957). The conceptual and methodological principles applied in this study are treated in Karl W. Deutsch, *Nationalism and Social Communication* (New York: Wiley, 1953); and Karl W. Deutsch, *Political Community at the International Level* (Garden City: Doubleday, 1954). The first-mentioned work provides the substance of the discussion of Part II of this paper.

[2] Ernst B. Haas, *The Uniting of Europe: Political, Economic and Social Forces, 1950-1957* (Stanford, Calif.: Stanford University Press, 1958). This study provides the substance of Part IV of this paper.

II

On the basis of an examination of ten closed cases of successful and unsuccessful unions of states in Europe and North America the Princeton study advances a series of general and specific findings on how "security-communities" are attained.[3] A "security-community" is a "group of people which has become integrated" and "integration" is defined as the "attainment, within a territory, of a 'sense of community' and of institutions and practices strong enough and widespread enough to assure, for a 'long' time, dependable expectations of 'peaceful change' among its population." [4] For practical purposes, however, the study proceeds in terms of two sub-types of security-community permitting of greater institutional specificity. Integration may be achieved through an "amalgamated" security-community, which implies the creation of a governmental structure, whether that of a unitary, federal or personal union type of state is immaterial. Roughly, the concept of the amalgamated security-community corresponds to the kind of regional arrangement which provides for a heavy dose of central decision-making, whether "federal" in the more restricted legal sense or not. On the other hand, integration may also be achieved through a "pluralistic" security community, any arrangement in which no true central decision-making unit is created and in which the constituent states retain their independence but which nevertheless provides for the kind of social interaction thought conducive to integration. Confederations and conventional international organizations at the regional level would fall into this category.

With commendable caution, the authors eschew a rigorous statement of which factors or conditions must be considered "necessary and sufficient" to bring about integration. They doubt that the successful isolation of a number of recurrent historical themes amounts to a truly "scientific" statement of a process. "When we call certain conditions *'essential,'* " they note, "we mean that success seems to us extremely improbable in their absence. Though essential, they also seem to us insufficient: even if all of them were present, we do not know whether any other conditions might be required which we may well have overlooked. A similar consideration applies to those conditions that we called *helpful* but not essential: we found that integration occurred in their absence, and might well recur in this way in future cases." [5]

---

[3] The study abstracts its findings from the examination of these cases: United States, 1789-1877; England-Scotland, middle ages to 1707; England-Ireland, until 1921; German unification, early 19th century until 1871; Italian unification, early 19th century until 1860; Hapsburg Monarchy, middle ages until 1918; Norway-Sweden, 1814-1907; Switzerland, 13th century until 1848; England-Wales, late middle ages; English unification, middle ages. The cases were selected to include both pluralistic and amalgamated security-communities, successful and unsuccessful attempts at unity. The authors assumed all their cases to be "closed" historically.

[4] Deutsch et al., *op. cit.,* p. 5.

[5] *Ibid.,* pp. 12-13.

Within this methodological context, the general findings are as follows. Pluralistic security-communities are easier to attain and maintain than more formal unions, provided that the central aim is merely the preservation of peace among the participants. This conclusion is not true if socio-political aims other than peace predominate. However, the actual attainment of either type of security-community cannot be judged readily by the passage of some "threshold" of integration. Successful integration is attained when the subjective criterion of certain élite expectations is met: if the expectations of key élites in the region converge toward demands for peaceful change and other benefits thought to be obtainable only through the union, integration is underway. Objectively speaking, integration can be considered achieved when the states in the region cease to prepare for war against one another, a condition which can be easily verified from military statistics and plans. It could be said that the "integration threshold" is passed when both criteria can be positively met, but since the subjective index is not considered easily verifiable, not much practical value is expected of the concept.

A range of conclusions were derived from the concept of social communication. First of all, successful integration is held to depend on the prevalence of mutually compatible self-images and images of the other actors participating in the process of unification. This involves first and foremost successful predictions on the part of one nationally identified élite of the behavior pattern of other élites active in the region. It is this type of sympathy feeling among the crucial actors which is held of importance, not verbal commitment to common symbols and propositions, such as "freedom," "peace" or "welfare." Further, successful integration tends to take place around a "core area," a region possessing superior administrative skills, military power, economic resources and techniques, as well as capacity for receiving and assimilating the demands of other regions so as to satisfy them. Actors in the weaker areas look to the core area for leadership and help in the satisfaction of their demands; sympathetic response on the part of the élites active in the core area then begets progressive integration without in the least implying any "balance of power" among participating units. A great deal of stress is placed on the "capacity" of the administrative system and the attitudes prevailing in the core area actively to respond to the needs expressed by others. In Karl Deutsch's terms, successful integration equals the balance of load and capability in the network of social communication.

The Princeton authors note that successful integration for both types of security-community is more likely if improvement of the communications network takes place before the actual burdens are spelled out in terms of political demands. They note also that war among the participating actors should cease to be a respectable mode of policy before the achievement of political union. Further, the nature of the élite structure is singled out as being of crucial importance. It is desirable for successful integration that a broadening of élites vertically in each political unit take place before the act of union, that rigid social stratification be weakened, that mass participation in public life increase. But it is equally desirable that horizontal contacts among élites of similar status and outlook in all the political units be made to flourish. Hence internal democratization was a prerequisite for the successful integration of Switzerland, Germany, Italy, Canada or the United States; but close "international" ties among political parties, trade associations, labor unions, religious organizations and the like are essential for larger regional integration. Put another way, the conditions and consequences associated with democracy and pluralism in modern western society emerge as crucial elements in the process of international integration.

"Take off," a concept adapted from the theoretical literature on economic development, is a central point in this explanation of growing regional unity. Whenever a given doctrine associated with integration has been adopted by a politically crucial élite as its own and thus lifted from advocacy initially confined to literary and philosophical circles, integration has acquired a momentum of its own; it has "taken off." Under what conditions does this happen historically? The Princeton authors argue that it happened in the cases they studied whenever a young generation developed aims implying a "new way of life" (e.g. the attainment of individual freedom and civil liberties) whose realization was thought to depend on a revolutionary change in established governmental institutions and on similar action by like-minded groups in neighboring states. Often such visions include claims for new governmental services which cannot, for administrative and ideological reasons, be satisfied by the established structure. Naturally such developments imply the prevalence of mutually compatible images among the internationally allied élites, the complementarity of values, a skill for compromise and for de-emphasizing issues which might strain the alliance. The use of force is more often an obstacle than an aid and the movement profits if its leaders de-emphasize integration for its own sake and present it merely as a means to other, more immediately desired, ends.

Such are the general findings applicable to regional integration, irrespective of institutional refinements. For "amalgamated" security-communities, the authors also argue that certain additional "essential" requirements could be isolated. Some of the initial expectations of élites—though by no means all—have to be satisfied to anchor the union. Some concrete "bonuses" may have to be paid to "persuade" hesitant élites to identify themselves with the union, usually specific financial or economic rewards. Administrative and economic growth in the core area must continue in order not to disappoint initial expectations. Leadership groups must continue to practice skill in de-emphasizing divisive values and in stressing common aspirations, in advancing successful mutual prediction of behavior patterns among élites and to facilitate easy interchange in group and personal roles in common tasks. And a generous range of all kinds of interpersonal, inter-group and international transactions (mail, trade, meetings, etc.) must continue to multiply non-national contacts, eventually implying a larger measure of institutional standardization.

As for essential requirements for successful "pluralistic" security-communities the authors stress merely the need for compatibility among the major value systems involved, the attendant capacity to receive, understand and sympathetically deal with demands of allied governments and élites —mutual responsiveness—and the need for successful mutual predictions of behavior patterns. Diplomacy by *fait accompli,* shifts in policy without consultation, unilateral threats and warnings are all incompatible with this requirement for successful regional growth among states retaining their independence.

These conclusions were drawn from historical cases outside the basic social context in which we live. The revolution in weapons technology making possible total war with a minimum of manpower had not occurred. Involvement in all corners of the globe for most of the participating units was less pronounced. The world was not divided into warring camps in disagreement on almost every aspect of life and thought. The industrial revolution had not yet affected equally all the states in question. Mass democracy and mass participation in politics was only a factor at the very end of the historical period under study and the concern with the welfare state was still to come. The "mass man" had not yet been discovered as an important political figure and the refinements of manipulation associated with totalitarian government were confined to the literature of political philosophers. In view of the difference in variables governing the Princeton cases and our own period, can we assume the validity of the conclusions for the study of regionalism in our time? For instance the Princeton authors note *inter alia* that unions based on initially non-political aims do not necessarily lead to political security-communities, thus throwing some doubt on the Mitrany thesis of functional international organization leading to peace and order; elsewhere they affirm that the existence of an external military threat may be a helpful condition to aid in regional integration, but that it is certainly not essential. If these conclusions apply to our own era, much of the logic underlying contemporary regional organizations and efforts seems misapplied if not fallacious. Without arguing dogmatically that the presence of the variables just listed *must* beget different conclusions, I suggest that the difference in context is sufficiently striking to make checking of these conclusions a necessity in the contemporary setting.

III

In our effort to check these historically derived findings in the context of contemporary efforts at regional integration it is first essential to raise a number of methodological points. One of these refers to the problem of *time.* When must mutual responsiveness among the interacting élites and actors come into existence? Before, during or after the onset of integrating relations? When must core area capability be well developed, before or during the "take off" period? Is an increasing flow of mail, trade, migration and personal contacts the cause or the result of integration? I submit that the question of *when* these conditions are thought to come about is vital when we seek to set up a rigorous conceptual scheme to explain the causes of integration. Especially in relation to indicators hinging on social communication we must know whether the transactions measured prevail among the élites to be integrated before the process starts or whether they come about as a result of events which characterize the region after the process has gone on for some years. If the latter is the case, we have merely defined an already functioning political community in terms of communications theory but we have not explained the steps through which it had to proceed before getting there.

Another fundamental question refers to the hierarchical *level* at which social action relating to integration is thought to take place. Does successful mutual responsiveness, communication, and the de-emphasis of divisive issues rest on mass participation in politics or on its minimization? Are numerically small groups of economic, industrial, administrative and military élites the crucial actors, or must the analytical focus be put on political parties and their constituencies? What is the role of doctrine, ideology, and mere issue-oriented pragmatic rationality in the inter-group contacts relating to integration?

Neither the issue of time nor of level is clearly isolated in the causative scheme implicit in the Princeton study. "Process" must be clearly differentiated from "background conditions" on the one hand, and from "consequent conditions" on the other. Unless this is done—and the task of differentiation would clearly imply some arbitrariness in view of the dynamic nature of the social data—we may forego the opportunity to use the study of regionalism as a device to learn something about the formation of larger political communities.

In one sense these problems of analytical method are mirrored in the dichotomy patent in the field of international organization between the existence of ambitious institutional structures and the relative absence of any obvious integrative consequences flowing from them. Are such structures the cause or a result of integration, or perhaps even unrelated to the process? Do they represent consensus at some elusive élite level or do they correspond to mass aspirations? Are they one of the background conditions from which community may develop, do they channel the process or are they irrelevant to this whole range of inquiry?

. . . .

IV

In identifying the background factors found to be directly related to continental European economic integration, emphasis will be focused on those ideologies, attitudes and expectations of articulate organized groups which prevailed between the end of World War II and 1950, the date of the first official federative proposal, Schuman's call for the European Coal and Steel Community (ECSC). Expectations will include "identical" aims, implying identical demands based on identical reasoning patterns regardless of the nationality of the group. These will be contrasted with "converging" expectations, i.e. aims based on a reasoning pattern peculiar to a given national group but sufficiently similar in aim to result in support for integrative proposals. Converging expectations make for regional unity instrumental in nature rather than being based on principle. Identical and converging expectations must finally be contrasted with aims of groups opposed to integration.

Thus we find that certain voices in all countries concerned advocated closer unity or federation because division of Europe was held responsible for military, cultural and political weakness, dependence on the United States, inferiority to the Soviet Union, and therefore inability to deal with internal aspects of the Communist threat to established and generally held European values. The same voices tended to defend a "third force" doctrine for a future United Europe and to preach economic revival through a regeneration of competition in a larger continental market, including the abolition of trade barriers and the destruction of cartels. Still others, sometimes identical with the groups just summarized and sometimes not, equated a United Europe with a general economic, social and cultural regeneration, achieving a new synthesis beyond the old issues of national hatreds, wars and class conflict.

These expectations were identical throughout the Continent. They were defended by the dedicated Federalists, for the most part intellectuals and professional people *not* overlapping with practical politics, industry, labor, agriculture or other entrenched élite groups. Among the political parties, only certain Christian-Democrats and a few Socialists subscribed to these ideas, including some Christian-Democrats but no Socialists in leading positions. It is fair to say that identical expectations united only certain politically peripheral persons. While they included the organized Federalists of all religious and secular persuasions it cannot be demonstrated that these people influenced the actual course of integration unless—as in the case of Adenauer, Schuman, Monnet, De Gasperi, Beyen and Pella—they also were active as politicians and negotiators.

Background conditions were otherwise when we focus on converging expectations. Here we find that German trade associations, trade unions and political parties—except the SPD—were one in favoring economic unification *if* this were the means for regaining German economic equality, i.e. if remaining allied occupation controls were removed simultaneously, including the ban on cartels. But we also find certain French trade associations, trade unions and the political parties of the Center and Moderate Right embracing economic federalism as a means for controlling an economically resurgent Germany, maintain in force allied decartellisation and deconcentration measures under "European" auspices, and assure for French industry non-discriminatory access to German coke and the southern German export market. All non-Marxist Italian parties and trade unions favored closer European unity because they saw in it the possibility for capital imports, unhampered exports of goods which could find a ready foreign market and above all the right for Italian workers to migrate. The general argument of freer trade appealed to organized business in Belgium, Holland and Luxembourg, but a very specific economic "bonus" was necessary to create a pro-integration bias among certain Belgian and Italian industrialists who feared extinction in a free larger market.

Opposition to economic federalism characterized trade associations convinced that without the protection of national tariffs and subsidies they would decline. It also applied to right-wing political parties (the RPF in France) whose attachment to the militarily independent national state is an important ideological tenet and to left-wing parties (the SPD and many of the Belgian Socialists) who saw in economic federalism merely a regionally cartellised but otherwise unreformed capitalism, whose impact on the national working class and national welfare was thought to be harmful. Opposition also characterized all major groups in industry, agriculture and politics in Great Britain for reasons too well known to require recapitulation.

The major conclusion on background expectations is one which the Princeton authors also discovered: a marked fragmentation in national attitudes prior to the initiation of the process of integration. Great Britain showed little disunity and hence non-participation in ECSC negotiations was not very controversial.

Fragmentation into opposing group opinions in each nation facilitated the *eventual* establishment of close links on a regional basis of communication among ideologically allied political and economic élites. In contrast to the Princeton findings, however, it must be stated that with the exception of the close ties among a few important Christian-Democratic politicians, the growth of this now striking communications network was the *result* of the establishment of federal institutions and not its cause. Contacts among trade unionists, industrialists, administrators and parliamentarians certainly existed before 1950; but they were lacking in intensity, in concrete programs, in consensus and in results. The background requirement of inter-élite responsiveness, of mutuality of values and willingness to de-emphasize clashing aspirations was in evidence only among a very narrow group of administrators and certain key politicians; it was not then a general phenomenon of regional inter-group relations.

My findings support the argument that the existence of a "core area" can be a vital consideration in regional unification. However, in the European context this meant a desire to unify in order to *control* such an area—the Ruhr—not to rely on it. On the other hand, many supporters of unification regarded Great Britain as a sympathetic core area around which unity should develop; their disappointment in the British refusal to accept this role was important in defeating EDC, but not in stopping regional integration in the economic field.

Nor do my findings support another key conclusion of the Princeton authors, the notion of the "new way of life." If the "new way of life" demanded by the younger generation is specified as a dedication to regional welfare economics, cultural regeneration and political mediation between Moscow and Washington, such a strand of thought can indeed be isolated among the background conditions surrounding European economic federation. However, it is typical of the "identical" demand patterns discussed above and therefore not consistently applicable to the policy-making élites. On the contrary, these seem often to have embraced unity as a device to protect an "old" way of life. If the "new" way be identified merely as a dissatisfaction with European international relations of the inter-war variety, however, then it becomes an important background factor, typical, however, of the old as well as the new generation.

These conditions and attitudes prevailing before 1950 clearly explain why Schuman's proposal for a federal approach to economic unity was eventually adopted: in view of the dominant national fragmentation of aspirations the scheme was a direct way to realize a new dispensation for a few, and instrumental toward achieving some very concrete and immediate economic benefits to many others. A definite change, or a "take off" did not take place until after the actual institutions of ECSC had been established. I stress, therefore, that new modes of conduct and new channels of communication among élites did not develop until *after* the institutional constitutive act. It was then that a closer rapport among trade unions, trade associations, political parties and senior civil servants began to develop, a process which eventually "spilled over" from the realm of coal and steel to the field of general economic unification—or the Common Market (EEC)—and acquired an independent momentum perhaps in 1955.[6]

The new institutions were called upon to realize the benefits expected of a common market restricted to coal and steel while being fully cognizant of the economic impossibility of acting meaningfully unless such related areas as foreign trade, taxes, wages, monetary policy and counter-cyclical measures were also subject to regional regulation. In this setting each

---

[6] The briefest, and yet accurate, descriptions of the ECSC and EEC Treaty rules are to be found in John Goormaghtigh, "European Coal and Steel Community," *International Conciliation* (May 1955), and Serge Hurtig, "The European Common Market," *International Conciliation* (March 1958). The economic issues of the common market are analyzed in Raymond Bertrand, "The European Common Market Proposal," *International Organization,* Vol. X, No. 4 (November 1956) and the political process of negotiation by Miriam Camps, *The European Common Market and Free Trade Area* (Princeton: Center for International Studies, 1957). See also the Economist Intelligence Unit, Ltd., *Britain and Europe* (London, 1957).

nationally organized group began to search for regional allies to aid in the implementation of a program for coal and steel considered beneficial to it. Interest groups coalesced in their efforts to influence the policy of the ECSC High Authority, as did the parliamentarians selected by national legislatures to control the High Authority in the ECSC Common Assembly. More important perhaps in the context of a "pluralistic" security-community, a special set of relations and a new code of conduct came to characterize the Council of Ministers and the associated national administrators, the organ to which the High Authority often deferred and which came to exercise the fundamental decision-making role in the expansive aspects of ECSC. Unlike the pattern in OEEC and other intergovernmental organizations, a presumption developed toward reaching consensus at a higher level of central action than that favored by the least federally minded member government. This resulted in progressive intergovernmental compromise toward more and more central economic planning, entrusted often to the High Authority. Eventually the process produced the Messina Conference of June 1955 and the Brussels Conference of Experts appointed to draft the EEC and Euratom agreements.

It could be argued, then, that a "take off" mentality did develop when significant decision-makers and élites realized that more economic benefits than sacrifices would develop as a result of further federal unity, and when they sought to influence the central institutions accordingly. The "take off" became an operational reality when groups previously indifferent or hostile toward integration turned to the advocacy of further unity by way of EEC, on the basis of their experience in ECSC institutions and with the effects of ECSC economic policy.

Successful "take off" is a manifestation of a previously successful "spill over": demands and expectations for further integrating measures are voiced as a result of performance in previously federated spheres of governmental activity. Performance is held inadequate because of an insufficient grant of powers or timid policy on the part of central authorities; hence the claim for new federal powers to achieve better performance is a direct outgrowth of the earlier institutional system and the realignment of group expectations produced through it. It becomes of the essence for the accurate statement of a regional process of political integration to state these realignments.

National trade associations affected by the initially created federal institutions may in principle persist in the positions analyzed in our discussion of the pre-federal background, but experience with European groups indicates that they adapt to new rules by changing policies, if not aims. Thus the initially anti-ECSC Belgian collieries became firm supporters of the federal authorities merely because they expected a more sympathtic treatment from them than from their national government. Other trade associations initially hostile become conditional supporters of the new system as they realize that the supranational authorities may be instrumental in achieving certain of their aims. This is illustrated by the eagerness of the French steel and coal industries to use ECSC for purposes of sustaining cheaper access to German coke and for increasing German production costs by "equalizing" social security and wage payments. Still others subscribed to the free market implications of the ECSC Treaty but opposed any granting of manipulative or planning powers to the supranational organs. Five years later such groups—for instance the German, Belgian and Dutch steel industries—still favor the same principles but exert themselves politically to minimize public regulation of the free market, especially in opposing anti-trust and anti-cartel measures. Their commitment to this political action compels them to work through the federal authorities. As for a "spill over," these groups favored EEC if it created a general free market but opposed strong central institutions to assert political control over it. Trade associations opposed to the continuation of economic integration, i.e. the adding of EEC to ECSC, were easily identified as the industries dependent on national protection, just as in 1950; in France and Italy this included the bulk of medium and small-sized manufacturing establishments and the major national trade associations.

National trade associations experience the necessity to combine supranationally in order to achieve common political goals once the new institutions are installed. While such combinations have occurred on a massive scale in Europe since 1950, there is little evidence that the allied industrialists are consistently receptive to each other's needs, expectations and values. Compromise occurs rarely; divisive aspirations are not usually de-emphasized successfully by leaders who emerge with a tacit mediating role; subordination of nationally-defined economic interests to common regional positions is not observable among industrialists after five years of experience in ECSC. The supranational alliances, then, remain *ad hoc* groupings for immediate tactical advantage. However, as EEC illustrates, integration is proceeding rapidly just the same.

But the picture is quite the reverse in the ranks of trade unions. All non-communist unions were in favor of economic integration in 1950, though with varying degrees of enthusiasm and by no means unconditionally. One of the conditions was the dedication of the federal institutions to direct measures for raising living and working standards. As ECSC in practice devoted little effort to this aim the unions were compelled to fashion themselves into a more potent political force in order to lobby more effectively; and in the process they had to achieve agreement on their aims. They successfully de-emphasized divisive aspirations on price policy, cartels, and migration by stressing the aims which unite them: regional collective bargaining for the standardization first of fringe benefits and eventually of wages and hours. Labor's radical supranational realignment and unity was obtained partly as a result of national economic demands pressing for a supranational equalization of cost factors and partly through the astute mediating role of certain key officials. Unlike the industrialists, the trade unionists display great mutual responsiveness and a good deal of role interchangeability in successfully combining alternating national leadership with consistent supranational compromise on common interests. What is more striking still, it can be easily demonstrated that these features developed rapidly over time and received a further decisive stimulus with the inauguration of EEC.

The process of integration since the debut of ECSC seems to have affected key political parties quite unevenly. The Christian-Democrats did not change in their unswerving support for integration. But about half of the Radicals in France abandoned their former instrumental and conditional support for economic federalism as their fear of Germany grew and their insistence on a French "national solution" hardened. On the other hand, many of the Moderates in France saw even more instrumental benefits in continuing integration than had been apparent in 1950; they supported EEC and even the expansion of ECSC powers—always on the assumption that certain French interests would thereby be favored. The German Liberals, similarly, concluded that growing unity among the Six is an obstacle to German reunification and therefore voted against EEC after having favored ECSC—for anti-allied reasons. The striking changes, however, occurred in Socialist ranks. The SPD maintained its opposition to ECSC until 1954 and switched thereafter to become one of the most consistent and forceful advocates of a regional planned economy functioning through democratic federal institutions. The SFIO, after overcoming its division on the EDC issue, now takes the same position, as does the Belgian Socialist Party which was split on ECSC and EDC. Finally the Nenni Socialists in Italy, who had opposed all European unity efforts, in 1956 aligned themselves with the, by then, general continental socialist position.

Doctrinal consensus on a trans-national basis has developed significantly as a result of activities in the ECSC Common Assembly (since 1958 the European Parliamentary Assembly, with control functions over ECSC, EEC and Euratom). Largely as a result of the increased opportunities to criticize meaningfully and continuously the activities of a true administrative agency, the Socialist deputies of six nationalities began to function as a supranational political party, showing a consistent record of successful internal compromise, deference to each other's wishes, alternating leadership and willingness to de-emphasize issues on which a unanimously endorsed doctrine proved unobtainable. Agreement reached by way of supranational activity proved highly significant in begetting the changed socialist positions in the home legislatures. Within the limits of the technical issues so far raised in the context of economic unification, the supranational group of Christian-Democratic deputies shows less doctrinal unity but functions smoothly as a general support for any "European" policy, exercising a role analogous to a national "government" party whereas the Socialists tend to act as the "loyal opposition." The Liberal Group shows no such unity and is rarely cohesive on concrete policy issues. Nevertheless, all three groups have developed into a permanent parliamentary élite conversant with the problems of integration and respected as such in their home legislatures. Again, however, this increase in trans-national communication and national prestige occurred *as a result* of the institutionalization of democratic parliamentary control functions at the regional level.

Realignments among governments are less patent. In essence, the positions of the three Benelux governments and of Italy are unchanged as compared to 1950: they still favor a maximum of economic unification and the creation of a sufficiently powerful federal political structure to administer the rules of the common market and implement its welfare objectives. Many statesmen in these four countries are frank to admit that they see in economic federalism the precursor to a full political union. These positions were expressed uniformly in the negotiations which resulted in the EEC and Euratom Treaties.

Things are otherwise in Germany and France. In 1950 these two governments agreed in favoring a maximum of political federalism for ECSC and in a minimization of intergovernmental features. During the EEC negotiations, there was a tendency for the German negotiators to minimize institutions for the common market and to oppose the insertion of provisions facilitating economic planning. The French by contrast were concerned mostly with minimizing the federal aspect of EEC so as to permit them to continue unilateral policies inconsistent with the EEC rules. However, the fact that an agreement was reached which subordinates national demands for the relaxation of the rules to the consent of EEC organs indicates that the degree of mutual responsiveness in these intergovernmental dealings was extraordinarily high. But it also illustrates the general finding on the process of integration that once governments have committed themselves —for whatever reasons—to certain common measures of fundamental importance to the daily lives of their entire citizenry they can resolve future problems of implementing the agreement only by means of further delegation of power to the center. This "administrative spill over" is an essential consequence of initial acts of integration in a crucial policy sector. Withdrawal from its implications is not possible—as in the case of NATO— when the external stimulant changes. Since the range of issues which gave rise to the initial step is woven completely into the contemporary preoccupation with welfare, withdrawal would imply a sacrifice of economic advantage —a step not taken lightly by elected politicians.

Given the background conditions we specified, given the initial act of institutional unification based on identical and converging aims and expectations, a realignment of political forces calculated by the actors on the basis of normal political expediency takes place. This realignment will result in the intensification of growth toward a regional political community *if the task of the center is expanded*. But the story of why the supranational task was expanded significantly in Europe since 1950 again confirms the earlier finding, stressed equally by the Princeton study, that demand for increased regional activity is based essentially on instrumental motives and only rarely on principle. If enough task expansion occurs the eventual condition characterizing the region will be a federal or unitary state, or a "pluralistic" institutional setting in which central decisions of ministerial organs are always implemented because there is no meaningful alternative to them. The lessons derived from the analysis of the process leading toward task expansion can now be summarized:

1. Groups subject to a process of integration are not uniformly responsive to each other's claims even though the institutional pressures are such as to make concerted supranational action politically reasonable and practically desired by most.
2. In the modern European setting, groups in the past exposed to active international value sharing find it easier to achieve this responsiveness. In practice, this has meant Socialist and Catholic labor and political groups.
3. Government negotiators and high civil servants working in isolation from political pressures and democratic accountability achieve mutual responsiveness more readily than groups resting on mass support.
4. Despite initial acts of integration, continuing rewards must be held out to participating groups in order not to alienate them. For labor this has meant the promise of an active welfare policy under EEC; for the French conservatives it has meant the "Europeanization" of investment programs in French Africa and the temporary waiving of some common market rules under EEC as applied in France; for Italy it called for the creation of the "European Bank"; for French and Belgian industrialists it resulted in the promise of some measures for the "equalization" of costs of production through higher social security contributions in Holland and Germany.
5. The contemporary process of integration need not include dedication to and inter-élite agreement on a "new way of life." On the contrary, it is my conclusion that integration is advocated as a means to defend some cherished aspect of an established way of life, even though this "way" may be transformed willy-nilly by the consequences of the integration process.

. . . .

Whether because of growing positive expectations of the new central institutions or because of the negative aim seeking to block institutional action at the center, the net result of the group realignment is an enhanced role for the center. The tendencies here outlined imply that all important groups are influenced in this fashion, that some opposition to integration is reconciled by its benefits while groups who continue to question central policy do so in the spirit of loyal opposition. This is the pattern uncovered in the five-year experience of ECSC. Whether it will prevail also under EEC is open to some doubt. . . . We must remember . . . that so far peasants, small retail businesses, artisans and family-size manufacturing establishments have remained unaffected by the progress of economic unification. It is these groups which furnish the bulk of the authoritarian and fascist constituency in Western Europe, utilizing appeals to exclusive national symbols and often rejecting supranational sharing of values on principle. Whether transitional economic protection and subsidies will suffice to woo these members of Europe's flourishing middle-class movements into the realignment pattern is by no means certain.

V

Our discussion shows that significant differences in background conditions, in the constituents of the process, in the kind and manner of élite participation can be discovered in the analysis of community formation at the regional level, depending on the historical setting and the functional preoccupation of the decision-makers. Lessons derived from pre-contemporary social contexts do not automatically apply to regional organizations now functioning and findings derived from NATO, for instance, cannot be automatically carried over into organizations dedicated to a different kind of task even when they function in the same cultural and time setting. In addition to the cultural and functional differentials between regional organizations, we must bear in mind marked structural variations. Does the integrative impact produced by inter-governmental organizations compare favorably with the role of various kinds of supranational, federal or confederate arrangements? To shed further light on these problems, the study of regionalism must be so generalized as to take account of the cultural, the functional and the structural variants in the contexts to be examined.

One approach to the study of regional integration in non-western settings is to focus on the relation of existing regional institutions and legal rules to the underlying social structure. Past and present findings in the European context agree in stressing the importance of fluid social relations, fragmentation of opinion and groups, widening of élites horizontally and vertically as important background conditions for integration. Do similar conditions exist in the Western Hemisphere setting, in the Arab world, in Southeast Asia, in the Caribbean? In all these regions international institutions of a consultative nature exist; but do they reflect merely the momentary aims of governments or are they tied to some basic social process whose nature could be studied by using the analogy of the European and Atlantic setting, at least as a point of departure? [7]

---

[7] Research hypotheses on differences and similarities in political behavior among western and non-western systems are developed by G. McT. Kahin, G. Pauker, and L. W. Pye, "Comparative Politics of Non-Western Countries," *American Political Science Review,* Vol. XLIX, No. 4 (December 1955). I consider many of the variables discussed there as applicable to work on international organizations. The same is true of hypotheses and research designs put forward by comparative politics specialists concerned with western systems. See G. A. Almond, T. Cole, and Roy Macridis, "A Suggested Research Strategy in Western European Government and Politics," *ibid.* Also Gabriel A. Almond, "Comparative Political Systems," *The Journal of Politics,* Vol. 18 (1956).

Existing institutions could serve a further research purpose. Our European lesson drives home the potential role of institutional forces in rechannelling and realigning previous group loyalties and expectations. Have OAS bodies, SEATO meetings, Arab League conferences and the like had similar consequences; or, since the answer is probably negative, why have no such consequences come about? The answer could reveal more information about the nature of background conditions in non-western settings as well as lead to insights on the relation between functional orientation and integrating results in regions other than the industrial-democratic setting analyzed thus far.

For that matter, the differences in integrating results observable from the work of economic organizations with slightly different functional missions but operating in the same region are not yet satisfactorily explained. Why did ECSC lead to EEC and Euratom, and therefore to greatly accelerated integration and why did OEEC and EPU, operating in the same context but with different powers and larger memberships, fail to expand? Why is it possible to argue that integration advances more rapidly as a result of decisions made in private by senior civil servants in the ECSC/EEC framework but that in OEEC the same technique yields no parallel consequences? [8] It might be suggested that all members of ECSC/EEC are marked by internal fragmentation and political movements looking for new solutions to old problems, whereas Britain and Scandinavia among the OEEC members are less plagued by this internal situation; but it would require more rigorous research into OEEC decision-making to substantiate this hypothesis.

The social background of the Arab effort at regional unity holds out fascinating questions for studies of this kind. It is here that the demand for a new way of life on the part of the younger generation might be demonstrated to be a background condition and a causative factor in the process of advancing *and* retarding regional political unity. Did the Arab League fail to produce unity because it was based on the negative consensus of groups identified with the status quo? Is Nasserism a more potent stimulus to unification because it self-consciously identifies itself with a new way of life, castigating the foreigner and promising domestic abundance? Further, the Arab cultural heritage might offer insights into patterns of achieving mutual responsiveness among élites which have no exact counterpart in the western setting.[9] But systematic research into regional decision-

[8] With very few exceptions, all discussions of OEEC are either institutional or economic in scope and intent. Some indications of political process may be gleaned from Robert Marjolin, *Europe and the United States in the World Economy* (Duke University Press, 1954); Lincoln Gordon, "The Organization for European Economic Cooperation," *International Organization,* Vol. X, No. 1 (February 1956); René Sergent, "Schritt für Schritt zum Gemeinsamen Markt," *Europa* (October 1955).

[9] To my knowledge, no discussions of political processes in the Arab regional organizations have appeared in English. Much information, however, can be gained from the diplomatic record alone. See T. R. Little, "The Arab League: A Reassess-

making would be required before adequate answers become available.

In the work of the Organization of American States and its predecessor bodies the notion of the core area might be subjected to a rigorous non-European test. To what extent did inter-American cooperation receive encouragement from the help and sympathy which the Colossus of the North might mobilize? But it might also be asked to what extent the OAS has its Latin raison d'être in a desire to achieve security *against* the United States by enmeshing the Colossus in a firm network of Latin-inspired legal obligations and institutional safeguards. In short, systematic research into the expectations entertained by Latin American élites with respect to the OAS might reveal an anti-American mutual responsiveness pattern which at the same time would imply a number of non-integrative consequences for the work of the OAS. But if this can be substantiated in the legal, social and economic aspects of the OAS program, would it explain the singular success of OAS efforts at maintaining collective security in the Western Hemisphere? In all likelihood a different range of factors would explain this strikingly integrative aspect of regional activity.[10]

Mutual responsiveness and the compatibility of élite aims could also be submitted to rigorous analysis in the study of SEATO and of the Baghdad Pact. Is fear of the communist enemy the unifying factor in these alliances? Is it the hope for rewards unilaterally proffered by the United States in the realm of military and economic aid? Or is it some local issue, say Kashmir, which bears no intrinsic relation to the basic function of the alliance? A study of the processes of compromising these aims in a setting of culturally heterogeneous members might prove instructive.

Generally shared expectations of economic gain are constituents of the process of integration found to recur with monotonous regularity. However, the degree of regional cohesion obtained through this expectation seems to vary sharply. True, in the EEC/ECSC setting it proved dominant and successful. The Princeton authors note that the disappointment of such expectations in the NATO framework may be partly responsible for the slow-down in Atlantic integration. But why did such expectations fail to yield a regional economic planning structure in the setting of the Colombo Plan? Why is their presence in the OAS the subject of many words but of little action? Why have essentially military pacts like SEATO stressed economic aid and development more than armaments? The uniformity of economic expectations and policies to meet them varies with the regional

ment," *Middle East Journal* (Spring 1956); Paul Seabury, "The League of Arab States: Debacle of a Regional Arrangement," *International Organization* (November 1949); B. Y. Boutros-Ghali, "The Arab League," *International Conciliation* (May 1954).

[10] Very little discussion of political processes in the OAS, as distinguished from institutional analyses and descriptions of actions in specific crises, is available. See, however, A. P. Whitaker, *The Western Hemisphere Idea* (Ithaca: Cornell University Press, 1954), and Martin B. Travis, Jr., "The Organization of American States: A Guide to the Future," *Western Political Quarterly*, Vol. X, No. 2 (September 1957).

setting and the functional preoccupation of the members, factors which themselves may be traced back to underlying conditions of social organization and communication.

Whatever the answers may be, they compel renewed attention to the phenomenon of regionalism as a fixed feature of our time. And to obtain them, there is no alternative to the systematic study of regional integration, combining institutional analysis with the study of political process. In doing so we may hit a rich lode of materials which might explain how nations cease to be nations, how they lose the self-consciousness which comes from having lived within the confines of a fixed set of frontiers, or how they develop loyalties extending over a broader geographic area, but which still display the earmarks of nationalism.

4. ARNOLD WOLFERS

The Anglo-American Tradition in Foreign Affairs

Political Theory and International Relations

Nowhere in English-speaking countries would the study of government and politics be considered complete that did not include political theory; in fact, at many universities theory is regarded as the very foundation on which all other aspects of the subject should be made to rest. This does not hold true, however, for the study of international politics. What a student of international relations may happen to learn about political thinkers of earlier centuries usually comes to him from outside the program of his specialty, and if he takes a course in political theory he is not likely to hear much about earlier thought on foreign policy.[1]

Reprinted from Arnold Wolfers and Laurence W. Martin (eds.), *The Anglo-American Tradition in Foreign Affairs,* pp. ix-xxvii, by permission of the Yale University Press.

[1] As far as the literature on international relations is concerned—and the same is true for the teaching in the field—there are exceptions to this rule of silence on political theory. There is Frank M. Russell, *Theories of International Relations* (New York, D. Appleton-Century, 1936), and notably the more recent book of readings by Hans J. Morgenthau and Kenneth W. Thompson, *Principles and Problems of International Politics* (New York, Alfred A. Knopf, 1950). These authors have chosen their material with a view to a series of topical subjects and have included both contemporary and earlier authors, Continental as well as English and American writers, statesmen as well as philosophers. The present volume [to which this selection is the introduction: ed.], on the other hand, is a selection of the contributions well known English and American philosophers and "statesmen-philosophers" have made to the theory of international politics in the four centuries between 1516 and 1919.

A cleavage exists between international relations and political theory, and it is a two-way affair. If specialists in international politics with rare exceptions have neglected political theory, the political theorists in turn, departing from older tradition, have paid little attention to what the thinkers of the past—Machiavelli not always excepted—have had to say on international relations. From reading the current histories of political doctrine, particularly as they deal with the political and moral philosophers representing the Anglo-American tradition, one might be led to believe that these thinkers had been interested in domestic problems exclusively.

Such mutual neglect, if that is what it should be called, is not a matter of accident. It has deep roots in the political experience of England and the United States and in the way this experience has been intellectually absorbed. The question today, however, is whether the reasons which explain this divorce between the two fields also justify its continuation; if they do not, the early "remarriage" which this book is meant to promote may commend itself to both parties.

As is well known, international relations as a special field of study made its appearance on the academic scene only after the close of World War I. It came as a fruit of Wilsonian idealism and the founding of the League of Nations. On the grounds that a "new era" had been ushered in and that the League if properly used and implemented would mark the end of European power politics, the study of international relations was meant to promote the cause of peace and international cooperation by showing how the new peace machinery should be used and developed. It was centered, therefore, on the "ought" of a better future order rather than on the "is" and "was" of the sorry conditions to which policy makers and their advisors had traditionally addressed themselves. Under these circumstances only those earlier thinkers deserved to be studied who, like Sully, Kant, Penn, or Bentham, had proposed schemes of international organization for peace and could thus qualify as precursors of the new prophets.

When in the 1930's disillusionment and a sharp reaction against this Wilsonian approach set in, the new realist school of thought, dominant today in academic circles, had reasons of a different kind for paying no attention to the doctrines of the past. The effort was now directed toward building up an empirical or causal science of international politics. Because its subject was now to be the "is" and "was" rather than the "ought" of external state behavior, the new program left even less incentive for concern with what was believed to be the exclusively normative outlook of political and moral philosophers of the past, Machiavelli alone being placed in a different category. Even if it had been realized that past thinkers on the subject had been anything but inarticulate about what they considered to be the actual workings of the state-system, their observations and generalizations on this aspect of the subject would probably have been discounted because of their lack of scientific methodology.

As in the 1930's, the climate of thought is undergoing another important change today, this time in a direction that may prove far more favorable to the study of political doctrine. It is no longer so confidently expected that an empirical science of international politics can meet all our needs; with new and growing interest in the theoretical bases of scientific work in this field, attention is being drawn to normative thought and philosophical speculation. Moreover, doubts have arisen whether new methods of investigation really allow the political scientist of today to dispense with such traditional tools as impressionistic observation, historical analogy, and common sense judgment, on which through the ages his predecessors relied for the validation of their assertions. Thus the road is being opened for a new appreciation of earlier contributions to the knowledge of international affairs.

The non-normative aspects of earlier thinking on the subject deserve to be emphasized first because they are less obvious. Much of the time the political philosophers of the past were preoccupied with the way statesmen and nations should behave toward each other. Yet they could not have felt justified in offering advice on rules to be followed had they not believed that they possessed knowledge of what would happen if their advice were accepted. This means, then, that some causal theorizing, however inadequate, was at least implicit in much of their normative effort. Thus Godwin states views about the way nations actually behave by declaring it "an improbable supposition" to conceive of a nation being attacked "so long as its own conduct is sober, acceptable and moderate." Hamilton's admonition not to continue wars to the point of the enemy's surrender if compromise should be possible, advice that deserves to be taken seriously in our time, rests on the explicit assertion that such surrender will cause the subsequent peace to be less secure. Some theorists quoted in this volume will be found to have made explicit propositions concerning some such cause and effect relationships; others have made them by implication. Hume's chapter on the balance of power offers a good illustration of a study directed primarily at empirical rather than normative theory. While Hume can be said to imply that governments should aim at balanced power in the world, his reasoning is based on generalizations concerning the way states as a rule have behaved in the past and are likely to behave in the future, the emphasis being on factors that induce them to push beyond the point of equilibrium. The bulk of the discussion of international relations by both Hobbes and Locke is of a similar kind. Because it serves them merely as an illustration of the state of nature, it is clearly directed toward a generalized description of what to them seemed to be the way sovereigns behave toward each other in fact; it was not intended as advice in matters of foreign policy.

Without any doubt, most of the sweeping generalizations that run through the writings of the political philosophers of the past are open to severe criticism. They are often crude, in many cases patently prejudiced, and as a rule presented without even the claim of meticulous verification. Hobbes "proves" to his own satisfaction that war coalitions cannot last beyond victory—a shrewd and prophetic hunch—by deducing his conclusion from premises he can hardly be said to have substantiated. Neither he nor others have been able to prove that men and nations are by nature enemies of one another and can therefore cooperate only as long as they are threatened by a common foe. Also from a scientific point of view, there is not one theorist or philosopher who cannot be blamed for a lack of clearly stated hypotheses and for the failure to validate them by means less open to prejudice than mere random experience and arbitrary choice of historical illustrations.

Yet before turning away contemptuously from the inadequate work of his predecessors, the social scientist of today who is struggling with the problems of international relations should ask himself how much better he is able to validate the hunches on which he is forced to base himself. He would have to remain within a narrow circle of rather marginal problems if he excluded all but scientifically unimpeachable investigations, particularly of the controlled-experiment or quantitative kind. For example, significant scientific work has been undertaken by psychologists and sociologists in recent years on the effects of insecurity and frustration on human behavior, some of it applicable to the behavior of nations. However, a political scientist called upon to evaluate the effects on foreign policy of frustration suffered by a nation in the wake of a punitive peace settlement, or of feelings of insecurity arising out of recollections of past invasions, while he would hardly refuse to express a scholarly opinion on the ground that there is no way open to him to "prove" his contentions, would have to rely heavily on personal experience and observations to supplement and qualify his tenuous scientific insight. Like the political philosophers before him, then, he would find himself mustering all the evidence which history, personal experience, introspection, common sense, and the gift of logical reasoning put at his disposal. If there is any difference between him and his predecessors—who, like himself, were confronted with such problems as alliance policy, the balancing of power, intervention in the affairs of other countries, and the pursuit of ideological goals—one would hope it might lie in a keener realization of the controversial and tentative nature of his reply, in a greater effort to consider alternative answers, and in a more conscious attempt to remain dispassionate and objective. Sometimes the scientifically minded scholar of today may turn out to be merely more pedantic in his formulations and less afraid of belaboring the obvious. In any case, analyses of national conduct undertaken by men of keen insight into human behavior and wide experience in the affairs of the political world cannot fail to be valuable to anyone seeking to understand what makes the clock tick in international relations. The reflections of the thinkers of the past—quoted in this volume on such matters as the advantages and weaknesses of the balance of power, the peculiarities of insular location, and the dangers of preventive war—are far removed from amateurish guesswork; the arguments as well as the evidence offered to sustain them are, in kind at least, the same as those used today in even the most scholarly debates on the same subjects.

Whether the political philosophers of the past have contributed much or little to empirical theory, the main test of their importance to the student of international relations today must rest on the continued value of their normative thought, which was undoubtedly their chief concern. They were seeking to decide when it is right or wrong for a nation to participate in "other peoples' wars," to interfere in the domestic affairs of others, to keep faith with allies, or to expand into new territory. They were also concerned with what they called the prudence of certain types of action, prudence meaning expediency guided and moderated by morality and wise judgment. To a considerable extent they were expressing value preferences —often couched in the form of "laws of nature"—and inquiring into the consequences which follow when nations fail to act in conformity with these preferences.

More and more it is coming to be appreciated that such moral preferences as well as broad assumptions about man and his motives are an inescapable starting point for even the most strictly empirical enterprise in matters of national behavior. Attempts to escape from this scientific dilemma merely lead to a lack of awareness of one's own presuppositions or to a failure to make them explicit. The very words that are used—self-preservation, aggression, imperialism, national interest—are loaded with emotional connotations, moral judgment, and prescientific assumptions. There might never have been any study of how to outlaw and prevent "aggressive" war had it not been for the tacit assumption that any *status quo* is morally preferable to a resort to international violence. It would make no sense to say or assume that nations must seek power adequate for survival if high value were not placed on the existence of independent nations. No expectations regarding the conduct of nations can be formulated that are not affected by either the optimistic hunch of a Locke, who entertained the belief that "calm reason and conscience" would guide the behavior of most men, or the pessimistic hunch of a Hobbes, to whom man appeared obsessed by fear and greediness. While the pessimist is likely to expect that peace will be maintained only if the power of all nations is held in check by a balance of their respective power, the optimist fears war only at times when the exceptional aggressor nations are not met with the unchallengeable predominance and solidarity of the great majority of peace-loving peoples. In this sense, all students in the field, consciously or unconsciously, belong to schools of moral and philosophical thought.

If this be so, the normative and speculative ideas of the great thinkers of the past are worthy of even more attention than are their clearly impressionistic insights into the realities and laws which explain the actual behavior of nations. Here is a wealth of explicit formulations and judgments concerning most of the problems of moral choice and prudence which plague the thinkers and practitioners of our time. Today there is still heated discussions of the respective values of the general human interest and the particular national interest, as Burke called them, and of the line to be drawn between justifiable and unjustifiable resistance to the demands of others. What this indicates is a search for standards, rational and moral, by which to judge policy—one's own and that of others—and by which to be guided in reaching decisions.

Although it is regrettable that value judgments in the past, as in the present, are often presented with assertions of fact as if there were no fundamental difference between them, the theorists which are included here left no doubt that most of the time they were seeking to guide statesmen and nations in choosing their ends and means with a view to maximizing desirable values or minimizing their sacrifice. If this meant treating the subject of values extensively, as in discussions about justice, weighing values against one another, and bringing them into conscious and discriminating perspective, it was an exercise which no policy science can avoid if it is to be useful.

While the student of international politics has every reason, then, to bridge the gulf which has separated him from political theory, it remains to be asked—remarriage requiring the consent of both sides—whether contemporary teachers of theory or of the history of doctrine may not have equally good reasons to break the silence they have maintained in respect to political matters transcending national boundaries.

Three factors may account for the lack of interest which political theorists are currently showing for anything but domestic government and politics: the first is the persistent impact of what until quite recently could be called the strategic insularity of both the British Isles and the American continent; the second is the striking contrast that exists for both countries between the internal and the external political scene; the third is a difference in the degree of moral opportunity offered by the domestic and the foreign field of political activity.

As long as the relative insular security of Britain and the United States lasted—or was thought to exist—it was possible to conceive of the development of institutions at home as being entirely separate from and independent of the events occurring beyond the frontiers of the nation. Where propinquity rather than isolation was characteristic of the relations between states, as on the Continent of Europe, domestic affairs could hardly be conceived except in interdependence with foreign affairs. In fact, the main emphasis was on the so-called primacy of foreign policy. In sharp contrast to this attitude the insular political theorists could choose to concentrate on internal politics, overlooking or leaving to the tender mercy of others the unsavory problems of international power politics and anarchy. Now that insular security has gone, this justification for aloofness from external problems has vanished too.

The second factor is also a phenomenon peculiar to Britain, the United States, and, in this instance, a few democracies in Western Europe. In these countries domestic political conditions stand in striking contrast to the conditions these nations face in their external relations: the domestic conditions are characterized by order, lawfulness, and peace arising from popular consensus on principles—a consensus so marked that some believe coercion has practically ceased to play a role here; but the external relations continue to be full of bitter struggle, violence, and Machiavellian practices. Obviously, no such contrast is experienced by peoples whose country is the frequent scene of revolution and domestic violence or suffers the cruel terrors of tyranny; to them "civil society," or "order under government," if it is experienced at all, possesses most of the objectionable features we attribute to international anarchy. The sharper the contrast between the domestic and the international scene, the greater, then, will be the inclination to treat the two fields of political activity separately and to overlook the traits they have in common. It is not a happy sign that much of what has been occurring in this century militates against the continued separation of the two fields. For the difference between them has been reduced, even to the observer in countries of democratic orderliness, not primarily because the international arena has taken on new and striking traits of lawfulness and order under government but because tyrannical suppression and persecution as well as revolutionary strife have come to be the order of the day in wide areas of the world. Thus government no longer appears as the safe panacea against the evils of Machiavellian practice or violence that set domestic affairs in sharp and unmistakable contrast to international anarchy. Working to lessen the lack of supranational government, for example in the case of the British Commonwealth, has not prevented close and friendly cooperation within this "anarchical" partnership. It would therefore seem that the two poles of the political continuum, civil society and international anarchy or power politics, are not so far apart in reality as they appeared at times, which suggests that a comprehensive theory of politics, including both foreign and domestic affairs, would make good sense.

This leads to the third, though closely related, factor: the difference in "moral opportunity." During the modern age England and the United States, together with a few Western countries, managed to put their sovereign control of internal affairs to excellent use for the progressive development of institutions of lawful government and civil liberty. This occurred in the course of the same four centuries during which the very existence of national sovereignty produced externally a multistate system with all the conflict, struggle, and war that this implies. Therefore, for political and moral philosophers the internal scene with its opportunity to promote the good life under civil government was as encouraging as the external scene was frustrating. One can hardly wonder that teachers of political theory, in the end, should have come to be interested far more in the way the theorists of the past had helped to solve the problems of government at home than in what they had to say about the comparatively barren and stagnant power politics of the multistate system. The more clearly normative their concern with politics, the more incentive they had to concentrate on the field in which sovereign control gave each people and government, individually, a high degree of power and opportunity to conduct itself according to its own moral precepts. There cannot fail to be a difference in moral opportunity between a realm in which every nation is at the mercy of the acts of others and one in which the course of events is predominantly shaped by its own decision. If there is to be less separation in the treatment of the two realms, the change must come from a growing realization that, after all, the single mind and will of the nation even at home is more fictitious than real and that moral opportunity is not so radically lacking in external politics as some impatient perfectionists of our time, impressed by the horrors of two world wars, are inclined to maintain.

If one may look forward, then, to a growing readiness to draw international relations and political theory closely together—as moral and political philosophers in past centuries were accustomed to do—the question is whether the student of international relations, awakened to this need, would do well to focus his attention, first, on the political thought of men with a particular national background and of a particular historical period.

. . . .

Political theorists writing in periods of multiple sovereignty are of major if not of exclusive interest to the study of international relations; and among them preference will necessarily go to those who since the age of Machiavelli and More were dealing with the behavior of political units similar in most respects to the nation-states of our own day.

This of course does not preclude the possibility that at some future time speculations and observations of medieval thinkers like Saint Augustine, Thomas Aquinas, or Dante will become relevant again in matters of world politics. Even today it is not fantastic to speak of recent changes within the international arena as pointing toward a kind of "new medievalism." The trend would seem to be toward complexities that blur the dividing lines between domestic and foreign policy. We are faced once again with double loyalties and overlapping realms of power—international communism versus nation-state, transnational affinity versus nationalism—as well as with wars like those recently fought in Korea and Indo-China that partake of the character of international and civil war simultaneously. Yet despite these novel developments, which deserve theoretical as well as practical attention, the traditional problems of interstate or intersovereign relations, predominant over the last four centuries, continue to occupy the center of the political stage whenever relations transcending national boundaries come into play. From this it follows that the theories dealing with interstate relations are at the present time most pertinent.

If drastic change has occurred in recent times, it has not taken the form of bringing to a close the modern era of interstate power politics, as many had hoped; it has merely brought to an end the "European Age" of such politics. The character of international relations has not been revolutionized, rendering obsolete earlier thought on these relations. . . .

While it makes sense, therefore, to draw insight primarily from those who have lived to see the modern multistate system at work, the question remains whether English and American thinkers deserve special attention. Obviously, theoretical discussion of international politics has not been the preserve of the English-speaking peoples. In fact, in matters of international relations the works of Continental authors such as Machiavelli, Grotius, Spinoza, and Kant have received much more attention than those of their Anglo-Saxon contemporaries. But the very silence that surrounds the latter provides one good reason for paying special attention to them. There are other, still more cogent, reasons for doing so. . . .

If insular security has been responsible, at least in part, for the divorce between political theory and international relations, it has had yet another and more important effect, this one bearing on the substance of the theory itself. It may be dangerous to lump together into two distinct categories all Anglo-American theorists on the one hand and all Continental theorists on the other, as if agreement within each camp had been the rule. On most points it has not. Yet in one vital respect it would seem permissible to so generalize about the two groups, even at the risk of doing injustice to exceptions.

It would be grossly misleading to suggest that all Continental thought in matters of international politics has been Machiavellian; passionate opposition to the views expressed in Machiavelli's *Prince* was voiced throughout the centuries that followed its publication. Friedrich Meinecke in his book on *Staatsräson,*[2] has given a brilliant account of the Continental debate between Machiavellians and anti-Machiavellians. Yet his discussion of Continental thought on foreign policy justifies the contention that Continental theory centered around the idea of the "necessity of state," which was the core of Machiavelli's argumentation. As the Continental political philosophers saw it, the main problem presented by conditions of multiple sovereignty was that of a deep conflict between morality and *raison d'état.* This was in line with the experience common to all Continental countries which in the face of constant external threats to their national existence believed themselves exposed to the compelling impact of forces beyond their control. The main question as they saw it was whether statesmen and nations were under moral obligation to put up resistance against these "compelling" demands of state necessity. While not all were ready,

[2] Friedrich Meinecke, *Die Idee der Staatsräson* (Munich, 1925). [See the bibliography below for the English version of this volume: ed.]

fatalistically or cynically, to advocate sheer resignation, there was ever present a feeling that nations were puppets in the hands of demonic forces, with little leeway if any to rescue moral values from a sea of tragic necessity.

English and American thought and experience traveled a different road. Even the concepts of necessity of state or reason of state remained foreign to the political philosophers of the English-speaking world. While the Continentals were arguing about the dilemma of statesmen faced by the irreconcilable demands of necessity and morality, English and American thinkers in turn were engaged in a debate about the best way of applying accepted principles of morality to the field of foreign policy. Here the assumption was that statesmen and nations enjoyed considerable freedom to choose the right path in their external conduct as they did in their internal policies. If there was any question about the compatibility of service to the national interest on the one hand and the avoidance of evil on the other, there was surely room, it was held, to decide for the good ends and to pursue them with the least evil of the available means.

This was a philosophy of choice, then, which was bound to be ethical, over against a philosophy of necessity, in which forces beyond moral control were believed to prevail. Choice presupposes freedom to decide what goals to pursue and what means to use in accordance with one's desires and convictions. Not to follow the dictates of moral conviction becomes a matter of guilt and subject to moral judgment. Thus from Thomas More to Woodrow Wilson the recurrent topics of concern and debate were questions such as the right of self-defense and its limits, the right and duty to intervene or not to intervene in the affairs of others, or the extent to which colonial rule and territorial expansion were justified under given circumstances.

Whereas the philosophy of necessity tends to lead to resignation, irresponsibility, or even to the glorification of amorality, the philosophy of choice lends itself to excessive moralism and self-righteousness as if the leeway for choice were unlimited and were of the same dimension for all. What saved most of the theorists of England and America from the pitfalls of such excesses was the care with which they defined to themselves the limitations that the need for national self-preservation—or the duty of self-defense as they might call it—sets on the freedom of choice. Nations were not being advised to sacrifice themselves on the altar of humanity or human liberty or to set the general interest above the national interest of self-preservation. There was no inclination to forget the rules of prudence for the rules of morality, prudence that taught men to use common sense and wise judgment in deciding where the duty of self-defense deserved primacy over other duties. Prudence also meant husbanding one's means and staying within these means even in the pursuit of good causes. There was room for hypocrisy in this argument. If there is a place for moral choice only within the limits set by a prudent concern for self-preservation, it becomes tempting to interpret and thus to justify, as a means of sheer self-preservation, almost anything seemingly reprehensible that one's own country may undertake in foreign affairs. Moreover, if in order to receive moral approbation every resort to violence must be strictly a matter of self-defense, there is much incentive to accuse others of evil aggression when they use force, while justifying one's own acts as purely defensive. On the whole it will be found, however, that the moral philosophers in question, rather than posing as apologists of their nation, placed themselves in the creditable role of serving as the conscience of the nation, reminding statesmen of the dictates of justice and reason.

Also, English and American theorists were not blind to the exceptional freedom of choice which insularity gave to their respective countries. Long before there was any science of geopolitics, More, Bolingbroke, Jefferson, and others praised the privileges offered their countries by the fact of insular location. The advantage, it was suggested, lay in the freedom to remain aloof from many international struggles without a sacrifice of national security, and thus in the chance of keeping one's hands clean of many of the morally more obnoxious vicissitudes of power politics to which others were subjected.

There may be some question whether all the thinkers whose work is presented below can be said to belong to the school of thought described here as typically Anglo-American. About a Locke, Godwin, Jefferson, or Wilson there can be little doubt. They were not merely urging nations to apply the Golden Rule in the conduct of their foreign policy to the maximum compatible with a moderate, prudent policy of self-preservation—they were confident that this was the road to peace and human happiness. But what about men like Hobbes, Bacon, Bolingbroke, Hamilton, or Mahan, usually characterized as conservatives, realists, and pessimists?

. . . .

Even among these representative exponents of what is now often referred to as the power political school of thought we find Bacon asserting that he would "never set politics against ethics," Hobbes maintaining that the state of nature when applied to sovereign nations allows for moderation in war and for self-restraint, Bolingbroke advising against acquisition of territory, and Hamilton agreeing with Locke that even the state of nature is "governed by moral law perceivable by reason" and advocating a foreign policy of moderation and vigilance in the exclusive service of self-preservation. Hume deserves to be mentioned as representing a middle road. He maintains that "the obligation to justice is less strong among nations than among individuals," thus suggesting a double standard of morality, one for individuals, the other for nations; but he leaves no doubt that his support of the balance of power, for example, is based on moral considerations as offering the best chance for "moderation and the preservation of the liberties of mankind."

Thus pessimists and optimists, realists and idealists, emphasize the moral aspects of political choice. While all of them take the right of national self-defense for granted, nowhere do they suggest that competition for power, conflict, struggle, or war could be regarded as signs of national health or heroism. If there is any awareness of a moral dilemma arising out of the conflicting demands of self-preservation on the one hand and the obedience to moral principle on the other, it is resolved, without apparent strain on the conscience, by reference to the analogous case of the individual who is considered morally justified in defending himself by force against external attack. This analogy is the weakest point in the argument. It fails to take into account how far more extensive and arbitrary than in the case of individuals are the claims that nations can label as self-defense. The emphasis placed on moderation and self-restraint indicates some awareness of this moral pitfall.

Moreover, for the two "island" countries external attack or invasion were unlikely contingencies most of the time, so that self-preservation in a strict sense of the term rarely came to place restrictions on the leeway they enjoyed in respect to other policy objectives. In matters of colonial expansion, for example, or of the spread of ideologies by means of intervention—often even of efforts to influence the outcome of other peoples' wars—there was much freedom to choose the road that appeared most consistent with one's scale of values. Here the door was wide open for soul-searching as well as for the exercise of wise judgment. Political theory in the Anglo-American tradition was full of such soul-searching, though the enjoyment of relative national security and an abiding confidence in reasonableness and common sense took much of the sting out of it.

. . . .

Inasmuch as the English and American theorists of the past applied a philosophy of choice to both internal and external politics, they had every reason to devote attention to both and to consider them closely related. Yet the two fields of policy differ in one important respect, with a cleavage within the theory of politics remaining to be noted. Since the dawn of the modern nation-state, domestic politics, particularly in the English-speaking world, constituted a gradual and progressive evolution from absolutism to constitutional government and democracy. Theory addressed itself here to a series of problems which presented themselves consecutively in the course of this historical process and found a solution as time went on. The theory that dealt with issues such as the relative place of church and state, the separation of powers, or the rights of the individual, all-important at some period, is on the whole a matter of historical and philosophical rather than of contemporary political interest, though it may again become pertinent in the latter sense within some new context. This accounts for the practice of treating the theory of internal politics as a history of political thought with emphasis on the interdependence between specific theories and the specific conditions prevailing at successive historical periods.

No similar evolution has taken place in international politics during the same four centuries in which the nation-state underwent its internal transformation. The essential features of the multi-state system and of the conduct of its members had changed little by the time Woodrow Wilson made his speeches from what they were when Thomas More wrote his *Utopia* in 1516. As a consequence, theorists contemplating the international scene have been responding throughout this period to one and the same pattern of events and addressing themselves on the whole to the same set of problems.

Because of this lack of evolutionary development there would seem to be no need to study the views of past theorists on international politics in the historical manner that is customary in matters of domestic politics. Theory here is related not to a particular period of multistate system but to a single persistent historical situation now extending back over more than four centuries. In this sense the theorists of this entire period must be considered contemporaries. The problems of self-preservation in the light of external danger, of expansion into new territories or of contraction, of intervention in the affairs of others, of alliances, peacemaking, and the conduct of wars are as much matters of concern and controversy today as they were when a More, Hume, or Bentham put their minds to them.

This contemporaneousness has its positive as well as its negative sides. To start with the latter, the inability of nations to fashion the world according to their wishes and thus to dispose of worrisome problems once and for all has meant that the theorists cannot generally be said to have moved step by step to the discovery of solutions of ever greater perfection. There is little reason to expect here the kind of accumulation of knowledge or increasing depth of insight that characterizes other parts of political theory. Had Hume written his classic chapter on the balance of power two centuries later, it is not likely that his treatment would have appeared outdated any more than Woodrow Wilson's argument in favor of a peace without victory would have seemed strange if stated a few centuries earlier.

For the student of international politics there is a great advantage, however, in what from other angles may seem to represent sheer stagnation and a source of frustration. Even if his interests were focused exclusively on the contemporary scene and the policy problems that statesmen of his own age are facing, he could still turn with profit to the discussions of theorists of the past. Except for one significant change in external conditions which will be discussed in a moment, and with one qualification necessitated by this change, the theorists of the last four centuries looked out on the same kind of world that he does and were seeking answers to the same questions which occupy his mind today. In this sense they are his contemporaries, too. To study their views is not a diversion satisfying a purely historical or what some might consider an antiquarian interest. Any reader will find himself on familiar ground in most of the texts reproduced in this volume if only he is prepared to take a few semantic and stylistic hurdles, like translating "kings and subjects" into "decision-makers and the public," or to recognize that if, for example, the old colonialism is coming to an end, territorial expansion of control continues to present a serious problem today.

But there is one qualification to this statement which needs to be emphasized and put in the form of a warning. If it was correct to relate the peculiar outlook of the English-speaking theorists—their philosophy of moral choice—to the insular security that their countries enjoyed, the disappearance of this security in our time, now an acknowledged fact, may call for a significant modification of the traditional philosophy. The leeway for choice which the two countries enjoyed in the past has been gravely curtailed. For all practical purposes they have become "Continental" in terms of the dangers and compulsions pressing upon them from the outside. While the multistate system has remained what it was before, their place in it has radically changed. The question is how they will and should adapt to this new situation not only their foreign policy but their way of thinking.

There are two extreme ways open to them, both tempting, both dangerous. One consists in swinging over to the Continental philosophy in its most extreme form, meaning the acceptance without qualification of a philosophy of necessity. All major decisions in foreign policy would then be conceived as dictated by external circumstances beyond human control, statesmen and people alike being absolved as a consequence from all moral responsibility. With resignation, anger, or glee the old quest for moral guidance would be laid aside to give free play to expediency and the concern for power. In this case the ideas of the old theorists would come to appear no less obsolete than the former insular policies with which they coincided; they would be condemned as naive and moralistic.

The other departure from tradition, more subtle than the first, would consist in closing one's eyes to the diminution of leeway that has taken place and to pretend that in doing under strong compulsion what was considered evil when undertaken by others was no longer evil when done by oneself. Thus if it became necessary to participate in wars in remote places, to threaten the use of force, or to build up military alliances in peace time, theory would provide the suitable moral labels, catering thereby to the sense of self-righteousness.

The lesson that can be learned from the theorists of the Anglo-American tradition points toward neither such cynicism nor such hypocrisy. As mentioned earlier, it was never suggested that national self-preservation itself should be sacrificed to moral principle. Instead, statesmen were urged to combine two basic goals: one, the primary though prudently conceived objective of self-preservation—call it the vital national security interest—the other, implied in such prudence, a fulfillment of the moral law to the maximum compatible with the primary duty of defense. If national security has come to occupy a much larger place in the policy of the two countries which have lost the advantages of insular remoteness, a break with tradition need not follow. Even now survival is not always at stake. Even now there is freedom of choice between more or less moderation, more or less concern for the interests of others, more or less effort to preserve the peace, more or less respect for justice, more or less of a sense of responsibility for the whole of mankind. In other words, there may be plenty of opportunity even now to justify the belief implicit in much of what is said in this volume that a wise interpretation and responsible pursuit of the national interest will be found to conform with the principles of morality, reasonably applied, and to the broader interests of mankind. If by the study of the theorists of the past the spirit which they expressed in happier days continues to influence Anglo-American thinking, it may prevent the adjustment which is imperative from leading to extremist theories; it may even help to keep the ship of English and American statecraft on an even keel.

5. E. H. Carr

The Twenty Years' Crisis

Morality in International Politics

The place of morality in international politics is the most obscure and difficult problem in the whole range of international studies. Two reasons for its obscurity, one general and one particular, may be suggested.

In the first place, most discussions about morality are obscured by the fact that the term is commonly used to connote at least three different things:

1. The moral code of the philosopher, which is the kind of morality most rarely practised but most frequently discussed.
2. The moral code of the ordinary man, which is sometimes practised but rarely discussed (for the ordinary man seldom examines the moral assumptions which underlie his actions and his judgments and, if he does, is peculiarly liable to self-deception).
3. The moral behaviour of the ordinary man, which will stand in fairly close relation to (2), but in hardly any relation at all to (1).

It may be observed that relationship between (2) and (3) is mutual. Not only is the behaviour of the ordinary man influenced by his moral code, but his moral code is influenced by the way in which ordinary men, including himself, behave. This is particularly true of the ordinary man's

---

Reprinted from E. H. Carr, *The Twenty Years' Crisis,* Chapter 9, by permission of Macmillan and Company, Ltd., St. Martins' Press. Copyright, 1939, 1946, by Macmillan and Company, Ltd., London.

view of political morality, which tends, more than personal morality, to be a codification of existing practice, and in which the expectation of reciprocity always plays an important part.

The monopoly of international studies between the two wars by the utopian school resulted in a concentration of interest on discussions of the question what international morality ought ideally to be. There was little discussion of the moral behaviour of states except to pass hasty and sweeping condemnation on it in the light of this ideal morality. There was no discussion at all of the assumptions of the ordinary man about international morality. This was particularly unfortunate at a period in which the popularisation of politics for the first time made the assumptions of the ordinary man a matter of primary importance; and the ever widening rift between the international utopia and international reality might have been described in terms of this divergence between the theory of the philosopher and practice based on the unexpressed and often unconscious assumptions of the ordinary man. Moreover, utopia met its usual fate in becoming, unknown to itself, the tool of vested interests. International morality, as expounded by most contemporary Anglo-Saxon writers, became little more than a convenient weapon for belabouring those who assailed the *status quo*. Here as elsewhere, the student of international politics cannot wholly divest himself of utopianism. But he will be well advised to keep his feet on the ground and rigorously maintain contact between his ambitions for the future and the realities of the present. Nor should this be too difficult. The anthropologist who investigates the moral codes and behaviour of a cannibal tribe probably starts from the presupposition that cannibalism is undesirable, and is conscious of the desire that it should be abolished. But he may well be sceptical of the value of denunciations of cannibalism, and will in any case not mistake such denunciations for a scientific study of the subject. The same clarity of thought has not always distinguished students of international morality, who have generally preferred the role of the missionary to that of the scientist.

The second obscurity is peculiar to the international field. Strange as it may appear, writers on international morality are not agreed among themselves—and are not always clear in their own minds—whether the morality which they wish to discuss is the morality of states or the morality of individuals. This point is so vital to the whole discussion that it must be cleared up on the threshold of our enquiry.

The Nature of International Morality

The period of absolute personal rule in which the modern state first began to take shape was not much troubled by distinction between personal and state morality. The personal responsibility of the prince for acts of state could be assumed without any undue straining of the facts. Charles I may have been a good father and a bad king. But in both capacities, his acts could be treated as those of an individual.[1] When, however, the growing complication of the state machine and the development of constitutional government made the personal responsibility of the monarch a transparent travesty, the personality (which seemed a necessary condition of moral responsibility) was transferred from the monarch to the state. Leviathan, as Hobbes said, is an "Artificial Man." This was an important step forward. It was the personification of the state which made possible the creation of international law on the basis of natural law. States could be assumed to have duties to one another only in virtue of the fiction which treated them as if they were persons. But the personification of the state was a convenient way of conferring on it not merely duties, but rights; and with the growth of state power in the nineteenth and twentieth centuries state rights became more conspicuous than state duties. Thus the personification of the state, which began as a liberal and progressive device, came to be associated with the assertion of unlimited rights of the state over the individual and is now commonly denounced as reactionary and authoritarian. Modern utopian thinkers reject it with fervour,[2] and are consequently led to deny that morality can be attributed to the state. International morality must, on this view, be the morality of individuals.

The controversy about the attribution of personality to the state is not only misleading, but meaningless. To deny personality to the state is just as absurd as to assert it. The personality of the state is not a fact whose truth or falsehood is a matter for argument. It is what international lawyers have called "the postulated nature" of the state.[3] It is a necessary fiction or hypothesis—an indispensable tool devised by the human mind for dealing with the structure of a developed society.[4] It is theoretically possible to imagine a primitive political order in which individuals are individuals and nothing more, just as it is possible to imagine an economic order in which all producers and traders are individuals. But just as economic development necessitated resort to the fiction of corporate responsibility in

[1] The Allied Governments in the Versailles Treaty attempted to revive this historic assumption by holding the ex-Kaiser personally responsible for acts of state; but the attempt was almost universally condemned as soon as passions began to cool. Modern dictatorships, however, helped to bring this conception back to fashion. Thus Professor Toynbee called the invasion of Abyssinia "Signor Mussolini's deliberate personal sin" (*Survey of International Affairs, 1935,* ii, p. 3), though he would probably have felt it incongruous to describe the Hoare-Laval Plan as the "personal sin" of Sir S. Hoare or Laval.

[2] Duguit, for example, calls it "valueless and meaningless anthropomorphism" (*Traité de droit constitutionnel,* i. ch. v.).

[3] Hall, *International Law* (8th ed.), p. 50; Pearce Higgins, *International Law and Relations,* p. 38.

[4] This does not, of course, mean that the state is a necessary form of political organisation, but only that, so long as the state *is* the accepted form, its personification is a necessary fiction. The same would apply to any other form (e.g. the class). The personification of the proletariat has gone far in Soviet Russia (e.g. the fiction that it "owns" the means of production).

such forms as that of the joint-stock company, so political development necessitated the fiction of the corporate responsibility of the state. Nor are the rights and obligations of these fictitious entities regarded as purely legal. A bank is praised for generosity to its employees, an armaments firm is attacked for unpatriotic conduct, and railways have "obligations to the public" and demand a "square deal"—all issues implying the relevance, not merely of legal, but of moral standards. The fiction of the group-person, having moral rights and obligations and consequently capable of moral behaviour, is an indispensable instrument of modern society; and the most indispensable of these fictitious group-persons in the state. In particular, it does not seem possible to discuss international politics in other terms. "Relations between Englishmen and Italians" is not a synonym for "relations between Great Britain and Italy." It is a curious and significant paradox that those utopian writers on international affairs who most vigorously denounce the personification of the state as absurd and sinister none the less persistently allocate moral praise and blame (generally the latter) to those imaginary entities, "Great Britain," "France," and "Italy," whose existence they deny.

Continuity is another element in society which makes the fiction of the group-person indispensable. The keenest objectors to the personification of the state will have no qualms about celebrating the 150th anniversary of *The Times* or the 38th victory of "Cambridge" in the boat race, and will confidently expect "the London County Council" to repay, fifty years hence, money which "it" borrows and spends today. Personification is the category of thought which expresses the continuity of institutions; and of all institutions the state is the one whose continuity it is most essential to express. The question whether the Belgian Guarantee Treaty of 1839 imposed an obligation on Great Britain to assist Belgium in 1914 raised both legal and moral issues. But it cannot be intelligently discussed except by assuming that the obligation rested neither personally on Palmerston who signed the treaty of 1839, nor personally on Asquith and Grey who had to decide the issue in 1914, neither on all individual Englishmen alive in 1839, nor on all individual Englishmen alive in 1914, but on that fictitious group-person "Great Britain," which was regarded as capable of moral or immoral behaviour in honouring or dishonouring an obligation.[5] In short, international morality is the morality of state. The hypothesis of state per-

[5] A striking example of confused thinking on this subject occurred in a recent letter to *The Times*. Commenting on the alleged British obligation to France in 1914, a distinguished professor of history wrote that "Grey may have regarded his personal honour as involved in support of France, but he certainly did not think that of the Cabinet was" (*The Times,* February 28, 1939). The promise, if any, to support France must have been given by Grey not on his own behalf, but on behalf of Great Britain. Unless he believed that the whole Cabinet was under the same obligation as himself to see that Great Britain's promise was honoured, he could not properly have given it at all.

sonality and state responsibility is neither true nor false, because it does not purport to be a fact, but a category of thought necessary to clear thinking about international relations. It is true that another moral issue was also raised in 1914—the obligation of individual Englishmen. But this was an obligation to "Great Britain," arising out of the obligation of "Great Britain" to "Belgium." The two obligations were distinct; and confused thinking is the inevitable penalty of failure to distinguish between them.

Curiously enough, this distinction seems to present more difficulty to the philosopher than to the ordinary man, who readily distinguishes between the obligation of the state to another state. In 1935, the Opposition in the House of Commons denounced the Hoare-Laval Plan as "a terrible crime." But it did not denounce Sir S. Hoare as a criminal or regard him as such; it found him guilty only of an error of judgment. In 1938, some Englishmen felt "ashamed" of the Munich Agreement. They were not "ashamed" of themselves; for they would have done anything in their power to prevent it. They were not "ashamed" of Mr. Chamberlain; for most of them admitted that he had acted honestly, though mistakenly, and one does not feel "ashamed" of anyone who commits an honest mistake. They were "ashamed" of "Great Britain," whose reputation had, in their view, been lowered by a cowardly and unworthy act. In both these cases, the same act which (in the view of the critics) represented an intellectual failure on the part of the individual represented a moral failure on the part of "Great Britain." The *mot* became current that the British loan of £10,000,000 to Czecho-Slovakia was "conscience money." The essence of "conscience money" is that it is paid by a moral delinquent; and the moral delinquent who paid the £10,000,000 was not Mr. Chamberlain, and not those individual Englishmen who had applauded the Munich agreement, but "Great Britain." The obligation of the state cannot be identified with the obligation of any individual or individuals; and it is the obligations of states which are the subject of international morality.

Two objections are commonly raised to this view.

The first is that the personification of the state encourages the exaltation of the state at the expense of the individual. This objection, though it accounts for the disfavour into which the personification of the state has fallen among liberal thinkers, is trivial. The personification of the state is a tool; and to decry it on the ground of the use to which it is sometimes put is no more intelligent than to abuse a tool for killing a man. The tool can equally well be put to liberal uses through emphasis on the duty of the state both to the individual and to other states. Nor can democracy altogether dispense with personification as a means to emphasize the duty of the individual. The most sophisticated of us would probably shrink from paying taxes to a group of individual fellow-citizens, though we pay them with comparative alacrity to a personified state. The same applies with greater force to graver sacrifices. "You would never have got young men to sacrifice themselves for so unlucky a country as Ireland," said Parnell, "only that they pictured her as a woman." [6] "Who dies if England live?" is not adequately paraphrased by "Who dies if other Englishmen live?" Moreover, it is difficult to see how orderly international relations can be conducted at all unless Englishmen, Frenchmen, and Germans believe (however absurd the belief may be) that "Great Britain," "France," and "Germany" have moral duties to one another and a reputation to be enhanced by performing those duties. The spirit of international relations seems more likely to be improved by stimulating this belief than by decrying it. In any case, it is clear that human society will have to undergo a material change before it discovers some other equally convenient fiction to replace the personification of the political unit.

The second objection is more serious. If international morality is the morality of fictitious entities, is it not itself fictitious and unreal? We can at once accept the view that moral behaviour can only proceed from individuals. To deny that "relations between Great Britain and Italy" means the same as "relations between Englishmen and Italians" is not to deny that "relations between Great Britain and Italy" depend on the actions of individual Englishmen and Italians. The moral behaviour of the state is a hypothesis; but we need not regard as "unreal" a hypothesis which is accepted in certain contexts as a guide to individual behaviour and does in fact influence that behaviour. So long as statesmen, and others who influence the conduct of international affairs, agree in thinking that the state has duties, and allow this view to guide their action, the hypothesis remains effective. The acts with which international morality is concerned are performed by individuals not on their own behalf, but on behalf of those fictitious group persons "Great Britain" and "Italy," and the morality in question is the morality attributed to those "persons." Any useful examination of international morality must start from recognition of this fact.

Theories of International Morality

Before we consider the moral assumptions which underlie current thinking about international affairs, we must take some account of current theories of international morality. For though it is the assumptions of the ordinary man, not the assumptions of the philosopher, which determine the accepted moral code and govern moral behaviour, the theories of philosophers also exercise an influence on the thought (and, less frequently, on the action) of the ordinary man, and cannot be left altogether out of the picture. Theories of international morality tend to fall into two categories. Realists—and, as we have seen, some who are not realists—hold

[6] Quoted in *Democracy and War*, ed. G. E. C. Catlin, p. 128.

that relations between states are governed solely by power and that morality plays no part in them. The opposite theory, propounded by most utopian writers, is that the same code of morality is applicable to individuals and to states.

The realist view that no ethical standards are applicable to relations between states can be traced from Machiavelli through Spinoza and Hobbes to Hegel, in whom it found its most finished and thorough-going expression. For Hegel, states are complete and morally self-sufficient entities; and relations between them express only the concordance or conflict of independent wills not united by any mutual obligation. The converse view that the same standard is applicable to individuals and to states was implicit in the original conception of the personification of the state and has found frequent expression not only in the writings of philosophers, but in the utterances of statesmen of utopian inclinations. "The moral law was not written for men alone in their individual character," said Bright in a speech on foreign policy in 1858, ". . . it was written as well for nations." [7] "We are at the beginning of an age," said Woodrow Wilson in his address to Congress on the declaration of war in 1917, "in which it will be insisted that the same standards of conduct and of responsibility for wrong shall be observed among nations and their governments that are observed among the individual citizens of civilised states." [8] And when in July 1918 the faithful House tried his hand at the first draft of a League of Nations, Article 1 ran as follows:

> The same standards of honour and ethics shall prevail internationally and in affairs of nations as in other matters. The agreement of promise of power shall be inviolate.[9]

No corresponding pronouncement was included in the Covenant. But Dr. Benes at one of the early Assemblies remarked that the League was "*ipso facto* an attempt to introduce into international relationships the principles and methods employed . . . in the mutual relations of private individuals." [10] In his famous Chicago speech of October 5, 1937, President Roosevelt declared that "national morality is as vital as private morality." [11] But he did not specifically identify them.

Neither the realist view that no moral obligations are binding on states, nor the utopian view that states are subject to the same moral obligations as individuals, corresponds to the assumptions of the ordinary man about international morality. Our task is now to examine these assumptions.

---

[7] John Bright, *Speeches on Questions of Public Policy*, p. 479.
[8] *Public Papers of Woodrow Wilson: War and Peace*, i, p. 11.
[9] *Intimate Papers of Colonel House*, ed. C. Seymour, iv, p. 28.
[10] *League of Nations: Fourth Assembly*, i, p. 144.
[11] *International Conciliation*, No. 334, p. 713.

Ordinary Assumptions about International Morality

It is noteworthy that the attempt to deny the relevance of ethical standards to international relations has been made almost exclusively by the philosopher, not by the statesman or the man in the street. Some recognition of an obligation to our fellow-men as such seems implicit in our conception of civilisation; and the idea of certain obligations automatically incumbent on civilised men has given birth to the idea of similar (though not necessarily identical) obligations incumbent on civilised nations. A state which does not conform to certain standards of behaviour towards its own citizens and, more particularly, towards foreigners will be branded as "uncivilised." Even Hitler in one of his speeches declined to conclude a pact with Lithuania "because we cannot enter into political treaties with a state which disregards the most primitive laws of human society";[12] and he frequently alleged the immorality of Bolshevism as a reason for excluding Soviet Russia from the family of nations. All agree that there is an international moral code binding on states. One of the most important and most clearly recognised items in this code is the obligation not to inflict *unnecessary* death or suffering on other human beings, i.e. death or suffering not necessary for the attainment of some higher purpose which is held, rightly or wrongly, to justify a derogation from the general obligation. This is the foundation of most of the rules of war, the earliest and most developed chapter of international law; and these rules were generally observed in so far as they did not impede the effective conduct of military operations.[13] A similar humanitarian motive inspired international conventions for the protection of the "backward races" or of national minorities, and for the relief of refugees.

The obligations so far mentioned have been obligations of the state to individuals. But the obligation of state to state is also clearly recognised. The number of synonyms current in international practice for what used to be called "the comity of nations" [14] shows the persistence of the belief that states are members of a comity and have obligations as such. A new state on becoming, in virtue of recognition by other Powers, a member of

[12] Speech in the Reichstag, May 21, 1935.

[13] The rules of war have since 1914 been exposed to an exacting test. The distinction between combatant and non-combatant grows less and less. A deliberate attack on so-called non-combatants may in fact promote important military objectives; and the conception of *unnecessary* suffering, which the belligerent is not entitled to inflict because it is not essential to his military purpose, becomes more and more restricted and difficult to sustain. In short, modern conditions of warfare are doing much to break down, in one important point, a previously existing and effective sense of universal obligation.

[14] Half a dozen synonyms, used quite indiscriminately, are quoted from recent documents by Dr. G. Schwarzenberger (*American Journal of International Law*, xxxiii, p. 59). There is no reason to suspect sarcasm in the reference, in a Japanese Imperial Rescript of 1933, to "the fraternity of nations."

the international community, is assumed to regard itself as automatically bound, without any express stipulation, by the accepted rules of international law and canons of international morality. As we have seen, the concept of internationalism was so freely used between the two wars for the purpose of justifying the ascendancy of the satisfied Powers that it fell into disrepute with the dissatisfied Powers. But this natural reaction was not a denial of the existence of an international community so much as a protest against exclusion from the privileges of membership. The result of the Versailles Treaty, wrote Dr. Goebbels, was "to expel Germany from the comity of powerful political countries," and the function of National Socialism was "to unite the people and once more lead it back to its rightful place in the comity of nations." [15] During Hitler's visit to Rome in May 1938, Mussolini declared that the common aim of Italy and Germany was "to seek between them and with others a regime of international comity which may restore equally for all more effective guarantees of justice, security and peace." [16] Constant appeals were made by both these Powers to the injustice of the conditions now imposed on them in the past and the justice of demands now made by them; and many people in these countries were beyond doubt sincerely and passionately concerned to justify their policy in the light of universal standards of international morality.

In particular, the theory that, since states have no moral obligations towards one another, treaties have no binding force, is not held even by those statesmen who exhibit least taste for international co-operation. Every state concludes treaties in the expectation that they will be observed; and states which violate treaties either deny that they have done so, or else defend the violation by argument designed to show that it was legally or morally justified. The Soviet Government in the first years of its existence openly violated not only treaties signed by previous Russian governments, but the treaty which it had itself signed at Brest-Litovsk, and propounded a philosophy which seemed to deny international obligation and international morality. But it simultaneously concluded, and offered to conclude, other treaties with the manifest intention of observing them and expecting others to observe them. The German Government accompanied its violation of the Locarno Treaty in 1936 with an offer to enter into a fresh treaty. In neither case is it necessary to doubt the sincerity of the government concerned. Violation of treaties, even when frequently practised, is felt to be something exceptional requiring special justification. The general sense of obligation remains.

The view that the same ethical standard is applicable to the behaviour of states as to that of individuals is, however, just as far from current belief as the view that no standard at all applies to states. The fact is that most people, while believing that states ought to act morally, do not ex-

[15] *Völkischer Beobachter,* April 1, 1939.
[16] *The Times,* May 9, 1938.

pect of them the same kind of moral behaviour which they expect of themselves and one another.

Many utopian thinkers have been so puzzled by this phenomenon that they have refused to recognize it. Others have sincerely confessed their bewilderment. "Men's morals are paralysed when it comes to international conduct," observes Professor Dewey;[17] and Professor Zimmern detects a "rooted prejudice against law and order in the international domain." [18] The discrepancy is less surprising than it appears at first sight. Casuists have long been familiar with the problem of incompatibilities between personal, professional and commercial morality. International morality is another category with standards which are in part peculiar to itself. Some of the problems of state morality are common to the whole field of the morality of group persons. Others are peculiar to the state in virtue of its position as the supreme holder of political power. The analogy between the state and other group persons is therefore useful, but not decisive.

Differences between Individual and State Morality

We may now turn to the principal reasons why states are not ordinarily expected to observe the same standards of morality as individuals.

(1) There is the initial difficulty of ascribing to the state or to any other group person, love, hate, jealousy and other intimate emotions which play a large part in individual morality. It seems plainly incongruous to say, as an eighteenth-century writer said, that "a nation must love other nations as itself." [19] For this reason, it is sometimes argued that the morality of the state must be confined to that formal kind of morality which can be codified in a set of rules and approximates to law, and that it cannot include such essentially personal qualities as altruism, generosity and compassion, whose obligations can never be precisely and rigidly defined. The state, like a public corporation, can—it is commonly said—be just, but not generous. This does not seem to be entirely true. We have already noted that group persons are commonly assumed to have moral as well as legal rights and obligations. When a bank or a public company subscribes to a Lord Mayor's Fund for assistance to victims of some great disaster, the act of generosity must be attributed not to the directors, whose pockets are not affected, and not to the shareholders, who are neither consulted nor informed, but to the bank or company itself. When the Treasury makes a "compassionate grant" in some case of hardship, the act of compassion is performed not by the official who takes the decision, and not by the Chancellor of the Exchequer in his individual capacity, but by the state. Some people expected "the United States" to remit the

---

[17] *Foreign Affairs,* March 15, 1923, p. 95.
[18] Zimmern, *Towards a National Policy,* p. 137.
[19] Christian Wolff, quoted in H. Kraus, *Staatsethos,* p. 187.

debts owing to them from European states after the first world war, and criticised their refusal to do so on moral grounds. In other words, paradoxical as it may appear, we do, in certain circumstances, expect states and other group persons, not merely to comply with their formal obligations, but to behave generously and compassionately. And it is precisely this expectation which produces moral behaviour on behalf of a fictitious entity like a bank or a state. Banks subscribe to charitable funds and states make compassionate grants because public opinion expects it of them. The moral impulse may be traced back to individuals. But the moral act is the act of the group person.

Nevertheless, while most people accept the hypothesis that group persons have in certain conditions a moral duty to act altruistically as well as justly, the duty of the group person appears by common consent to be more limited by self-interest than the duty of the individual. In theory, the individual who sacrifices his interests or even his life for the good of others is morally praiseworthy, though this duty might be limited by duty to family or dependents. The group person is not commonly expected to indulge in altruism at the cost of any serious sacrifice of its interests. A bank or public company which failed to pay dividends owing to generous contributions to charities would probably be thought worthy of censure rather than praise. In his presidential campaign of 1932, Franklin Roosevelt referred tauntingly to Mr. Hoover's reputation for humanitarian activities in Europe, and invited him to "turn his eyes from his so-called 'backward and crippled countries' to the great and stricken markets of Kansas, Nebraska, Iowa, Wisconsin and other agricultural states." [20] It is not the ordinarily accepted moral duty of a state to lower the standard of living of its citizens by throwing open its frontiers to an unlimited number of foreign refugees, though it may be its duty to admit as large a number as is compatible with the interests of its own people. British supporters of the League of Nations who urged Great Britain to render assistance to victims of "aggression" did not maintain that she should do this even to the detriment of her vital interests; they argued that she should render the assistance which she could reasonably afford [21] (just as a bank can reasonably afford to give 500 guineas to the victims of an earthquake). The accepted standard of international morality in regard to the altruistic virtues appears to be that a state should indulge in them in so far as this is not seriously incompatible with its more important interests. The result is that secure and wealthy groups can better afford to behave altruistically than groups which are continually preoccupied with the problem of their

[20] Speech at the Metropolitan Opera House, New York, reported in the *New York Times*, November 4, 1932.

[21] The League of Nations Union "advocates sanctions only in cases where the number and resources of the governments co-operating on the League's behalf make it reasonably certain that the would-be aggressor will abandon his intention, so that war will not break out at all" (*Headway*, December 1937, p. 232).

own security and solvency; and this circumstance provides such basis as there is for the assumption commonly made by Englishmen and Americans that the policies of their countries are morally more enlightened than those of other countries.

(2) It is, however, not merely true that the ordinary man does not demand from the group person certain kinds of moral behaviour which are demanded from the individual; he expects from the group person certain kinds of behaviour which he would definitely regard as immoral in the individual. The group is not only exempt from some of the moral obligations of the individual, but is definitely associated with pugnacity and self-assertion, which become positive virtues of the group person. The individual seeks strength through combination with others in the group; and his "devotion to his community always means the expression of a transferred egoism as well as of altruism."[22] If he is strong, he converts the group to the pursuit of his own ends. If he is weak, he finds compensation for his own lack of power to assert himself in the vicarious self-assertion of the group. If we cannot win ourselves, we want our side to win. Loyalty to the group comes to be regarded as a cardinal virtue of the individual, and may require him to condone behaviour by the group person which he would condemn in himself. It becomes a moral duty to promote the welfare, and further the interests, of the group as a whole; and this duty tends to eclipse duty to a wider community. Acts which would be immoral in the individual may become virtue when performed on behalf of the group person. "If we were to do for ourselves what we are doing for Italy," said Cavour to D'Azeglio, "we should be great rogues."[23] The same could truthfully have been said by a great many directors of public companies and promoters of good causes. "There is an increasing tendency among modern men," writes Dr. Niebuhr, "to imagine themselves ethical because they have delegated their vices to larger and larger groups."[24] In the same way we delegate our animosities. It is easier for "England" to hate "Germany" than for individual Englishmen to hate individual Germans. It is easier to be anti-Semitic than to hate individual Jews. We condemn such emotions in ourselves as individuals, but indulge them without scruple in our capacity as members of a group.

(3) These considerations apply in some measure to all group persons, though they apply with particular force to the state. There are, however, other respects in which we do not ordinarily demand from the state even the same standard of moral behaviour which we demand from other group persons. The state makes an altogether different kind of emotional appeal to its members from that of any other group person. It covers a far larger field of human activities, and demands from the individual a far more intensive loyalty and far graver sacrifices. The good of the state comes

[22] R. Niebuhr, *Moral Man and Immoral Society,* p. 40.

[23] Quoted in E. L. Woodward, *Three Studies in European Conservatism,* p. 297.

[24] R. Niebuhr, *Atlantic Monthly,* 1927, p. 639.

more easily to be regarded as a moral end in itself. If we are asked to die for our country, we must at least be allowed to believe that our country's good is the most important thing in the world. The state thus comes to be regarded as having a right of self-preservation which overrides moral obligation. In the *Cambridge History of British Foreign Policy* published after the war, Professor Holland Rose condones the "discreditable episode" of the seizure of the Danish fleet at Copenhagen in 1807 on the ground of Canning's belief that "the very existence of Great Britain was at stake." [25] Those who take a different view commonly argue that Canning was mistaken, not that he should have acted otherwise if his belief had been correct.

Other differences between the standards of morality commonly expected of the state and of other group persons arise from the fact that the state is the repository of political power and that there is no authority above the state capable of imposing moral behaviour on it, as a certain minimum of moral behaviour is imposed on other group persons by the state. One corollary of this is that we are bound to concede to the state a right of self-help in remedying its just grievances. Another corollary is the difficulty of securing the observance by all of a common standard; for while some moral obligations are always thought of as absolute, there is a strong tendency to make the imperativeness of moral obligations dependent on a reasonable expectation of the performance of the same duty by others. Conventions play an important part in all morality; and the essence of a convention is that it is binding so long as other people in fact abide by it. Barclays Bank or Imperial Chemicals Limited would incur moral censure if they employed secret agents to steal confidential documents from the safes of rival institutions, since such methods are not habitually employed by public companies against one another. But no stigma attaches to "Great Britain" or "Germany" for acting in this manner; for such practices are believed to be common to all the Great Powers, and a state which did not resort to them might find itself at a disadvantage. Spinoza argued that states could not be blamed for breaking faith; for everyone knew that other states would do likewise if it suited their interest.[26] One reason why a higher standard of morality is not expected of states is because states in fact frequently fail to behave morally and because there are no means of compelling them to do so.

(4) This brings us to the most fundamental difficulty which confronts us in our analysis of the moral obligations currently attributed to the state. It is commonly accepted that the morality of group persons can only be social morality (a state or a limited liability company cannot be a saint or a mystic); and social morality implies duty to fellow members of a community, whether that community be a family, a church, a club, a nation or humanity itself. "No individual can make a conscience for him-

[25] *Cambridge History of British Foreign Policy,* i, pp. 363-4.
[26] Spinoza, *Tractatus Politicus,* iii, § 14.

self," writes T. H. Green; "he always needs a society to make it for him." [27] In what sense can we find a basis for international morality by posting a society of states?

Is There an International Community?

Those who deny the possibility of an international morality naturally contest the existence of an international community. The English Hegelian Bosanquet, who may be taken as a typical representative of this view, argues that "the nation-state is the widest organisation which has the common experience necessary to found a common life," [28] and rejects with emphasis "the assumption that humanity is a real corporate being, an object of devotion and a guide to moral duty." [29] The reply to this would appear to be that a corporate being is never "real" except as a working hypothesis, and that whether a given corporate being is an object of devotion and a guide to moral duty is a question of fact which must be settled by observation and not by theory, and which may be answered differently at different times and places. It has already been shown that there is in fact a widespread assumption of the existence of a world-wide community of which states are the units and that the conception of the moral obligations of states is closely bound up with this assumption. There is a world community for the reason (and for no other) that people talk, and within certain limits behave, as if there were a world community. There is a world community because, as Señor de Madariaga puts it, "we have smuggled that truth into our store of spiritual thinking without preliminary discussion." [30]

On the other hand, it would be a dangerous illusion to suppose that this hypothetical world community possesses the unity and coherence of communities of more limited size up to and including the state. If we examine the ways in which the world community falls short of this standard of coherence, we shall have a clue to the underlying reasons for the shortcomings of international morality. It falls short mainly in two ways: (1) the principle of equality between members of the community is not applied, and is indeed not easily applicable, in the world community, and (2) the principle that the good of the whole takes precedence over the good of the part, which is a postulate of any fully integrated community, is not generally accepted.

The Principle of Equality

(1) The principle of equality within a community is difficult to define. Equality is never absolute, and may perhaps be defined as an absence of discrimination for reasons which are felt to be irrelevant. In Great Britain,

[27] T. H. Green, *Prolegomena to Ethics,* p. 351.
[28] B. Bosanquet, *The Philosophical Theory of the State,* p. 320.
[29] B. Bosanquet, *Social and International Ideals,* p. 292.
[30] S. de Madariaga, *The World's Design,* p. 3.

the reasons for which some receive higher incomes or pay more taxes than others are (rightly or wrongly) felt to be relevant even by most of those in the less-favoured categories, and the principle of equality is not therefore infringed. But the principle would be infringed, and the community broken, if people with blue eyes were less favourably treated than people with brown, or people from Surrey than people from Hampshire. In many countries, minorities *are* discriminated against on grounds which they feel to be irrelevant, and these minorities cease to feel, and to be regarded, as members of the community.[31]

In the international community such discrimination is endemic. It arises in the first place from the attitude of individuals. Gladstone is said on one occasion to have exhorted an audience of his fellow-countrymen to "remember that the sanctity of life in the villages of the Afghan mountains among the winter snows is no less inviolable in the eyes of the Almighty than your own." [32] It may safely be said that the eyes of the Almighty are not in this respect those of the great majority of Englishmen. Most men's sense of common interest and obligation is keener in respect of family and friends than in respect of others of their fellow-countrymen, and keener in respect of their fellow-countrymen than of other people. Family and friends form a "face-to-face" group, between whom the sense of moral obligation is most likely to be strong. The members of a modern nation are enabled, through a more or less uniform education, a popular national press, broadcasting and travel facilities, and a skilful use of symbols,[33] to acquire something of the character of a "face-to-face" group. The ordinary Englishman carries in his mind a generalised picture of the behaviour, daily life, thoughts and interests of other Englishmen, whereas he has no such picture at all of the Greek or the Lithuanian. Moreover, the vividness of his picture of "foreigners" will commonly vary in relation to geographical, racial and linguistic proximity, so that the ordinary Englishman will be likely to feel that he has something, however slight, in common with the German or the Australian and nothing at all in common with the Chinese or the Turk.[34] An American newspaper correspondent

[31] It is only in recent times that there has begun to be even a presumption that all inhabitants of a territory are members of the community. Like Jews in Nazi Germany, the coloured inhabitants of the Union of South Africa are today not regarded as members of the community. In the United States, most white Southerners would hesitate to admit that the negroes are members of the community in the same sense as they are themselves.

[32] Quoted by the Delegate of Haiti in *League of Nations: Fifteenth Assembly,* 6th Committee, p. 43.

[33] "Moral attitudes always develop most sensitively in person-to-person relationships. That is one reason why more inclusive loyalties, naturally more abstract than immediate ones, lose some of their power over the human heart; and why a shrewd society attempts to restore that power by making a person the symbol of the community" (R. Niebuhr, *Moral Man and Immoral Society,* pp. 52-3).

[34] The variations of feeling are naturally also influenced by current political prejudices.

in Europe is said to have laid down the rule than an accident was worth reporting if it involved the death of one American, five Englishmen, or ten Europeans. We all apply, consciously or unconsciously, some such standard of relative values. "If it was not that China was so far away," said Neville Chamberlain in the House of Commons on the occasion of Japanese bombing of Chinese cities, "and that the scenes which were taking place there were so remote from our everyday consciousness, the sentiments of pity, horror and indignation which would be aroused by a full observation of these events might drive this people to courses which perhaps they had never yet contemplated." [35] The same *motif* recurred in his national broadcast during the Czecho-Slovak crisis on September 27, 1938: "How horrible, fantastic, incredible it is that we should be digging trenches and trying on gas-masks here because of a quarrel in a far-away country between people of whom we know nothing." [36] These words were criticised in many quarters. But there is little doubt that they represented the initial reaction of the ordinary Englishman. Our normal attitude to foreigners is a complete negation of that absence of discrimination on irrelevant grounds which we have recognised as the principle of equality.

This attitude of the individual is reflected in the attitude of states to one another; and the difficulty is intensified by the structure of the international community. Even if equality between individuals of different countries is recognised, the inequalities between states would be none the less flagrant. The existing inequalities among a handful of known states subject to no external control are infinitely more glaring, more permanent and more difficult to forget than inequalities between the anonymous mass of citizens subject, at any rate in name, to the same law. The importance attached to the idea of equality in international politics is shown by the number and insistence of the demands based on it. "Most-favoured-nation treatment," the "Open Door," "freedom of the seas," the Japanese claim for the recognition of racial equality in the Covenant of the League of Nations, the old German claim to "a place in the sun," the more recent German claim to *Gleichberechtigung* or "equality of status," have all been demands for the application of the principle of equality. The praises of equality were repeatedly sung in the Assemblies and Committees of the League of Nations—mainly, if not exclusively, by delegates of minor Powers.[37] Yet there is little attempt at consistency in the use of the term.

---

[35] House of Commons, June 21, 1938: *Official Report,* col. 936. A correspondent in *The Times,* commenting on "the inconsistencies of compassion" in the international sphere, enquires whether "the world's conscience" regards "100 dead or destitute Chinese as equivalent to one persecuted Jew," or whether it is "simply that the Jews are near at hand, while the Chinese are a very long way away, and yellow at that" (*The Times,* November 25, 1938).

[36] N. Chamberlain, *The Struggle for Peace,* p. 275.

[37] Of the Great Powers only France, largely dependent for her position on the support of minor Powers, consistently advocated the principle of equality. "There

Sometimes it merely means formal equality of states before the law. In other contexts, it may mean equality of rights, or equality of opportunity or equality of possessions. Sometimes it seems to mean equality between Great Powers. When Hitler argued that "according to all commonsense, logic and the general principles of high human justice . . . all peoples ought to have an equal share of the goods of the world," [38] he hardly intended to convey that Lithuania ought to enjoy as much of "the goods of the world" as Germany. Yet if we assume that equality of rights or privileges means proportionate, not absolute, equality, we are little advanced so long as there is no recognised criterion for determining the proportion. Nor would even this help us much. The trouble is not that Guatemala's rights and privileges are only proportionately, not absolutely, equal to those of the United States, but that such rights and privileges as Guatemala has are enjoyed only by the good will of the United States. The constant intrusion, or potential intrusion, of power renders almost meaningless any conception of equality between members of the international community.

The Good of the Whole and the Good of the Part

(2) The other capital shortcoming of the international community is failure to secure general acceptance of the postulate that the good of the whole takes precedence over the good of the part. Great Britain possesses a common national consciousness because the man from Surrey will normally act on the assumption that the good of Great Britain is more important than the good of Surrey. One of the chief obstacles to the growth of a common German national consciousness was the difficulty in persuading Prussians, Saxons and Bavarians to treat the good of Germany as more important than the good of Prussia, Saxony and Bavaria. Now it is clear that, despite pious aspirations, people still hesitate to act on the belief that the good of the world at large is greater than the good of their own country. Loyalty to a world community is not yet powerful enough to create an international morality which will override vital national interests. Yet the conception of a community implies recognition of its good as something which its members are under an obligation to promote, and the conception of morality implies the recognition of principles of a universally binding character. If we refuse altogether to recognise the overriding claims of the whole, can any world community or any kind of international morality be said to exist at all?

---

is not, and we trust there never will be," said M. Blum on one occasion (*League of Nations: Sixteenth Assembly,* Part II, p. 28), "an order of precedence among the Powers forming the international community. Were a hierarchy of States to be established within the League of Nations . . . then the League would be ruined, both morally and materially"—a remarkable statement in view of the hierarchical constitution of the Council.

[38] Speech in the Reichstag of April 28, 1939.

This is the fundamental dilemma of international morality. On the one hand, we find the almost universal recognition of an international morality involving a sense of obligation to an international community or to humanity as a whole. On the other hand, we find an almost equally universal reluctance to admit that, in this international community, the good of the part (i.e. our own country) can be less important than the good of the whole. This dilemma is, in practice, resolved in two different ways. The first is the method, which Hitler borrowed from the Darwinian school, of identifying the good of the whole with the good of the fittest. The fittest are by assumption "the bearers of a higher ethic";[39] and it is only necessary to prove in action that one's country is the fittest in order to establish the identity of its good with the good of the whole. The other method is that of the neoliberal doctrine of the harmony of interests, of which Woodrow Wilson, Lord Cecil and Professor Toynbee have been quoted as representatives. This doctrine, like every doctrine of a natural harmony of interests, identifies the good of the whole with the security of those in possession. When Woodrow Wilson declared that American principles were the principles of mankind, or Professor Toynbee that the security of the British Empire was "the supreme interest of the whole world," [40] they were in effect making the same claim made by Hitler that their countrymen are "the bearers of a higher ethic"; and the same result is produced of identifying the good of the whole international community with the good of that part of it in which we are particularly interested. Both these methods are equally fatal to any effective conception of international morality.

There is no escape from the fundamental dilemma that every community, and every code of morality, postulates some recognition that the good of the part may have to be sacrificed to the good of the whole. The more explicitly we face this issue in the international community, the nearer we shall be to a solution of our problem. The analogy of the national community, though imperfect, is once more helpful. Modern liberalism, wrote Hobhouse shortly before 1914, "postulates, not that there is an actually existing harmony requiring nothing but prudence and judgment for its effective operation, but only that there is a possible ethical harmony to which . . . men might attain, and that in such attainment lies the social ideal." [41] The word "ethical" betrays the break in the argument. The nineteenth-century "harmony requiring nothing but prudence and judgment for its effective operation" was a harmony of interests. The "ethical harmony" is one achieved by the sacrifice of interests, which is necessary precisely because no natural harmony of interests exists. In the national community, appeals to self-sacrifice are constantly and successfully made, even when the sacrifice asked for is the sacrifice of life. But even in the

---

[39] Hitler, *Mein Kampf,* p. 421.
[40] See pp. 77, 79.
[41] L. T. Hobhouse, *Liberalism,* p. 129.

national community, it would be erroneous to suppose that the so-called "harmony" is established solely through voluntary self-sacrifice. The sacrifice required is frequently a forced one, and the "harmony" is based on the realistic consideration that it is in the "interest" of the individual to sacrifice voluntarily what would otherwise be taken from him by force. Harmony in the national order is achieved by this blend of morality and power.

In the international order, the role of power is greater and that of morality less. When self-sacrifice is attributed to an individual, the sacrifice may or may not be purely voluntary. When self-sacrifice is attributed to a state, the chances are greater that this alleged self-sacrifice will turn out on inspection to be a forced submission to a stronger power. Yet even in international relations, self-sacrifice is not altogether unknown. Many concessions made by Great Britain to the Dominions cannot be explained in terms either of British interests or of submission to the stronger. Concessions made by Great Britain to Germany in the nineteen-twenties, ineffective as they were, were dictated, not wholly by British interests or by fear of Germany's strength, but by a belief in some conception of international morality which was independent of British interests. Any international moral order must rest on some hegemony of power. But this hegemony, like the supremacy of a ruling class within a state, is in itself a challenge to those who do not share it; and it must, if it is to survive, contain an element of give-and-take, of self-sacrifice on the part of those who have, which will render it tolerable to the other members of the world community. It is through this process of give-and-take, of willingness not to insist on all the prerogatives of power, that morality finds it surest foothold in international—and perhaps also in national—politics. It is, no doubt, useless to begin by expecting far-reaching sacrifices. The standard of what we can reasonably afford must not be pitched too high. But the course most detrimental to international morality is surely to pretend that the German people are the bearers of a higher ethic, or that American principles are the principles of humanity, or that the security of Great Britain is the supreme good of the world, so that no sacrifices at all by one's own nation are in fact necessary. When Professor Zimmern urges "the ordinary man" to "*enlarge* his vision so as to bear in mind that the *public affairs* of the twentieth century are world *affairs*," [42] the most concrete meaning which can be given to this injunction is that the recognition of the principle of self-sacrifice, which is commonly supposed to stop short at the national frontier, should be extended beyond it. It is not certain that ordinary man will remain deaf to such an appeal. If the Chancellor of the Exchequer were to attempt to justify an increase in the income-tax on the ground that it would make us better off, we should dismiss him as a humbug; and this is the kind of argument which is almost invariably used to justify any international policy involving apparent sac-

[42] Zimmern, *The Prospects of Civilisation,* p. 26.

rifice of interests. A direct appeal to the need of self-sacrifice for a common good might sometimes prove more effective.

But it is necessary to clear up a further point on which many illusions are current. In the national community, we assume that in this process of self-sacrifice and give-and-take the giving must come principally from those who profit most by the existing order. In the international community, the assumption is commonly made by statesmen and writers of the satisfied Powers that the process of give-and-take operates only within the existing order and that sacrifices should be made by all to maintain that order. International peace, said Mr. Eden once, must be "based on an international order with the nations leagued together to preserve it"; and to this international peace "each nation makes its own contribution because it recognises that therein lies its own enduring interest." [43] The fallacy latent in this and many similar pronouncements is fatal to any workable conception of international morality. The process of give-and-take must apply to challenges to the existing order. Those who profit most by that order can in the long run only hope to maintain it by making sufficient concessions to make it tolerable to those who profit by it least; and the responsibility for seeing that these changes take place as far as possible in an orderly way rests as much on the defenders as on the challengers.

6. Arnold Wolfers

Statesmanship and Moral Choice

Throughout the ages moralists have expressed horror at the way princes and sovereign states behave toward each other. Behavior which would be considered immoral by any standard can obviously be detected in all realms of life; but nowhere does the contradiction between professed ethical principles and actual behavior appear so patent and universal as in the conduct of foreign relations. Governments spy on each other and lie to each other; they violate pledges and conduct wars, often at the cost of millions of lives and untold misery. No wonder, then, that in western democracies if not elsewhere indignation over such practices should be voiced with vehemence. In our day it frequently expresses itself in wholesale

Published in *World Politics,* Vol. I, No. 2 (January 1949), pp. 175-95.

[43] Anthony Eden, *Foreign Affairs,* p. 197.

denunciations of the multi-state system on the ground that sovereign states cannot deal with each other except by the use of immoral means, derogatorily called power politics. Some draw the cynical conclusion that morality has no place in international politics, while others would have men fulfill their moral duty by substituting world government for the present immoral political system.

This sweeping moral condemnation of foreign policy as pursued by all nations points to a striking and disturbing contradiction in our public life. Most of our statesmen claim to be pursuing policies of peace and enunciate high moral principles upon which their policy is supposed to be based; they and many publicists praise the democracies for the moral superiority of their conduct of foreign affairs over that of aggressive and ruthless dictators. Yet at the same time many respected students in the field of international relations insist that all sovereign states alike are compelled by the "system" to play the evil game of power politics. The two positions would seem to be incompatible. Either our statesmen and their supporters are deceiving themselves and others or those who without discrimination condemn all power politics as immoral are overstating the case. In a country like the United States where moral passion tends to run high and where the question of morality in politics is a matter of genuine and wide concern, it is important to try to resolve this contradiction.

. . . .

The fundamental discrepancy which seems to exist between the morality of "state" and private behavior would disappear only if it could be shown that politics conducted in a multi-state system is not necessarily any more immoral than average private behavior, or that the chief difference pertains not to the degree of immorality prevailing in the two spheres of human action but to the circumstances under which men are required to act. Much of what strikes people as immoral practices of governments may prove to be morally justified by the peculiar and unhappy circumstances which the statesman has to face and which, moreover, he may often be unable to change.

Any ethical perfectionist will be shocked at such a suggestion. He will deny that any action that would be evil under one set of conditions could be morally justified under another. If men are held to be morally bound to act in accordance with an absolute ethic of love such as the Sermon on the Mount, obviously no set of circumstances, even circumstances in which the survival of a nation were at stake, could justify acts such as a resort to violence, untruthfulness, or treaty violation. The concern for self-preservation and power in itself would have to be condemned as evil. This being the case, the ethical perfectionist can offer no advice to statesmen other than that they give up public office and turn their backs on politics. As a matter of fact, in order to be consistent, the perfectionist, as some have pointed out, must give the same advice to private citizens, requiring of them that they abandon their concern for their own family, for welfare or business. If, as Hans Morgenthau holds, "the very act of acting destroys our moral integrity," only a life of saintliness could come close to satisfying perfectionist moral commands.[1]

We must address ourselves exclusively then to the non-perfectionist who demands of man, not that he follow an absolute code of ethical rules—what Max Weber calls the "natural law of absolute imperatives"—but that he make the best moral choice which the circumstances permit.[2]

. . . .

There is nothing peculiar to international politics in this impact of circumstance. Our conscience revolts at the idea of men putting other men to death. Yet non-perfectionist moralists throughout the western world agree in condoning the acts of those who kill in self-defense, in obedience to an order to execute a criminal, in war, or possibly in the case of tyrannicide. In other cultures it has been considered morally proper, if not a moral duty, to put the first born, aging parents, or widows to death. One and the same act, then, will be judged differently depending on the context within which it is performed and depending also, of course, on the ethical standards by which behavior in general is judged.

This is not the place to enter upon the age-old discussion of what the standards of a non-perfectionist ethic should be, nor is such a discussion necessary for our purpose. However much non-perfectionists may disagree on ethical standards and thus on the nature and hierarchy of values, they hold in common the process by which they reach their moral judgements. They start with the conviction that there can be no escape from sacrifices of value whether, as theologians maintain, because of man's original sin and essential corruption, or because of the dilemmas of a world in which man is faced with incompatible moral claims. With this as a basis they hold that men, statesmen and private individuals alike, are morally required to choose among the roads open to them the one which under the circumstances promises to produce the least over-all destruction of value or, positively speaking, points toward the maximization of value.[3]

---

[1] Hans J. Morgenthau, *Scientific Man vs. Power Politics,* p. 189.

[2] See Max Weber, "Politics as a Vocation," *From Max Weber: Essays in Sociology,* New York, Oxford Press, 1946, pp. 120 ff.

[3] Max Weber's "ethic of responsibility," ("Politics as a Vocation," pp. 118 ff.) comes closer to what is here described as a non-perfectionist ethic of maximization of value than it might appear from some of his statements. Weber, it is true, declares that, "from no ethics in the world can it be concluded when and to what extent the ethically good purpose 'justifies' the ethically dangerous means and ramifications" (p. 121). He is here taking issue with the revolutionary fanatic who from the point of view of an "ethic of ultimate ends" considers every act of violence justified so long as it serves his ultimate end. But when Weber goes on to demand of men that they hold themselves responsible for the consequences of their acts, especially of

Moral condemnation, according to non-perfectionist ethics, rests not on the fact that values have been destroyed, however deplorable or downright evil such destruction may be judged. Instead it is based on the conviction either that the action in question rested on false ethical standards or that in terms of agreed ethical standards a less destructive choice could and should have been made.[4]

Thus a private citizen who breaks family ties in order to serve what he considers a higher cause may find himself condemned because his cause is not considered worth the sacrifice or because there were other less costly ways of attaining his end. Similarly a statesman who decides to break off diplomatic negotiations rather than to accept the terms of the opposing side may be judged wrong because he placed undue value on an increment of national prestige which was at stake or because he failed to appreciate properly the dangers involved in his choice of action. There is no difference either in the method of evaluation or in the ethical standards, whether the case be one of political or private behavior. In that sense the ethic of politics is but a part of general ethics. The question which remains to be answered, however, is why the sacrifices of value in international politics should be as widespread, continuous, and shocking in extent as they so obviously are. Is it because the circumstances under which foreign policy is conducted are so different and so unalterably different from those under which private citizens make their choices?

German writers on international politics have emphasized what they consider a unique and all-pervasive circumstance characteristic of inter-state relations. Writing in the heyday of German "Realpolitik" Ratzenhofer declared categorically that the relations between sovereign states are unalterably relations of enmity.[5] His assertion reminds one of the no less dogmatic Marxist proposition according to which the relations between capital and labor in a capitalist economy are relations of enemies engaged in a class war.[6]

---

their acts of violence, he does not refute their moral right to "contract with the diabolic powers of violence" which as political men they must do, but implicitly calls on them to choose the road which will minimize the evil consequences for which they bear responsibility.

[4] Morgenthau, *Scientific Man vs. Power Politics,* following in the footsteps of Max Weber, also emphasizes the "ethical paradoxes" of politics. "Political ethics" he says, "is indeed the ethics of doing evil" (p. 202). Yet he too concludes that "it is moral judgement," meaning presumably the best a man can morally do, "to choose among several expedient actions the least evil one" (p. 203).

[5] See Gustav Ratzenhofer, *Wesen und Zweck der Politik,* Leipzig, 1893.

[6] Carl Schmitt, in *Der Begriff des Politischen,* Munich, 1932, modifies Ratzenhofer's thesis by declaring that inter-state and, in fact, all truly political relations are in the nature of "friend-foe" relations. While he does not claim that relations between all states at all times are inevitably hostile, he maintains that nations always group themselves as friends and foes and that there could be no such thing as statehood or politics if it were not for the existence of potential enmity, by which he means the possibility of deadly physical combat.

If one looks at the facts of history and of the contemporary world, one cannot subscribe to this German view. Instead it seems as if the relations between sovereign states no less than the relations between other groups or individuals run the whole gamut from almost complete amity—take Canadian-American or Anglo-Canadian relations—to almost unmitigated enmity, as in the days of war. Amity and enmity appear as the two extreme poles of a wide scale of human relationships. It remains true, however, and a matter of great political and moral consequence, that the multi-state system, for reasons which cannot be analyzed here, has a tendency to push relations between at least some states in the direction of enmity—and, for that matter, more so in our century than in the last. . . . The causes of enmity in inter-state relations are significant to the moral problem only to the extent to which statesmen may be responsible for bringing about or for not eliminating enmity, and thus become responsible for the consequences of such enmity.

One can imagine a condition of complete enmity between states. There would be no trace of community between them, no sense of commonly held values or of common interest. Each individual state would have to be looked upon as an entirely separate entity operating in the social vacuum of absolute anarchy. There would exist a state of latent if not actual war all the time, turning diplomacy into warfare with other means. With good reason nations could consider themselves in a constant state of emergency with all the things gravely endangered to which they attached value. It would be a situation, as we know it from experience of total war, in which the sheer quest of survival would justify almost any course of action. "Out-group morality" of the most extreme type would prevail.

Take the other extreme, that of amity or the "friend-to-friend" relationship. While there would be no complete identification a sense of community would exist sufficient to eliminate mutual fear and suspicion. There would be no expectation of violence and therefore no need for preparations with which to meet the dangers of conflict. Despite the fact that each state would be sovereign, or rather because each state would be free to handle its own affairs, such friendly nations could behave toward each other according to the codes of "in-group morality" and live in peace with each other.

The more relations between states degenerate toward enmity the more nations are justified in fearing for the things they cherish and the more reason they have to make and require sacrifices by which inimical claims can be defeated. Greater enmity therefore increases the likelihood that Machiavellian practices will become necessary and morally justified. The degree of amity or enmity thus appears as a morally portentous circumstance. While in a state of amity statesmen are likely to be able to choose between different avenues toward cooperation, compromise and conciliation. Enmity, however, may preclude such choices and place before the statesman a different set of alternatives. He may be able to take steps which will promise to mitigate if not to eliminate existing enmity. Often, however, he will have to choose between efforts to deter his opponent, thereby neutralizing the effects of enmity, and efforts to defeat him.

This cannot be said to be a peculiarity of international politics or of the multi-state system. The same phenomenon can be found in the relationship between father and son, employer and employee, white and colored man. There may be complete amity between them with no trace of distrust, no shadow of fear, no concern for self-protection, no awareness of conflicting demands or expectations. But here, too, relations may degenerate into fierce hostility for reasons too numerous to detail. Behavior then may change beyond recognition.

Two friends may live in almost perfect harmony. But let suspicion arise that one is seeking to exploit their hitherto harmonious relationship in some treacherous fashion. The other will feel justified in spying on his onetime friend. He may start laying traps. The case may end with one man killing the other. What is important to remember in this connection is that the killer may be judged to have been neither legally nor morally guilty, provided the treachery was flagrant enough. Not only our courts but public opinion in our country recognize the excuses of self-defense and unbearable provocation.

Similarly, strife between such groups as industrialists and workers may lead to property damage, kidnapping, or even open violence. Here, again, moral judgement will take the circumstances into account. Public opinion has been aroused at times by the employment of industrial police in labor disputes and by acts of violence on the part of striking workers. In each case, however, condemnation on the part of fair-minded judges of human behavior has been based not so much on the fact that the group in question used tactics of power politics as on the conviction that the provocation or grievances in a given instance were not sufficient to justify acts of coercion and violence.

It will be objected, and rightly so, that intra-state relations do reach a degree of hostility that would call for the use of violence and other Machiavellian devices.[7] The state protects many of the values to which people are attached. The state can also prohibit the use of means to which society is opposed and can enforce its prohibition—though only by the

[7] Some writers while agreeing that the ethical problems of political and private life are basically the same nevertheless stress the difference, if only quantitative, which makes international power politics the domain of evil "par excellence." In his earlier works Reinhold Niebuhr stresses the peculiar selfishness and immorality of human communities including the state, as indicated by the title of his book, *Moral Man and Immoral Society,* New York, Charles Scribner's Sons, 1936. Later, however, he places more emphasis on the fact that all life is a "contest of power" and that international war and conflict are but a revelation of the general character of human existence and human sinfulness. (See his *Christianity and Power Politics,* New York, Charles Scribner's Sons, 1940, especially pages 11, 12, and 103.)

very means which the components of that society have renounced for themselves. This holds true, however, only for well organized states where the government can marshal sufficient authority and police power to prevent family feuds and social or racial conflicts from breaking into the open and degenerating into violence and the use of other Machiavellian means. But while the pacifying influence of such a state and its influence on human behavior should not be minimized, exponents of world statehood tend to exaggerate the case for government.[8] The kind of government and therefore the kind of internal peace which this country enjoys at this time represents the exception rather than the rule. Our government operates under conditions, not wholly state-made, of widespread amity between most of the groups that are powerful enough to influence the course of domestic events. It is recognized as legitimate by practically everyone and is ordinarily obeyed not because it has the force of coercion but because its authority is freely accepted. If one looks at the performance of other governments either in the contemporary world or in past periods of history, one finds no lack of examples of governments operating under quite different conditions and with quite different results.

Some governments are strong and ruthless enough to suppress the hostilities that would otherwise break out between warring factions, ethnic, social, or religious, but they do so by means of suppression, often tyrannical or terroristic. Rather than eliminate Machiavellian practices, such governments merely monopolize them. To what extremes of behavior this may lead has been drastically demonstrated by the way modern totalitarian regimes have persecuted the "enemies of the people." Other governments are too weak to control the forces of internal enmity; then there are bloody revolts or civil wars. When that happens enmity often reaches a degree of fierceness which relations between states rarely approximate. Machiavellian practices of the most extreme kind become the order of the day.

Government or statehood, whether national or world-wide, is therefore no panacea against those aspects of power politics which are morally deplorable. The real evil is enmity and its threat to values to which people are devoted.

However, the moralist needs to be reminded of the fact that there is not only no sure way to eliminate the fateful circumstance of enmity but that at a given time there may be no way at all. Certainly the elimination of the multi-state system itself, whether in a region such as Europe or on a world-wide scale is not one of the objectives statesmen are free to choose and therefore morally obliged to choose under all circumstances. Even if a radical change in the existing order were morally desirable because there was no reason to suppose that a regional federation or a

[8] Mortimer Adler, *How To Think about War and Peace,* New York, Simon and Schuster, 1944, declares anarchy to be the only cause of war and defines anarchy as "the condition of those who try to live without government" (p. 69).

world government would create circumstances of greater amity than exist today, the psychological prerequisites for a concerted move of major nations toward such a goal are beyond the control of governments.

If it be true that statesmen cannot at all times choose to work for conditions of world-wide amity under world government, is it not their moral duty at least to promote amity at all times and at all costs? Once it is conceded that enmity requires and justifies sacrifices of value often of the most shocking kind, it would seem as if no price paid for amity could be considered too high. Yet statesmen would be rendered incapable of maximizing values if, without respect for the context in which they were forced to operate in a given instance, the quest for amity were taken as the sole measure of their actions. Amity is a condition passionately to be desired; but there are times when efforts to bring it about will lead to disaster. It takes two to make friends. An attempt to establish bonds of friendship may be interpreted as a sign of weakness; the result may be aggression. Again the demands of the opponent may call for sacrifices of value greater than those connected with continued enmity. Firmness and even resort to force may under certain circumstances require less loss of life, less human suffering, less destruction of faith and principle than the most sincere attempt to eliminate the causes of hostility by concessions.

This is not the same as saying that power politics generally preclude the opportunity for persistent and active pursuit of amity—or of justice for that matter. There are many occasions when disputes can be settled peacefully and when enmity can be eliminated or avoided, provided one side at least has enough courage, imagination and initiative. Sometimes a spirit of conciliation or even of generosity can do wonders in evoking a ready and sincere response. Whenever the lines of enmity are not irreparably drawn, there may remain room for moderation and self-restraint, for better understanding of each other's true designs and for fair compromise. While it is true that in the end it needs two to make friends, it is not always the other side which must take the first step.[9]

Only those who extol the value of national "virility" which is supposed to express itself in obstinate resistance to compromise, or those who are afraid of being the suckers will insist that the "necessity of state" is always on the side of toughness and unrelenting assertion of national claims. . . .

To the extent that enmity exists and cannot be eliminated at a given moment it would appear to dictate to the statesman a course of action that

---

[9] Winston Churchill, *The Gathering Storm,* Boston, Houghton Mifflin, 1948, p. 320, testifies admirably to these oportunities for statesmanship. He says "those who are prone by temperament and character to seek sharp and clear-cut solutions of difficult and obscure problems, who are ready to fight whenever some challenge comes from a foreign Power, have not always been right. On the other hand, those whose inclination is to bow their heads, to seek patiently and faithfully for peaceful compromise, are not always wrong. On the contrary, in the majority of instances they may be right, not only morally but from a practical standpoint. How many wars have been averted by patience and persisting good will!"

will often run counter to his moral preferences. Does this not mean that those exponents of "Realpolitik" are right who claim that the statesman, instead of being able to make moral choices, is left with virtually no leeway, having to bow to the dictates of the "necessity of state"?

It confuses the moral issue to state the case in this way. The "necessities" in international politics and for that matter in all spheres of life do not push decision and action beyond the realm of moral judgment; they rest on moral choice themselves. If a statesman decides that the dangers to the security of his country are so great that a course of action which may lead to war is necessary, he has placed an exceedingly high value on an increment of national security.

Necessities of a similar kind are known to private citizens. Parents may decide that in order to save the family business they must try to get their son to enter the family firm. Although they know that they are asking him to choose a career he abhors, they are ready to sacrifice his happiness to the "necessity of family." A trade union leader who calls a strike which he knows to be ruinous to patrons to whom he is devoted makes and requires a painful sacrifice for the "necessities" of the labor movement. In every such case conflicting values, interests and loyalties call for choices in which what it deemed to be the higher cause or value calls for submission to its necessities.

It is no play on words to say that the necessity or reason of state is but another of these necessities of life which become compelling only as a particular pattern of values is accepted. If the position of the statesman differs from that of private citizens it is because he must take upon himself the responsibility for sacrifices of value in order that others, as a nation, may protect or attain the things which they treasure. He may feel in duty bound to do so even though in a given instance he may disagree with the moral judgement of those to whom he is responsible. In that sense if in no other it may be justifiable to speak of the peculiar "demonic" quality of politics and public office, as Max Weber and other writers frequently do.

There is good reason why the controversy about the relationship between necessity of state and ethical standards should be rife in our culture. It points to a clash between two sets of ethical standards, one Christian or humanistic, the other nationalistic. Nationalistic ethics place what are called vital national interests—and not national survival only—at the very pinnacle of the hierarchy of values. The preservation or attainment of these values—territorial integrity, colonial possessions, "Lebensraum," treaty rights or economic interests—are therefore assumed to justify the sacrifice of almost every other value whether it be life, generosity, humane treatment of others, truthfulness or obedience to the law. Especially, the interests of other nations count for little, if anything, on a nationalistic scale of values.

While those who adhere to non-perfectionist Christian or humanistic ethical views accept the fact that sacrifices of value are inescapable, as non-nationalists they may nevertheless, in the case of any policy decision, question whether a particular national interest is worth the sacrifices required or could not be protected by a less costly method. This may not seem to hold true when national survival itself is unquestionably at stake. It could properly be said that the multi-state system, since it rests on the co-existence of a multitude of independent states, is incompatible with any ethic which would forbid sacrifices necessary for national survival. Moral advice not to submit to the necessities of survival would not only be advice to commit national suicide but would tend to wreck the multi-state system itself.[10]

As a matter of fact, the controversy between exponents of nationalistic and non-nationalistic ethical standards in our culture is not over the moral right to pay the price of survival. None but the perfectionists or absolute pacifists deny a nation which is engaged in a life and death struggle the right to make and demand every sacrifice necessary for victory.

But this is not the same as saying that the non-perfectionist must capitulate before every alleged "necessity of state." Nations engaged in international politics are faced with the problem of survival only on rare occasions. How otherwise could it be explained that most of the nations which have attained independence in recent centuries have survived when surely most of them most of the time have been devoted to anything but an unrestrained quest of power? If ever any country did employ Machiavellian principles consciously and methodically it was Hitler's Germany, but with the result that she lost her independence as conclusively as few great nations have done.

As a rule, not survival but other "national interests" are at stake, such as the preservation of outlying bases and possessions, the protection of treaty rights, the restoration of national honor, or the maintenance of economic advantages. While it is a prerequisite of the system that nations attach a high if not the highest value to their survival, the same cannot be said of these other national interests. As a matter of fact, the moral dilem-

[10] It is not surprising that authors who believe that international politics is essentially a struggle for national survival should reach very pessimistic ethical conclusions. Thus, Nicholas J. Spykman, *American Strategy in World Politics,* New York, Harcourt, Brace, 1942, bases his case on the proposition that "the struggle for power is identical with the struggle for survival" and that states can survive only by constant devotion to power politics. Although the use of power "should be constantly subjected to moral judgements" (p. 12), Spykman concludes that the "statesman can concern himself with values of justice, fairness and tolerance only to the extent that they contribute to or do not interfere with the power objective," meaning the quest for survival. In his further statement that the quest for power is not made for "the achievement of moral values" he is taking issue with those exponents of nationalistic ethics who place supreme moral value on national survival. See also in this connection Mortimer Adler's statement that "so long as national self-preservation remains the dominant end for which prudence must choose means, the principles of morality cannot be reconciled with the counsels of prudence," *How To Think about War and Peace* (p. 78).

mas with which statesmen and their critics are constantly faced revolve around the question of whether in a given instance the defense or satisfaction of interests other than survival justify the costs in other values. Does the expropriation of American investments abroad, for instance, justify the choice of military intervention rather than of unpromising negotiation? Is it morally preferable to risk a loss of prestige with its possible dangerous consequences for the safety of the country rather than to insist on maintaining a position which threatens to provoke hostilities? In every case the interpretation of what constitutes a vital national interest and how much value should be attached to it is a moral question. It cannot be answered by reference to alleged moral necessities inherent in international politics; it rests on value judgments.

Even national survival itself, it should be added, is a morally compelling necessity only as long as people attach supreme value to it. In that sense the multi-state system itself depends on a value pattern in which there is an element of nationalism. If at any time those who have the power to decide over the foreign policies of the major countries should come to attach higher value to the attainment of world government than to the preservation of independence, the psychological, though not necessarily all other practical, obstacles to world government would be removed.[11] Until that happens nations are likely to consent to all kinds of Machiavellian practices, however much they may abhor them, whenever they are convinced that their independence can be saved in no other way.

International politics offer some opportunities and temptations for immoral action on a vast and destructive scale; they tend to present themselves in the guise of "necessity of state." Statesmen in command of the machinery by which public opinion can be manipulated may make it appear as if they were acting for the sake of objectives to which the people attach high value when in fact they are out to serve material personal interests or to satisfy personal ambitions for power. Where men wield as much power as they do in international politics there is room for an infinite variety of abuses for which the "necessity of state" can serve as a convenient cloak. Then again, statesmen may sincerely believe that a particular course of action is dictated by vital interests; but judged by non-

---

[11] R. M. MacIver, *The Web of Government*, New York, MacMillan, 1947, suggests that these basic value judgements may change as the old myths of national sovereignty and national interests lose their grip on people, while Arnold Toynbee, *A Study of History*, New York, Oxford University Press, 1947, p. 299, passing moral judgement, denounces the "pagan worship of sovereign nation-states," calling it "a monstrous product of the impact of parochialism on the Western Christian Church." See also, in this connection, Harold Lasswell, *World Politics and Personal Insecurity*, New York, McGraw-Hill, 1935, who devotes Chapter XI, "In Quest of a Myth: The Problem of World Unity," to the problem of how, by the use of symbols, myths, and other practices, human value judgements might be changed in favor of world unity.

nationalistic standards of ethics they may be placing undue value on certain interests of their people or underestimating the value of things not pertaining to their nation which their policy would sacrifice.

While this makes moral criticism and self-criticism imperative, the difficulties which stand in the way of their proper use in international politics need to be emphasized. If it is hard for statesmen to make proper moral choices, it is not any easier for others to do justice to their conduct of foreign policy.

. . . .

The trouble about much of the moral condemnation of foreign policies and with much of the moral advice tendered to statesmen goes back to a lack of appreciation of the kind of knowledge required for proper and useful moral criticism in international affairs. From a non-perfectionist point of view the circumstances, however technical, have to be taken into consideration; moral conviction and high ideals, much as they are needed to guide moral judgment, cannot by themselves offer an answer. Nor is this true in international politics only. It needs some knowledge of economics to judge whether an industrialist is exploiting his workers; he may be paying the highest wages the traffic will bear. It needs psychological understanding to decide whether in a particular situation divorce represents morally the least evil choice.

Similarly, in international politics where the circumstances are no less involved and technical, moral convictions cannot tell what roads are open to a statesman under the specific conditions under which he is forced to act, nor can they reveal what the political consequences and therefore the relative costs in terms of value of any one of several courses of action are likely to be. Will an alliance provoke war or will the failure to make a commitment tempt an aggressor? Will an appeal to the United Nations in a given case help bring about a peaceful settlement or instead create graver tension, perhaps even going so far as to destroy the organization? Disarmament may be morally the best choice under one set of circumstances; it may be downright evil in another in which it would place a nation—and small nations dependent upon it for their security—at the mercy of an ambitious conqueror. The same holds true for all the other panaceas or devices so dear to the heart of those who are most quickly ready to give moral advice to policy-makers or to condemn them for their actions. In one context it may be right to offer concessions whereas in another it may constitute "appeasement" with all of its evil consequences.

. . . .

Despite the difficulties of doing justice to the statesman and of avoiding the pitfalls of politically dangerous as well as morally untenable condemnations, men who have non-perfectionist and non-nationalistic moral convictions dare not evade the task of moral judgement whether of their own political acts or of the acts of others. Where there is so much room for moral choices as there is in international politics and where the destiny of entire nations depends on these choices, attempts to evade, silence or ignore moral judgement merely play into the hands of those who relish the uncriticized use or abuse of their power. The Nazi leaders were helped by the climate of moral cynicism which prevailed in Germany. It made it easy for them to justify even the most brutal acts on the grounds of necessity of state or to glorify their freedom from any "decadent" moral inhibitions.

The world will not fail to suffer from the immoral acts of statesmen as of other men in the future as it has in the past, nor does it look as though nations would soon be freed from the bitter consequences of international enmity, or from the appalling sacrifices inflicted and justified in the name of national interest and survival. A single powerful government, engaged, for whatever reasons, in a policy of aggression and aggrandizement, may force all others into line with its Machiavellian practices, provided these others have the will to survive. In such cases moral exhortations and intentions will serve little unless the causes of such aggression and the dangers inherent in it are removed.

Yet international politics are not beyond the pale of non-nationalistic, non-perfectionist morality. Statesmen need not be fooling either themselves or others if they contend, as they frequently do, that in specific instances they have restrained their nation's quest for power; nor need they apologize if on occasion, they choose a conciliatory or even a generous course of action, though a more egotistical policy would promise more tangible national benefits. Despite the continued strength of nationalist sentiment in all parts of the world, there is no reason to assume that people value national benefits only. They often attach a great deal of value to a good record of international collaboration and at times applaud a leader who takes risks for the good will, the amity or the interests of other nations—or seeks to keep his own conscience and that of his people clear.

This explains why under certain circumstances a national government might receive the backing of its people even in sacrificing national independence itself, particularly if it were done for the purpose of establishing a better international order, perhaps a world-wide federation. From the point of view of non-nationalistic ethics such national self-sacrifice for world government might appear morally justified if there was assurance of enough amity and all-round consent to permit the establishment and functioning of an orderly and humane government of the world; it might be condemned if it led to world tyranny or world anarchy. There are historical instances when such sacrifice of independence has justified itself in the eyes of almost everybody, as when the thirteen American states federated successfully.

Under the circumstances usually prevailing in a multi-state system painful limitations are set on policies of self-negation, generosity or restraint of power. It would be utopian to expect drastic changes in this respect. But to say that the field of international politics is reserved for selfishness, brutality, self-righteousness or unrestrained ambition for power is not only cynical but manifestly unrealistic.

C. SELECTED BIBLIOGRAPHY

1. "Historical sociology" of International Relations

Aron, Raymond, *Introduction à la philosophie de l'histoire* (Paris: Gallimard, 1948).

———, "De l'analyse des constellations diplomatiques," *Revue Française de Science Politique,* Vol. IV, No. 2 (April-June 1956), pp. 237-51.

———, *War and Industrial Society* (London: Oxford University Press, 1958).

Association Française de Science Politique, *La politique étrangère et ses fondements* (Paris: A. Colin, 1954).

Behrendt, Richard, "Der Beitrag der Soziologie zum Verständnis internationaler Probleme," *Zeitschrift für Volkwirtschaft und Statistik,* Vol. 91, No. 2 (June 1955), pp. 145-70.

Brinton, Crane, *The Anatomy of Revolution,* Revised edition (New York: Vintage Books, 1957).

Coulborn, Rushton (ed.), *Feudalism in History* (Princeton: Princeton University Press, 1956).

Deutsch, Karl, et al., *Political Community and the North Atlantic Area* (Princeton: Princeton University Press, 1957).

Friedrich, Carl J., *Foreign-Policy in the Making* (New York: W. W. Norton, 1938).

Gottmann, Jean, "Geography and International Relations," *World Politics,* Vol. III, No. 2 (January 1951), pp. 154-73.

———, *La politique des Etats et leur géographie* (Paris: A. Colin, 1952).

Gross, Feliks, *Foreign Policy Analysis* (New York: Philosophical Library, 1954).

Haas, Ernst B., and Whiting, Allen, *Dynamics of International Relations* (New York: McGraw-Hill, 1956).

———, "Regional Integration and National Policy," *International Conciliation,* No. 513 (May 1957).

———, *The Uniting of Europe* (Stanford: Stanford University Press, 1958).

Herz, John H., *International Politics in the Atomic Age* (New York: Columbia University Press, 1959).

Neumann, Sigmund, "The International Civil War," *World Politics,* Vol. I, No. 3 (April 1949), pp. 333-50.

Renouvin, Pierre, *Histoire des Relations Internationales,* Vol. I (Paris: Hachette, 1953), Introduction.

"Research Approaches to the Study of War and Peace," *The Journal of Social Issues,* Vol. XI, No. 1 (1955).

Russell, Frank M., *Theories of International Relations* (New York, Appleton-Century, 1936).

Sprout, H., and M. Sprout, *Man-milieu relationship hypotheses in the context of international politics* (Princeton: Princeton University Press, 1956).

Wright, Quincy, *A Study of War* (Chicago: University of Chicago Press, 1942).

Zimmern, Sir Alfred, *The Study of International Relations* (Oxford: Clarendon Press, 1931).

2. Political Philosophy and International Relations

Carr, E. H., *The Twenty Years' Crisis* (London: Macmillan and Co., 1939).

Corbett, Percy, *Morals, Law and Power in International Relations* (Los Angeles: J. R. Haynes and D. Haynes Foundation, 1956).

Elliott, William Y., *The Pragmatic Revolt in Politics* (New York: Macmillan, 1928).

Friedrich, Carl J., *Inevitable Peace* (Cambridge: Harvard University Press, 1948).

Kant, Immanuel, *The Philosophy of Kant,* Carl J. Friedrich (ed.) (New York: The Modern Library, 1949).

Machiavelli, *The Prince* and *The Discourses* (New York: The Modern Library, 1940).

Meinecke, Friedrich, *Machiavellism: The Doctrine of Raison d'Etat and Its Place in Modern History* (New Haven: Yale University Press, 1957).

Niebuhr, Reinhold, *Moral Man and Immoral Society* (London: Scribner's, 1941).

———, *The Children of Light and the Children of Darkness* (New York: Scribner's, 1944).

Schiffer, Walter, *The Legal Community of Mankind* (New York: Columbia University Press, 1954).

Thompson, Kenneth W., "Beyond National Interest: A Critical Evaluation of Reinhold Niebuhr's Theory of International Politics," *Review of Politics,* Vol. 17, No. 2 (April 1955), pp. 167-80.

Waltz, Kenneth N., *Man, the State and War* (New York: Columbia University Press, 1959).

Wolfers, Arnold, "Statesmanship and Moral Choice," World Politics, Vol. I, No. 2 (January 1949), pp. 175-95.

———, and L. W. Martin, *The Anglo-American Tradition in Foreign Affairs* (New Haven: Yale University Press, 1956).

Index